CECIL RHODES
AND THE
CAPE AFRIKANERS

CECIL RHODES AND THE CAPE AFRIKANERS

The Imperial Colossus and
the Colonial Parish Pump

M. Tamarkin
Tel Aviv University

FRANK CASS
LONDON • PORTLAND, OR.

First published in 1996 in Great Britain by
FRANK CASS & CO. LTD
Newbury House, 900 Eastern Avenue, London IG2 7HH

and in the United States of America by
FRANK CASS
5804 N.E. Hassalo Street, Portland, Oregon 97213-3644

Copyright © 1996 M. Tamarkin

British Library Cataloguing in Publication Data

Tamarkin, M.
  Cecil Rhodes and the Cape Afrikaners:
  Imperial Colossus and the Colonial
  Parish Pump
  I. Title
  968.04092

    ISBN 0-7146-4627-X (cloth)
    ISBN 0-7146-4267-3 (paper)

Library of Congress Cataloging-in-Publication Data

Tamarkin, M (Mordechai), 1938–
  Cecil Rhodes and the Cape Afrikaners : the imperial colossus and
  the colonial parish pump / M. Tamarkin.
    p. cm.
  Includes bibliographical references and index.
  ISBN 0-7146-4627-X (cloth)   ISBN 0-7146-4267-3 (paper)
    1. Rhodes, Cecil, 1853–1902. 2. Afrikaners—History. 3. Cape of
  Good Hope (South Africa)—History. I. Title.
  DT1851.R56T36 1996
  968.704′092—dc20   95-30907
                                                                CIP

Typeset by Vitaset, Paddock Wood, Kent
Printed in Great Britain by
Bookcraft (Bath) Ltd, Midsomer Norton, Avon

*In memory of my late father Eliahu,
to my mother Yafa, to my wife Aviva and to my
children Ilan, Ofra and Yael.*

Contents

Preface

In the long period in which I conducted the research for this study I have spent much time in archives and libraries. In this endeavour I have enjoyed the efficient, helpful and friendly help from a host of librarians. In particular, I would like to thank the staff of the Cape Archives in Cape Town, of the South African Library in Cape Town, of the South African Parliament Library in Cape Town, of the Jagger Library in the University of Cape Town, of the Stellenbosch University Library, the University of South Africa Library in Pretoria and the Rhodes House Library in Oxford. I am greatly indebted to Professor Shula Marx, the Institute of Commonwealth Studies in the University of London, Professor Hermann Giliomee from the Department of Political Studies at the University of Cape Town and Dr Iain Smith from the Department of History at the University of Warwick, who have dedicated much time reading the first draft of this book, and provided me with very constructive critiques. They gave me the benefit of their knowledge and insights from their respective scholarly vantage points. In shaping the final draft I have paid diligent attention to their comments and suggestions. They share, however, no responsibility for any failings of this study. Finally, I would like to thank my wife Aviva and my children Ilan, Ofra and Yael for understandingly and gracefully enduring my long absences and the long hours I have spent at my desk and by my PC.

M. Tamarkin
Tel Aviv University

Abbreviations

BG	*Burgersdorp Gazette*
BPP	British Parliamentary Papers
CT	*Cape Times*
CA	*Cape Argus*
DFA	*Diamond Fields Advertiser*
DRC	Dutch Reformed Church
GR	*Graaff Reinetter*
OC	*Onze Courant*
OL	*Ons Land*
PRP	Public Record Office
VOC	Dutch East India Company
ZA	*Zuid Afrikaan*
ZABBB	Zuid Afrikaansche Boeren Bescherming Vereeniging

Introduction

This study has not been conceived primarily as an addition to the long list of biographical accounts, memoirs and studies, whose subject is Cecil John Rhodes. Rhodes has received more than his fair share of academic attention. Nevertheless, this study of the relations between him and the Cape Afrikaners[1] may fill some gaps in his political biography. The Cape Afrikaner dimension was critical in Rhodes's political career. As J.T. Molteno, a contemporary Cape politician, stated: 'Rhodes had owed everything political to Hofmeyr and the Afrikaner Bond and without Hofmeyr and the Bond Rhodes would have been a rich man only, not a world name and an empire-builder ... Hofmeyr and the Afrikaner Bond were the basis and foundation of the political power of Rhodes.'[2] Yet, this dimension suffers from relative neglect in Rhodes's biographies, including Rotberg's recent voluminous one. The main reason is that these authors have rarely consulted the abundant Cape Afrikaner sources. This study, in using these sources, and in focusing on Rhodes's relations with Cape Afrikaners, may contribute to a better understanding of his political career.

While not being primarily concerned with British imperial history, it may also contribute to the study of the roots of the Anglo-Boer war which suffers from a similar deficiency. Studies of the origin of the Anglo-Boer war in the West are almost invariably Anglo-centric. In the context of studying the 'official mind' this is a perfectly legitimate bias.[3] However, the war for British supremacy in South Africa was also premised on the crucial question of the loyalty of Cape Afrikaners to the British empire and their attitude towards their ethnic brothers in the Transvaal. From this broader perspective, a Cape Afrikaner perspective on these questions, drawing on Cape Afrikaner discourse, may prove beneficial to a better understanding of the roots of the war.

Likewise, while the Cape is the background, rather than the focus of this study, a thorough investigation of the relations between Rhodes and Cape Afrikaners may shed light on a critical period in Cape history.

This study has a definite Cape Afrikaner bias. I am mainly interested in the evolution of the Cape Afrikaners in the late nineteenth century.

1

Rhodes, who appeared on the political scene of the Cape Colony in the 1880s, played an important role in the shaping of Cape Afrikaner political outlook and practice throughout much of the last two decades of the century. Consequently, the study of his relations with the Cape Afrikaners can serve as a useful prism through which to look upon this community and understand important elements in their history – the evolution of their ethnic identity and consciousness, and their attitude towards fellow English-speaking colonists, the British empire and their republican ethnic brothers. The bias towards Cape Afrikaners is also reinforced by the fact that in a study of such relations, an understanding of the role of so complex a community requires more than the study of one person, even one as energetic and volatile as Rhodes.

The study is divided into three chronological chapters, using the metaphors of courtship, marriage and divorce, corresponding respectively to the 1880s, to the period of Rhodes's premiership and his alliance with the Afrikaner Bond from 1890 to the Jameson raid at the close of 1895, and to the post-raid period culminating in the 1898 general election.

The title of this study conveys an apparent asymmetry in the relations between Rhodes and the Afrikaner Bond, the political arm of Cape Afrikaners. Jan Smuts referred to this salience: 'Many observers had animadverted upon the unnatural Bond–Rhodes alliance ... That derided parish pumpers should so complacently range themselves under the banner of an imaginative imperialist seemed to the outside world inexplicable ...'[4] The study has to account for the emergence of this 'unnatural' alliance and its flourishing during Rhodes's premiership. To facilitate this, the analysis was informed by the concept of a common ground, or space, shared by Rhodes and the Afrikaner Bond, representing Cape 'Afrikanerdom', which was conducive to their political cohabitation. The first chapter, presenting the profile of the prospective allies, delineates and analyses this common ground.

The vast difference in space allocated to the respective partners, reflects the inherent asymmetry in sketching the profile of an individual and a large-scale community, alluded to earlier. The profile of Rhodes is not only more straightforward, but also well researched and presented in numerous studies, biographical and other. The difficulty in outlining the profile of Cape Afrikaners, as an ethnic community, is compounded by the fact that they are grossly under-researched in the relevant period. Furthermore, although this study focuses on the political behaviour of Cape Afrikaners, this was informed by political consciousness and ideology, which in turn reflected the overall balance of colonial experience of that ethnic community.

Consequently to account for the political consciousness and ideological inclinations of Cape Afrikaners, which prepared them for the alliance with Rhodes, I had to go beyond the topical and chronological confines of the subject. To understand the ideological outlook and political behaviour of Cape Afrikaners in the late nineteenth century, it is vital to comprehend the process of their integration and socialisation into the British imperial and colonial world. This process was fed by a complex interaction between economic, social, cultural and political forces. Since there is no other satisfactory outline of this process, the rather lengthy account of the evolution of the Cape Afrikaner community under British rule from the beginning of the nineteenth century is not superfluous. It is this evolution which shaped, from a Cape Afrikaner perspective, the common ground and ripened them for the alliance with Rhodes. In delineating the common ground questions relating to the evolution of Cape Afrikaner ethnic identity and consciousness have to be addressed. Keen attention is devoted to the intense ideological and political discourse unfolding within this evolving ethnic community. It is argued that the apparent common ground between Rhodes and the Cape Afrikaners at the particular historical juncture was at the root of their political alliance.

However, to understand fully the evolution of the relations between Rhodes and the Bond through courting, marriage and divorce, another analytical concept has been introduced. Rhodes and the Bond, the inhabitants of the common ground, while keenly interested in cohabitation, were also subjected to the pull of conflicting external forces. Although diligently cultivating the common ground and courting the Afrikaner Bond, and Cape Afrikaners more generally, Rhodes was primarily a British imperialist. Ultimately he could not resist the call of empire. For Cape Afrikaners the pull of ethnic solidarity with their republican brothers, especially in the Transvaal, in crisis situations, was all but irresistible. Thus, both Rhodes and his Afrikaner partners were potentially responsive to the opposing tunes of their respective sirens. For the courting to be consummated and for the marriage to be stable, the sirens had to be silent, or at least only faintly heard. This, as we shall see, was the case until the end of 1895. In initiating the Jameson raid, Rhodes succumbed to the call of the empire, and in violating the independence of the Transvaal he compelled the Bond to respond to the call of the ethnic blood.

Thus, the broad historical context had a direct critical bearing on the evolution of the relations between Rhodes and the Cape Afrikaners. Indeed, the relevant historical scene had been undergoing dramatic changes in the last three decades of the nineteenth century. The discoveries of diamonds in Kimberley in the late 1860s, and gold in the Rand in 1886, changed the economic scale and scope of the Cape and South Africa considerably. This newly discovered economic wealth not only stimulated the growth of the economy, but also attracted increasing imperial attention and involvement. It was intensified, in the second half of the 1870s, paradoxically as part of a strategy of disengagement from direct involvement. The annexation of South West Africa by Germany in 1884, albeit with British consent, marked the beginning of the scramble for southern Africa. The discovery of gold in the Rand, which shifted the South African economic balance from the Cape Colony to republican Transvaal, further fed British interest and involvement which escalated until the Anglo-Boer war at the turn of the century. Thus, the backdrop of the evolving relations between Rhodes and the Cape Afrikaners, was not the parochial, dormant environment of the Cape but rather a volatile, explosive southern Africa.

The sources consulted for this study are extensive and varied. There are private papers of contemporaries including the Rhodes Papers, the Hofmeyr Papers, the Dr Te Water Papers, the F.S. Malan Papers, the Bower Papers and others, as well as edited versions such as the selected correspondence of J.X. Merriman, J.R. Innes, P.A. Molteno, Jan Smuts, Alfred Milner, Olive Schreiner, and the selection of Rhodes's speeches. The reports of the Cape Parliament (Hansard) contain useful information regarding the political discourse at that level. Reports of the congresses of the Afrikaner Bond were also consulted. There are also useful autobiographical accounts like those of J.T. Molteno, F.L. Dormer, J.R. Innes, T.E. Fuller, D.P. Faure, G.A.L. Green and C.W.H. Kohler. Extensive use has been made of the local press and particularly the Dutch and Afrikaans press in the Cape and the republics. Dutch newspapers in the Cape mushroomed in the last decades of the nineteenth century not only in the big urban centres but also in small peripheral areas. These sources contain a wealth of information related to the ideological and political discourse of Cape Afrikaners generally and to their relations with Rhodes in particular. Of particular value is the *Zuid Afrikaan* (*ZA*), amalgamated in 1894 with *Ons Land* (*OL*), which was closely identified with the top leadership of the Afrikaner Bond. Numerous biographical studies have also been consulted. There are the numerous biographies of Rhodes, mostly scholarly, but some also by his friends and contemporaries. There are also biographical studies of other contemporaries like J.X. Merriman, J.H. Hofmeyr, Jan Smuts, W.P. Schreiner, J.H. de Villiers, S.J. du Toit, D.C. de Waal, F.S. Malan and T.P. Theron. There is the pioneering work of T.R.H. Davenport on the Afrikaner Bond which proved very helpful. I have also benefited from numerous dissertations, mainly from the University of Cape Town, but also from elsewhere in South Africa and beyond, on subjects directly and indirectly related to this study. Finally I have used extensively studies, books and articles, on imperial, south African and Cape history.

4

NOTES

1. In the period under study, the term Afrikaner was rather ambiguous, describing an ethnic, as well as a voluntary territorial political community. In this study this term relates to the ethno-cultural community comprising the speakers of Dutch and/or the local Dutch dialect (Afrikaans) among the white settlers in South Africa.
2. J.T. Molteno, *The Dominion of Afrikanerdom* (London, 1923), p. 80.
3. See, for example, R. Robinson and J. Gallagher, with A. Denny, *Africa and the Victorians: the Official Mind of Imperialism* (London and Basingstoke, 1961), pp. 410–61.
4. W.K. Hancock and J. van der Poel, *Selection from Jan Smuts Papers* (Cambridge, 1962), Vol. i, June 1886–May 1902, p. 26.

1

The bridegroom and the bride

Cecil John Rhodes and the Afrikaner Bond, the first fully fledged party representing Cape Afrikaners' interests, made an almost simultaneous appearance on the Cape Colony's political scene. On 31 October 1878, Jan Hendrik Hofmeyr and others founded in the western Cape the Zuid Afrikaansche Boeren Bescherming Vereenigen (Farmers' Protection Union) (ZABBV) to promote and defend farmers' interests.[1] In mid-1879 Stephanus Johannes du Toit from Paarl called for the establishment of an Afrikaner Bond, as a more embracing and ambitious political organisation.[2] In 1880–81 this organisation came into being.[3] In a congress held in Richmond in May 1883 the two organisations amalgamated to form the Afrikaner Bond en Boeren Bescherming Vereeniging.[4] As a result of the 1884 general election the Bond became the dominant political party in the Cape, and Cape Afrikaners made a dramatic appearance on the local political stage. The Bond was primarily concerned with the promotion of the material interests of its predominantly rural constituents.

On 1 September 1870, at the age of 17, Cecil John Rhodes landed in South Africa in search of fame and fortune.[5] By 1880 he had made a small fortune in the diamond fields at Kimberley and had also spent sufficient time in Oxford to be influenced by the spirit of British imperialism prevailing in certain quarters in this British intellectual Mecca.[6] In 1881, he entered the Cape House of Assembly, as a Member for Barkly West, one of the constituencies of the newly annexed Griqualand West.[7] This would prove to be the first step in a determined pursuit of political fame.

By 1890 the two novices in the Cape political arena, Rhodes and the Afrikaner Bond, had struck a political alliance which secured Rhodes the premiership of the colony. The next chapter will attempt to give an account of the political courtship which culminated in 1890 in a seemingly strange political marriage between Rhodes and the Afrikaner Bond. Why did Rhodes court the Bond, and Cape Afrikaners more generally, so persistently and so enthusiastically? And perhaps more importantly and intriguingly, why did the Bond respond so willingly and unreservedly? However, to understand the courtship and the marriage, we must first become acquainted with the bridegroom and the bride. They are the subject of the present chapter.

THE BRIDEGROOM

While this study is not another attempt to resolve the mystery of Rhodes's personality, a working outline of Rhodes's motivation is essential to the understanding of his approaches to the Cape Afrikaners, and to the Afrikaner Bond in particular.

Rotberg, in his recent voluminous and exhaustive biography of Rhodes, argues against the conventional wisdom, shared by most of Rhodes's numerous biographers, that he was motivated, in all his later endeavours, by the imperial vision which had captured his soul in the second half of the 1870s. Thus, he discounts Flint's argument that Rhodes's entry into the Cape Parliament was part of a long-term strategy. The following is Rotberg's account:

> In 1881, Rhodes, the successful amalgamator, the advocate of railways and of the rationalization of diamond mining, entered the lower house of the parliament of the Colony of the Cape of Good Hope. Ten months later, after completing his degree at Oxford, Rhodes returned to South Africa to make money from diamonds, to advance his political career, and to develop and then enlarge upon an array of projects which together, after a time, constituted Rhodes's personal imperial imperative.[8]

Rotberg takes a similar view of Rhodes's vision of northern expansion, arguing that in the early 1880s he was not motivated by 'the promise of regions beyond the Limpopo'.[9] He also adopts this incremental interpretation regarding Rhodes's relations with the Afrikaner Bond:

> The support of the Bond . . . was essential. But it is incorrect to suggest that Rhodes shifted ground politically in the 1880s solely in order to accomplish his dreams of northern glory. As before, and as almost always, Rhodes was a tactician, an incrementalist. He had ideas and visions, but those ideas were options, and Rhodes always toyed simultaneously with several desirable objectives.[10]

Presenting Rhodes in the early 1880s as a mere tactician runs against the evidence used by the priests of the conventional wisdom. In the first place, there is Rhodes's famous first will from 1877. As puerile and naive as it may seem to our post-colonial, post-imperial cynical eyes, it should be taken seriously as representing young Rhodes's inner motivation. After all, what can be more serious than a young man in his early twenties contemplating his death and writing a will and testament? In this will,

Rhodes instructed that his worldly possessions be used for the establishment of a secret society to be charged with the following tasks:

> The extension of British rule throughout the world ... the colonization by British subjects of all lands where the means of livelihood are attainable by energy, labour and enterprise, and especially the occupation by British settlers of the entire continent of Africa, the Holy Land, the Valley of the Euphrates, the islands of Cyprus and Candia, the whole of South America, the islands of the Pacific not heretofore possessed by Great Britain, the whole of the Malay Archipelago, the seaboard of China and Japan, the ultimate recovery of the United States of America as an integral part of the British Empire.[11]

That this will represented a deeply-seated motivation rather than an emotional outburst is proven by the fact that five years later Rhodes saw fit to entrust its execution to a more trustworthy agent.[12]

On 2 June 1877, Rhodes put the following thoughts in writing:

> It often strikes a man to enquire what is the chief good in life; to one the thought comes that it is a happy marriage, to another great wealth, to a third travel and so on; as each seizes the idea, for that he more or less works for the rest of his existence. To myself thinking over the question the wish came to render myself useful to my country.[13]

A friend from his Kimberley days wrote in his memoirs: 'On Wednesday, the 23rd May, 1877, Cecil Rhodes confided to me the objects to which he intended to devote his life, and he did devote it ...'.[14] Jameson, Rhodes's close friend and confidant, recalled that, as early as 1878, 'Cecil Rhodes, then a man of twenty-six or twenty-seven, had mapped out, in his clear brain, his whole policy just as it has since been developed'.[15] And Sydney Shippard remembered that in early 1878 he and Rhodes 'discussed and sketched out the whole plan of British advance in south and central Africa'.[16] Rotberg's remark that Shippard did not 'indicate whether the details of the plan bore any real resemblance to the eventual shape of Rhodes' activities' is hardly relevant. Neither is the claim that Rhodes, at the time of the Bechuanaland crisis of 1884–85, 'had no real sketch of "Rhodesia" in his head',[17] a proof that his vision of imperial expansion developed incrementally. In fact, Ralph Williams, who wrote that Rhodes, at that time, 'knew nothing of the country' (Rhodesia), also writes that 'it was the lake countries of Tanganyika and the lakes to the north of it which Rhodes then wished for and his primary object was to keep the road thither open'.[18] L. Michell tells us that around 1881 Rhodes was seen with his hand on the map of Africa declaring: 'That is my dream, all English.'[19] In fact, this evidence may serve as a proof that, in pursuit of his grand imperial design, Rhodes was a reductionist rather than an incrementalist. Indeed, that he did not have a detailed plan for expansion, or that he viewed 'Rhodesia' as a corridor to Tanganyika does not undermine the argument that already by the late 1870s Rhodes was primarily motivated by his imperial African dream.

It is hardly surprising that Rhodes's vision of imperial expansion unfolded gradually and did not follow his original plan closely. As a free-lance imperialist he could not, of course, fulfil his dream as *deus ex machina*. Geopolitical circumstances, economic conditions and numerous constraints affected Rhodes's fortunes as an empire-builder. However, it is quite clear that, over and above contextual constraints and tactical exigencies, the combined impact of the intellectual frontier at Oxford,[20] the economic frontier in Kimberley and the imperial frontier in southern Africa produced in young Rhodes a most compelling, indeed obsessive sense of imperial mission. This sense of mission became a most powerful driving force. It guided him and served as an ideological cement giving meaning and coherence to his multifarious activities. Thus, with Rhodes, imperial vision had preceded imperial practice. Imperial vision was not an incremental outcome of tactical exploits and successful responses and reactions. Rather, operative plans, tactics and strategy served a vision which had possessed Rhodes long before his first imperial endeavour. True, Rhodes was tactical and responsive. However, it is difficult to account for the zeal and determination of his reaction to the crisis in Bechuanaland in 1883–85, to take one example, unless we accept the compelling vision which drove him. Even Rotberg agrees that 'it is impossible to ignore, dismiss, or deride Rhodes's visionary impulses as inconsequential'. Indeed, as he himself writes, 'one aspect of Rhodes's greatness lies in the breadth of his genius – the sweep from grand design to minutiae'.[21] Rhodes was not satisfied with dreaming of an ultimate British global order; he always asked himself, 'what's to be done?'

In understanding the interaction between grand design and tactical minutiae, it is important to focus on Rhodes's role as free-lance empire-builder in an age of intensive, multinational imperialist competition. In September 1888, Rhodes recalled his predicament during the Bechuana-land crisis of the mid-1880s: 'From my humble point of view I felt I was embarking upon a project without an atom of support at my back.'[22] This was, however, a self-inflicted predicament, as Rhodes viewed himself as a high priest of the *vision* of British imperialism rather than as an agent of the British government. He believed that he had discovered the secret of Britain's imperial destiny. He likened himself to an inventor who was not sure that he would live long enough to complete the registration of his patent.[23] This greatly sharpened his political senses and was a source of permanent internal tension and anxiety.

Rhodes's misfortune was that he assumed the imperial mantle at a time when the fortunes of aggressive, formal imperialism in Britain were in decline. In fact, Rhodes was captivated by the vision when the goddess of imperialism was still smiling, during the imperialist revival of the last Disraeli government. Young Rhodes must have been thrilled by the annexation of the Transvaal in 1877 and the general manifestation of imperial resolve and aggression by the High Commissioner Sir Bartle Frere. And if there was a setback in the battle of Isandlwana against the Zulu in 1879, there was also the satisfaction of a prompt and decisive imperial response. It is hardly surprising that, in 1877, Rhodes appointed the Secretary of State for Colonies as one of the executors of his first will.

Any hopes that the British government would fulfil its imperial destiny vanished with the general election of 1880. Little England won the day and Gladstone, who in his Midlothian campaign rode the wave of anti-imperialism, was swept to power. The humiliating defeat at Majuba Hill in 1881 at the hands of the Transvaal Boers gave the change in Britain's imperial fortunes a painful South African touch. Worse still, the defeat was met not by revenge, but rather by concession. F.J. Dormer, the then editor of the *Cape Argus*, wrote that Rhodes was 'one of those whom the stirring events of 1880–81 left in an attitude of violent antagonism towards a settlement which was based upon the undeniable defeat of British arms'.[24] Rhodes himself spoke subsequently of the 'vacillation of the Home Government, which never knew its own mind about us' when he entered Cape politics: 'Many Englishmen cried out at the surrender after Majuba but the real humiliation was borne by those who, relying on the Imperial pledges, had stood firm in the Transvaal for the old flag.'[25] No wonder that in 1882 he struck the Secretary of State for Colonies from his will and appointed his trusted friend Pickering as an executor. Then came the Bechuanaland crisis of 1884–85. Although the Warren expedition was sent and Bechuanaland was eventually saved for the empire, the handling of the crisis by the British government and some of its local agents left Rhodes frustrated and exasperated. At a time when Germany, Portugal and Transvaal were engaging in a scramble for southern Africa, the British failed to demonstrate the imperialist zeal and determination hoped for by Rhodes. British imperialism had to find a more effective agent if the British were to fulfil their cosmic destiny.

This was the background which transformed Rhodes from a mere visionary and enthusiastic observer and supporter into the foremost empire-builder of his time. While exhibiting interest in imperial expansion and consolidation further afield, Rhodes concentrated his resources, zeal and energy in British expansion to southern Africa, his particular imperial frontier. According to a Cape parliamentary gallery reporter, Rhodes, at the beginning of his parliamentary career, in the early 1880s, 'never gave the House ... an inkling of his great plans'.[26] Gradually, however, the full scope of his imperial grand design was unfolded. On

18 July 1883, speaking in the debate on the Basutoland Annexation Bill, he stated: 'I have my own views as to the future of South Africa, and I believe in a United States of South Africa, but as a portion of the British Empire.'[27] At about that time, Rhodes told his constituents some five years later, he found himself 'studying Cape politics from what I may humbly suggest was a broader platform'.[28] As it became clear from his activity until 1890, this 'broader platform' included the whole area from the Cape through Bechuanaland to the Zambesi and beyond.

This was not an undertaking for 'reluctant imperialists'. British 'reluctant imperialism' was manifested in a reluctance to invest both financial and power resources for the attainment of imperial glory. Rhodes's contribution to British imperialism was primarily in developing local financial and power resources and committing them to the imperialist cause. The importance which he attributed to the role of his private financial resources in his imperial scheme was already manifested in his first will of 1877, in which he left all his worldly assets for the furtherance of British expansion. Discussing railway schemes in China, Rhodes told Colquhoun: 'You'll never do anything with it, Colquhoun; you've got no money.' Better known is his astonishment upon hearing from General Gordon that he had refused to accept a small fortune offered to him by the Chinese government: 'I would have taken it and as many more rooms-full as they offered me: it is no use having big ideas if you have not the cash to carry them out.'[29] Thus, it is wrong to view Rhodes's money-making operations in the early 1880s as unrelated to his grand imperial vision.[30] The linkage between South African financial resources controlled by Rhodes and his imperialist designs came to full light during the negotiations leading to the final amalgamation of the diamond industry in Kimberley. The only real opposition on the part of Barney Barnato, the last obstacle to the amalgamation, was related to Rhodes's ideas regarding the non-economic role of De Beers. As Turrell put it:

> Rhodes wanted the monopoly to be the basis for a colonial exploration and investment company with a wide range of political powers; Barnato had to be persuaded that this grand scheme could be built on the profits of diamond mining.[31]

When he finally succumbed he told Rhodes: 'Some people have a fancy for one thing, some for another. You want the means to go north, if possible, so I suppose we must give it you.' The result was that De Beers became a veritable imperialist agency controlled by Rhodes.[32] Subsequently Rhodes used De Beers's financial resources for his northern expansion. Rhodes exploited similarly the resources of his Goldfields of South Africa Limited.[33]

Thus, Rhodes was not, as was argued by Hobson and by many subsequent radical critics, merely a greedy capitalist out to accumulate material wealth. Of this type there were many in contemporary South Africa. Rhodes developed and cultivated his enormous wealth also as a means to further his imperialist plans. In arguing for the primacy of the political ideal over purely economic considerations, I do not wish to present Rhodes as a net product of an idealist inspiration. Indeed, as I pointed out earlier, Rhodes was, like many others, a product of his material and economic environment, and it is impossible fully to understand his evolution as an ardent imperialist without regard to his experience on the new frontier of aggressive capitalism in Kimberley. Equally, it is impossible to account fully for his political manoeuvres without regard to the requisites of his financial operations. Finally, it is impossible to grasp fully his imperialist drive in southern Africa without regard to the broad movements and dynamics along the volatile economic, capitalist frontiers of the region. Rhodes was, however, more than that. As I argued before, the combined impact of the intellectual, economic and imperial frontiers which Rhodes straddled during his formative years produced in him an overarching, overriding and compelling imperialist vision and drive which had an autonomous existence and which became his prime and ultimate motive and guide. It is from this premise that I argue that Rhodes placed his economic resources at the service of his imperialist enterprise.

Financial resources however, on their own, were not sufficient, especially in an age when the 'scramble' became a European competition for African territories. If Rhodes was to implement his imperial dreams, metropolitan reluctance had to be made good by his own political power base. Galbraith argues that, indeed, the urge for power was Rhodes's foremost driving force.[34] As in the case of money, the question arises: power for what purpose? Galbraith dismisses Rhodes's admirers' assertion that Rhodes dedicated himself selflessly to the imperial ideal. He argues that all that Rhodes did was for his own self-realisation.[35] This is probably true, but it is a truism that ordinary people, as well as historical heroes are ego-centred. What is significant for the understanding of Rhodes is that in his search for self-realisation he employed both his financial and power resources, as well as his remarkable charisma, in a relentless campaign for the expansion of the British empire, particularly in southern Africa.

Since the British government was not trusted to fulfil Britain's manifest imperial destiny, an alternative power base had to be cultivated in South Africa itself. Thus, Rhodes courted and cultivated local imperial agents such as the Governor and High Commissioner, Sir Hercules Robinson, and other officials in the imperial civil and military establishment.[36] Since these were ultimately responsible to the imperial government they could offer auxiliary services. Rhodes needed, in addition, a local political base. His choice was the Cape Colony which, having received responsible government in 1872, was an autonomous regional player. On 7 June 1885, in connection with the Bechuanaland affair, Rhodes wrote to Lord Harris of the Colonial Office:

> I had to consider the best mode of permanently checking the expansion of the Boer republics in the interior. The only solution I can see is to enclose them by the Cape Colony. The British public I feel will never stand the permanent expense of a Crown Colony so far removed from the sea . . .'.[37]

However, the Cape, alas, was not a powerful launching pad for Rhodes's grand imperial design. In the debate on Basutoland in the Cape parliament in 1883 he said: 'Are we a great and independent nation? No! we are only the population of a third-rate English town, spread over a vast country.'[38] Indeed, there was an inherent discrepancy between Rhodes's imperial vision and the available powerbase for its fulfilment. In trying to overcome this weakness, Rhodes demonstrated his ability to operate simultaneously at the levels of vision, strategy and tactics. Thus, he argued for relinquishing the Cape's control over densely populated black regions, like Basutoland and the Transkei, and handing them over to direct imperial control.[39] This, from Rhodes's perspective, would free the Cape to fulfil its imperial destiny, namely, becoming the dominant state in South Africa and serving as the base for imperial expansion northwards. Addressing the Cape Parliament on 16 August 1883, he said:

> I look upon this Bechuanaland territory as the Suez Canal of the trade of this country, the key of its road to the interior. The House will have to wake up to what is to be its future policy. The question before us really is this, whether this Colony is to be confined to its present borders, or whether it is to become the dominant state in South Africa – whether, in fact, it is to spread its civilisation over the interior.[40]

This was the first time that Rhodes divulged in public the full scope of his expectations from the Cape – that it should become dominant in the South African state system and that it should serve as a launching pad for northern expansion. As he told Parliament a year later in the debate on Bechuanaland, they had to annex this territory in order to strengthen their claim to be the 'dominant faction and mover in that Union [the Union of South Africa]'.[41]

Thus, Rhodes adopted the Cape, and South Africa more generally, not only as his home but also as the medium through which he wished to express his personality and his imperial vision. At the beginning of his political career Rhodes said in parliament: 'I have adopted the Colony as my home . . .'.[42] Referring, in a speech to his constituents in 1888, to the allegation that he wished to secure for himself a seat in the British Parliament, he said: 'I have not the slightest idea of quitting South Africa for any other country. Here I can do something; but were I to go to England as a politician, I should be lost in obscurity.'[43]

The seed of collaboration between Rhodes and the Cape Afrikaners originated, as we shall see later, in the scheming mind of the former. This seed would not have come to blossom in a full-blown alliance between the two, however, unless it had fallen on very fertile ground. Therefore, to understand the development and nature of this alliance we have to turn to the Afrikaner field and to the causes for its remarkable fertility.

THE BRIDE

The attitude of Cape Afrikaners towards Rhodes and the political alliance between the latter and the Afrikaner Bond cannot be properly and fully understood without reference to the multi-dimensional process of socialisation into the British colonial and imperial world which Cape Afrikaners had undergone since the onset of the British occupation at the beginning of the nineteenth century. It was this process, approaching a climax towards the end of the century, which made Cape Afrikaners so receptive and responsive to Rhodes's advances. This broad and complex process was fuelled by the increasing economic integration of the Cape into an expanding British imperial economy and on concomitant processes of modernisation. These, in turn, produced social changes which transformed Cape Afrikaner society. This transformation was enhanced by a parallel impact of the culture of the imperial masters. Cape Afrikaners were also absorbed into the institutional web of the colonial state at the level of both local and central government. All these influences, converging on Cape Afrikaner society, played a major role in shaping their collective identity and their ideological and political outlook. Grievances and complaints notwithstanding, by the end of the nineteenth century Cape Afrikaners as a whole, and certainly those who provided them with ideological and political guidance, were sufficiently satisfied with the imperial connection to view it as beneficial rather than as an unmitigated evil.

The integration of Cape Afrikaners into the British imperial economy.

At the root of the process of socialisation lay, as indicated above, the increasing integration of the Cape into the fast-expanding British imperial economy and indeed the global economy during the nineteenth century. The conventional view emphasises the stagnation of the Cape economy under the Dutch East India Company (VOC) and the dramatic economic transformation in the wake of the British occupation.[44] In opposing the portrayal of the Dutch period as economically static and stagnant, Ross emphasises the dynamic and expansive nature of the economy during the Dutch period and concludes:

> The agricultural history of the colony during the 19th century ... is therefore basically the story of a steady intensifying on the basis of the widespread, if low level, commercialization achieved by the end of the VOC period.[45]

There is little doubt that the VOC period was anything but economically stagnant and that it presents an impressive narrative of expansion and adaptation to both ecological and market conditions. However, by over-emphasising the continuity between the two periods and by portraying the change as one only of quantity and pace, we may underestimate the far-reaching changes which the Cape economy was undergoing during the nineteenth century. The absorption of the Cape by the foremost modern industrial state, which was also the dominant imperial power, set in motion processes of change which transformed the scale, the scope and the nature of the economic order, and the physical and demographic landscape of the country. This was to have a considerable impact on the evolution of Cape Afrikaner society and its collective consciousness.

Perhaps the degree of continuity has been exaggerated because, until the early 1870s, agriculture continued to be the foundation of the Cape economy, and it was dominated by the farming community whose origin was in the VOC period. Such an impression may also be enhanced by the fact that the economic transformation and the improvement of the Cape's economic fortunes were not immediate or dramatic. The Cape had to find and exploit profitable economic niches if it was to benefit from its British connection. This was not an easy task in an empire which was moving away from mercantilism into a new economic era premised on the concept and practice of free trade. Since significant mineral discoveries were only made in the late 1860s and the second half of the 1880s, economic growth had to rely solely on the expansion of the productive potential of the agricultural sector.

The Cape's agriculturally based economy, adjusting well to the ecological environment, to the infrastructural deficiencies and to the limited scope of domestic and foreign markets, had developed, during the VOC period, on subsistence, exchange and market lines, with wine, grain and livestock as its main products. The local market inherited by the British was very limited in scope, largely because the VOC discouraged immigration and maintained a very limited administrative presence in its colony. This changed in the course of the nineteenth century with striking economic consequences. In 1819 the British government decided to encourage immigration to the Cape Colony which it had annexed formally four years earlier. This new policy resulted, a year later, in the immigration of some 4,000 English settlers.[46] Although such an effort of organised immigration was not repeated, a stream of immigrants, mainly English but also others, continued. Consequently, the European population increased from a mere 26,568 in 1806 to 109,921 by 1855.[47] The stream turned into a minor flood with the discovery of diamonds in Griqualand West in the late 1860s and by 1891 the Cape had some 377,000 Europeans.[48] From an economic point of view, the mere increase in scale was not insignificant. However, the main contribution of the new immigration to the economic development of the Cape was primarily qualitative.

The new European immigrants formed the nucleus, indeed the bulk, of a fast growing urban population. They gave an impetus to a phenomenal urban growth in the Cape during the nineteenth century. The dramatic process of urbanisation[49] of the overwhelmingly rural Cape was also boosted by a considerable expansion, both in space and in scale, of the civil service of the colonial state. Between 1815 and 1860, the size of the civil service increased fivefold and the number of administrative units in the Cape rose from six in 1806 to 43 in 1860.[50] The administrative headquarters contributed to the establishment of new urban centres or provided impetus for existing ones.

Urban development under the rule of the VOC was very rudimentary. Outside Cape Town most small urban centres like Stellenbosch, Paarl and Tulbagh were in the western province. Swellendam, which was established in 1743 some 130 kilometres east of Cape Town, was until 1786 the furthest town from the VOC's headquarters. Graaff Reinet, which was established in the east in that year, was not much of an urban centre in the early 1800s. Uitenhage in the eastern Cape, founded by the Batavian administration in 1804, was the last Dutch contribution to the urbanisation of the Cape.[51]

During the nineteenth century, under British rule, the growth of urban centres dramatically changed the Cape's landscape. Most of the towns and villages which existed at the end of the century had, in fact, been established before 1854.[52] Between 1806 and 1860 the number of these increased tenfold.[53] In 1855 there were 45 towns and villages in the Cape. However, most towns and villages were very small, the proportion of people living in these centres rose between 1806 and 1855 only from a quarter to a third of the entire population.[54] The proportion increased markedly in the wake of the discovery of diamonds in the late 1860s.

The increasing urban population, in towns throughout the colony, considerably expanded the local market, providing ready consumers for the agricultural output produced mainly by the Afrikaner farmers. Thus, in response to the growing local demand, the farmers considerably increased the production of foodstuffs.[55] However, even in the late nineteenth century the total urban population of the Cape could not have exceeded that of an average English city. Clearly, if the Cape was to develop its agricultural productive potential it had to look for markets further afield. Indirectly and directly the British were instrumental in considerably expanding the regional economic horizons of the Cape colonists. Indirectly, the British were responsible for the establishment of the two Boer republics which became part of the economic hinterland of the Cape. With the discovery of gold in the Transvaal during the 1880s this hinterland became a lucrative market for Cape produce. Furthermore, as the scramble for southern Africa unfolded during the last two decades of the century, British expansion also broadened the economic horizons of the Colony.

However, the regional hinterland acquired a considerable economic importance for the Cape only from the second half of the 1880s, in the wake of the gold discoveries on the Rand and the establishment of Rhodesia. By then the Cape economy had become crucially dependent on the economy of its imperial master. From being an outpost of a declining commercial company the Cape was linked to the most developed, dynamic industrial country in the world. Britain had no intention of developing its colonies as competing industrial societies. Rather, the colonies were perceived as markets for the steadily expanding British industrial output. The colonial economies were also expected to develop their mineral and agricultural potential for supplying the growing demand of the British industrial economy and society. The growing British investments in the colonies during the nineteenth century were geared primarily to developing this potential.

It was not at all easy for the Cape to benefit from the expansion of its economic horizons. Cape wheat, for example, could not compete on the export markets and depended solely on the increase in local demand. In general, however, exports did rise considerably under British rule.[56] Cape wine made the first major break into the British market in the wake of the second British occupation in 1806. Government encouragement and preferential tariffs boosted the export of inferior Cape wines to Britain.[57] The gradual removal of this protection which began in 1825 and culminated in the Cobden Treaty in 1860 brought about a sharp decline in wine production.[58] Thus, wine production, which was also limited to the Western Cape, did not provide the economy with the key to sustained economic growth and prosperity.

It was the export of wool from the 1840s which transformed the Cape economy, linking it more firmly to the world market and launching it on a course of progress and relative prosperity. In the development of this industry the British connection, both local and metropolitan, was much more crucial than in the case of wine. The dramatic growth of wool production in the Cape was triggered by the growing demand of the fast developing wool industry in Britain.[59] Wool, unfortunately, was not a traditional Cape product. In the predominantly pastoral Cape economy sheep production had, for a long time, been a major occupation. However, the local fat-tailed sheep, well adjusted to the Cape ecological conditions and to traditional subsistence, exchange and market requirements, were no providers of suitable wool. Sheep production had to be transformed if the Cape was to benefit from the opening in the British market. The task was not easy. The Batavian administration, at the beginning of the century, tried, to no avail, to encourage conservative Cape farmers to introduce Merino wool-producing sheep. During the British period a combination of government encouragement, local initiative and stimulation by enterprising merchants established and then expanded wool production. The number of wool-producing sheep rose from 15,000 in 1824 to 4,828,000 in 1855 and the value of wool exports increased from £2,000 in 1820–24 to £984,000 in 1855–59.[60]

The expansion of wool production drew more closely into the market economy areas like the Midlands, the eastern Cape and the Karoo, which had previously been relatively marginal. The impact of the increase in scale and spatial scope of this economic development was at the root of the rapid growth of villages and towns across the Cape. The new towns and *dorps* became the focal points of a commercial network which mainly serviced the expanding wool industry. There developed a commercial chain leading from London through major urban centres, to regional centres and then to local *dorps*. At the end of this chain was the *smous*, the itinerant trader, who brought the message of the market economy to the most isolated farmer. The story of the Mosenthal brothers who, after having established themselves in Port Elizabeth, opened a branch in Graaff Reinet which, in turn, served as a centre for sub-branches in outlying centres like Richmond, Murraysburg, Burgersdorp, Hopetown and Aliwal North, was by no means unique.[61]

However, these centres could not activate the productive potential of such vast areas and gear it to the world market, unless the necessary infrastructure was developed. Unlike the wine-growing areas, the sheep-producing areas were a long way from the only harbour, which had been built during the Dutch period. The *trek boers*, who developed the pastoral economy, spread far and wide in this vast colony. In a period in which the ox-wagon was the main mode of transport, most areas were too remote from the local market or from the Cape Town harbour to be involved intensively and regularly in the market economy. The problem

18

of distance was exacerbated by the topography of the Cape. Especially when the main product of market value was bulky, any large-scale market-oriented commercial development was uneconomic. Thus, the Hottentots-Holland range isolated the Swellendam area from Cape Town, only some 130 km away.[62] The much more distant Graaff Reinet area, which in 1795 produced half of the sheep and a third of the cattle in the colony, had only limited access to the only proper market in Cape Town.[63]

Because of the distance, cost and technical difficulties, the development of roads during the British period had a slow start. Only during the 1840s did John Montagu begin to develop the transport system, upgrading the Cape Town harbour and building roads, mountain passes and bridges across the Cape.[64] However, before the advent of railways, surface transport by ox-wagon was no solution for long-distance trade. The solution lay in the development of new ports along the long Cape coast – in Port Beaufort, at the mouth of Breede River in 1816, in Mossel Bay in 1848, in Knysna in 1817, in Port Elizabeth in 1815 and in East London in 1845.[65] The shift of the economic balance eastward, in the wake of the wool boom, was manifested by the fact that the value of merchandise handled by the Port Elizabeth port exceeded, by 1860, that of Cape Town.[66] Each port, supplemented by local roads, was the focal point of growing regional commercial networks which were, in turn, linked to the overall Cape commercial system and to the world markets. It is in these ports that the big mercantile houses established themselves and from which they sent their tentacles inland. The best account of the evolution of such a regional system is the telling story of the commercial enterprise of Joseph Barry and Nephews which expanded from their base in Port Beaufort.[67] Yet, even within these smaller-scale commercial systems, the surface transport and communication was slow and erratic.[68] The constraints on commercial activity stemming from this were only removed with the construction of railway lines across the colony during the last three decades of the century.[69]

Thus, with the development of ports and a more reliable and faster transport system, the economic distances between producers and markets, locally and externally, were sharply reduced. The introduction of modern communication means also had a most beneficial effect on the economic life in the Cape. Mail service within the Cape and between it and the outside world improved steadily throughout the nineteenth century.[70] Much more important, for the shortening of economic distance and speeding up the commercial pace, was the introduction of the telegraph service. The first telegraph line, between Cape Town and the naval base in Simonstown, was launched in 1860, and by 1878 various centres throughout the Cape were served by 2,700 miles of telegraph lines.[71] The economic importance of the telegraph service was highlighted by the fact that financial institutions were its main customers.[72]

As the transport and communication systems in the Cape were improving, the commercial system became more compact and closely knit, with villages and towns serving as its focal points. In order to function and to prosper, the system needed a financial network to provide it with the essential flow of capital and credit. It was in this crucial economic field that the British imperial connection proved very useful. During the Dutch period credit facilities were rudimentary and even under British rule there was no immediate improvement. Until 1837, the provision of banking services was the domain of the government and of merchants offering discount. The first private bank, the Cape of Good Hope Bank, was established only in 1837. By 1860, 23 local banks were in operation, mainly in the western and eastern provinces.[73] The spread of local banks was indicative of both the increasing demand for banking facilities and the availability of surplus local capital.

Soon, however, British banks were attracted to the Cape. Surplus capital was available in Britain to service the economic development of the dependent colonial economies. The consecutive wool, diamond and gold booms turned the Cape, and South Africa more generally, into an attractive field for metropolitan banking ventures. The interest shown by British capital in banking operations in the Cape was timely because local capital could not satisfy the increasing need for credit for the expansion of productive and commercial operations.[74] The first imperial bank, the London and South African Bank, was incorporated by royal charter on 17 November 1860. The second, the Standard Bank of British South Africa, which was to have a crucial impact on the economic development of South Africa, was established in 1862.[75] By 1885, imperial banks, with branches spread across the Colony, overshadowed the local banks and ten years later they virtually monopolised the banking system.[76]

The development of the physical and economic infrastructure, which was generated by the wool production, also stimulated the commercial exploitation of existing agricultural resources and the introduction of new ones. Thus, the construction of harbours along the coast boosted the export of skins, hides and horns before the occurrence of the wool boom.[77] In the late 1850s Angora goats were introduced to the Mossel Bay and Oudtshoorn areas and to the midlands and eastern province. Between 1869 and 1874 the export of mohair increased in value from £15,000 to £107,000.[78] Another new development was the production of ostrich feathers, in response to the growing demand by the European fashion industry. The concomitant rise in price boosted the value of the export of feathers from £70,000 to £206,000 between 1869 and 1874.

A contemporary farmer and politician wrote in 1881: 'another animal was added to our domesticated list, and new life and vigour thrown into our farming population at the Cape.'[79]

The Cape's export trade was geared mainly to the British market. As the items of export were primary products, the consequent dependence also exposed the Cape to the fluctuations of demand and prices in the British markets. An interesting, though by no means crucial, case of rise and decline of fortunes stemming from this dependence is that of horse breeding.[80] More serious, though temporary, was the drop in wool production which resulted from the trade depression of the mid-1860s.[81] In the first half of the 1880s there was a severe decline in agricultural exports.[82] However, by that time the Cape economy was sufficiently diversified, and assisted by the mineral revolution of the 1870s and the 1880s it was able to recover.

The increase in the export trade provided Cape colonists with cash income they could use for consumption. A contemporary wrote in 1860 about the impact of the introduction of wool-bearing sheep in the Colesberg area in the Karoo:

> That the introduction of the Merino gave a great and permanent impulse to the prosperity of the community is obvious. In the first place, then, wool more than doubled the farmers' income; and, being a ready-money transaction, gave him annually the command of a considerable amount of cash.[83]

In the same year the civil commissioner of Cradock reported that it was not unusual for an 'ordinary farmer' in the district to earn from £5,000 to £7,000 a year, an 'almost fabulous' sum in South Africa.[84] The newly acquired cash income not only created a space for conspicuous consumption, but also encouraged the trade in basic necessities. Thus, as Ross writes, 'In 1865, Graaff Reinet, where Barrow could not buy bread, had eleven bakers, as well as 26 boot and shoemakers, 35 blacksmiths, and 108 "merchants, wholesale and retail dealers".' By then only 25 per cent of the 4,000 persons in these occupations in the Cape resided in Cape Town.[85]

The growing prosperity of the colonists was also manifested in the marked expansion of the import trade. Even in the late nineteenth century the manufacturing industry in the Cape was very rudimentary.[86] Even after the Cape had acquired fiscal autonomy, with Responsible Government in 1872, the Cape government did little to foster the development of local industries.[87] Thus, with the expansion of exports there also developed a flourishing import trade, mostly with Britain and its colonies.[88] The value of imports rose from £423,277 in 1830 to £9,372,019 in 1882.[89] In the case of imports, as in the case of exports, the trade definitely followed the flag. British shipping also prospered from the steady growth of the Cape's foreign trade, British ships almost monopolising maritime transport to and from the Colony.[90]

In the overall economic development of the Cape during the nineteenth century the imperial nexus was of vital importance. The colonial government made, as we have seen, a substantial contribution in upgrading the infrastructure which was essential to economic and commercial expansion. The imperial government and its local agents also played a direct role in facilitating and encouraging economic development. When the British first took over in 1795, the Cape as a whole was grossly underdeveloped. A memorandum submitted to the British authorities by F. Kersteins on 26 September 1795 blamed VOC policies for the economic decline of the Cape.[91] Even if, as has been conventionally argued, the economic malpractices of the VOC were not abolished,[92] the advent of British rule brought at least some economic relief. Between 1795 and 1803, the first period of their occupation of the Cape, the British authorities removed all the restrictions on trade which had existed in the VOC period.[93] Thus, at the very beginning of its rule, Britain considerably expanded the economic space of Cape colonists. In fact, Britain had a keen interest in exploiting the economic potential of the colony to its fullest. Unlike the declining commercial company, which had a limited interest in the economic development of the Cape, Britain was the foremost power in the world. Under British rule the Cape became an important link in a global defence system and part of a powerful imperial economic network. Furthermore, the British had a much more systematic and constructive approach to the government of its colonies than the VOC. From all these perspectives, the British government and its local agents had a keen interest in the development of the indigenous economic resources for the sake of financing the expanding government and with a view to transforming the Cape into a profitable component of the British industrial economy.

The Cape under the VOC had not prepared the Afrikaner colonists for playing this new role. Under the monopolistic practices of the VOC with its minimalistic economic and developmental approach, there could not flourish the skills, attitudes and agents essential for the beneficial integration of the local economy into the highly dynamic and competitive British economy. In particular, the Cape lacked a sufficiently large entrepreneurial class such as was the agent of the capitalist revolution in Britain and elsewhere in Europe. With a radical change in the immigration policy under British rule, the door opened for the influx of a predominantly English-speaking entrepreneurial class.

The qualitative contribution of this entrepreneurial class, from the big mercantile houses down to the itinerant trader, to the economic development of the Cape was immense. The alien entrepreneurs not only brought with them the aggressive, adventurous spirit of capitalist Europe, but also possessed the necessary skills, had knowledge of the British and European markets and had vital access to capital. Thus, the Mosenthal Brothers in the east, Thalwitzer in the west, Barry and Nephews in the Overberg, and others, played a vital role in the development of the wool industry which ushered in the first real economic boom.[94] This is equally true for the introduction of Angora goats and the systematisation and expansion of ostrich farming which made an important contribution to the economic prosperity of the colony. Immigrants were also arch modernisers. Thus, the first incubator for breeding ostriches and the first reaping machine for grain harvesting were introduced by British settlers.[95] Above all, the immigrants were the backbone and the engine of the fast-developing urban system with its shops and mercantile companies, with its banks and other financial institutions which were the hearts and the vessels introducing capitalism to the Cape's rural economy.

The imperial government itself, through its local agents, was directly involved in promoting the economic development of the Cape. By initiating settlement in the eastern Cape and through its efforts to stabilise the eastern frontier, the imperial government opened a new zone of development and prosperity for white settlers, which tilted the economic balance within the colony towards the east. In 1813, the government instituted, instead of the VOC land loan system, a perpetual quitrent tenure, which increased land-holding security and was conducive to long-term rural planning, investment and development.[96] For as long as they could, the local imperial agents at the Cape also tried to maintain the structure of labour relations to the advantage of the commercial farmers.[97] Even after the abolition of slavery in the 1830s the government continued to favour the white farmers, allowing them to unashamedly exploit black labour.

The government was also keenly interested and involved in promoting the improvement of Cape agriculture. As early as 1800, the British government sent W. Duckitt to the Cape 'to superintend the establishment of model farms in suitable localities, as everything in the shape of cereals, hay etc., was so inferior and fearfully expensive'. Duckitt spread the message of modern, progressive agriculture among conservative Afrikaner farmers through open-minded farmers like the Van Reenens.[98] In 1811 the Cape Governor drew the attention of farmers to the expansive potential of the wine industry and offered financial inducements to successful ones.[99] Improvement in wheat farming and the introduction of modern machinery was stimulated by two government experimental farms.[100] The biographer of Lord Charles Somerset, who began his long Governorship in 1814, writes:

Lord Charles, always eager to introduce a new idea, if he considered it would increase the productivity of the country, offered rewards to progressive and inventive farmers; established experimental farms, not only for breeding but also for crop raising; imported the newest kind of agricultural machinery which he tested to establish its suitability in local conditions; and introduced legislation to improve South African wines.[101]

He also showed an interest in Merino sheep production. Pure-bred flocks were developed in government farms in the west and the east and sheep were offered to farmers at low prices. He showed a particularly keen interest in the development of horsebreeding. On a government stud farm, crossbreeding between horses and donkeys produced draught animals for the expansion of wheat growing.[102]

The pull of the market and the developmental input by the government and other agencies transformed the Cape rural scene. During the 1850s a beginning was made in moving away from the traditional, wasteful method of herding the sheep during the day and kraaling them at night. Barbed wire fencing was adopted in order to rationalise sheep production and prevent the deterioration of the pasture associated with the traditional system.[103] Sheep farmers resorted to building dams and installing lifting pumps on a small scale during the 1850s. In the wake of the drought in the eastern province in the 1860s, more farmers were motivated to build dams and sink wells.[104] Since the improvements in sheep farming entailed considerable capital investment, only the more successful farmers adopted them. The domestication and systematisation of ostrich farming, which required considerable capital outlay, was another response to new market opportunities.[105] The substantial expansion of the local market centres also created new opportunities for those who could make the necessary adjustments. Thus, systematic pig breeding on an unprecedented scale was undertaken towards the end of the nineteenth century.[106] To supply the demand for dairy products for the growing urban population, British dairy cows were cross bred with existing Afrikander and Friesland cows to produce the Cape cow.[107]

The development and improvement of agricultural production introduced a degree of sophistication unheard of in the Dutch period. The transformation of agricultural pursuits encouraged the development of large farming units in which economies of scale facilitated the introduction of improvements. The enlargement of scale and the intensification of agriculture also called for a new attitude towards farm management. Management had to be not only foresighted and innovative but also systematic and rational. The best account available of such an approach to farm management relates to Reitz, Breda, Joubert and Company in the Swellendam and Bredasdorp areas which controlled vast areas.[108] Effective, rational and economically sound farm management was a prerequisite for success. It was undoubtedly exercised, to a greater or lesser degree, by many large-scale farmers. This, in turn, must have also influenced smaller-scale farmers who wished to survive in a highly competitive market environment.

The considerable increase in the scale and pace of agriculture also encouraged co-operation. Traditional individualism was unsustainable in the new era when physical and economic distances were drastically reduced and when the farming community was increasingly pulled by the forces of an expanding modern market economy. Under the new prevailing circumstances there was the scope and the need to pool resources through cooperation for the pursuit of common goals. This was manifested in the evolution of agricultural societies in different parts of the Cape.[109] The main task undertaken by the agricultural societies was the promotion and organisation of agricultural shows and fairs in which farmers exhibited their products and competed for prizes. Fairs and sales were organised to improve market opportunities. There were local shows as well as regional ones and Cape produce also participated in the International Kensington Exhibition of 1862.[110]

The physical and economic landscape of the Cape was definitely changing dramatically during the nineteenth century. Although there were temporary depressions and setbacks, the general trend was one of improvement and progress. The farming community, which was, at the level of production, until the early 1870s virtually the sole agent of economic development, benefited handsomely from the improvement in the economic fortunes of the Colony. The impact of economic development is rarely equal. In the Cape, English farmers, on the whole, were in the forefront of the development of the agricultural economy. The impact of economic development was varied within the Afrikaner farming community. However, Afrikaner farmers, many of whom had lived on the economic margins of the colony, increasingly integrated into the expanding market economy. On the whole, many of them responded positively, indeed enthusiastically, to the new economic challenges and opportunities. This process of economic transformation not only occurred under the aegis of the British empire and its local agents; it had, in fact, a distinct British imprint in all its dimensions and manifestations.

The effects of economic development on Cape Afrikaner society

Economic development brought in its wake social change which had a dramatic impact on the socio-economic profile of Cape Afrikaner society. During the VOC period only the south-western Cape and especially the areas closer to Cape Town were intensively within the orbit of the market economy. As we have seen, even the Overberg, just over a hundred kilometres from Cape Town, had great difficulties in maintaining an effective contact with a viable market. Areas further north and east, inhabited mostly by *trek boers*, lived on the margins of the market economy. This did not immediately change with the advent of British rule. John Fraser, who was born in 1840 in Beaufort West in the Karoo, has conveyed the sense of remoteness and isolation of this peripheral area.[111]

Since the British occupation was not, initially, very disruptive administratively and since economic development largely proceeded, until the rapid expansion of wool production, along previous lines, there was also, correspondingly, a large measure of continuity in the social structure of the Afrikaner segment of the Cape population. As Ross shows, there were, in the south-western Cape on the eve of the first British occupation, only a handful of agrarian plutocrats like the Melcks or the Cloetes of Constantia. The backbone of western Cape society was composed of middle-level, mainly wine and wheat farmers. According to Ross, this Cape gentry consisted of 'a relatively undifferentiated broad mass of farmers, rather than a very small élite'.[112]

British occupation did not meaningfully alter the economic and social fortune of this group. They continued to enjoy economic well-being, social status and some political influence. With the quickening of the economic pace and the deepening of commercial penetration, new economic spaces were opening which reinforced the ranks of the Cape gentry. Thus, the development of coastal trading in Port Beaufort at the mouth of the Breede River from about 1820 created opportunities not only for established wealthy families like the Van Reenens, the Van Bredas and the Van der Byls, but also for many smaller-scale Afrikaner farmers in the Overberg and along the Breede river as far as the Little Karoo.[113] The expansion of coastal trading further east, in creating markets for the products of livestock farmers, encouraged the process of social stratification among them as well.

It was, however, the large-scale expansion of wool production and subsequently ostrich farming from the 1840s which boosted the ranks of the Cape Afrikaner gentry. This expansion was also facilitated by the availability of more land, as a result of the immigration of the voortrekkers and the appropriation of African lands. In his work on Graaff Reinet Dubow shows how the capitalisation of agriculture in that district brought in its wake social change which swelled the ranks of this group of land owners.[114] The Civil Commissioner of Colesberg, in the Karoo, gave an account in 1860 of the impact of wool production on the level of economic affluence and the changing lifestyle and expectations of the hitherto marginal sheep farmers of that area.[115] The mineral discoveries of the late 1860s and 1880s, in providing capital and markets, gave a further boost to the processes of capitalisation and social stratification of the agricultural sector.[116] A list of prize winners at the agricultural shows in Graaff Reinet between 1854 and 1866 provides clear proof that many Afrikaner farmers were taking the challenge of modern farming seriously.[117] The socio-economic significance of the eastward economic movement was not only in the increased size of the rural élite but also in its tremendous spatial expansion. The Cape Afrikaner gentry, which had been previously largely restricted to the west and south western Cape, was now spread throughout the length and breadth of the colony. This broad, upwardly mobile group became increasingly integrated in and dependent on the colonial and imperial economy.

The expansion and intensification of the agrarian economy which swelled the ranks of the Cape Afrikaner gentry also contributed to the emergence of less fortunate groups in the rural areas. The expansion of agriculture was only partly facilitated through a generous disposal of Crown and African lands. As the process of capitalisation of agriculture intensified it also involved the dispossession of existing marginal and unsuccessful white farmers. Thus, the growth of the Cape gentry was accompanied by a concomitant increase in the number of Afrikaner *bijwoners* (squatters) and poor whites, mainly Afrikaners.[118]

The development of the Cape economy, which rested until the 1870s almost solely on the agricultural resources of the colony, created additional avenues and agencies for socio-economic mobility, change and stratification. A most important area which increasingly attracted Cape Afrikaners was that of commerce, artisanship and, to a lesser extent, industry. The arenas for these pursuits were the fast developing and expanding urban centres. The expansion of commerce in the nineteenth century was particularly dramatic. During the VOC period commerce offered very limited opportunities to the settlers. To the extent that the company allowed burghers to pursue commerce, it involved the company's trade contracts and monopolies. These restrictive policies allowed individual burghers like Dirk Gijsbert van Reenen to flourish but greatly restricted the opportunities of others.[119]

The British government was interested in promoting and encouraging local economic enterprise rather than getting involved directly in commercial activity. This created new economic opportunities for individuals possessed of skill, capital and the entrepreneurial spirit. As we have seen, British immigrants were the main beneficiaries from this new economic space. They possessed the necessary attributes and contacts which the predominantly rural Afrikaners lacked. But gradually Afrikaners with entrepreneurial spirit or those who could not fulfil their material aspirations through farming, ventured into the commercial field. Piet Retief, the future famous Voortrekker leader, presented an unsuccessful early attempt to take advantage of the many and varied openings in this field.

Having failed as a farmer in his native Stellenbosch area, he secured, in 1813, a government contract to provision the troops on the eastern frontier. Having failed in this venture, he subsequently tried, and failed again, to make a living first in Uitenhage and then in Grahamstown, as a 'general dealer, baker, miller, butcher, liquor trader, auctioneer, timber merchant and building contractor'.[120] Had he been as successful as he was resourceful, Afrikaner mythology would probably have lost one of its most cherished heroes. In G. Maritz, another prominent Voortrekker leader, the Cape lost a very successful wagon-builder. There were many other success stories like that of the two de Villiers Graaff brothers who had been forced to leave the farm of their unsuccessful father and became very wealthy businessmen in Cape Town, or D.C. de Waal who began his adult career as a farmer and who in 1878 opened, in partnership with H. de Vos de Kock, a hardware business which, by 1895, had become the biggest of its kind in the Cape.[121] In Stellenbosch, G. Krige, in addition to farming, was a wine merchant and a distiller, while A.B. de Villiers combined farming with wine trading and hotel keeping.[122] In Graaff Reinet, F.K. Te Water was an agent and the largest landed proprietor in the town.[123] These are a few examples of what obtained in most urban centres.

Cape Afrikaners were also extensively involved in the development of local financial institutions, featuring prominently in many of the local banks.[124] They also ventured into the developing insurance business,[125] and into joint economic enterprises like the South African Whaling Company, the Paarl Omnibus Company, the Spirit Distillery Company and the Worcester Omnibus Company.[126] Progressive Afrikaner wine farmers in the west formed companies to improve the marketing of wine. They also joined the mineral revolution by investing in diamond- and gold-mining companies.[127]

The economic development of the Cape offered many Afrikaners opportunities in small-scale business and artisanship. The *Cape Almanac* of 1855 provides interesting information on the occupations of the inhabitants of the small village of Piketberg. Among the 25 Afrikaners the following was the occupational distribution: a 'capitalist', three retail shopkeepers, a lodging house keeper, an auctioneer, a wagonmaker, a blacksmith, a tailor, a mason, a thatcher and a carter.[128] Not all those who flocked to the urban centres became self-employed businessmen and artisans. As the list shows, the socio-economic stratification went further. Piketberg also had 'an agent and vendu clerk', and three labourers among its Afrikaner inhabitants.[129] Larger urban centres naturally offered much more scope in these and other occupations.

Towns and villages were also the locus of another major agent of socio-economic mobility and differentiation, namely the educational system. Looking at the development of education in the Cape from the vantage point of the late nineteenth century, it would hardly be an exaggeration to state that the British had effected an educational revolution. By the end of the Dutch period only elementary education was provided in schools run by parish clerks. The only other education, preparing children for confirmation, was given by *meesters* hired by farmers.[130] The establishment of an effective educational system during the British period proceeded very slowly. The intention to anglicise Cape Afrikaners through the agency of an English educational system was more easily stated than implemented. A shortage of teachers and funds and Afrikaner resistance to the exclusion of Dutch greatly hampered the expansion of education among Afrikaners outside Cape Town.[131] It was not until 1829 that the South African College was founded in Cape Town to provide higher education up to the level of matriculation.[132]

It was only with the introduction of the Education Act of 1865 that the educational system began to penetrate the *platteland* (countryside). Two years later the Superintendent General of Education reported that 'there is scarcely a village or hamlet in the Colony without a public school'. Indeed, the mushrooming of towns and villages throughout the Cape greatly facilitated the spread of education. A report from 1876 indicates that Afrikaner farmers were keen that their children learn English.[133] More colleges of higher education were also established in different areas.[134] Through this expanding educational system increasing numbers of young Afrikaners were exposed to modern English education, and many of them excelled.[135] University education was offered to matriculants at the University of Good Hope.[136] Many bright young Afrikaners pursued university education overseas, mainly in Britain, and in Edinburgh there existed an Afrikaner students association.[137] Many South Africans who were to be famous in the twentieth century, like Jan Smuts, F.S. Malan and J.H.H. de Waal, had studied in Europe in the late nineteenth century.[138]

While it would be an exaggeration to claim that all educated Afrikaners were assimilated, there is no doubt that as the nineteenth century progressed an increasing number of emerging educated Afrikaners did assimilate or at least acquired, through the anglicised education system, a knowledge of English. In 1890, the *Zuid Afrikaan* (ZA) complained that almost all the teachers in the public schools were English and Scottish or South Africans with a limited knowledge of Dutch and that the teachers and professors in the colleges and teacher training colleges were also English and Scottish.[139] Later that year, Jan Hofmeyr complained of people who in public meetings spoke in favour of Dutch while giving their children English education and even allowing, for their sake, prayers in English at home.[140] Many educated Afrikaners became more proficient in English than in Dutch. Indeed, in 1854, a supporter of the

Dutch language conceded that 'the language of Holland is largely unintelligible to the colonists'.[141] And the local Cape Dutch dialect had to go a long way before it could challenge English. Thus, when T.F Burger, future president of the Transvaal, went to Holland to further his education, he was at home in English but had great difficulties writing Dutch.[142] In 1869, when J.H. de Villiers was asked to address an election meeting in Dutch, he said that all his reading and writing were in English and that he had difficulty delivering an address in Dutch. In the middle of the 1870s, by then a Chief Justice, he predicted that English would become the common mother tongue of South Africa.[143] J.H. Hofmeyr ('Onze Jan'), who was to become a proponent of the Dutch language, started his career as an editor of the *Volksvriend*, writing editorials in English and then translating them into Dutch. He also addressed a public meeting in Stellenbosch in English as late as 1875.[144]

The anglicised education system provided emerging generations of educated Afrikaners with a linguistic tool which facilitated their integration into the steadily expanding bureaucracy. This offered Cape Afrikaners avenues of socio-economic mobility and contributed to the process of social differentiation among them. Many Cape Afrikaners were employed by the state in clerical positions while fewer rose to higher positions of responsibility and prestige.[145] Increasing numbers of Afrikaners joined the professional élite as advocates, attorneys, notaries, medical practitioners, accountants and land surveyors.[146]

Most of these, like the Cape Afrikaners who were involved in business, became concentrated in the old and new urban centres across the colony, from Cape Town down to the small villages. These were not only centres of economic activity but also foci of a developing urban culture modelled on that of Victorian England.[147] The Cape proponents of this culture were English-speakers who regarded themselves as a fragment of the imperial British nation and wished to replicate Victorian Britain in the Cape environment. This urban culture with its pursuit of progress, education, religion and benevolence, with its reading habits, with its newspapers, debating, literary, scientific and musical societies, with its horse racing, cricket matches, theatre and brass bands, gradually and partially spread from the major towns to the villages. The English education system, which imparted not only linguistic skills but also culture in the broad sense, prepared many Cape Afrikaners, whether fully anglicised or not, for gradual integration into this urban culture. One of the most conspicuous manifestations of this adopted urban culture was the pursuit of goals and the promotion of interests through co-operation and association. Cape Afrikaners were increasingly involved in associations, unions, societies, committees, commissions and so on, which promoted both culture and welfare.[148]

30

The process of urbanisation of the Afrikaners was also closely linked to the development of the Dutch Reformed Church (DRC). In many cases the newly founded church was the nucleus of a new town or village. The characteristic neglect of the public sphere during the Dutch period was also manifested in the religious life of the Cape. By the end of the VOC's rule in 1795, there were only six DRC congregations in the Cape and they had no central organisation or guidance.[149] The impact of this neglect on the general state of the Afrikaner population in much of the Cape was captured by the Commission of Circuit sent to inspect the eastern province in 1811. They reported that parents feared 'that their children, growing up without education, without a knowledge of the first principles of religion and morality, would at best be like nothing else than savages'.[150] The expansion and growth of the DRC during the nineteenth century was dramatic. By 1854 there were 49 DRC congregations throughout the length and breadth of the colony.[151] In 1824 the first synod of the Cape DRC was held in Cape Town and it was subsequently held every five years. With it the DRC acquired a central guiding and co-ordinating body which deliberated and dealt with all aspects of life affecting the Afrikaners – ecclesiastical as well as social, educational and political. Subsequently the Cape was divided into regional rings which dealt on a more regular basis with matters affecting the different congregations.[152] In 1859 the Stellenbosch Seminary was established to facilitate the local training of clergymen for the fast expanding DRC network.[153] On the one hand the church operated at the grassroots, reaching out for the isolated farmers, while on the other it developed a colonywide hierarchical organisation.

In its promotion of education, its social concerns and community-oriented activities, and its spiritual and moral guidance, the DRC played a crucial role in the transformation of Cape Afrikaner society. It functioned as one of the most important agents of regularisation and socialisation of this society into the colonial world. From this perspective it was significant that the evolution and expansion of this religious-social organisation took place under the wings of the colonial state. It was only in 1843 that the church was granted complete autonomy to regulate its affairs. Until then it was part of the colonial administration, its ministers being civil servants.[154] Not less important was the role played by Scottish clergymen like Dr Thom, the Murray clan, McGregor, Fraser, Innes, Robertson and many others, in the growth of the DRC. While most of these married into Afrikaner families and their descendants were Afrikanerised, the impact of their British background on this major agent of socialisation had a definite effect on the nature of this process. The DRC, with few exceptions, was a bastion of the local Dutch language and culture. However, with the spread of knowledge of English among

Cape Afrikaner youths, the pressure for the use of this language in church services increased. Preaching in English was allowed and in 1870 the synod passed a resolution that *predikants* must be able to preach in English.[155]

Cape Afrikaners and the colonial state

In understanding the process of integration of Cape Afrikaners into the colonial and imperial ambience it is important to consider their attitude to, and interaction with, the colonial state in its governing and administrative manifestations. One of the most outstanding aspects of the transition to British rule was the ease with which Cape Afrikaners initially accepted their new colonial masters. This is, in fact, hardly surprising since the British until the late 1820s effected little change in the government of the Cape. Initially, the British did not wish to mould the Cape in the British image. As in Quebec earlier on, the policy was not to impose a new British order on newly conquered colonies inhabited by non-British. Thus, the British inherited many of the existing central and local ruling and administrative institutions, structures and practices, which included autocratic governors collaborating with the local oligarchy, the financial system, the Dutch-Roman legal system, the central government functionaries and the burgher senate and the local administration with the *landdrosts* and the *heemraden*. They also continued the practices, or rather malpractices, of the VOC period, with official corruption, abuse of power and favouritism. Effective government was more in the realm of intent than reality and until the late 1820s it was the local society with its dominant oligarchy which shaped colonial rule rather than the reverse.[156]

When the radical reform in the government of the Cape were implemented from the late 1820s, a generation of Afrikaners had already been born under British rule. This reform represented a determined effort to break with the inherited mercantilistic, corrupt and inefficient past and to launch the Cape on a course which would integrate her into the emerging liberal, free-trade British imperial polity. The new colonial state began to infringe on the privileges of the old colonists. Ordinance 33 of December 1827 abolished the Boards of *Landdrosts* and *Heemraden* which had been the bastion of power of the local oligarchies and a source of patronage and personal material benefits. The judicial and executive functions which were exercised by the *landdrosts* were separated and invested respectively in resident magistrates and in civil commissioners. Resident magistrates were required to be trained in British jurisprudence and civil commissioners to abide by standards of bureaucratic efficiency and moral propriety.[157] The efficiency of the local administration was further enhanced by the creation of new districts. The moral propriety of civil servants improved as they began to be remunerated through salaries rather than through perquisites for services rendered, as before.[158] At the centre, the burgher senate, the bastion of the Cape oligarchy was abolished and a new supreme court was established to replace the governor in his role as a court of final appeal. A chief justice and an attorney general were brought from England.[159]

The Cape Afrikaner oligarchy lost much of their power through this transformation, which also augured some other disadvantageous innovations like the elimination of monopolies, a change in the disposition of land, Ordinance 50 of 1828 which improved the status of the Coloureds and ultimately the abolition of slavery in 1834. A frontier farmer expressed the bewilderment and disenchantment of his fellow farmers:

> Now we have a Civil Commissioner to receive our money for Government and Land Surveyors, a Magistrate to punish us, a clerk of the Peace to prosecute us, and get us in the Tronk [prison], but no Hccmraad to tell us whether things are right or wrong ... The Englishman is very learned ... They and the Hottentots will squeeze us all out by degrees.[160]

As Peires argues, the radical changes in the policies of the colonial government were at the root of the great trek.[161]

The administrative revolution, while inflicting immediate damage, had long-term benefits, and with the passage of time, and as the new administrative system consolidated, Afrikaners learnt to appreciate the higher standards of efficiency and professionalism introduced by administrators and members of the judicial system. Thus, as early as 1828, 100 Paarl 'householders' petitioned the government to appoint 'a Justice of the Peace or other Magistrate'. This request having been granted, Paarlites continued to press for the further extension of judicial and administrative facilities.[162] While it is true that Cape Afrikaners had lost much of their influence in the central government, they maintained a significant position at the local level. The number of Afrikaner civil commissioners, which replaced the *landdrosts*, rose from three in 1832 to seven in 1855 and to 14 in 1865, and we also find Afrikaners well represented among the Justices of Peace. In most divisions Afrikaners monopolised the position of field cornets which were 'indispensable to the internal administration'.[163] Afrikaners were also able to promote their interests through their participation in local government bodies like the boards of public roads or the courts for granting wine and spirit licences.[164] After 1836, they could promote their local interests also through their elected representatives in the municipal councils,[165] and after 1855 they almost monopolised the newly formed divisional councils in most divisions.[166]

33

While at the local level Cape Afrikaners never lost their influence in matters concerning their interests, it took them a long time to recover influence at the centre of power. This recovery was closely linked to the evolution and culmination of Representative Government in the Cape. Only in 1853, after much pressure from the colonists, was the Cape granted Representative Government with a bi-cameral parliament. The process of constitutional progress culminated with the granting of Responsible Government in 1872.[167] The advent of Representative Government in 1854 afforded the Cape population an opportunity to participate in the political process through exercising legislative checks on the executive, the latter being still the prerogative of the governor. With the granting of Responsible Government the stakes in representative politics considerably increased, since the government was formed by the parliament and was responsible to it. This change in political fortunes did not immediately stimulate Cape Afrikaners to greater political efforts. Until the late 1870s they participated in parliamentary politics as individuals, rather than as members of political blocks representing the collective interests of their ethnic community.

The evolution of Cape Afrikaners' ethnic consciousness and politics

Looking back from the vantage point of the 1870s, the balance of integration of Cape Afrikaners into the different spheres of colonial life was mixed. Indeed, colonialism and capitalism produced contradictory impacts and consequences in the changing Cape Afrikaner society. Inevitably, there were winners as well as losers. As will be further elaborated, colonialism and capitalism also generated grievances and dissatisfaction. However, increasing numbers of Cape Afrikaners exploited the new economic opportunities as farmers, businessmen and professionals. They took advantage of the improved educational system to acquire proper education for themselves and/or for their children. They valued the stability and security which the colonial state provided. They gradually occupied positions of influence in public life – in the administration, in local government and ultimately in the central representative institutions. Among many Cape Afrikaners these benefits definitely outweighed the grievances. Such a balance-sheet hardly provides fertile ground for anti-colonial resistance.

Even Afrikaner 'nationalist' historians have not discovered traces of Afrikaner 'nationalism' in the Cape until late in the nineteenth century.[168] Referring to the period around 1815, Van Jaarsveld comments that in addition to general satisfaction with aspects of British rule, 'the Colonists, who were conservative and religious, had a natural respect for the authority placed over them and consequently became loyal subjects of the new regime'.[169] It was only with the administrative revolution of the late 1820s that British rule caused severe dislocations and produced serious grievances. The great trek was, as we have seen, a direct response to the new colonial order.[170]However, the fact that it was a withdrawal rather than resistance, the narrow regional basis of the movement and its fragmentary nature point to the weakness of Afrikaner identity and cohesion and to the absence of a strong social basis which could have sustained anti-colonial protest. This was underlined by Piet Retief who said in 1832 that Afrikaners would 'rather go and live in a desert land' than openly resist the British government.[171] The ZA, representing the emerging Cape Afrikaner élite of the western Cape, condemned the trek, expressing the hope that the trekkers would be again subjected to British rule,[172] and in 1837, a specially convened DRC synod came out strongly against the trekkers.[173] From the point of view of the relations between Cape Afrikaners and the colonial state, the great trek, having offered an outlet to the more dissatisfied and adventurous souls, functioned as a safety-valve, removing from the Cape those who might have otherwise been driven to anti-colonial resistance.

The first major political agitation in the Cape under the British rule was the anti-convict movement in 1848–49. However, this resistance to the settling of convicts in the Cape was not an Afrikaner one. It was a manifestation of a growing common ground between English-speaking colonists and Cape Afrikaners.[174] In those years, politically informed and conscious Cape Afrikaners laboured to foster understanding and unity between members of the two white settler communities. When English-speaking settlers expressed fears that the Afrikaners would use their numerical superiority under Representative Government against them, the ZA strongly denied that there was a need to protect the interests of English speakers from Afrikaner infringement. The newspaper also strongly denied that the convict question had aroused any anti-English feeling, as was suggested by the governor.[175] This disposition also informed the ZA's attitude towards the Boer republics. Thus, it hailed the annexation of Natal in 1842 and that of the trans-Orange region in 1848 to the British empire, while strongly condemning the British withdrawal from the latter.[176] In 1848 the government secretary, John Montagu, observed that 'a community of thought, habit, and sentiment' was being formed among English and Dutch settlers.[177]

Afrikaner historians, like Scholtz and Van Jaarsveld, agree that, at least until the 1870s, there was little evidence of Afrikaner national consciousness and assertion. On the contrary, there were abundant manifestations of increasing loyalty to the British Crown. On the occasion of the granting of Responsible Government in 1853, neither the ZA nor leading Cape Afrikaners raised objections to the exclusion of the Dutch language from Parliament, and this constitutional progress was accompanied by expressions of loyalty to Britain.[178] The *ZA* took advantage of the visit of the Duke of Edinburgh in January 1870 to reject allegations of disloyalty and to express pride in the British connection. Scholtz, referring to this manifestation, laments that 'reverence for British authority and for British ideals increasingly obtained among the [Cape] Afrikaners above loyalty to their own national character [*volksaard*]'.[179] Loyalty to the colonial government and more broadly to the British empire and Crown was not limited to the educated élite who, in the process of socialisation, not only acquired a knowledge of the English language, but also an appreciation and admiration for British culture and institutions. Loyalty and submission to the colonial authorities was also inculcated among the non-anglicised Afrikaners by the DRC. The synod which condemned the great trek warned members of the church to be submissive towards those whom God had chosen as his servants.[180]

By 1872, with the transition to Responsible Government, many Cape Afrikaners had few reasons to withdraw their loyalty from Britain. By then the material benefits of British rule were all too evident. The introduction of Merino sheep, Angora goats and ostrich farming had spread the benefits of the market economy throughout the colony. Diamond mining held great promise as a lucrative source of income and as a stimulant to the local trade in farm produce. Cape Afrikaners, having asserted themselves at the local level of government, were now well poised to take advantage of the new constitutional dispensation and to make their mark on the centre of power. Direct imperial presence greatly diminished as colonial interests and initiatives became paramount.

It was some six years from the granting of Responsible Government before the Cape Afrikaners began to organise politically on an ethnic basis, another six years before they began fully to exploit the political space opened to them by the 1872 constitution and yet another six years to ripen for the alliance with Rhodes. In investigating the roots and evolution of the alliance between Rhodes and the Afrikaner Bond we must direct our attention to this process of Cape Afrikaner political assertion. It is in the context, nature and dynamic of this process that we have to seek explanations for the willingness, indeed eagerness, of Cape Afrikaners to ally themselves to the arch-imperialist, Cecil John Rhodes.

The political pregnancy which culminated in the alliance between the Bond and Rhodes spread throughout much of the 1880s, a decade in which the socialisation of Cape Afrikaners into the colonial and imperial world progressed apace. Indeed, the alliance would be incomprehensible without reference to this process. This assertion, however, runs against an important thrust of the Afrikaner 'nationalist' historiography, namely that the early 1880s witnessed the 'awakening' of broad ethnic nationalism among Cape Afrikaners. Having failed to find explanations for this 'awakening' in the bilateral relations between Cape Afrikaners and the imperial authorities, they discover them in the former's response to imperial encroachments on their republican brothers' interests. The British partiality towards the Basuto in their struggle against the Orange Free State in 1868, the annexation of Griqualand West to the British empire in 1871, and ultimately the annexation of the Transvaal in 1877 and the first 'war of liberation' in 1880–81, sparked off the fire of ethnic nationalism among Cape Afrikaners.[181] M.C. van Zyl wrote in 1979 on the relevant impact of this war: 'This led to a common feeling of nationhood and resulted in a general Afrikaner nationalism. Thereafter Afrikaner nationalism in South Africa could not be arrested.'[182] Van Jaarsveld writes similarly that this war, 'notwithstanding their [Afrikaners] political borders, united them spiritually, and made them nationally and historically conscious. This led directly to Afrikaner nationalism and gave rise to the concept of an Afrikaner *volk* and Afrikaner nation'.[183]

From the perspective of this claim it should be asked: why did Cape Afrikaners, who had condemned the Great Trek and expressed the hope that the trekkers would soon be reincorporated in the British empire, who had hailed the annexation of the trans-Orange region and denounced British withdrawal therefrom and who had at least until 1868 shown 'no sentimental attachment' to the Transvaal,[184] discover, all of a sudden, their common pan-Afrikaner nationality and destiny? The 'nationalist' answer is that Cape Afrikaners were provoked by the manifestations of imperial aggression. They were particularly 'infected' and inspired by the response of their republican ethnic brothers to this aggression.

The position taken in this study is that in accounting for the evolution of Cape Afrikaners' ethnic consciousness and political assertion, we need to focus on the Cape itself. Giliomee, in breaking away from the 'nationalist' paradigm, has made an important contribution to a better understanding of Afrikaner collective identity and politics. In analysing the socio-economic dimensions of these phenomena he points to vast and rich research avenues. However, from a restricted Cape vantage point, it seems that further analytical focusing may advance our understanding. Giliomee rightly rejects the notion of 'awakening' of Afrikaner nationalism because of its deterministic implications.[185] There was, indeed, no dormant Afrikaner nation waiting to be awakened. It cannot be denied, especially from the vantage point of the last decade of the present century, that ethnic nationalism and political mobilisation have been major ideological and political options in the last two centuries. However, their appearance on the historical scene have not been predetermined and inevitable. In seeking to understand these historical phenomena, we must focus on the particular circumstances which brought them about.

In order to focus more clearly on the roots of Cape Afrikaner ethnic consciousness and mobilisation, two conceptual shackles must be removed. First, it should be stressed, as Giliomee does, that there is not a necessary congruity between the manifestations of Afrikaner ethnic consciousness in the late nineteenth century and in the twentieth century.[186] In stating in a later article that 'over the past century the wine and wheat farmers of the Western Cape have arguably been the firmest pillar of support for the Afrikaner nationalist movement which today rules South Africa',[187] he shows, however, how tempting is the 'nationalist' paradigm. The late nineteenth century Cape phenomenon must be studied on its own merits and not as part of an assumed historical continuum. Secondly, we must free ourselves from another 'nationalist' axiom, namely that the evolution of ethnic consciousness and mobilisation in the late nineteenth century Cape was an integral part of the growth of a unified pan-Afrikaner nationalism.

To focus on the evolution of Afrikaner ethnic consciousness and mobilisation in the late nineteenth century Cape as a specific, concrete historical phenomenon, the introduction of two analytical distinctions may prove fruitful. First, a distinction should be made between ethnic nationalism and ethnic mobilisation. Though sharing a common parentage these two phenomena are politically distinct. They both rest on a sense of ethnic identity and represent manifestations of a developed ethnic consciousness. They both translate this consciousness into political action. Ethnic nationalism is distinguishable in that it represents a desire for ethnic exclusivity and political self-determination. As Gellner argues, a nation, which is engendered by the spirit of nationalism, exists when 'men will to be politically united with all those, and only those, who share their culture'.[188] Ethnic mobilisation, on the other hand, occurs when a self-conscious ethnic group accepts the ethnic diversity of the state and mobilizes in order to improve its share in the political and material spoils of it. This is the essence of ethnic politics in most, if not all, black Africa's multi-ethnic states; it is derogatively termed 'tribalism'. Under certain circumstances ethnic mobilisation can be transformed into full-blown ethnic nationalism. There is also a way back from ethnic nationalism to ethnic mobilisation. The two-way movement underlines the contextual nature of both phenomena.

The second useful analytical distinction is that between ethnic core and ethnic diaspora. This distinction is vital for understanding the evolution of Afrikaner ethnic consciousness and mobilisation in the period under consideration, because the Afrikaners through much of the nineteenth century lived in different states under different regimes and circumstances. It was only in 1910, with the advent of Union, that Afrikaners became subjects of one state. The nature of the political consciousness and behaviour of the different Afrikaner communities was primarily determined by the particular circumstances in their respective ethnic core. There existed ethnic solidarity between cores and diasporas, which varied in essence and manifestations according to particular historical circumstances. However, on the whole, the interaction between the ethnic core and the ethnic diaspora played a relatively minor role in the evolution of the ethnic consciousness of the core community. From a Cape Afrikaner perspective the Afrikaners in the Transvaal and the Free State were ethnic diaspora. From the latters' perspective, it goes without saying, Cape Afrikaners were their ethnic diaspora. This distinction not only directs our attention to Cape Afrikaners and their particular circumstances, but also gives us a better perspective on the impact of events in the republics on their political consciousness and behaviour.

Another methodological hurdle is that relating to the beginning of Afrikaner ethnic consciousness. Giliomee, in rejecting Van Jaarsveld's notion of 'awakening', rightly prefers 'beginning' as a more neutral term. The question is, however, when was the beginning? Giliomee claims that 'the gradual and often tentative growth of Afrikaner cultural and political ethnic awareness was rooted firmly in historical changes that occurred after 1870'.[189] Indeed, especially from a pan-Afrikaner perspective, the Transvaal crisis in the late 1870s and early 1880s, having sparked off South Africa-wide manifestations of ethnic solidarity, offers an attractive point of departure. However, it would prove difficult to account for the almost instant success of Cape Afrikaner ethnic mobilisation unless we take a longer view of the process of ethnic-consciousness formation. In dealing with ethnic assertion we have to account not only for the overt manifestations of ethnic mobilisation but also for the deep, at times invisible, current of group ethnic-consciousness formation.

More thorough local research is required before we can have a conclusive picture of this process. Giliomee, as we have seen, traces the beginning of broad Afrikaner ethnic consciousness only in the last decades of the nineteenth century.[190] However, if we restrict ourselves to the Cape and look for the origin of Cape Afrikaner ethnic consciousness and mobilisation, rather than for the beginning of pan-Afrikaner nationalism, we can find evidence that the manifestations of the 1870s and 1880s were rooted in a long, cumulative process. While the evidence is not abundant and dramatic, it is sufficient to indicate that, by then, the formation of Cape Afrikaner ethnic consciousness was well under way and that it was also manifested in concrete ethnic responses and initiatives.

The ethnic 'revival' of Cape Afrikaners presents a special case in which the modern manifestation of ethnic consciousness was not rooted in real or presumed primordial foundations. There was no ancient historical or prehistorical Afrikaner tribe or kingdom. In our search for the origin of this group we cannot go further back than 1652, the year in which Jan van Riebeeck landed on the shores of the Cape to establish a station for the VOC. Indeed, the foundation stones for the evolution of Cape Afrikaners' ethnic identity and consciousness are traceable in the Dutch period. This period provided a historical melting pot which amalgamated people of diverse origins – mainly Dutch, German and French – into a distinct ethnic group. Despite regional and economic differences, this group shared in common sufficient attributes which served as a basis for the evolution of ethnic identity and consciousness. The group had quite clear boundaries. There was the racial boundary, not always rigid, which distinguished them from the non-white neighbours. There was also a boundary which separated them from the Company's officials and other transient European expatriates. They perceived themselves as sons of Africa, hence the term Afrikaner which gained wide circulation towards the end of the Dutch period. The relative isolation of many Afrikaner farmers also carved a cultural boundary between themselves and the mother country. The cultural gap between Holland, perhaps the most progressive, sophisticated and cultured country in Europe, and the Cape Afrikaner farmers grew so wide that most of the latter could not be construed as a fragment of the former. The evolution of a local Cape Dutch dialect underlined the process of cultural estrangement between the mother country and the Cape colonists. This may also have been enhanced by the multi-ethnic origin of the Cape settlers.

Within these boundaries Cape Afrikaners shared a common language and the Dutch Reformed Church. Farming was an occupation shared by the vast majority of the Afrikaners. Finally, they shared the experience of constant struggle for well-being and survival as a white group in the African environment. During the Dutch period, these common attributes within defined external boundaries nurtured a sense of ethnic identity and consciousness. During this period, however, the process of collective identity formation was embryonic, not being manifested in broad cultural, social or political movements. The isolation of most Afrikaner farmers, breeding individualism and parochialism, was not conducive for that. Furthermore, the impact of the ineffectual and remote VOC was too weak to create the conditions which could have transformed the Afrikaner farmers spread throughout this vast colony into a compact community and to generate universal grievances which could have triggered a broad and sustained collective political response.[191]

During the British occupation there developed conditions which encouraged the evolution of Cape Afrikaner ethnic identity and consciousness and precipitated more overt manifestations of ethnic assertion. Giliomee argues, from a broad pan-Afrikaner perspective, that 'during the second half of the nineteenth century two interlinked forces impeded the development of such ethnic consciousness', namely imperialism and capitalism.[192] However, looking at the nineteenth century as a whole from a Cape perspective, we see that the penetration of British capitalism and imperialism played a critical role in stimulating and shaping Cape Afrikaner ethnic consciousness. The British introduced to the Cape the 'triple revolution' – economic, administrative and educational – which in Europe was, as A.D. Smith argues, at the root of ethnic revival and nationalism.[193]

Giliomee links the beginning of 'political ethnic self-consciousness' partly to the 'rapid expansion consequent upon the opening of the Diamond Fields in 1869'.[194] The discovery of diamonds certainly gave a considerable boost to the capitalist thrust in the Cape. However, in linking the evolution of Afrikaner ethnic consciousness and assertion to capitalism, a broader and longer-term view may prove instructive. The impact of the diamond industry on Cape Afrikaner ethnic consciousness cannot be fully appreciated without reference to the economic development of previous decades, especially since the introduction and expansion of wool production. Through involvement in production for export, through the elaborate urban system which became the focus of expanding communication and financial networks, rural Cape Afrikaners throughout the colony became part of an expanding capitalist market economy. In creating a broad, centralised common Cape market and in breaking physical, geographical barriers, capitalism, before and after the mineral discoveries, lessened considerably the distance between the different segments of Cape Afrikaner society. Afrikaners throughout the Cape were increasingly becoming an integrated community. Furthermore, the ethno-economic dichotomy between English-speaking people and Afrikaners created optimal conditions for the emergence of ethnic consciousness and mobilisation. *Vis-à-vis* the predominantly English-speaking townsmen, merchants and capitalists, and also the 'progressive' farmers, the primarily conservative Afrikaner farming community felt not only distinct but also marginalised and threatened, despite sharing in the economic development of the country. Thus capitalism created among Cape Afrikaners two ideal conditions for the evolution of ethnic consciousness and mobilisation. First, it created a convergence between a cultural group and an economic community.[195] Secondly, it engendered among the ethno-economic group a sense of threat. Ethnic mobilisation is very often primarily defensive, ethnic groups closing ranks for the sake of protection. The need for economic protection was certainly, a major concern and motive among Cape Afrikaners. It is largely from this perspective that they became increasingly aware of the role of the colonial state.

British imperialism, through the agency of the colonial state, also played a very important role in the evolution of Cape Afrikaner identity and consciousness. British occupation created, instantaneously, a much clearer cultural dividing line between rulers and ruled, between colonisers and colonised. The consolidation of a culturally alien rule provided a political-cultural antithesis against which Cape Afrikaner collective self-perception could be forged. It was, however, as we have seen, only after the administrative revolution of the late 1820s that the alien regime became relatively intrusive throughout much of the colony. From this perspective, the Great Trek, while definitely not an early manifestation of pan-Afrikaner nationalism, can be construed as a collective ethnic, regional response to the imposition of alien rule and norms on the rural Afrikaner population. This sense of alienation was exacerbated by the policy of assimilation which sought to give the colonial state and society a distinct English character. Cape Afrikaners did not offer aggressive resistance to the assimilation thrust. However, while the lukewarm anglicisation thrust produced a small minority of fully anglicised Afrikaners, it increased the cultural alienation of the majority and did not even erase the ethno-cultural identity of many educated Afrikaners.

The cultural alienation was further exacerbated by the influx of English settlers who, in creating islands of British culture, reinforced the alien nature of the colonial state. Furthermore, while being a minority, they not only occupied the heights of the economy but also were over-represented in the bureaucracy and the central representative institutions. In May 1883, in a speech in Bloemfontein, J.H. Hofmeyr described the sense of alienation among Cape Afrikaners:

> To the North of the River [Orange] there is a lively feeling, that Government and people are one, but to the South that feeling is either completely absent or very uncertain ... If it comes to the election of a Parliamentary representative (at any rate up till recently), then the influential Oom Piet and Oom Klaas felt that he ought not to offer himself as a candidate, because he could speak no English. If the Dutch farmer in the Colony is summoned to appear before the Court, then his case is taken in a language which he does not understand, and then he repeatedly has to see acting as interpreter between the magistrate and himself a Kafir, who is far below him in society, but who now looks down on him, because he understands two languages against the farmer's one. If he is called up to serve on commando, then he must serve under the command of a man, whom he has not elected, who does not know his language, who does not understand his character, and who despises him.[196]

In addition, the cultural arrogance displayed by many English settlers towards the Afrikaners infringed on the latter's sense of personal and collective dignity. The following tirade by 'John Bull' in the *Eastern Star* on 15 April 1879 might have been a bit extreme but not an exception:

> a Colony inhabited by cowardly, traitorous, yet boasting and senseless Dutch Boers ... such brutes ... It would indeed be a bright day for the Cape if every Dutch Boer was driven out of it, or even if they were deprived of their privileges and treated as the wretched, disloyal, ungrateful foreigners they really are.[197]

Attack on the dignity of a culturally defined group can be transformed into a powerful motivating force for ethnic mobilisation.

The colonial state stimulated the evolution of Cape Afrikaner ethnic identity and consciousness in yet another important way. This state was much more centralised, organised and effective than its VOC predecessor. As the capitalist thrust reduced economic and geographic distances, so the British colonial state shortened the lines of control and communication between rulers and ruled. As capitalism forged an integrated common Cape market, so the colonial state gradually created an integrated common political market. Consequently, the distance between different segments of the ruled diminished. The increasingly intrusive state became a focus of broad Cape Afrikaner concern because its actions and abstentions were directly relevant to their well-being. An intrusive colonial state, indeed any state, is an inevitable source of grievances. While the grievances of different regions or different economic sub-groups may have been different, they all shared a common parent. The colonial state was also the object of common expectations and demands. Finally, especially with the introduction of Representative Government, the colonial state created a central arena for political contest over its favours and spoils and, ultimately, its control. In all these, the colonial state offered ideal conditions for the growth of ethnic consciousness and the emergence of ethnic mobilisation among Cape Afrikaners.

In conclusion, economically, socially, culturally and politically Cape Afrikaners, despite benefiting in more than one way from British rule, occupied a distinctly marginal niche in their own land. This multiple, overlapping marginality gave a tremendous boost to the evolution of Afrikaner ethnic consciousness and mobilisation.

In view of the ethnic dichotomy between the British colonial state and Cape Afrikaner society, it is hardly surprising that Cape Afrikaner ethnic assertion took, for a long time, a predominantly cultural shape. The existence of Dutch newspapers from the 1820s, without interruption, reflected the determination of Cape Afrikaners, even those who had access to English education, to conduct public discourse in their own language. Similarly, many Cape Afrikaners resisted the temptations of assimilation and gave their children Dutch education.[198] The DRC, another foundation of Afrikaner ethnicity, was also an arena in which the cultural struggle was waged. While English made some inroads into the church, no less important was the struggle for the preservation of Dutch as the language of worship.[199] With the advent of Representative Government, in 1854, the political ramifications of the language question became all too obvious and evident to at least some Cape Afrikaners. In 1850 the mere possibility that Representative Government would be introduced created among Afrikaners great expectations, according to an English teacher in George: 'The Dutch show a great unwillingness to have their children taught in English; ... they say there will be no need of it now that they are to have Representative Government, ... henceforth all will be Dutch.'[200] On the eve of Representative Government a reader wrote to the *ZA*:

> If the electors in the *platteland* will have to put forward and elect only people who know English we will have not a free but a forced choice, because in many districts people who enjoy the full trust of the public and possess all the local knowledge and capabilities do not master the English language, whereas the few who know English have little or no knowledge of local affairs and in many cases enjoy no public trust.[201]

The fact that English was recognised as the only official language of political discourse under Representative Government reinforced the alienation of many Cape Afrikaners and was a source of a major ethnic grievance.

It is against this politicisation of the language question that we must interpret the warning sounded by Dr Changuion in August 1857: 'In each people language, nationality and worship are very closely interconnected, so that if one is lost the others lose their power.'[202] In 1856, the request of the Member for Albert in the Legislative Assembly to address the Assembly in Dutch was refused. In 1857 and 1858 petitions were submitted to that effect, a motion in Parliament was rejected, and in the Dutch press correspondents and leaders urged the use of Dutch in public life.[203] In 1856 all the nine field cornets of Graaff Reinet appealed to the governor to publish parliamentary legislation in Dutch too.[204]

The ethnicisation of Cape Afrikaners was also manifested, in 1858, in opposition to state-sponsored immigration from Britain. Earlier, in 1856, when state-sponsored immigration was discussed, the *ZA* called for immigration from Holland, Germany and Switzerland rather than from Britain.[205] Between 1845 and 1861 efforts were made to encourage youth immigration from Holland and 664 Dutch youths actually settled in the Cape.[206] There were also manifestations of solidarity with Holland, like the collection of more than £1,000 for the victims of floods in the Netherlands.[207] It is perhaps not coincidental that in the same period there were other manifestations of Cape Afrikaner cultural self-assertion like the establishment of the Paarl Gymnasium in 1859, the attempt by *Het Cradocksche Nieuwsblad* in 1861 to use the Cape Dutch dialect to communicate with ordinary Afrikaners and the foundation in 1862 of *Aurora Rederykskamer*, a Dutch dramatic and debating society.[208]

All this indicates that Afrikaner ethnic consciousness was simmering below the surface. Though not yet politically organised, Afrikaner ethnicity was definitely being politicised. In fact, the political apathy of *platteland* Afrikaners, before the 1870s, could be construed, in view of the culturally alien nature of the state and of the political process, as a positive political statement. On the other hand, the increasing number of Cape Afrikaners who did show interest in parliamentary politics, in particular farmers from the east, and the beginning of the struggle for the use of Dutch in parliament in the second half of the 1850s, show that an assertive ethnic political consciousness was forming. A study of the Graaff Reinet district shows that in this town there were cases of Afrikaner electoral ethnic mobilisation before the advent of the Afrikaner Bond.[209] In 1882, Janse van Rensburg, the first president of the Bond, recalled that 15 years earlier an association was formed in Cradock with the aim of electing farmers to parliament.[210] During the election campaign in 1869 the *Cape Argus* wrote: 'On the hustings and at some of the meetings men of position and ability stated amid the applause of their hearers that they or their candidates were Afrikanders.'[211] Ethnic solidarity was becoming a political asset.

The introduction of Responsible Government in 1872, in entrusting to the colonists the executive as well as the legislature, transformed the colonial state. It presented a great opportunity and provided an incentive to potential ethnic mobilisers, because the control of the colonial state was not only desirable but also possible. It is in this context that the increased resources of the state in the wake of the diamond revolution contributed to the advent of Afrikaner ethnic mobilisation. The parliament was now responsible for the disposition of increasing state revenues. Between 1870 and 1881 government expenditure rose from £795,695 to £5,472,263.[212] Politics was becoming much more relevant to the economic well-being of Cape Afrikaner farmers than ever before. In 1878, in search of additional revenue, the Sprigg government imposed excise on spirits, producing a major grievance among the more modernised and politicised, and also economically hard-pressed, wine farmers in the western Cape. It was this economic grievance which pushed them to exploit the new political space created by Responsible Government more systematically and more determinedly. It was manifested in the establishment of the ZABBV, the first Cape Afrikaner political party, which, after amalgamating with the Afrikaner Bond, set out to secure a dominant influence in the central institutions of the colonial state.

Against the background of the gradual evolution of Cape Afrikaner ethnic consciousness and assertion, the sudden outburst of ethnic mobilisation and its almost instant political success in the late 1870s and the first half of the 1880s make more sense than the pan-Afrikaner nationalist interpretation. The content and political orientation of this consciousness were almost a pure product of the Cape Afrikaners' colonial experience.

Because British occupation was a critical formative stage in the evolution of Cape Afrikaner ethnic consciousness, the combined impact of British capitalism and colonialism not only precipitated its advent, but also left a deep imprint on its nature. As we have seen, the impact of both capitalism and imperialism was complex, indeed contradictory. While offering scope and space for beneficial integration, they also marginalised Cape Afrikaners throughout much of the nineteenth century. The concurrent cultural thrust of British imperialism had a similarly contradictory effect on Cape Afrikaner society. What informed the emergent Cape Afrikaner ethnic consciousness was neither fully satisfactory integration nor total alienation, but rather a mixture of integration and marginalisation. This blend not only created a niche for a particular ethnic identity, but also shaped the content of the evolving ethnic consciousness. The ambiguous nature of the integration and socialisation of Cape Afrikaners into the colonial state was reinforced by concomitant processes of modernisation and social change. This was reflected in diverse, contradictory outcomes and responses among them.

British colonialism announced the birth of a more progressive era, but brought with it the pangs as well. Economic development offered new opportunities but also produced grievances. There were Afrikaners who accumulated considerable land and wealth, but also those who paid the price in dispossession and abject poverty. There were Cape Afrikaners who adopted the ethos of progress and those rejecting it in the name of conservatism. There were those who were fully anglicised and those who adhered to their mother tongue. There were those who integrated into the multi-cultural social life and those preferring their own. There were those who in religious affairs were inclined towards liberalism and even left the DRC, and those who fortified themselves in their fundamentalist religious *laager*. There were those who fully identified with the colonial state and those who rejected it. There were those who joined the political game and those who abstained. There were those, like J.W. Sauer, who became non-racial liberals and those who believed that the black man's burden was to carry the white man's one. There were those who played cricket, dressed in white, and those who preferred to mount a horse and hunt with *veldschoene* on their feet.

What informed the ethnic political consciousness of Cape Afrikaners and their attitude towards the colonial state and the British empire, as a distinct cultural group, was the balance of integration with all its contradictory manifestations. As the nineteenth century progressed, for many Cape Afrikaners this balance progressively improved, breeding increasing satisfaction with colonial rule and the imperial connection. Consequently, the goals of ethnic mobilisation were rectifying grievances and improving opportunities rather than breaking the imperial, colonial nexus. Indeed, Cape Afrikaners became increasingly colonial-Cape-centric. In 1892, the *Express* from Bloemfontein gave a republican perspective of this salience:

> The truth is hard but it cannot be hidden. The Cape and Orange are two. The Afrikaner here is different from the one there ... The colony is a colony! Orange is a republic. Around us the wind of freedom blows while above our heads blows the flag of independent Orange. There the freedom thirsty Afrikaners dwell under the broad and soft wings of the British Queen.[213]

From a Cape Afrikaner perspective, the Cape was an ethnic core, while their republican Afrikaners were the ethnic diaspora.

The impact of relations between core and disaspora on Cape Afrikaners

It is against this background that the impact of the imperial intervention against the republics on the Cape Afrikaners' political consciousness and mobilisation should be analysed and understood. My basic argument is that the imperial intervention, which culminated in the 1877–81 Transvaal crisis, stimulated the development of Afrikaner ethnic mobilisation in the Cape ethnic core, rather than 'awakened' them to their pan-Afrikaner national destiny.

Informed Cape Afrikaner opinion took an interest in the affairs of the republics only when political events of particular importance took place. Thus, as we have seen, the Dutch press hailed the annexation of the Orange Free State in 1848 and condemned British withdrawal therefrom in 1852. In 1868 in the wake of successive battles between the Basuto and the Free State, when the British intervened on the side of the former, sharp criticism of British action appeared in the pages of the Dutch press, and in Cape Town a play on the Great Trek was staged. However, this does not satisfy an Afrikaner historian who criticises Cape Dutch newspapers for displaying loyalty to the crown and propagating 'the principle of brotherhood and amalgamation between the two white populations of the country'. A big shock was needed, he concludes, in order to break this nationalist apathy.[214]

47

The annexation to the British empire, in 1871, of Griqualand West, where diamonds had been discovered, aroused mixed reactions in the Cape. On the one hand there was bitter opposition, but on the other hand J.H. Hofmeyr, an editor who must have been aware of the mood of his readers, while not condoning British behaviour, put forward a case for imperial annexation.[215] Scholtz claims that this episode brought about 'a lively and full consciousness of their own nationality' among Cape Afrikaners.[216] Hofmeyr's biographer is more specific with regard to the impact of this episode: '... and it was possible to come out more openly with one's sentiments, and to press the claims of the Dutch language more frequently and with more insistence'.[217] In other words, the annexation of the diamond fields contributed to the growth of Afrikaner ethnic consciousness and assertion in the Cape core, rather than pan-Afrikaner nationalism.

More central and crucial to the nature of the politicisation of Cape Afrikaners was the impact of the Transvaal crisis which culminated in the first short Anglo-Boer war in 1880–81. There is no doubt that well before this crisis there had been among Cape Afrikaners a widespread sense of identification with, and solidarity towards, their Dutch-speaking brothers in the republics. This sentiment rested on shared language and culture, on a perception of a common collective birth on the African soil and also on family connections. The Afrikaners' colonial-republican connection was highlighted at the time of the crisis by the fact that the two presidents of the republics were prominent ex-Cape Afrikaners. The criticism of British injuries to republican interests was motivated, primarily, by a sense of solidarity and sympathy towards their co-ethnics in the republican diaspora. This was articulated by Hofmeyr in a memorial to Gladstone: 'Connected with the Boers of the Transvaal by the ties of descent, language, religion, and – many of us – of inter-marriage and friendship, we feel that their wrongs are our wrongs, and services rendered to them are services rendered to us.'[218] Addressing his own people, Hofmeyr was more sanguine:

> The Annexation of the Transvaal has had its good side. It has taught the people of South Africa, that blood is thicker than water. It has filled the Africanders, otherwise grovelling in the mud of materialism, with a national glow of sympathy for the brothers across the Vaal, which we look upon as one of the most hopeful signs for the future.[219]

It would, however, be misleading to view these articulations as the birth of pan-Afrikaner nationalism. A close scrutiny of the Cape Afrikaners' political behaviour during the Transvaal crisis and its aftermath reveals ambiguities and complexities, rather than a clear march of pan-ethnic nationalism. The crisis highlighted the basic dilemma facing a core ethnic community, torn between ethnic solidarity towards its diaspora and particular interests and inclinations. The pull of the core was particularly strong, since an improving balance of interests fostered among conservative Afrikaner farmers a strong attachment not only to their colonial form of government but also to their imperial and monarchical connection. Consequently, the Transvaal crisis which hastened the political ripening of Cape Afrikaners produced neither a pan-Afrikaner nationalism nor even a Cape Afrikaner nationalism. It did produce a mild form of Cape Afrikaner ethnic mobilisation aimed primarily at immediate core-related issues. Emerging Afrikaner politics failed the test of ethnic nationalism because it manifested no desire for either ethnic self-determination or ethnic exclusiveness.

There was no lack of manifestations of solidarity towards the Transvaal: memoranda signed by thousands of Cape Afrikaners condemning the annexation, delegations to the governor, assistance to a delegation from the Transvaal and determined opposition in parliament to an attempt by Premier Sprigg to promote confederation before the disannexation of the Transvaal. The Transvaal burghers were even encouraged to offer passive resistance, and when the war broke out money was collected, and medical assistance rendered.[220] Yet Hofmeyr, who played a prominent role in assisting the Transvalers, favoured confederation. He told the governor that the withdrawal of Britain from South Africa would be a disaster, promising that if the annexation was annulled he would do his best to promote confederation under the British flag. In a speech in Parliament, while opposing confederation under the prevailing circumstances, he revealed that he was disappointed that the annexation had dashed his hopes of directing 'the stream of *South African*[221] nationalism into the canal of British loyalty' and inducing the republican Boers to forgo independence. Unhappy with the prospect of an uprising, in the wake of the Transvaal burgers' meeting at Paardekraal, Hofmeyr advised Transvalers that if passive resistance failed, they should try to secure a Cape-like liberal constitution and amalgamate with the Colony. When the war broke out his recipe was solidarity with the republican brothers combined with loyalty to Britain. His behaviour during the war and his efforts to secure peace highlighted the ambivalence of many Cape Afrikaners, torn between the call of the blood and their genuine loyalty to the empire. Deeply concerned with the prospect of eventual Boer defeat and the ramifications of a prolonged war on Cape Afrikaners, he urged General Joubert to demonstrate 'tangible proof of submission' despite their victories on the battlefield.[222]

The true impact of the Transvaal crisis on mainstream Cape Afrikaners emerged in the wake of the Pretoria convention of 1881 which concluded the conflict. It was articulated by Hofmeyr in Parliament, on 31 October

1881, when he moved to thank the British government for the generous terms of peace with the Transvaal. Reacting to accusations that Cape Afrikaners were inclined towards republicanism, he stated:

> For all that it cannot be denied that blood is thicker than water ... It cannot be denied that since the annexation of the Transvaal, the feeling of Dutchmen towards the Crown has to some extent grown cool. All that feeling will now be done away with by the concessions accorded to the Transvaal. That will not only remove any momentary feeling of opposition towards British institutions and the British Government, but it will do more than this in establishing a new feeling in the hearts of Dutchmen which never existed before. Instead of resting upon simply a cool and calculating feeling as to the material advantages of British rule, they will now have a warm-hearted feeling of thorough attachment to the Crown, just such a feeling as animates the most loyal and patriotic Englishman. If this has been the result of the Transvaal war, then that war has not been in vain.[223]

Any commentary is superfluous. From the perspective of the relations between the Cape Afrikaners and the empire the Transvaal crisis was, indeed, a collective catharsis.[224]

The emergence of organised Cape Afrikaner politics and the evolution of their ideological and political outlook

The moderate response of Cape Afrikaners to the Transvaal crisis was also manifested in the nature and concerns of the political organisations which sprang up during the late 1870s and early 1880s. Contributing to a heightened ethnic consciousness, there is little doubt that the crisis expedited the evolution of organised Cape Afrikaner ethnic politics. However, as we have seen, the immediate cause leading to the formation of the ZABBV in 1878 was a parochial one, namely, the imposition of excise duty on local brandy. In the original constitution of that body there is no mention of the crisis or of other strictly ethnic issues. In fact, even the word Afrikaner is not to be found and the ethnic nature of the association can be deduced only from the language in which the document was written. The stated object of the association was 'to watch over and protect the Farming Interests of the Colony'.[225]

The Albert Boeren Bescherming Vereeniging, formed in 1879 in the east, appears both more ethnic and more strictly political than its western counterpart. D.P van den Heever, the charismatic leader from the east, in outlining to the founding meeting the objectives of the association, placed high on the agenda the struggle to use the *moedertaal* (mother tongue) in Parliament. This was a clear manifestation of ethnic assertion in response to an ethno-cultural grievance. He concluded with his vision of the new association: 'Not only Farmers' Protection Committee but an Afrikaner Bond, a compact bound together by loyalty and interest in which every Afrikaner may feel at home. Then South Africa will become what it must be, and then the alien tongue will no longer dominate South Africa.'[226] This fiery message is, in fact, much more mild than appears at first glance. 'Loyalty' (to the British crown) placed a clear boundary to both geo-political and political scope of the association. In the context of the Cape, the ideal was cultural non-domination rather than ethno-cultural domination and exclusiveness, as it would have been in the case of a fully-fledged ethnic nationalism. The concern with the language, which was absent from the ZABBV, was, perhaps, not merely a response to the cultural campaign of S.J du Toit and the *Patriot*, as suggested by Davenport.[227] If Du Toit's message had more resonance in the east, it was, perhaps, because it happened to be a local grievance with less salience in the west, where knowledge of English was more prevalent. Indeed, the language barrier excluded aspiring politicians from fully participating in the political life of the Colony. It was primarily a colonial grievance to be rectified, rather than a source of organic ethnic nationalism. As we have seen, the east had pioneered the language struggle already in the late 1850s. 'Loyalty and interest' reflected the Cape, colonial essence and boundaries of this association.

The Genootschap van Regte Afrikaners, established in 1875 'to stand for our Language, our Nation and our Land' represented a clearer and more overt and assertive ethno-cultural thrust. As in the case of many nationalist movements in Europe, the Genootschap sought to rescue a vernacular language from oblivion by elevating it to a medium of literary performance, and transforming it into the foundation stone for con-structing a nation. As in Europe, behind this movement in the Cape stood cultural entrepreneurs, clerics and teachers, who were provoked into action by the threat from a dominant alien culture.[228] In publishing *De Afrikaanse Patriot*, a history of Afrikaans, grammar books and literary work in the local Dutch dialect, S.J. du Toit, in particular, made a remarkable contribution to the political awakening of Cape Afrikaners.[229] In retrospect he is perceived as one of the fathers of the Afrikaner ethnic nationalism. Indeed, with its emphasis on Cape Dutch (Afrikaans) as an indigenous Afrikaner creation, and with the elaboration of a highly patriotic ethnic *volk* history, this movement had definite organic ethnic nationalist overtones and potential.

It is, however, pertinent to probe, from a late nineteenth century perspective, the resonance and impact it had among Cape Afrikaners. The Genootschap was predominantly a Paarl phenomenon, inspired primarily by the experience of cultural entrepreneurs straddling the Cape cultural frontier. Among its moving spirits we find immigrants from Holland. S.J. du Toit, the volatile, erratic leader of the new movement, was inspired by the religious-cultural tradition of the anti-modernist movement in Paarl led in the 1860s by the Dutch churchman Van der Lingen to which he gave a new twist.[230] Prominent alongside S.J. du Toit we find other Dutchmen like the teachers A. Pannevis and C.P Hoogenhout and the churchman Jan Lion Cachet. As in some cases of small 'unhistoric' subjugated small nations in Europe, it was foreigners who showed greater interest in the upgrading and rescuing of local vernaculars.[231] S.J. du Toit was also influenced by the doctrines of the Dutch theologian Abraham Kuyper and his anti-liberal, neo-Calvinist Christian National movement.[232]

The Paarl Genootschap faced stiff opposition from the Cape Afrikaner intelligentsia. The DRC upheld high Dutch, the language of worship, and most members of the non-cleric intelligentsia also preferred high Dutch and looked down upon the attempt to elevate the 'inferior' local patois which was considered by the educational authorities as a 'Kaffir language'.[233] This preference of educated Afrikaners was reflected in the fact that whereas there were many Dutch newspapers in the Cape, the *Patriot* remained, until the end of the century, the only Afrikaans newspaper. It was also manifested in the establishment of a second language movement, in 1890, to promote high Dutch which was a foreign language to many ordinary Afrikaners. The competition between High Dutch and the Cape Dutch vernacular considerably hampered the prospect of ethnic nationalism in the Cape. First, there no agreement among cultural entrepreneurs which language to uphold and promote. Secondly, and perhaps more importantly, support for the vernacular, the 'inner language', which was so critical in the evolution of organic ethnic nationalism in Europe,[234] as the cultural medium of Cape Afrikaner ethnic assertion, was marginal. The Paarl language movement also did not reflect the experience and concerns of Cape Afrikaner farmers, struggling on the economic frontier, who formed the bulk of the emerging Cape Afrikaner ethno-political community.

The circumscribed nature of the Paarl ethno-cultural movement was reflected in its public appeal. The *Afrikaanse Patriot*, the organ of the Genootschap, began with 50 subscribers; by 1877 their number had increased to 400, hardly reflecting great enthusiasm. The increase to over 3,000 by 1881 was most probably a reward for its outspokenness with regard to the Transvaal crisis and to the politicisation it had precipitated among Cape Afrikaners.[235] It is noteworthy, however, that the annexation of the Transvaal did not immediately prompt the cultural entrepreneurs in Paarl to transform their enthusiasm into ethnic political organisation. It was only on 20 June 1879, some two years later, that S.J. du Toit called for the formation of an Afrikaner Bond. Considering the crisis facing 'Afrikanerdom' the prospective Afrikaner Bond, as outlined by Du Toit, lacked even the nationalist fervour of some of his earlier writings. It had pan-South African, rather than a pan-Afrikaner traits. The proposed Bond was to be an ethnically inclusive, rather than exclusive, organisation, while on the crucial language issue it did not go beyond equality with English. As the Transvaal crisis was moving towards confrontation it was, surprisingly, only very mildly anti-British.[236] Even so, it went too far for Hofmeyr to heed the call. Towards the end of 1879 Du Toit renewed his call but to no avail, and it was only in the second half of 1880 that two or three Bond branches were formed in the Karoo.[237] Thus, even the outbreak of the war in the Transvaal did not immediately inspire Cape Afrikaners into more determined political mobilisation and action. It seems that the military performance of the Transvalers and the honourable end of the war in early 1881 finally broke the ice. By September 1882 at least 59 Bond branches had been established, mainly in the midlands and the eastern province.[238]

By that time the ideological colours of S.J. du Toit, the originator and propagator of the Afrikaner Bond, were sharper and clearer. His militancy had been manifested in encouraging the Transvalers to take up arms to regain their independence. His enthusiastic support for the republican cause and for Kruger earned him the job of Inspector of Education in the Transvaal. Before leaving the Cape in February 1882, to take up his appointment, he left behind a Program van Beginselen (programme of principles) for the Bond. This ideological testament represented a much clearer manifestation of organic ethnic nationalism than his 1879 proposals. First, the definition of the nation (*volk*) was considerably narrowed down to include mainly the descendants of Dutch and Huguenot colonists. Secondly, while accepting that the British authority represented the will of God, it stated that 'the ultimate object of our national development must be a *united South Africa under its own flag.*'[239] It thus contained the two crucial components of a fully fledged ethnic nationalism, namely, ethnic exclusiveness and ethnic self-determination. The 'glorious' outcome of the war may have encouraged him to come out of his ideological closet.

It would, however, be erroneous to equate the sudden popularity of the Bond, in the aftermath of the war, with the attraction of the ideology of its originator. Much more research has to be done before we can satisfactorily explain why Afrikaners in the midlands and the east preferred the Bond to the ZABBV, making it by far the stronger of the two, spatially and numerically. The original Afrikaner Bond had far too short an independent existence to offer a fruitful field for a comparative class analysis.[240] The short history of the Bond, until its amalgamation with the ZABBV, does, however, provide sufficient evidence that there was no ideological convergence between the bulk of its leadership and S.J. du Toit. In an address to a visiting government minister on 25 October 1881, the committee of the Graaff Reinet branch of the Bond stated:

> Your Honour cannot be unaware of the fact that there are some Colonists who look upon the Bond, as a proof of dissatisfaction with the British rule; and having revolutionary intentions. Therefore we candidly make use of this public opportunity, to throw such an indignant accusation far away from us, as we do not intend doing anything else, but to make use of those privileges which Her Majesty granted us in a free Constitution, and to use for that purpose only such means as are constitutional.[241]

There is certainly no trace here of Du Toit's radical, fiery stuff. In a Bond Congress held in Graaff Reinet in early March 1882, a resolution expressing confidence in Hofmeyr, the conservative and pragmatic leader, as 'the leader of the Afrikaner party in the Cape Colony', was unanimously adopted. Rather than discuss Du Toit's programme of principles, they referred it to the branches. Little wonder that the *Patriot* was rather unhappy with the outcome of this congress.[242]

In the following Bond congress, held in September 1882 in Cradock, D.P van den Heever, one of the most influential leaders of the organisation, stated bluntly during the debate on a South African confederation: 'I am happy with this government and if anybody dragged the English flag through the mud, we can and must shoot him dead.'[243] Of particular interest were the views of Hofmeyr, who had joined the Bond to rescue it from the ideological excesses of its initiator. On the eve of the congress he published a direct attack on S.J. du Toit's notion of a united South Africa 'under its own flag'. He viewed it as 'an extremely venturesome thing' to associate the Bond with such a goal, reminding his readers that on two recent solemn occasions 'every one was full of enthusiasm, of attachment to Her Majesty the Queen and to her rule'. While viewing 'the independence of the whole of South Africa as an inevitable eventuality', his position on this crucial issue was radically different from that of his ideological rival in two main respects. First, as a true conservative pragmatist he expected it to happen as a result of historical evolution rather than as the outcome of a conscious effort by the Afrikaners. In fact, he expected it to happen as a result of British military defeat at the hands of another European power. Secondly, Hofmeyr's concept of the Afrikaner nation was not ethnically defined. He argued that independence would not be a blessing to the country before 'we ... first acquire a sane feeling of nationality'. He went on to propose a voluntary rather than an organic notion of nationalism:

> Only if both elements [Dutch and English] learn to respect one another, will the cohesive force of a true national feeling be acquired ... If in the

course of time we have acquired a true nationality of our own – then, and not before, shall we be ripe for independence, and then it will matter little, what language shall be our national language, then we may even, like the most patriotic nation in the world, the Swiss, speak three or four languages.[244]

At the subsequent congress he used a similar argument in opposing D.F. du Toit who had introduced an amendment stating that a united South Africa under its own flag was an objective of the Bond. Hofmeyr carried the day, the amendment being defeated by 55 votes to five.[245]

The congress at Richmond, in May 1883, the objective of which was the amalgamation of the Bond and the ZABBV, was opened by the popular chairman, Janse van Rensburg, who reminded the delegates that it was the anniversary of 'our Honourable Queen', and asked them to show their loyalty by offering her three cheers. This was done, according to the official minutes, 'with the greatest enthusiasm and was repeated'.[246] Hardly a promising start for ethno-republicanism. On the two crucial controversial issues, the constitution adopted for the Cape Afrikaner Bond was an unqualified victory for Hofmeyr. The first article confirmed the inclusive, voluntary definition of the Afrikaners: 'The Bond knows no nationality at all except that of the Afrikaners, and regard as belonging thereto, anyone, of whatever origin, who strives for the welfare of South Africa.' The second article defined a united South Africa as the *eind bestemming* (destiny) rather than the *einddoel* (final goal) of the Bond. This semantic difference is not inconsequential. It is the difference between patiently and passively awaiting the historical process to ripen naturally and actively working towards its expedition. It is the difference between pragmatic conservatism and Jacobin radicalism. At Richmond the former clearly carried the day.

This disposition of the Bond, before and upon amalgamation, was manifested also in the balance of issues occupying the attention and time of its leaders and members. Out of the 34 items on the agenda of the Cradock congress only two had broad ideological, political ramifications. Most of the rest dealt with local, immediate interests and grievances affecting mainly the Cape Afrikaner farming community.[247] The picture in the amalgamation congress at Richmond was even clearer. Only one item of major ideological importance, the programme of principles, was proposed as an item on the agenda, and that by only two branches. The remaining 32 were of a parish pump nature.[248] This narrow Cape outlook of the Bond was articulated and legitimised by Janse van Rensburg, who became the first chairman of the amalgamated Afrikaner Bond. He said that 'the aim of *Afrikanderisme* is primarily to promote it here before we move across the borders. Let us rather first sort out things here and than we shall look at other matters ... there is enough to be done here.'[249]

Clearly, the leadership and the rank and file of the original Afrikaner Bond had more in common with the ZABBV than with S.J. du Toit and his fancy ideas. The choice of Hofmeyr as the unchallenged, though uncrowned, leader of the amalgamated Bond was, indeed, natural.

During the rest of the 1880s and until the Bond struck an official alliance with Rhodes in July 1890, these major ideological, or rather non-ideological, and political themes and orientation of the Bond were further confirmed.

Less than two years after the amalgamation of the Bond at Richmond, its loyalty to Britain stood the test of the Bechuanaland crisis.[250] The British government, haunted by the memories of Majuba and anxious to consolidate the Cape as a collaborating sub-imperial agent in southern Africa, expected the worst. They feared not only a political crisis but also another South African war engulfing the Cape Afrikaners as well.[251] The evidence suggests that these anxieties reflected British paranoia rather than Cape Afrikaner disposition.

In a debate in the Cape parliament on 15 July 1884 on Sprigg's proposal to annex the disputed territory to the Cape, Afrikaner MPs were either lukewarm or positive.[252] When the crisis erupted, in the wake of the annexation of the republic of Goshen by the Transvaal, the parliament was in recess. Resolutions adopted by various branches of the Bond, while manifesting some sympathy towards the Transvaal and the Boer settlers in the minuscule republics, betrayed no anti-imperial feelings. They were mostly concerned lest the agitation by the 'jingoes' create ill-feeling between English and Afrikaners in the Cape. The Swellendam branch passed the following resolution on 1 November 1884: 'This meeting is of the opinion that there is no better Government for us than the English, and desires no other flag save the English and to continue to be loyal English subjects.'[253]

The debate on Bechuanaland in the Cape parliament in late June and the beginning of July 1885, soon after the storm had subsided, enables us to evaluate the impact of the crisis on Afrikaner Bond MPs. D.C. de Waal's claim, that 'if the opposition had carried its point, there would have been war not only in the Transvaal, Free State and the Cape Colony, but even in Cape Town', sounds more like someone letting off steam, *ex post facto*, than a reflection of the views and sentiments of this respectable and wealthy farmer and businessman.[254] Janse van Rensburg, the Bond's chairman, was more representative of the prevailing Cape Afrikaner mood when he assured parliament that 'no born Englishman could be more loyal than he was himself'.[255] J.A de Wet stated that 'there were no more loyal people in the country' than the Afrikaners, adding that only their loyalty prevented them from being driven to rebellion against the Queen.[256] The ultimate expression of loyalty was offered by

A.S. le Roex, the non-anglicised MP for the remote Karoo constituency of Victoria West: he said he was also a member of the Africander Bond, but notwithstanding that he would fight and die for the Queen if it were necessary. If it came to pass that South Africa would have to fight for England, then he was sure that every Bondsman would offer his life and blood for it, but he was afraid that the merchants and advocates, those ringleaders of the late meetings (by which he meant the English Jingoes), would hide themselves away.[257]

T.D. Barry, an English-speaking Bondsman, assured Parliament that he 'had never heard a disloyal word uttered' in the Bond and that 'he did not believe there were more than two or three Bondsmen who wished the British flag out of South Africa'.[258] The Bechuanaland crisis, like the Transvaal one before it, rather than triggering disloyalty, was an occasion for Cape Afrikaners to restate their loyalty to Crown and Empire.

The jubilee year of Queen Victoria in 1887 offered Cape Afrikaners an outlet for amazing manifestations of love and loyalty, in town and country, in verse and prose. The Afrikaner Bond congress in its official address to the Queen gave the lead:

> We the undersigned, representatives of the Afrikaner Bond of the Colony ... wish to approach you with our heartiest and most sincere congratulations on this blessed occasion ... We assure you humbly and respectfully [of] our true loyalty to your throne, and we feel proud that in the great British Empire there are not more loyal subjects than those we represent.

It was signed by 'the humblest, loving and most loyal subjects of Your most Blessed Majesty'.[259] In Paarl, the capital of 'Afrikanerdom', representatives of the Genootschap van Regte Afrikaners and the Afrikaner Bond were present at the local celebration with their flags, while the main speaker expressed his joy at the impressive presence of the burghers which proved Paarl's loyalty to the Queen.[260] The local Dutch newspaper ran a special supplement including a long poem, full of praises for the Queen, by Oom Jan.[261] Such celebrations were not restricted to major urban centres. A correspondent from Van Rhijnsdorp boasted that 'although our village is small and miserable we have demonstrated our loyalty to our honourable Queen Victoria'.[262] A rural Bond branch in the east held a banquet on a farm. According to the correspondent, 'the house was beautifully decorated and the flag which during thousands of years [sic] withstood the blows of the storm flew merrily high, a striking proof of our Bondsmen's loyalty'.[263]

In 1887 Hofmeyr was a member of the Cape delegation to the first Colonial Conference held in London. In a proposal combining a mild preferential treatment for colonial produce with a scheme to finance imperial defence, Hofmeyr made the most important contribution to the idea of strengthening the imperial connection. According to one observer Hofmeyr's speech marked 'a new epoch in the history of the, up to that time, shadowy idea of Imperial Federation, to which now for the first time form and substance had been given'. Lord Knutsford, the Colonial Secretary, also acknowledged that '*the* speech of the Conference was made by Mr Hofmeyr'.[264]

Loyalty seems to have been contagious. The following somewhat poetic report which appeared in the *Patriot*, on the toast drunk in honour of the Queen at the Bond congress of 1888, captured the prevailing spirit:

> The chairman got up and said that it was decided to propose a toast to the Queen on the occasion of her birthday (loud and continuous applause) ... The glasses were filled and the toast drunk with such enthusiasm that only Bondsmen can demonstrate – yes, even the warmest Englishman could not have drunk it with greater enthusiasm ... Professor Jan de Villiers jumped to his harmonium and the English anthem was sung by all ... 'God Save the Queen' was sung in such a way that even the world famous 'Paarl Rock' bowed in respect as the canon fired 21 shots.[265]

Little wonder then, that in an interview given to a London newspaper, D.F. du Toit, the editor of the *Patriot* and the leader of the more extreme faction in the Bond, said that 'the Bond was as loyal as it was possible' and that in England they spoke of a republic more than in the Cape.[266]

Demonstrations of loyalty were not restricted to party congresses and festive royal occasions. Loyalty became an integral part of the internal ideological-political discourse in the Bond at the local, branch level. Thus addressing a Bond meeting in the east, in 1888, D.P van den Heever said that he was 'proud and glad to be a Bondsman and a British subject ... The Bond and the Bondsmen want to make South Africa one land under the flag of our beloved Queen.'[267] Speaking in a similar vein two years later, in an election campaign in Stellenbosch, did not prevent W.A. Krige from securing an overwhelming victory.[268] On 12 July 1890, on the eve of the formation of Rhodes's government, M.L. Neethling, a prominent Bondsman, addressing a meeting in Malmesbury attended by 130 farmers, reminded the audience that the Bond was loyal: 'Its first principle is respect for the Queen and submission to her government. I will be the first to strike my name off if the Bond adopts a disloyal direction.' P.B van Rhijn, also a member of parliament, said that he joined the Bond only a year before because he had thought earlier that the Bond was disloyal.[269]

The second major trend which manifested itself in the formative years of organised Cape politics, and which gained impetus during the 1880s, was the desire to join hands with the English-speaking colonists and ultimately to amalgamate with them in a great white non-ethnic nation.

Thus, the *ZA* declared in July 1887 that 'the Bond did not distinguish between born Afrikaners and the English who realized that it was their duty and interest ... to support the cause of the Colonists'.[270] Accordingly, the Bond opened its ranks to English speakers. Hofmeyr, in fact, saw the recruitment of Englishmen as a testament to the Bond's success, preferring five of them to 100 Afrikaners.[271] From this perspective as well, 1887 was a special year. The Bond's annual congress in April was held in Uitenhage, where the integration between ethnic Afrikaners and English speakers in the local Bond branch was the most successful. In his reply to the greetings of the local English-speaking branch chairman, the Bond chairman expressed his joy at witnessing the love towards South Africa that was manifested by English speakers. In a report back on the congress to his Paarl branch, a delegate told of his astonishment to find 'among the Englishmen many who were Afrikaners in heart and soul and who belong to the Bond'.[272] Referring to Hofmeyr's speech upon his return from the Colonial Conference in London, the *ZA* elaborated: 'there is no reason why the Colonists of the two great nationalities which exist here, together with others, will not form in the long run a truly South African nation.'[273] This spirit was echoed by a small branch in the east which expressed the hope that the Queen would live to see 'the happy day when all race differences between English and Dutch-speaking Afrikaners would cease to exist'.[274] In the Bond congress of 1888 the *rapprochement* between the Bond and the English sector of the Cape population found expression in the participation of delegates from the Farmers Association with the right both to participate in the deliberations and to vote. Elated Van den Heever preached to the congress: 'All the differences of nationality must be set aside, and we must march together shoulder to shoulder as one *volk*. If there was a day that I was proud this was the day. I did not believe that I would experience it. I extend to the English friends the hand of friendship. (loud applause)'[275] In February 1889 the *ZA* argued that the differences between English and Dutch speakers did not prevent them from forming one nation.[276] The willingness, indeed eagerness, of Bondsmen to collaborate with their English compatriots was also manifested in their support from 1884 of Upington and Sprigg as prime ministers. One of the reasons for the Bond's refusal to form the government was its fear that this would exacerbate the tension between English and Afrikaners.

Not everybody was happy with the new spirit of brotherhood emanating from Bond circles towards the English. In March 1887, the *Patriot* criticised the Bond and the *ZA* for propagating love between Afrikaners and English.[277] In June 1888 it surmised that the improved tone towards the Bond in the English press resulted from the Bond becoming more *Engelsgesind* (English-inclined) than before.[278] Neither was the *Patriot* happy with the persistent parochial nature of the Bond. The *Patriot* claimed that there were two parties within the Bond – the parish-pump party centred in Cape Town and a 'high politics' party represented by it:

> The best of them are colonial and think and work only for the colony, while a whole group want to be nothing more than an agricultural society. Politics, high politics is our struggle. No politics, but better wool and better wine is their aim.[279]

The *Patriot* was also unhappy about the enthusiastic loyalty expressed by the Bond. Criticising D.P. van den Heever for saying that the Bond was established to promote loyalty, the newspaper, while confirming its own loyalty, reminded its readers that the organisation was formed 'to care for us and our children'.[280] It was also critical of Hofmeyr's zealous imperialism as manifested in his contribution to the Colonial Conference.[281] Although the *Patriot* had moderated its positions during the 1880s, the pro-English excesses of the Bond were too much for it to swallow.

Clearly, however, as the 1880s wore on, the 'high politics' party in the Bond was marginalised, as the loyal, colonial-centric Afrikaners consolidated their hold on the party. This emerged conclusively from the outcome of the controversy over the programme of principles. From the inception of the amalgamated Bond this ideological 'hot potato' was thrown from congress to branches and from one congress to another. When the 1889 congress finally decided the issue, the programme bore little resemblance to the original neo-Calvinist, ethno-cultural and republican proclivities of S.J. du Toit.[282] It was a clear victory for Hofmeyr's pragmatic conservatism.

The causes of the Afrikaner Bond's moderate political-ideological disposition

How can we account for the political-ideological outlook of the Bond as it evolved during the 1880s? How did it happen that, in the wake of the 'national' crisis, the Bond moved not in the pan-Afrikaner, ethno-nationalist trajectory, but rather in one the political and ideological parameters of which were largely prescribed by the colonial imperial experience and boundaries? At the height of the Transvaal crisis in the early 1880s, Hofmeyr exclaimed: 'Blood is thicker than water.' How did it transpire that by the end of the decade water rather than blood was flowing in the political veins of the Cape Afrikaner Bond? These questions are most pertinent to our investigation. The consummation of the relationship between Rhodes and the Afrikaner Bond in a political marriage in 1890 resulted not only from the courting of the bridegroom but also, perhaps principally, from the disposition of the bride.

As a point of departure it should be stated that Cape Afrikaners, upon encountering British occupation, possessed only a rudimentary collective-consciousness. The process of collective consciousness formation among them took place largely, as we have seen, under the aegis of British rule. Generations of Afrikaners had been born as British subjects before this process matured in the 1870s in ethnic political mobilisation. British colonial experience, with all its contradictory ramifications, left a deep impression on their evolving collective consciousness. The manifestations of loyalty by the Afrikaner Bond serve as clear evidence thereof. It may sound somewhat speculative, but the admiration and love for the Queen may suggest that she played a role in the formation of Cape Afrikaner group identity and consciousness. They seem to have adopted Queen Victoria as a collective mother figure. Praising and congratulating the Queen on her birthday in 1890, the *ZA* suggested that if a president were to replace the Queen, the centrifugal forces in the Cape would increase.[283] Cape Afrikaners seem to have internalised their imperial monarchical experience. Beyond that, it was the balance of their colonial experience which influenced their disposition. We have seen that on the whole this balance, though mixed, was positive. Particular attention must be given, however, to the evolution of this balance during the 1880s, the decade that provides the immediate background to the emergence of overt Cape Afrikaner politics.

Economically, the decade of the 1880s was an eventful one. The Cape economy was, on the whole, more complex and dynamic than before. However, during the first half of the decade it was afflicted by another depression. By 1886 this was over and with the gold discoveries in the Witwatersrand the economic horizons brightened,[284] and the economic prospects of South Africa as a whole now seemed better than ever before. For the Cape, however, the blessings were mixed as Cape farmers, and particularly the wine farmers, could not find profitable markets for their produce. When Hofmeyr came back from the Colonial Conference in London he told his Cape audience:

> When I brought forward my plan, I looked at the situation from a broad Imperial stand point, but the interest of my own place was not on that account altogether absent from my mind. I thought of my electors at Stellenbosch. I thought of the Paarl, of Cape wines, raisins, dried fruits, etc., and of the market which they might get under a favourable tariff in England and the Colonies.[285]

The dependence of the Cape Afrikaners went beyond the economic field. This broader dependence informed the world outlook and the strategy of the Afrikaner Bond. This broader dependence was more acute than the economic one, being related not merely to their economic well-being as farmers, but also to the prospect of their very survival on the African soil. This sense of acute dependence, stemming from a strong sense of weakness in the face of a perceived threat to their survival, was a very important determinant of the collective Afrikaner psyche. It was an important part of their formative individual and collective experience as a small group of white settlers in what was perceived as a hostile black continent. The perceived threat to their survival was exacerbated after the encounter with the better organised, more numerous Xhosa people on the eastern frontier from the late eighteenth century. It was further reinforced by the experience of their republican brothers in the interior. Indeed, the *swart gevaar* (black danger) was not the invention of the National Party in the aftermath of the Second World War. It was also uppermost in the collective consciousness of Cape Afrikaners who were associated with the Bond in the last two decades of the nineteenth century.

Like other white settler groups in new continents inhabited by 'barbarians', Cape Afrikaners aspired to achieve total domination. Domination was perceived as a vital determinant of prosperity and survival. However, under the weak and ineffectual VOC, it was impossible. Consequently, along the frontier in the east, the relations between white settlers and African groups were characterised by a combination of confrontation and symbiosis. The advent of British imperialism changed the balance of power between whites and blacks. While not always performing to the full satisfaction of Cape Afrikaner settlers, British rule eliminated the threat to their physical survival. Thus, Sir Bartle Frere left a positive impression on Cape Afrikaners, despite his Transvaal policy, because of his strong-arm policy against the Zulu and other African groups.[286] In its attitude towards the British imperial connection the Bond favoured a symbiosis between Cape Afrikaners and the empire, geared to eliminate the *swart gevaar* and secure white domination. From this perspective loyalty to the empire, far from being merely a manifestation of sentimentality, was definitely functional. In the 1880s with the scramble for southern Africa attracting new powers to the region, particularly Germany, the imperial connection was seen as a protection against foreign aggressors. Hofmeyr, for example, was beset by the prospect of German intervention.

Having relieved Cape Afrikaners of the external threat to their physical survival, British rule exposed and exacerbated another area of threat and crucial dependence. For their economic well-being, the Afrikaners were dependent on the availability of two major means of production, namely, land and labour. With the expansion of commercial farming and the growth of population additional land and labour were badly needed to avert economic and social decline. Cape Afrikaner interests, as proclaimed by the Bond, required free access to African land and free exploitation of African labour. They minced no words in spelling out their ideal of racial aristocracy. In May 1890 the *ZA*, in reference to the crucial labour question, stated bluntly that it was the role of Africans to be transformed into a working class. It claimed that there were two alternatives – either the 'Natives', would work for the colonists or the colonists would have to leave South Africa.[287] The most persistent and pressing grievance articulated by Bond circles was the unwillingness of the imperial authorities to adopt an appropriate 'native policy'. This was highlighted in the bitter criticism of British policy in Bechuanaland.[288] The view was repeatedly expressed that, had the British government adopted a 'correct' policy regarding the relations between white settlers and 'natives', the devotion and loyalty of the Afrikaners to the empire would have known no bounds.[289]

The attitude towards the empire seems to have somewhat improved from 1886 with the assumption of office by Salisbury's Conservative government. This government was praised for not interfering in the internal affairs (namely 'native affairs') of the colony. Its recognition of the rights of the settlers in the 'New Republic' in Zululand and the approval of the Voters' Registration Act of 1887 were perceived as proofs that on the vital issue of 'Native affairs' the British government was moving in the right direction.[290] Even Sir Hercules Robinson, the governor, who had come under strong criticism for his policy in the interior, enjoyed a *bonne presse* towards the end of his term in 1889. His departure speech which extolled the virtues of 'colonialism' as against imperialism was received with amazement and admiration.[291] The bitter attacks were shifted from the government to the British parliament and public opinion, the bastions of 'wretched' liberalism and humanitarianism.[292] In emphasising its essential satisfaction with Britain, the *ZA* argued that 'the best is the enemy of the good'.[293]

Imperialism was 'good' also because the imperial component in the colonial experience decreased markedly with the advent of Responsible Government in 1872. The democratisation of the colonial state created a space within which Cape Afrikaners could assert themselves, pursue their interests and promote their visions. As a result, the goal of political mobilisation was primarily to exploit the space provided by the imperial government. With the advent of organised Afrikaner politics in the late 1870s, Afrikaners were well poised to take advantage of their numerical superiority and to make their mark on the colonial state. As early as 1882 they managed to secure the introduction of Dutch as a language of parliamentary deliberations, opening parliamentary politics to many who had been previously excluded or marginalised, and removing a major ethnic grievance.

In the wake of the 1884 general election the Bond became the dominant parliamentary group. In bringing down the Scanlen government in 1884 and being the main force behind the incoming Upington government, the Bond established itself as the kingmaker of Cape politics. Cape Afrikaners were no more passive objects of the colonial state; they became a major component and determinant thereof. In June 1888 Theron, the Bond's secretary, stated in Parliament that a government which was supported by the Bond governed according to its spirit.[294] Little surprise that Afrikaner leaders were happy with the transformed colonial state. The *ZA* explained that the loyalty demonstrations occasioned by the Queen's jubilee expressed 'the feeling that Afrikaner-dom enjoys under the generous rule of Her Majesty the Queen'.[295] D.C. de Waal told a Bond congress banquet that neither he nor other Bondsmen wanted to change British rule for another: 'They are happy with the privileges they enjoy and viewed the monarchical rule we have here as the best.'[296] R.P. Botha, the Bond's chairman, while confessing that in his heart he was a republican, rejected an allegation that the Bond strove for a republic. After criticising the regime in the republican north he concluded: 'Hence my opinion is that the constitutional government that now exists here is the best for this Colony.'[297]

Thus, during the 1880s, the alienation of Cape Afrikaners from the colonial state diminished considerably. Furthermore, they became an integral part of the colonial white ruling class. In other colonial situations the alienation and exclusion of the indigenous peoples from the colonial state power structure were at the roots of anti-colonial resistance. In Europe a similar alienation and exclusion of small ethnic nations stimulated the emergence of ethnic nationalism.[298] In the Cape the absorption of the Afrikaners by the colonial state denied ethno-nationalist entrepreneurs the basic conditions for success. Having become the arbiters of political power, politically conscious Cape Afrikaners could also identify with the British empire which was the legitimiser of the benevolent colonial state.

The new political space opened for Cape Afrikaners under Responsible Government was shared, however, with the English-speaking colonists. Even though the Bond controlled, from 1884, the single largest parliamentary group, they did not possess an outright majority. Indeed, Responsible Government, while offering new opportunities, also exposed and exacerbated another critical area of Afrikaner weakness and dependence. The English-speaking minority could not be taken for granted. First, they were a minority which played a crucial economic role. Secondly, though a minority, their representatives were in the majority in parliament. Thirdly, they could enlist the support of the 'home' government.

Thus, in order to shape Cape politics to suit their interests and taste, a symbiosis, or alliance, with at least a segment of the English-speaking population was essential. This requisite also reinforced the symbiotic strategy towards the empire, as was candidly articulated by the *ZA*: 'Is it possible, at this stage, to think of separating the Cape from England? Everybody knows that this is not possible without a civil war.'[299] It was the fear that Bond domination, by exacerbating the tension between English and Afrikaners, would impair the prospect of domestic symbiosis that prompted the Bond to support successive English prime ministers and governments in which they had only a minor share. In refusing to assume the premiership in 1884 Hofmeyr explained: 'Because if I formed a Ministry, my opponents would raise the racial issue, and I hate racial issues.'[300] Thus, the propagation of 'colonialism' rather than ethnic nationalism and the non-ethnic definition of Afrikanerdom made good political sense. The reference to Upington, by the Bond's chairman, as 'the Afrikaner from Cork'[301] was not cynical.

If there was not more collaboration and more amalgamation between Cape Afrikaners and Englishmen, it was not for lack of will on the part of the former. The Bond was not prepared to collaborate on any terms. There were three important issues, on which they held clear positions and which they expected to be respected by potential partners: recognition of their cultural heritage and equalisation between English and Dutch; protection of farmers against debilitating competition; the adoption of a 'native policy' which would guarantee the flow of a cheap, obedient labour supply and reduce the electoral power of the Africans.

For many English-speaking politicians it was difficult to adjust to the new parliamentary reality shaped by the sudden political assertion of Cape Afrikaners. They were reluctant to resign themselves to the fact that the good old days of Afrikaner apathy and 'carpet bagging', which gave them absolute control of Parliament and government, were over, and that colonial democracy had come home to roost.[302] In June 1884, C.T. Jones from Port Elizabeth, responding to a request that Bills be printed also in Dutch, reminded Afrikaner MPs that 'this is an English colony and an English Parliament'.[303] There were English politicians who, out of genuine liberal persuasion, or for more mundane electoral reasons, wished to expand the black vote entrenched by the non-racial Cape constitution. With the incorporation of the Xhosa areas in the Cape the scope for black political participation increased considerably. Bond politicians viewed the courting of the black vote as an attempt by frustrated English politicians to deprive them of the dominant position they had acquired. While the Bond reluctantly accepted the non-racial franchise as part of the democratic dispensation which was the source of their own power, they were determined to limit the black franchise to prevent the Cape being dominated by English liberals supported by black voters. Worse still, there was the ultimate danger of black domination. The *Patriot* expressed bluntly what most Bond politicians would have subscribed to: 'The white man must be the boss ... If the black man will ever be the boss, it will be time for us to trek.'[304] A domestic *swart gevaar* which had replaced the external one obsessed, indeed haunted, the Bondsmen.

In some cases English-speaking liberals were elected in constituencies in which black voters held the electoral balance. The *ZA* was clear about the political implications of the alliance between white liberal politicians and black voters:

> At a time in which the anti-colonial party will be strengthened unless the electoral law is changed and a suitable solution to the Transkei question is found, it is supremely important that the Dutch do not separate themselves, like the Irish, but instead ally with the English who share their views.[305]

The *ZA* was candid in stating that 'Sprigg deserves support only on account of his position with regard to the Native question'.[306] The strategy of the Bond was premised on an alliance with English-speaking elements as a means to dominate the blacks. The strategy of English-speaking liberals to secure power through alliance with the black electorate was the main grievance of the Bond against them and the foremost obstacle to collaboration with them.[307]

Afrikaner political power, however, was becoming a reality that no aspiring and pragmatic English politician could afford to ignore. Sprigg discovered it in 1881, to his dismay, when he was ousted from office mainly because the Afrikaner group strongly opposed his Basutoland policy.[308] In joining the Scanlen government in 1881, Hofmeyr signalled the entry of the Afrikaners into active politics. However, his resignation in November of that year, in response to John X. Merriman's outburst against Afrikaner ethnic politics, highlighted the uneasy, contradictory nature of the new alliance between Cape Afrikaners and English-speaking politicians.[309] Afrikaner MPs, from 1883 as Bondsmen, who continued to support Scanlen, albeit lukewarmly and reservedly, turned against him in 1884, mainly because of his intention to hand the Transkei over to Britain.[310]

The assumption of power by the Upington government marked the transition to an era of more formal coalition-making, with the Bond playing a dominant role. On 8 May 1884 a meeting of 38 Bond supporters in parliament elected Sir Thomas Upington as their candidate for the premiership. Only then was he summoned by the governor and entrusted with the formation of a new government. The new cabinet included only one representative of the Bond – the Secretary for Native Affairs, J.A.

de Wet.[311] The real head of the government, however, was Sprigg – whom the Bond accepted only reluctantly. In consenting to his inclusion the Bond demonstrated their ultimate commitment to colonial interests rather than to ethnic sentiment, having had to put aside their dislike of Sprigg for his attitude towards the Transvaal and his past anti-Afrikaner stance, because Upington refused to form a government without him.[312] By 1886 they had accepted him as prime minister because he was a staunch 'colonialist', and especially because he subscribed to the Bond's 'native' policy.[313] Although the prime minister and most ministers were English, the British colonial secretary reminded British MPs that the 'Cape Government is at present time a Dutch Government'.[314]

The alliance between the Bond and Upington and Sprigg was a marriage of convenience rather than love, confirming the Bond as a pragmatic rather than an ethnically purist party. The balance sheet of the alliance, from a Bond perspective, was, on the whole, positive. In April 1886, at a dinner for Bond's parliamentarian, D.C de Waal expressed the party's satisfaction with the government.[315] In June 1886, the *ZA* complimented the Upington government for dedicating itself to the elimination of 'racial hatred' (English–Afrikaner hatred) and for supporting a truly colonial party.[316] Bond MPs must have been delighted to hear Colonel F. Schermbrucker, a cabinet member, upholding the alliance with the Bond, praising it for its loyalty and political respectability, strongly defending the Bond-inspired government policy in the Bechuanaland crisis and expounding a perfect 'colonial' creed.[317] Another minister defended the Bond's dominant position in Parliament. The *Mercury*'s sharp criticism of the minister, and its complaint that 'we languish under the damned Afrikaner yoke', could only have increased Afrikaner satisfaction.[318] An English-speaking government supporter even spoke in favour of equality for Dutch in the public service.[319] Relations between the Bond and the government were not always harmonious. Sprigg was not as protectionist as they would have liked him to be,[320] and in 1888 they differed over regional issues.[321] However, although the government's 'Afrikaner sentiment was limited' it was perceived as the best under the circumstances.[322] This pursuit of, and satisfaction with, the politics of the possible again highlighted the pragmatic, moderate nature of the Bond. The satisfaction with the vital white trans-ethnic alliance further weakened the case for a more exclusive Cape Afrikaner ethnic political strategy.

The pragmatism and moderation of the Bond was a true reflection of its perception of the balance sheet of its relations with the empire and its domestic English-speaking collaborators. However, in order to account fully for this perception and consequent political orientation, we need to focus on the socio-economic basis of the Bond.

67

The impact of British imperialism and capitalism, which precipitated radical socio-economic transformations among the predominantly rural Afrikaners, led to the emergence of an educated elite. In similar situations, members of this group frequently played an important role as ethno-national entrepreneurs and mobilisers.[323] Yet, in the Cape, as ethnic politics appeared among Afrikaners, most of them were not available. Many members of the Cape Afrikaner intelligentsia were fully anglicised, and were not interested in the ethnic politics of the Bond. *ZA* lamented that, with the language, educated Afrikaners acquired English ways of thinking and became more English than Afrikaner in their ideas.[324] Professor N. Mansvelt condemned the denationalising impact of the educational system.[325] The Bond also had very limited support among the DRC clergy, whose counterparts in Europe were instrumental in the emergence of nationalism among small nations.[326] In fact, the DRC, the most effective social institution among Cape Afrikaners, not only preached loyalty and submission to the colonial state, but also challenged the Bond on the crucial 'native question'.[327] Having very limited support from members of the religious and secular intelligentsia, the Bond lacked people of 'reading and debating ability' in Parliament.[328] The *ZA* justified the employment of Dutchmen, rather than Cape Afrikaners, in the Transvaal civil service by asking: 'How many educated Afrikaners join the Bond?'[329] A confident, yet vulnerable, ethnically conscious intelligentsia living on the cultural frontier could have given the Bond a more radical and purist touch. Well-educated young Afrikaners, like Jan Smuts and F.S. Malan, who were beginning to join the Bond around the mid-1890s, had been absent in its formative years.

The economic development which enabled accumulation by enterprising farmers also marginalised many less fortunate ones. This process of pauperization which began a few decades before the establishment of the Bond and gained momentum with the increasing pace of the capitalisation of Cape agriculture, swelled the ranks of *bijwoners* (squatters) and 'poor whites' (mainly Afrikaners).[330] Under other circumstances such groups, having lost both economic stake and social status, could have provided fertile recruitment grounds for radical, militant ethnic politics. The process of politicisation of such deprived, marginal groups is, however, long and complex. In the late nineteenth century Cape, these groups were far from being ripe for any politics. As John Molteno, a contemporary Cape politician, observed: 'The Poor Whites and *Bywoners* class of Dutch Afrikanders was not noted at any time for patriotism: bread, not patriotism, was of more account in their scheme of philosophy.'[331] When, in the twentieth century, poor Afrikaners became politicised, they offered much socio-political scope for chauvinist ethno-nationalist entrepreneurs. In the late nineteenth century Cape this class of poor Afrikaners began to be the passive objects of the socio-moral concern of the Afrikaner ethnic leadership. It was only in the early 1890s that Bond leaders began to view the pauperization of many Cape Afrikaners as a threat to ethnic survival.

As the upper and lower social strata were beyond the reach of ethnic politics, the Bond was inspired by, and appealed to, what might be termed the socio-economic centre. Its social base consisted primarily of members of the Afrikaner land-owning farmers. This group was not homogeneous, embracing sub-groups with economic, regional and occupational differences. There were, for example, wine and wheat farmers, mainly from the western province and stock farmers from the south-west, the Karoo, Namaqualand, the midlands and the eastern province. There was also considerable wealth differentiation among them. While their interests did not always converge, they were all land-owning farmers who, in various degrees, were effectively linked to the market economy. As such they all had a keen interest in the distribution of resources and opportunities by the state, and in the effect of its policies on their economic fortunes. As they were culturally distinct from the minority of English-speaking farmers and had particular cultural grievances in common, in addition to economic interests, ethno-cultural mobilisation made sense. The ethnic disposition of this group was also fed by the tradition of antagonism between Afrikaner and English-speaking farmers in the east, the latter having collaborated with the merchants against the perceived interests of the Afrikaner farmers.[332] The Bond also attracted a number of successful commercial entrepreneurs like D.C. de Waal, D. de Villiers Graaff, G.J. Krige, A.B. de Villiers, C.W.H. Kohler, N.F. de Waal, P.G. Wege, M.M. Venter, and others. Many of these, however, were born on farms and were themselves also farm owners. Furthermore many of them represented in Parliament predominantly rural constituencies.

For the members of this backbone of Cape Afrikaner society, the colonial state was becoming increasingly congenial. They exploited the economic spaces that opened up with the expansion of the capitalist economy. They valued the stability and security provided by the colonial state. Members of this group played leading roles in the public life of their communities. They were to be found in agricultural societies, on school and church committees, and in cultural and benevolent societies. They were also prominent on municipal boards and in divisional councils. They controlled most Bond branches and their representatives formed the vast majority in the Bond's congress. Ultimately their representatives became the arbiters of power in parliament. Indeed, their moderation is hardly surprising. Furthermore, it is usual for especially individualistic land-owning farmers to be extremely conservative. As the leaders of the

Graaff Reinet Bond branch put it to a visiting minister, in October 1881: 'for the most of us are landed proprietors, and it is a well known fact, that landed proprietors are conservative ...'.[333] Rejecting the *Cape Times*'s allegation that the Bond strove for the victory of republicanism, the *ZA* stated that the Cape Afrikaners were happy with the Queen's rule as long as constitutional liberties were upheld. The reason for it was simple: 'Why, then, would the Afrikaner public, which is as conservative as one can find, strive for a republican system of government.'[334] Early in 1885 the *Patriot* portrayed a stereotypical profile of the Cape Afrikaner farmers on the eve of their political awakening:

> Our farmers who form the core of our Afrikaner population are docile and peaceful by nature. The Dutch-Afrikaner farmer is the happiest man if he can cultivate his farm peacefully and undisturbed and promote his affairs. If he gets an adequate price for his produce so that he can pay taxes, rents and other accounts ... then he is satisfied in his home and family circle ... To attend public meetings for political goals is a bother for him.[335]

The conservative Cape Afrikaners were thus, instinctively and by natural inclination, averse to politics, let alone radical politics. That politicisation did strike roots among this group and that they turned to ethnic political mobilisation, was due to the fact that the colonial cup was only half full. This half reinforced the moderation and conservatism of Afrikaner farmers. The other half, filled with grievances, produced ethnic politics. Those responsible for the political awakening of the Cape Afrikaner farmers were, according to the *Patriot*, 'the foreign fortune seekers and Jingoes' who not only took advantage of his apathy and denied him his rights but also 'ridiculed, scorned and slandered' him. According to the newspaper, 'this situation was intolerable ... a confrontation was unavoidable ... it came and it continues ... this is all the story.'[336] This was also the main theme in the address of T.P. Theron to the 1887 Bond congress. He argued that the main motivation behind the formation of the party was the grievances of the Afrikaner farmer who had been 'like a beast of burden'. Indeed, as he recalled, the initial response of the farmers to their predicament was political apathy and withdrawal. This came to an end when people like Hofmeyr in the west and D.P. van den Heever in the east 'came forward in the dark days, impelled by the true love of fatherland, to protect the interests of the Boer, and the means used by them was the formation of an association known by the name of the Farmers' Protection Association solely for the protection of the Boer'.[337]

Two years earlier, Van den Heever himself saw fit to raise his voice against the allegations that the Bond was mainly concerned with the elimination of imperial and English influence in South Africa. As the founder of Afrikaner politics in the east, this firebrand reminded his Afrikaner readers that the Bond was not established to deal with these issues of high politics. 'I know,' he wrote, 'what was the basis for the Afrikaner political awakening because I was the first in the East to initiate it.' According to him there were three main causes for this awakening: (a) the excessive government expenditure which landed the colony in heavy debts; (b) the language grievance; (c) the neglect of Afrikaner interests by the rulers of the Colony. Consequently, the Afrikaners realised that the only way to promote the welfare of *land* and *volk* was by electing their own representatives to Parliament. He concluded that 'the goal of the Bond is no more and no less than to strive for the welfare and prosperity of South Africa'.[338] The centrality of these grievances in motivating and sustaining the Bond emerges also from the address of the Bond chairman at the opening of its 1890 congress. In 'lamenting' the demise of the ultra-English and jingoistic South African League, the chairman claimed, not altogether cynically, that its decline had been a greater loss to the Bond than to its founders:

> We needed them in order to awaken our brothers. If the League existed and was effective we would have had twice as many branches ... Our main threat is apathy. Why are there no representatives from western districts like Oudshoorn and others? Is it not mainly because there is no immediate danger to the Afrikaner cause in their areas and thus there is no need for them to harness themselves to and have an interest in, this cause?'[339]

Conservative land proprietors such as those who formed the backbone of the Bond, would have lent their support to a radical ideology and militant strategy only if their vital interests were seriously threatened over a long period. As the *ZA* claimed, a political change in the Cape would occur only if the British government were deliberately to support the anti-colonial minority represented by the *Cape Times* 'against the majority whose loyalty is undisputed'.[340] Such support would have been perceived not simply as a gross act of political ingratitude; in supporting the world outlook and policies of the Cape liberals the British would have jeopardised the vital interests, indeed the very survival, of the conservative Afrikaner farmers. Thus, had the conditions which brought about Afrikaner ethnic mobilisation persisted or became more pronounced, the case for a more assertive and radical ethnic nationalism could have been established. However, during the 1880s no such development occurred. In fact, the Bond's almost instant success eliminated many of the grievances which had motivated its formation. The Bond became the Cinderella of Cape politics. From 'beasts of burden' the Bondsmen were transformed, almost instantaneously, into 'kingmakers'. With the equalisation of Dutch and English in Parliament in 1882, the foremost cultural grievance disappeared. During the second half of the 1880s, as economic conditions improved, British imperialism became less intrusive and more accommodating. Collaborative relations were established with a docile and obliging English-led government and an increasing number of English speakers joined the Bond. These were not the conditions in which an assertive, radical Afrikaner ethnic nationalism could strike root, let alone flourish. It is hardly surprising that the conservative Bondsmen cold-shouldered S.J du Toit and his Paarl collaborators in their attempt to infuse warmer, purer ethno-nationalist blood into the veins of the Bond. The *Patriot* had to admit that the nationalist sentiment among the Afrikaners was 'too weak' and that for most people the material pocket was more important than the nationalist heart.[341]

Thus, there was a close correlation between the ideological and political orientation of the Bond and the interests of its leaders and members. The manifestations of loyalty to Crown and empire and the desire to merge with the English speakers into a new non-ethnic Afrikaner nation were not merely platitudes to please external audiences. They stemmed from the depth of their colonial experience, from the perception of their vital interests and from their innermost convictions and desires. For all that, conservative, moderate, pragmatic, loyal Bondsmen did have a strong sense of ethnic identity which was manifested in the two language movements which were established in 1875 and 1890 to promote the Cape Dutch dialect and Dutch respectively. They also showed genuine solidarity towards their ethnic brothers in the republics, and the Transvaal in particular, during the recurring conflicts between them and the British empire.

Indeed, the ethnic consciousness, ideological outlook and political practice of Cape Afrikaners, as manifested in the Bond, were informed by varied and contradictory influences. They were shaped by a definite ethnic identity and solidarity, and by a mixture of ethnic grievances and trans-ethnic interdependence. Not surprisingly, therefore, their consciousness and outlook were marked by ambivalence, which was reflected in the very meaning of the term Afrikaner. This term was used by Cape Afrikaners interchangeably to convey ethnic, as well as non-ethnic, meanings. Thus, while the official definition of the Afrikaner by the Bond was non-ethnic, the same word was used to describe ethnic identity, grievances and desires.[342] While the Bond appealed to ethnic identity and experience in the process of political mobilisation, it also celebrated its de-ethnicisation through the recruitment of English speakers. While the language, the innermost core of their ethnic identity, was a major grievance and an object for nurturing and promotion, the goal was equality with English rather than the supremacy of Dutch. This found expression in an open letter from Bond branch members in the east. On the one hand they stated: 'We feel ... that if a *volk* is denied of its language, it is denied everything, because *de taal is gansch het volk*' (the language is the people). On the other hand it was clearly implied that the removal of this grievance would unite Afrikaners and Englishmen: 'because of this there is discord; because of this the bond of love between Englishmen and Afrikaners has been torn'.[343] Hofmeyr, addressing the 1888 Bond congress, gave a more explicit expression to this ambivalence when referring to the progress in securing equality between Dutch and English: 'If we shall follow this path we shall become one *volk*.'[344] This ambivalence revealed itself also in the attitude of Bondsmen towards their republican brothers. While the Bond exhibited ethnic solidarity towards their republican diaspora in 1888, its secretary could speak with equanimity on the prospect of Transvaal's becoming an English republic.[345]

The domestic ethnic grievances and external ethnic crises obviously did not converge to produce radical ethnic nationalism. In fact, paradoxically, they watered down the ethnic content of Cape Afrikaner political consciousness as manifested in the Bond. In precipitating the advent of organised politics, colonial grievances and republican crises combined considerably to improve Cape Afrikaner fortunes. Effective settler colonial democracy denied the more committed and radical ethnic nationalist entrepreneurs the constant conflict with an unyielding colonial state which in other colonial situations was at the root of anti-colonial struggles. The ethnic nationalist ideology paid the price of the almost instant political success of the Bond. Consequently, the Cape Bond was a manifestation of ethnic mobilisation, designed to utilise the readily available political space to eliminate grievances and improve opportunities, rather than to promote ethnic nationalism.

Furthermore, the improving colonial balance sheet engendered, at least among some Bond leaders, an urge to resolve the contradictions and ambivalence and to reach a new harmony. As D.C. de Waal told the 1887 congress, the Bond's goal was not to fulfil an ethnic destiny, but rather to create the conditions which would obviate the need for its existence as an ethnic mobilizer: 'The old national prejudices are fortunately fast disappearing, and the time is approaching when our children will speak the two languages. And now the fourth question, where is the Bond going? It is moving towards the time when there will be here neither Dutch nor English and all will be Afrikaners.'[346] N.F. de Waal, the Bond's assistant secretary, went even further when addressing a De Beers banquet in honour of delegates to the Bond congress in Kimberley in March 1891:

The Bond was working for one nation, into which all differences were to be sunk; and if one day there was no more need for the Bond, then there would be no more talk of nationality; then there would be one language and one country and the object of the Afrikaner Bond ... would be accomplished.[347]

It was this striving for harmony which informed the political goal of the Bond – neither ethnic exclusiveness and domination nor separation from the British empire. This disposition of Bond leaders is reminiscent of the acceptance by members of small, marginal 'unhistoric' nationalities, in nineteenth century Europe, of the liberal assumption that, while not totally losing their ethnic identity, they were destined to merge with the larger, viable, 'historical' nationalities. At least some Bond leaders would have probably subscribed to what Revd Griffiths said in 1847: 'Let it [the Welsh language] die fairly, peacefully and reputably. Attached to it as we are, few would wish to postpone its euthanasy. But no sacrifice would be deemed too great to prevent its being murdered.'[348] From this perspective, it is quite possible that there were Afrikaner Bond leaders who viewed with resignation, if not satisfaction, the prospect of becoming part of the Cape, if not South African, fragment of the large British nation spread across the world. The Bond was essentially a truly white non-ethnic Home Rule party. Its colonial, Cape-centric orientation and dynamic affected the organisational fortunes and scope of the Bond. It was established in 1883 as a South Africa-wide organisation but by the end of the decade its republican branches degenerated and the Bond remained a Cape colonial party.[349]

This was the political-ideological dowry of the bride whom Rhodes coveted as a partner in implementing his imperialist vision. And the attention and space dedicated to its description are not superfluous, because as in human relations, the success of political courtship is often determined more by the disposition of the bride-to-be than by the enthusiasm and persistence of the suitor.

NOTES

1. T.R.H. Davenport, *The Afrikaner Bond* (Cape Town, London and New York, 1966), p. 16.
2. Ibid., pp. 35–8.
3. Ibid., pp. 39–43.
4. Ibid., pp. 67–70.
5. R.I. Rotberg, *The Founder: Cecil Rhodes and the Pursuit of Power* (Johannesburg, 1988), p. 36.
6. J.S. Galbraith, *Crown and Charter: the Early years of the British South Africa Company* (Berkeley, Los Angeles and London, 1974), p. 18.
7. B. Roberts, *Cecil Rhodes: Flawed Colossus* (London, 1987), pp. 42–3.
8. Rotberg, *The Founder*, pp. 125 and 127.

9. Ibid., p. 151.
10. Ibid., p. 216.
11. B. Williams, *Cecil Rhodes* (London, 1921), p. 51.
12. L. Michell, *The Life of the Right Honourable Cecil John Rhodes* (London, 1910), Vol. i, p. 138.
13. W.T. Stead, (ed.), *The Last Will and Testament of Cecil John Rhodes* (London, 1902), p. 58.
14. J.M. Orpen, *Reminiscences of Life in South Africa from 1846 to the Present Day* (Cape Town, 1964), p. 2.
15. 'Imperialist', *Cecil Rhodes: a Biography and Appreciation, with Personal Reminiscences by Dr. Jameson* (London, 1897), pp. 391–2.
16. Rotberg, *The Founder*, p. 150.
17. Ibid., p. 175.
18. Sir R. Williams, *How I Became a Governor* (London, 1913), p. 123.
19. Michell, *Cecil Rhodes*, Vol. i, p. 52.
20. On the contribution of Rhodes's Oxford experience on his imperial drive see Rotberg, *The Founder*, pp. 94–6 and 100–3.
21. Ibid., p. 235.
22. 'Vindex', *Cecil Rhodes: His Political Life and Speeches* (London, 1900), pp. 214–15.
23. J. Marlowe, *Cecil Rhodes: the Anatomy of Empire* (London, 1972); for Rhodes's belief that he would not live beyond the age of 50, see Molteno, *The Dominion of Afrikanerdom*, p. 35.
24. F.J. Dormer, *Vengeance as Policy in Afrikanerland: A Plea for a New Departure* (London, 1901), p. viii.
25. Michell, *Cecil Rhodes*, Vol, i, p. 93.
26. Ibid., Vol. i, p. 93.
27. Vindex, *Cecil Rhodes*, p. 52.
28. Ibid., p. 213.
29. Williams, *Cecil Rhodes*, p. 52.
30. Rotberg, *The Founder*, p. 127.
31. R.V. Turrell, *Capital and Labour on the Kimberley Diamond Fields* (Cambridge, 1987), p. 227.
32. Rotbert, *The Founder*, p. 209.
33. A. Mabin, 'The course of economic development in the Cape Colony, 1854–1899: a case of truncated transition' paper presented to Economic History Conference, Durban, 1984, p. 11.
34. Galbraith, *Crown and Charter*, p. 19.
35. Ibid., p. 21.
36. P. Maylam, *Rhodes, the Tswana and the British: Colonialism, Collaboration and Conflict in the Bechuanaland Protectorate, 1885–1899* (London, 1980), p. 128.
37. J.I. Rademeyer, *Die Land Noord van die Limpopo in die Expansie Beleid van die Suid Afrikaanse Republiek* (Cape Town and Amsterdam, 1949), p. 153.
38. Michell, *Cecil Rhodes*, Vol. i, p. 96.
39. Ibid., pp. 96–7.
40. Vindex, *Cecil Rhodes*, p. 62.
41. *Hansard*, 15 July 1884, p. 346.
42. T.E. Fuller, *The Right Honourable Cecil John Rhodes* (London, 1910), p. 19.
43. Vindex, *Cecil Rhodes*, p. 209.
44. H. Houghton, 'Economic development, 1865–1965', in M. Wilson and

L. Thompson, *The Oxford History of South Africa* (Oxford, 1975), Vol. ii, pp. 1–2.
45. R. Ross, 'The origins of capitalist agriculture in the Cape Colony: a survey', in W. Beinart, P. Delius and S. Trapido, *Putting the Plough to the Ground: Accumulation and Dispossession in Rural South Africa, 1850–1930* (Johannesburg, 1986), pp. 66 and 86; see also R. Ross, 'The Cape of Good Hope and the world economy, 1652–1835', in H. Giliomee and R. Elphick, *The Shaping of South African Society, 1652–1840* (Cape Town, 1989).
46. A.J. Christopher, *Southern Africa* (Folkestone, 1976), p. 64.
47. Ibid., p. 96.
48. N.C. Pollock and S. Agnew, *An Historical Geography of South Africa* (London, 1963), p. 185.
49. In the process of urbanisation I include cities and towns as well as *dorps* (villages).
50. Christopher, *Southern Africa*, pp. 87–8.
51. Ibid., p. 51.
52. A. Mabin, 'The making of colonial capitalism: intensification and expansion in the economic geography of the Cape Colony, South-Africa' (PhD thesis, Simon Fraser University, Vancouver, 1964), p. 63.
53. Christopher, *Southern Africa*, p. 87.
54. Ibid., p. 94; Mabin, 'The making of colonial capitalism', p. 64.
55. M.H. De Kock, *Selected Subjects in the Economic History of South Africa* (Cape Town and Johannesburg, 1924), pp. 175–6, 184–6, 191–2, 194–5, 213–18, 223–5.
56. Christopher, *Southern Africa*, p. 59.
57. Ross, 'The Cape of Good Hope and the world economy, 1652–1835', pp. 248–9; Christopher, *Southern Africa*, p. 59.
58. J. Du Plessis, 'Colonial progress and countryside conservation: an essay on the legacy of Van der Lingen of Paarl, 1831–1875' (MA thesis, University of Stellenbosch, 1988) p. 134; Christopher, *Southern Africa*, p. 59; M. George, 'John Bardwell Ebden, his business and political career at the Cape, 1806–1849', (MA thesis, University of Cape Town, 1980), p. 80; de Kock, *Selected Subjects*, pp. 195–7.
59. T. Kirk, 'The Cape economy and the expropriation of the Kat River settlement, 1846–1853', in S. Marks and A. Atmore, *Economy and Society in Pre-Industrial South Africa* (New York, 1980), pp. 227–9.
60. Christopher, *Southern Africa*, p. 59.
61. C.G. Henning, *Graaf Reinet: A Cultural History, 1786–1886* (Cape Town, 1975), p. 39.
62. E.H. Burrows, *Overberg Outspan* (Cape Town, 1952), p. 232.
63. Christopher, *Southern Africa*, p. 51.
64. W.A. Newman, *Biographical Memoir of John Montagu*(London, 1855), pp.158–218; C. Pama, *Bowler's Cape Town: Life in Cape Town in Early Victorian Times, 1834–1868* (Cape Town, 1977), pp. 38–9.
65. Christopher, *Southern Africa*, p. 100.
66. Ibid., p. 97.
67. Burrows, *Overberg Outspan*.
68. Mabin, 'The making of colonial capitalism', p. 130; A.J. Purkis, 'The politics, capital and labour of railway building in the Cape Colony, 1870–1885' (PhD thesis, Oxford University, 1978), pp. 43–5.
69. Purkis, 'The politics, capital and labour of railway building in the Cape Colony', 1870–1885, pp. 42–6; Mabin, 'The making of colonial capitalism', pp. 132–40,

259–71 and 285–89; J. van der Poel, *Railway and Customs Policy in South Africa, 1885–1910* (London, 1933), pp. 7–10.
70. R.F.M. Immelman, *Men of Good Hope: the Romantic Story of the Cape Town Chamber of Commerce, 1804–1954* (Cape Town, 1955), p. 99; J.J. Redgrave, *Port Elizabeth in Bygone Days* (Wynberg, 1947), pp. 289–90; Pama, *Bowler's Cape Town*, p. 38.
71. Mabin, 'The making of colonial capitalism', pp. 128–9.
72. A. Mabin, 'Concentration and dispersion in the banking system of the Cape Colony, 1837–1900', *South African Geographical Journal*, Vol. 67, No. 2 (1985), p. 149.
73. Mabin, 'Concentration and dispersion ...', pp. 142–3.
74. Ibid., p. 146.
75. E.H.D. Arndt, *Banking and Currency Development in South Africa (1652–1927)* (Cape Town and Johannesburg, 1928), pp. 255–7.
76. Mabin, 'Concentration and dispersion ...', pp. 142–4.
77. Ross, 'The Cape of Good Hope and the world economy', p. 253.
78. Mabin, 'The making of colonial capitalism', pp. 110 and 123; Henning, *Graaf Reinet*, p. 42; de Kock, *Selected Subjects*, pp. 226–7.
79. Mabin, 'The making of colonial capitalism', pp. 110 and 123.
80. Burrows, *Overberg Outspan*, pp. 157–8.
81. Mabin, 'The making of colonial capitalism', p. 105.
82. Ibid., p. 68.
83. Houghton, 'Economic development, 1865–1965', pp. 4–5.
84. K. Schoeman, *Olive Schreiner: 'n lewe in Suid-Afrika, 1855–1881* (Cape Town and Pretoria, 1989), p. 159.
85. Ross, 'The origins of capitalist agriculture in the Cape Colony: a survey', p. 65.
86. De Kock, *Selected Subjects*, pp. 282–3.
87. Ibid., p. 284.
88. See, for example, *The Cape of Good Hope Almanac and Annual Register (Cape Almanac)* (1855), pp. 58–9.
89. D.W. Rush, 'Aspects of the growth of trade and the development of ports in the Cape Colony, 1795–1882' (MA thesis, University of Cape Town), p. 41.
90. See, for example, *Cape Almanac* (1855), pp. 58–9.
91. Immelman, *Men of Good Hope*, pp. 11–13.
92. R. Ross, 'The rise of the Cape Gentry', *Journal of Southern African Studies*, Vol. 9, No. 2 (1983), pp. 197–200.
93. Immelman, *Men of Good Hope*, pp. 14–5.
94. Henning, *Graaff Reinet*, p. 40; M. Kaplan, *Jewish Roots in the South African Economy* (Cape Town, 1986), pp. 32 and 34–9; L. Herrman, *A History of the Jews in South Africa* (Johannesburg and Cape Town, 1935), p. 102; Burrows, *Overberg Outspan*, pp. 114–15 and 255–69; T.A. Van Ryneveld, 'Merchants and Missions: development in the Caledon District, 1838–1850' (BA Honours thesis, University of Cape Town, 1990), pp. 6–15.
95. Mabin, 'The making of colonial capitalism', pp. 110–11; Burrows, *Overberg Outspan*, p. 162.
96. De Kock, *Selected Subjects*, pp. 150–5.
97. Ross, 'The rise of the Cape Gentry', p. 216.
98. H.J. Duckitt, *Hilda's Diary of a Cape Housekeeper* 1902, reprinted Braamfontein, 1978, p.1; *Dictionary of South Africa Biography*, Vol. i, pp. 257–8.
99. De Kock, *Selected Subjects*, p. 195; C.L. Leipoldt, *300 Years of Cape Wine* (Cape Town, 1952), pp. 82–7.

100. De Kock, *Selected Subjects*, p. 186.
101. A.K. Millard, *Plantagenet in South Africa: Lord Charles Somerset* (Cape Town, London and New York, 1965), p. 71.
102. De Kock, *Selected Subjects*, pp. 220, 229 and 231.
103. Burrows, *Overberg Outspan*, p. 112; Christopher, *Southern Africa*, p. 24.
104. Mabin, 'The making of colonial capitalism', p. 107.
105. Ibid., pp. 110–11.
106. De Kock, *Selected Subjects*, pp. 232–3.
107. Ibid., pp. 213–21.
108. Burrows, *Overberg Outspan*, pp. 108–11 and 157– 9.
109. Immelman, *Men of Good Hope*, pp. 67–8, 75, 77, 233–4 and 237–9; C.G. Henning, *A cultural history of Graaff Reinet 1786–1886* (PhD thesis, University of Pretoria, 1971), pp. 87 and 89; Burrows, *Overberg Outspan*, p. 120.
110. Immelman, *Men of Good Hope*, pp. 231, 233 and 235–7; Burrows, *Overberg Outspan*, pp. 21 and 110; Henning, *Graaff Reinet*, pp. 41 and 46.
111. J.G. Fraser, *Episodes in my Life* (Cape Town, Port Elizabeth, Uitengage and Johannesburg, 1922), p. 2.
112. Ross, 'The rise of the Cape Gentry', pp. 207–8.
113. Burrows, *Overberg Outspan*, p. 264.
114. S. Dubow, 'Land, labour and merchant capital: the experience of Graaff Reinet District in the pre-industrial rural economy of the Cape, 1852–1873' (University of Cape Town, Centre for African Studies, 1982), pp. 53–60.
115. Houghton, 'Economic development', pp. 4–5.
116. Dubow, 'Land, labour and merchant capital', p. 87.
117. Henning, *Graaff Reinet*, Appendix xii.
118. Dubow, 'Land, labour and merchant capital', pp. 53–60; C. Bundy, 'Vagabond Hollanders and runaway Englishmen: white poverty in the Cape before Poor Whiteism', in W. Beinart, P. Delius and S. Trapido, *Putting the Plough to the Ground* (Johannesburg, 1986).
119. Immelman, *Men of Good Hope*, pp. 3–13; *Dictionary of South African Biography*, Vol. ii, pp. 796–7.
120. *Dictionary of South African Biography*, Vol. ii, pp. 585–6.
121. Ibid., pp. 188 and 267–8.
122. P. Scully, 'The bouquet of freedom: social and economic relations in Stellenbosch District, 1879–1900' (MA thesis, University of Cape Town, 1987), pp. 38 and 59.
123. K.W. Smith, 'From Frontier to Midlands: a history of the Graaff Reinet District, 1786–1910', Occasional Paper No. 20 (Institute of Social and Economic Research, Rhodes University, Grahamstown, 1976), p. 273.
124. See for example, *Cape Almanac*, 1855, pp. 159–65, Henning, *Graaff Reinet*, p. 47; H. Giliomee, 'Aspects of the rise of Afrikaner capital and Afrikaner nationalism in the Western Cape, 1870–1915', in W.A. James and M. Simons, *The Angry Divide: Social and Economic History of the Western Cape* (Cape Town, 1989), p. 69.
125. *Cape Almanac*, 1845, p. 323.
126. *Cape Almanac*, 1832, p. 203; 1855, pp. 191 and 195.
127. Davenport, *Afrikaner Bond*, p. 102; Scully, 'The Bouquet of freedom', pp. 34 and 74–6.
128. *Cape Almanac*, 1855, p. 184
129. Ibid., p. 184.
130. M.F. Katzen, 'White settlers and the origins of a new society, 1652–1778', in

M. Wilson and L. Thompson, *Oxford History of South Africa* (Oxfprd. 1969), Vol. i, p. 230.

131. P. van Schalkwyk, 'The response of the Afrikaners to the policy of anglicisation in the Cape Colony, 1806–1870' (BA honours thesis, University of Cape Town, 1990), pp. 28–43.

132. W. Ritchie, *The History of the South African College, 1829–1919* (Cape Town, 1918), pp. 26–55.

133. Scholtz, J. Du Plessio, *Die Afrikaner en sy Taal, 1806–1875* (Cape Town, 1939), pp.187–8.

134. E. Drus, 'The development of education at the Cape from 1859–1892' (MA thesis, University of Cape Town, 1940), p. 86.

135. Henning, *Graaff Reinet*, p. 123; *Het Oosten*, 17 June 1897.

136. *Standard Encyclopedia of Southern Africa*, Vol. 10 (Cape Town, 1974), p. 15.

137. B. Cloete, *Die Lewe van Senator F.S. Malan*(Johannesburg, 1946), p. 58.

138. F.S. Malan Papers, 'An ex journalist looks back', p. 3.

139. *ZA*, 1 May 1890.

140. Ibid., 11 Nov. 1890.

141. Henning, *Graaff Reinet*, p. 98.

142. S.P. Engelbrecht, *Thomas Francois Burgers: a Biography* (Pretoria and Cape Town, 1946), p. 4.

143. Scholtz, *Die Afrikaner en sy Taal*, p. 172; Davenport, T.R.H. 'The consolidation of a new society: The Cape Colony', in M. Wilson and L. Thompson, *Oxford History of South Africa*, Vol. i, (Oxford, 1969), p. 277.

144. Scholtz, *Die Afrikaner en sy Taal*, pp. 168 and 173.

145. See for example *Cape Almanac*, 1865, pp. 48–61.

146. See for example, *Cape Almanac*, 1865, pp. 86–90.

147. On the urban élite culture of the Cape in the mid-nineteenth century see E. Bradlow, 'The culture of a colonial élite, the Cape of Good Hope in the 1850s,' *Victorian Studies*, Vol. 29, No. 3 (Spring 1986), pp. 387–403.

148. *Cape Almanac*, 1832, pp. 110–7; 1845, pp. 180–2; 1855, pp. 143–58, 182–3, 187–8, 191, 194, 196–7, 205, 210 and 245; 1865, pp. 134–43; 1877, pp. 248, 287–8, 295–6, 298, 305, 307 and 309–10. Henning, *Graaff Reinet*, pp. 111–14 and 194–212; B. Booysens, *Ek heb Geseg, die Verhaal van ons Jongeliede en Debatsvereenigings* (Cape Town, 1983), pp. 11–33.

149. A. Du Toit and H. Giliomee, *Afrikaner Political Thought: Analysis and Documents* (Cape Town and Johannesburg, 1983), Vol. 1, 1780–1850, p. 22–3.

150. Henning, *Graaff Reinet*, p. 91.

151. Du Toit and Giliomee, *Afrikaner Political Thought*, p. 23.

152. Henning, *Graaff Reinet*, pp. 96–7.

153. Davenport, 'The consolidation of a new society', p. 277.

154. Henning, *Graaff Reinet*, p. 96.

155. Scholtz, *Die Afrikaner en sy Taal*, pp. 182–3 and 195–6; Van Schalkwyk, 'The response of the Afrikaners', pp. 44–63.

156. J. B. Peires, 'The British and the Cape, 1814–1834', in R. Elphick and H. Giliomee, *The Shaping of the South African Society* (Cape Town, 1989), pp. 472–80 and 490–3; Du Toit and Giliomee, *Afrikaner Political Thought*, pp. 10–13.

157. J.B. Peires, 'The British and the Cape', pp. 496–7.

158. Du Toit and Giliomee, *Afrikaner Political Thought*, p. 23; Davenport, 'The consolidation of a new society', p. 329.

159. Peires, 'The British and the Cape', p. 496.

160. Ibid., pp. 498–9.
161. Ibid., pp. 499–510.
162. J. du Plessis, 'Colonial progress and countryside conservatism', pp. 137–8.
163. See for example *Cape Almanac*, 1832, 1845, 1855 and 1865; it should be noted that because the figures are calculated on the basis of surnames absolute accuracy is impossible; F.A. Van Jaarsveld, 'Die Veldkornet en sy aandeel in die opbou van die Suid Afrikaanse Republiek tot 1870' (MA thesis, University of Pretoria), *Archives Year Book of South African History* (1950), Vol. ii, p. 204.
164. See for example, *Cape Almanac*, 1855.
165. Davenport, 'The consolidation of a new society', pp. 318–9; *Cape Almanac*, 1845, 1855 and 1865.
166. Davenport, 'The consolidation of a new society', p. 319; *Cape Almanac*, 1865.
167. Davenport, 'The consolidation of a new society', pp. 320–4; J.L. McCracken, *The Cape Parliament, 1854–1910* (Oxford, 1967), pp. 18 and 24.
168. Scholtz, *Die Afrikaner en sy Taal*; F.A. Van Jaarsveld, *The Awakening of Afrikaner Nationalism* (Cape Town, 1961).
169. Ibid., p. 33.
170. Peires, 'The British and the Cape', pp. 499–506.
171. Ibid., p. 505.
172. Scholtz, *Die Afrikaner en sy Taal*, pp. 52–3.
173. J.A. Coetzee, 'Politieke groepering in die woording van die Afrikanernatie' (PhD University of South Africa, 1949), pp. 54–5.
174. Du Toit and Giliomee, *Afrikaner Political Thought*, p. 27.
175. Scholtz, *Die Afrikaner en sy Taal*, pp. 54–5.
176. Van Jaarsveld, *The Awakening of Afrikaner Nationalism*, p. 35.
177. Scholtz, *Die Afrikaner en sy Taal*, p. 55.
178. Van Jaarsveld, *The Awakening of Afrikaner Nationalism*, p. 35.
179. Scholtz, *Die Afrikaner en sy Taal*, pp. 165–6.
180. Coetze, 'Politieke groepering', pp. 53–4.
181. Scholtz, *Die Afrikaner en sy Taal*, pp. 162–4 and 166–7; Van Jaarsveld, *The Awakening of Afrikaner Nationalism*, pp. 195–201.
182. Cited in H. Giliomee, 'The beginnings of Afrikaner Nationalism, 1870–1915', *South African Historical Journal*, Vol. 19 (1987), p. 122.
183. F.A. van Jaarsveld, *Omsingelde Afrikanerdom: Opstelle oor die Toestand van ons Tyd* (Pretoria and Cape Town, 1978), p. 12.
184. Van Jaarsveld, *The Awakening of Afrikaner Nationalism*, p. 44.
185. H. Giliomee, 'The beginnings of Afrikaner ethnic consciousness, 1850–1915', in L. Vail (ed.), *The Creation of Tribalism in Southern Africa* (London, 1989), p. 21.
186. Ibid., pp. 21–2.
187. H. Giliomee, 'Aspects of the rise of Afrikaner capital and Afrikaner nationalism in the Western Cape', p. 63.
188. E. Gellner, *Nations and Nationalism* (Oxford, 1983), p. 55.
189. Giliomee, 'The beginnings of Afrikaner ethnic consciousness', p. 22.
190. Ibid., p. 23.
191. M.F. Katzen, 'White settlers and the origin of a new society, 1652–1778', pp. 228–32; Du Toit and Giliomee, *Afrikaner Political Thought*, pp. 3–4; G. Schutte, 'Company and colonists at the Cape, 1652–1795', in R. Elphick and H. Giliomee, *The Shaping of South African Society*, pp. 284–317.
192. Giliomee, 'The beginnings of Afrikaner ethnic consciousness', p. 23.

193. A.D. Smith, *The Ethnic Origins of Nations* (Oxford, 1886), pp. 130–38.
194. Giliomee, 'The beginnings of Afrikaner ethnic consciousness', p. 28.
195. Giliomee, 'Aspects of the rise of Afrikaner capital and Afrikaner nationalism in the Western Cape', p. 65.
196. J.H. Hofmeyr, *The Life of Jan Hendrik Hofmeyr (Onze Hab)* (Cape Town, 1913), p. 235.
197. Ibid., p. 214.
198. Scholtz, *Die Afrikaner en sy Taal*, pp. 66–72.
199. Ibid., pp. 88–100.
200. Ibid., p. 66.
201. Ibid., pp. 64–5.
202. Ibid., p. 111.
203. Ibid., pp. 116–18.
204. Ibid., p. 123.
205. Ibid., pp. 107–8.
206. A.J.D. De Villiers, 'Die Hollandse Taalbeweging in Suid Afrika', *Annale van die Universiteit van Stellenbosch* (Cape Town, September 1936), p. 89.
207. Ibid., p. 89.
208. Du Plessis, 'Colonial progress and countryside conservatism', pp. 176–7; Scholtz, *Die Afrikaner en sy Taal*, pp. 211–14; De Villiers, 'Die Hollandse Taalbeweging', p. 90.
209. Smith, 'From Frontier to Midland', pp. 245–6 and 273.
210. *Patriot*, 29 Feb. 1882, Byvoegsel.
211. *CA*, 25 May 1869, quoted in J.L. McCracken, *The Cape Parliament*, p. 109.
212. Giliomee, 'The Beginning of Afrikaner Nationalism', p. 129.
213. *ZA*, 2 Feb. 1892.
214. Scholtz, *Die Afrikaner en sy Taal*, pp. 162–6.
215. Ibid., pp. 166–7; Hofmeyr, *Hofmeyr*, pp. 119–20.
216. Scholtz, *Die Afrikaner en sy Taal*, p. 167.
217. Hofmeyr, *Hofmeyr*, p. 79.
218. Hofmeyr Papers, 7A, Address to Gladstone.
219. Hofmeyr, *Hofmeyr*, p. 64.
220. Hofmeyr, *Hofmeyr*, pp. 161–74.
221. Italics added; note that he alluded to territorial (South African) rather than ethnic nationalism.
222. Hofmeyr, *Hofmeyr*, pp. 173–6; Hofmeyr Papers, Box 7/C, telegraphic communication between Hofmeyr and General Joubert, March 1881.
223. Hofmeyr Papers, Misc.8, Box 18.
224. *ZA*, 26 Jan. 1888.
225. Hofmeyr, *Hofmeyr*, pp. 643–5.
226. Davenport, *Afrikaner Bond*, p. 21.
227. Ibid., p. 21.
228. B. Anderson, *Imagined Communities: Reflections on the Origin and Spread of Nationalism* (London and New York, 1983), pp. 69–77; M. Hroch, *Social Preconditions of National Revival in Europe* (Cambridge, 1985), pp. 62–3, 76–7, 98–9 and 107.
229. D.A. Scholtz, 'Ds. S.J. du Toit as kerkman en kultuurleier' (PhD thesis, Stellenbosch University, 1975); J.D. du Toit, *Ds. S.J. du Toit in Weg en Werk* (Paarl, 1919).
230. Du Plessis, 'Colonial progress and countryside conservation', pp. 233–6.
231. Hroch, *Social Preconditions*, pp. 11 and 86.

232. L. Van Niekerk, *De Eerste Afrikaanse Taalbeweging en sijn Letterkundige Voortbrengsten* (Amsterdam, 1916), pp. 1, 11, 13 and 29; Davenport, *Afrikaner Bond*, pp. 28–31; du Toit, *S.J. du Toit*, pp. 9, 80–1 and 84.
233. de Villiers, 'Die Hollandse Taalbeweging in Suid Afrika', pp. 95–7.
234. Smith, *The Ethnic Origins of Nations*, p. 171.
235. Van Niekerk, *De Eerste Afrikaanse Taalbeweging*, p. 10.
236. Davenport, *Afrikaner Bond*, pp. 35–6.
237. Davenport, *Afrikaner Bond*, pp. 38–40.
238. *Notulen van het Afrikaansch Nationaal Congress gehouden te Cradock* (Notulen), 12 Sept. 1882, pp. 7–9.
239. *Notulen*, Richmond congress, 22 May 1883, pp. 43–4.
240. Giliomee, 'The beginning of Afrikaner ethnic consciousness', p. 38.
241. Henning, *Graaff Reinet*, p. 162.
242. Davenport, *Afrikaner Bond*, pp. 56–7, *Patriot* 17 March 1882.
243. *Patriot*, 29 Sept. 1882, Byvoegsel.
244. Hofmeyr, *Hofmeyr*, pp. 204–5.
245. Ibid., p. 207.
246. *Notulen*, Richmond, 22 May 1883, p. 9.
247. *Notulen*, Cradock, 12 Sept. 1882, pp. 3–7.
248. *Notulen*, Richmond, 22 May 1883, pp. 42–3.
249. *Patriot*, 29 Sept. 1882.
250. D.M. Schreuder, *The Scramble for Southern Africa, 1877–1895: the Politics of Partition Reappraised* (Cambridge, 1980), pp. 160–172.
251. Ibid., p. 168.
252. *Hansard*, 15 July 1884, pp. 342–3, 347, 349 and 351.
253. *British Parliamentary Papers* (*BPP*), Africa, 38, Transvaal Sessions 1884–85, pp. 698, 714, 725, 736 and 750–1.
254. *Hansard*, 1 July 1885, p. 320.
255. Ibid., 3 July 1885, p. 340.
256. Ibid., 1 July 1885, p. 311.
257. Ibid., 3 July 1885, p. 342.
258. Ibid., 3 July 1885, p. 340.
259. *ZA*, 25 June 1887.
260. *Paarl*, 2 July 1887.
261. Ibid., 18 June 1887.
262. *ZA*, 7 July 1887.
263. Ibid., 16 July 1887.
264. Hofmeyr, *Hofmeyr*, pp. 299–301.
265. *Patriot*, 1 June 1888; Paarl Rock is a most impressive rock overlooking the town of Paarl.
266. *ZA*, 6 March 1890.
267. Ibid., 17 Nov. 1888.
268. Ibid., 15 May 1890.
269. Ibid., 15 July 1890.
270. Ibid., 29 July 1886.
271. Hofmeyr, *Hofmeyr*, p. 374.
272. *ZA*, 10 May 1887.
273. Ibid., 18 June 1887.
274. Ibid., 16 July 1887.
275. *Patriot*, 25 May 1888.
276. *ZA*, 21 Feb. 1889.

THE BRIDEGROOM AND THE BRIDE

277. *Patriot*, 15 March 1887.
278. Ibid., 1 June 1888.
279. Ibid., 18 March 1887; *ZA*, 24 March 1887.
280. *Patriot*, 15 April 1887.
281. Ibid., 1 July 1887.
282. Hofmeyr, *Hofmeyr*, pp. 652–3.
283. *ZA*, 24 May 1890.
284. Mabin, 'The making of colonial capitalism', pp. 220–47.
285. Hofmeyr, *Hofmeyr*, p. 302.
286. *ZA*, 11 Sept. 1886; T.R.H. Davenport, *South Africa: a Modern History* (Bergvlei, 1987), pp. 196–7.
287. *ZA*, 29 May 1890.
288. Ibid., 29 June 1886, 14 Aug. 1886, 12 and 15 Nov. 1887.
289. See, for example, ibid., 22 March 1887.
290. Ibid., 1 Nov. 1887 and 5 March 1889.
291. Ibid., 16 and 30 April 1889; Graham Bower Papers, Item 5.
292. Ibid., 9 Feb. 1889 and 9 April 1889.
293. Ibid., 31 March 1888.
294. *Hansard*, 17 July 1888, p. 295.
295. *ZA*, 13 Dec. 1887.
296. Ibid., 14 April 1887.
297. Ibid., 17 April 1888.
298. Hroch, *Social Preconditions*, pp. 8–10.
299. *ZA*, 20 Dec. 1887.
300. Hofmeyr, *Hofmeyr*, p. 247.
301. *ZA*, 7 March 1889.
302. J.P.V. Vanstone, 'Sir John Gordon Sprigg: a political biography' (PhD thesis, Queen's University, Canada), pp. 219–20.
303. *Hansard*, 24 June 1884, p. 230.
304. *Patriot*, 15 July 1887.
305. *ZA*, 6 July 1886.
306. Ibid., 25 June 1887.
307. Ibid., 3 April 1886.
308. Vanstone, 'Sprigg', p. 219.
309. Hofmeyr, *Hofmeyr*, pp. 186–94.
310. Ibid., pp. 238 and 245–7.
311. Ibid., p. 247.
312. Ibid., p. 247; Vanstone, 'Sprigg', p. 224.
313. Ibid., p. 225; *ZA*, 25 June 1887.
314. Schreuder, *The Scramble for Southern Africa*, p. 166.
315. *ZA*, 22 April 1886.
316. Ibid., 1 June 1886; see also 21 and 28 Aug. 1886.
317. *Hansard*, 1 July 1885, pp. 323–7.
318. *ZA*, 24 Feb. 1887.
319. Ibid., 10 March 1887.
320. *Hansard*, 16 June 1884, p. 180.
321. *ZA*, 7 Aug. 1888, 4 Sept. 1888 and 2 Oct. 1888.
322. Ibid., 6 Oct. 1888.
323. Hroch, *Social preconditions*, pp. 145–8 and 156–8; see also, Anderson, *Imagined Communities*, pp. 65–79, on the role of members of the intelligentsia in Europe as cultural, linguistic entrepreneurs in the service of emerging nationalism.

83

324. *ZA*, 27 July 1886.
325. Ibid., 10 May 1890.
326. *Patriot*, 28 Nov. 1889; Hroch, *Social Preconditions*, pp. 139–45.
327. *Patriot*, 28 Nov. 1889.
328. *ZA*, 24 July 1886.
329. *ZA*, 9 Feb. 1888.
330. Bundy, 'Vagabond Hollanders and runaway Englishmen' pp. 101–28.
331. Molteno, *The Dominion of Afrikanerdom*, p. 81.
332. B.A. LeCordeur, *The Politics of Eastern Cape Separatism, 1820–1854* (Cape Town, 1981), pp. 31, 54, 138–9, 221, 227–30, 248, 250, 273, 282, 285–6; M. Streak, 'The Afrikaners as viewed by the English, 1795–1854', (PhD thesis, Rand Afrikaans University, 1972).
333. Henning, *Graaff Reinet*, p. 162.
334. *ZA*, 9 Nov. 1887
335. *Patriot*, 30 Jan. 1885.
336. Ibid., 30 Jan. 1885.
337. Orpen Collection, Vol. 10, Theron's lecture (1887), pp. 2–5.
338. *ZA*, 5 Feb. 1885.
339. *Notulen*, 1890 congress, pp. 4–5.
340. *ZA*, 19 Nov. 1887.
341. *Patriot*, 6 May 1887 and 16 Sept. 1887.
342. See for example, Orpen Collection, Vol. 10, Theron's lecture (1887); *ZA*, 4 Dec. 1886.
343. Ibid., 4 Dec. 1886.
344. Ibid., 29 May 1888.
345. *Hansard*, 3 Aug. 1888, p. 389.
346. *ZA*, 14 April 1887.
347. *CA*, 1 April 1891. He certainly did not envisage the assimilation of English speakers.
348. E.J. Hobsbawm, *Nations and Nationalism since 1780: Programme, Myth, Reality* (Cambridge, 1990), pp. 31–45.
349. Davenport, *Afrikaner Bond*, pp. 95–110.

2

Courtship, 1880s

EARLY BEGINNINGS

The feasibility of Rhodes's Cape sub-imperialist strategy wholly depended on his ability to induce the dominant political force in this self-governing colony, namely the Afrikaner Bond, to collaborate. According to L.S. Jameson, as early as 1878 Rhodes told him: 'The Dutch are the coming race in South Africa and they must have their share in running the country.'[1] This early allusion to the Afrikaners indicates, at the least, that Rhodes did not share the anti-Afrikaner prejudices of many English-speaking politicians who viewed the Cape as a purely British colony and the Afrikaners as political guests in their own homeland.

There is firm evidence that the strategy of harnessing the Cape Afrikaners to his imperial wagon originated in 1881, soon after he had taken his seat in the Cape parliament. Preparing for himself a congenial political space, Rhodes acquired influence in the *Cape Argus* by assisting the editor, Francis Dormer, to become the proprietor of the newspaper. According to Dormer, Rhodes was at that time frustrated and incensed by the humiliation to British arms and flag at Majuba. When discussing the policy of the newspaper he argued that in the wake of Majuba the paramount issue was whether Dutch or English would predominate in South Africa. Dormer's solution was 'each in its own sphere'. Rhodes's initial response betrayed his frustration: 'You don't think we ought to have sat down under that licking, although I know that Solomon and you think we deserved it, and yet we are to accept the situation.' Dormer advised caution and refused to follow an active anti-Afrikaner line. After some contemplation Rhodes responded:

> I suppose you are right ... I think we understand one another. I don't dislike the Dutchmen. Your plan of working with Hofmeyr is the best – Sprigg impossible – Solomon, he'd wreck an empire for what he is pleased to call his principles – and there's nobody else. But let us understand one another. We are not going to be trampled upon by these Dutchmen.[2]

In accordance with this strategy, Dormer joined the Bond's Cape Town branch to assist Hofmeyr in rescuing the organization from the Paarl zealots.[3]

The choice of Cape Afrikaners as possible collaborators was, at that stage, largely a choice by elimination. As Rhodes said, 'there's nobody else'. If the Cape was to fulfil its imperial role, its political community would have to be appropriately inspired and its political potential mobilised. However, as Rhodes reminisced in 1888, 'Cape politics ... were very localised; and the mist of the Table Mountain covered all'.[4] To his chagrin, as he subsequently recalled, the lack of resolve of the British government was compounded by the weakness of those in the Cape who should have come forward as allies: 'The English party in the Cape Assembly was hopelessly divided and individually incapable. And it had no policy beyond that of securing office.'[5] In fact, there was no English party at all. Before the establishment of the Bond there had been no political parties in the Cape parliament, political allegiance being given mainly on a personal basis.[6] Furthermore, as Merriman complained, 'our mercantile classes [predominantly English] are so bound up with Government contracts, and so anxious to do a shot on each other, that they allow themselves to be slaughtered ...'[7]

At the same time, as Rhodes recalled, 'on the other side was a compact body of nominees of what afterwards came to be called the Afrikaner Bond, who acted all together at the dictation of Hofmeyr'.[8] Recalling discussions with Rhodes in the mid-1880s J.R. Innes claimed that the latter was 'enormously impressed by the potentialities of the new political machines [the Bond]'. He thought that 'the Dutch farmer would always get the better of the English shopkeeper, for he was a born politician'. Consequently, he concluded that 'the keys of Cape politics hangs in the White House'.[9] By that time it was apparent, as Merriman complained, that, indeed, 'the White House ... are the arbiters of our destiny'.[10]

Thus, any plan to use the Cape as an imperial springboard had to rest on an alliance with the Bond. Jameson recalled Rhodes's attitude in this regard: 'The means to that end were the conciliation, the winning of the Cape Dutch support. They were the majority in the country, he used to say, and they must be worked with.' According to Jameson, Rhodes intended to transform the Cape Afrikaners into British imperial agents: 'I mean to have the whole unmarked country north of the colony for England, and I know I can only get it and develop it through the Cape Colony – that is, at present, through the Dutch majority.'[11] Rhodes not only intended using Cape Afrikaners as political allies, but also viewed them as the ideal pioneers and settlers in his new imperial domains.[12]

The critical question was whether the political and pioneering energies of the Afrikaners could be harnessed in the service of British imperialism.

If he consulted his friend Merriman, Rhodes would have been warned that it was a hopeless effort. The former, like many other Englishmen, viewed the Bond as extremely anti-British.[13] In the early 1880s the South African believed 'Mr. Hofmeyr is one of the hottest agitators, anti-English to the backbone'.[14] Rhodes himself subsequently told a Cape Town audience that when he first sat as a member in the House he was told that the Afrikaner Bond was worse than a Fenian organisation and that he ought to have nothing to do with it.[15] Rhodes, apparently, thought differently. Referring to his early days in Cape politics he said:

> Hofmeyr was, without doubt, the most capable politician in South Africa, and if he concealed in his breast aspirations for a United South Africa in which Great Britain should have no part or lot, the concealment was very effective.[16]

On 18 July 1883, in a debate in Parliament on Basutoland, Rhodes pressed Hofmeyr on this point. Referring to the Bond's Richmond congress earlier that year, Rhodes noted with satisfaction D.P. van den Heever's positive reference to the British flag in South Africa. He was not sure, however, where Hofmeyr stood: 'I would like to hear whether he [Hofmeyr] is still in favour of a United States of South Africa under its own flag.'[17] Rhodes must have believed Hofmeyr when he replied that he had told members of the Bond that 'if those words "under its own flag" were carried he would retire from the Bond at once.'[18]

Rhodes's courting of the Bond progressed in two main phases. The first phase, from 1881 to 1885, was hesitant and vacillating. The second, from 1886 to 1890, was much more determined, aggressive, single-minded and purposeful. In the first phase Rhodes was a novice to Cape politics. He had to sort out his goals and his strategies and to establish a power base in a political system which was in a state of flux. Dormer provides firm evidence that at the beginning of his political career, Rhodes sanctioned the exploration of an avenue of co-operation with Hofmeyr and his political troops. There is also evidence that Rhodes himself began to cultivate positive relations with Cape Afrikaner politicians at about the same time. Hofmeyr reminisced about his early encounter with Rhodes at the time of the Transvaal war in 1881: 'But when the war was over we had a talk with one another and I said: "it is an awful pity that the war broke out". I was surprised when Mr Rhodes said, "No it is not. I have quite changed my opinion. It is a good thing. It has made Englishmen respect Dutchmen and made them respect one another."' 'Well', added Hofmeyr, 'when an Englishman could speak like that to a Dutchman, they are not far from making common cause with one another.'[19] Rhodes must have specially targeted Hofmeyr whose influence was particularly strong among Afrikaner parliamentarians.

L. Michell, Rhodes's banker, friend and biographer, wrote that at the beginning of his parliamentary career Rhodes also courted the friendship of other Afrikaner Members of Parliament, paying them visits on their farms.[20]

There were also occasions for political collaboration in parliament. Thus, in 1881 Rhodes joined Hofmeyr and his followers in defeating the Sprigg government over its Basutoland policy and forcing its resignation.[21] In 1882 Rhodes supported Hofmeyr's Bill allowing the use of Dutch in parliament, thus co-operating in removing the most pressing ethnic grievance of Cape Afrikaners.[22] If the political ears of the Afrikaner MPs were sensitive, they must have noted with satisfaction Rhodes's support for flogging diamond thieves in 1882 and his views on the Sotho: 'nothing can be done with this uncivilised race until we show them that we are masters'.[23] However, at the same time, Rhodes also adopted positions which could not have been popular with Cape Afrikaner politicians. Thus, he proposed a heavy excise duty on Cape spirits and as a free trader he opposed the protection of farmers against foreign competition.[24] While favouring direct imperial rule in Basutoland, as well as in the Transkei, Afrikaner politicians favoured collaboration with the Orange Free State to the detriment of the Sothos.[25] Rhodes definitely sent conflicting messages to Cape Afrikaner politicians. There were, as yet, no bargains and no deals between them. From Rhodes's perspective it was casual flirting rather than determined courting. He was not only a newcomer to Cape parliamentary politics; he represented an area which had only recently been incorporated into the Cape and lacked both familiarity and a political base. Being a political newcomer and an outsider was, however, not without advantages. In his search for potential allies he was free from prejudices which marred the relations between those who spoke English and the Afrikaners. For a highly ambitious young politician, possessing both substantial economic interests to protect and a far-reaching political vision to promote, a virgin political soil was readily available.

If Rhodes believed, as he told Dormer in 1881, that 'high politics had better be left to take care of themselves' he was quickly made aware of the reality of the changing regional circumstances which forced him to the centre of the political arena. In 1883 he was soon involved in the affairs of Bechuanaland and in 1884–85 he was engulfed by the Bechuanaland crisis.[26] This crisis revealed the contradictory nature of the relations between Rhodes and Cape 'Afrikanerdom', as represented by the Bond. The contradiction was inherent because for Rhodes the Bond was a means, rather than a goal, and it was bound to surface when a change in circumstances dictated a change in strategy. The contradiction could have disappeared only if there had developed a full convergence of goals. Around the mid-1880s this was certainly not the case. Rhodes knew that he would have to enlist the support of the Bond, but he was clearly not prepared to forego his imperial goals for the sake of an alliance with the Bond.

Rhodes caught the attention of the Bond's mouthpiece when he addressed Parliament on the Basutoland Annexation Bill on 18 July 1883. In opposing Hofmeyr's proposal for an alliance with the Orange Free State to deal with Basutoland, Rhodes advocated direct imperial rule over it. In his speech Rhodes stated clearly his goal of a united South Africa 'as a portion of the British Empire' and tried to convince Afrikaner MPs to give precedence to Cape interests: 'We have heard so much about the Free State and so much about the Transvaal that I begin to think it is just time to think of the interests of the Cape Colony.' Rhodes clearly addressed primarily the Afrikaner Bond contingent, trying to convert them to a more Cape-centric outlook.

The *ZA* perceived the speech by a parliamentary novice as sufficiently important to warrant an editorial. It rated it one of the best in the debate: 'He promises to be, in the long run, one of our most capable speakers and one of the most influential *volksvertegenwoordiger* [people's representative].' Commending his knowledge of the subject, the writer was particularly impressed by Rhodes's 'native' perspective: 'One has to have a clear sight and *unprejudiced* [italics added] soul to understand Native questions, but whoever is endowed with it understands them within a short time.' At the same time, the writer did not like Rhodes's distinction between 'true Afrikaners' (who agreed with him on Basutoland) and the 'false Afrikaners' (who did not). The bottom line was that, while Rhodes possessed good potential, he still had a lot to learn.[27]

Soon after his entry into Cape politics a threat arose to the road to the north as Boer frontiersmen and adventurers got involved in local African disputes in Bechuanaland south of the Molopo river. In May 1882 he drew the attention of Parliament to the dark clouds gathering on their northern border. His warnings were not heeded by Parliament which was embroiled in the more pressing Basutoland problem. In 1883 Rhodes managed to get Scanlen, the Cape prime minister, to appoint a commission to look into the borders of Griqualand West with Bechuanaland. As a member of the commission Rhodes got involved in the affairs of Bechuanaland beyond the call of duty. He negotiated with the parties to the conflict and put heavy telegraphic pressure on Scanlen to annex the southern part of the disputed area to the Cape. The parochial Cape government, however, was not prepared to take bold action.[28]

By the time Rhodes brought the matter to Parliament, in mid-August 1883, at least one of the two minuscule Boer republics, Stellaland, had been founded in Bechuanaland. At that stage Rhodes only proposed to appoint a Resident to represent the colonial government at the court of Chief Mankoroane in the southern part of the disputed territory. This modest measure, however, was designed to stake a claim in an area which he presented as crucial to the future of the Cape: 'On our dealing with Bechuanaland depends the future of this colony; for [I] looked on that territory as the Suez Canal for our trade with the interior.' Rhodes warned Parliament that 'if we departed from the control of the interior and its interests, we should fall from the position of a paramount state in South Africa to that of a minor state'. In his speech he clearly courted the Afrikaner MPs, knowing that their opposition would seal the fate of his proposal. In expressing the hope that the problem be settled 'without any Imperial factor being introduced into it', he clearly presented expansion into the interior as a Cape rather than an imperial project. Other themes in the speech were also directed to soft Afrikaner spots. Thus, Rhodes ignored the claims of the African chief concerned and declared candidly: 'I am no negrophilist, and I hold to the distinct view that we must extend our civilization beyond our present borders.' To make sure that this arrow hit the target he emphasised that he differed from the liberal MPs who perceived such an attitude as immoral: 'Now I have not these scruples.' To appeal to the natural *trek geest* (trekking spirit) of the Afrikaners he said: 'I feel that it is the duty of this colony, when, as it were, her younger and more fiery sons go out and take land, to follow in their steps with civilised government.' In line with this, he declared that 'what we now want is to annex land, not natives'. To the wine farmers he offered a free trade route to the interior for their products. It was the first occasion on which he tried publicly to persuade Cape Afrikaners that the economic potential of the interior could be best exploited through Cape sub-imperialism. Finally, while propagating the paramountcy of Cape interests, he showed an understanding of the Cape Afrikaners' ethnic concern for their republican brothers: 'Of course, we must not disregard any legitimate interest of the Transvaal.'[29]

However, this demonstration of submission to Afrikaner prejudices, interests and sensitivities was to no avail. Hofmeyr was not impressed. He was 'ready to do anything for the promotion of colonial trade and interests'; however, he added, 'Mankoroane had been always considered as an enemy to the Transvaal and if we now sent a Resident with him, the act might be regarded by the Transvaal as inimical to their interests'.[30] The *ZA* was more critical of Rhodes's first public presentation of his broad strategy, depicting his policy of thwarting Transvaal's expansion 'as dangerous as it is foolish'. It was dangerous because it would precipitate a conflict with the Transvaal. It was foolish because the true civilising mission in the interior, which Rhodes used as an argument, would be better promoted by 'a people with the customs and outlooks of the

Transvalers than by the inhomogeneous Cape society'. The writer added, referring to Rhodes's previous advice to relinquish Basutoland, that 'if there was here the unity they have in the Transvaal, we would have subjugated Basutoland, instead of evacuating it'.[31] The memories of the Transvaal crisis of 1880–81 were too fresh for the ethnic solidarity to wane, and Bondsmen clearly believed that an amicable agreement with the Transvaal regarding free passage to the interior was possible and would suffice to safeguard the Cape's vital commercial interests. Clearly, Rhodes had to do much more courting to win the hearts and minds of Afrikaner Bondsmen.

Soon he had another opportunity to do so. The London Convention of February 1884, supplanting the Pretoria Convention of 1881, delineated the western borders of the Transvaal in a way which left Bechuanaland out of its reach. Britain stepped in and declared a protectorate over the disputed area of southern Bechuanaland. However, the presence of the two petty republics in that area continued to be a source of friction and anxiety. These were exacerbated when J. Mackenzie, a missionary and a crusader for African interests, was appointed to administer the protectorate and sort out the disputes between republican settlers and African chiefs. Afrikaner Bondsmen were infuriated by the appointment and by the treatment meted out to the Stellaland settlers by Mackenzie. As a result, when the latter urged Governor Sir Hercules Robinson to send reinforcements to the area, the latter did not even approach the Upington government which ruled by grace of the Bond.[32] In July, partly in response to representations from Upington and Hofmeyr, Robinson recalled and dismissed Mackenzie.[33]

Rhodes was given a wonderful opportunity to shape the future of the vital corridor northwards when Robinson appointed him as Mackenzie's successor. Shortly before his appointment Rhodes supported the prime minister's motion in Parliament to empower the government to negotiate the annexation of Bechuanaland to the Cape, broadly repeating the same themes he had enunciated a year earlier, when he had proposed to appoint a resident with chief Mankoroane.[34] The *ZA*, while bitterly criticising Robinson for making such a nomination without consulting the government, welcomed the nominee: 'Rhodes is certainly someone who, as far as ability and colonial spirit are concerned, has got a good name here.' It expressed confidence that, unlike his predecessor, he would not precipitate a war.[35] At the end of August 1884, shortly before Rhodes reached an agreement with the Stellalanders, the *ZA* expressed the hope that he would succeed in his negotiations.[36]

His assignment in Bechuanaland was, from the perspective of our investigation, an important formative experience for Rhodes. It was for him an exercise in Cape sub-imperialism, which contained most of the components of his grand strategy. It was about keeping the road to the north open by forestalling the expansion of the Transvaal in order to maintain the dominant position of the Cape in a future union of South Africa. Cape politics, as well as the British government, were directly involved, and in the regional background there was, from August 1884, the German threat from the Atlantic flank of southern Africa. Rhodes had an opportunity to prove his worth, not only as a preacher, but also as a strategist and an operator. Bechuanaland was the training ground for the big game.

The unfolding strategy for the resolution of the Bechuanaland crisis foreshadowed his future grand strategy. It entailed collaboration with the moderate section of the Afrikaner settlers as a basis for dealing with the more militant ones: 'My policy ... is contained in a few words viz. to try and effect a reconciliation with the Van Niekerk party [Stellaland] and obtain their co-operation in dealing with the people at Rooi Grond, or at least their neutrality.'[37] 'I fully rely on your co-operation' he subsequently wrote to Van Niekerk.[38] Bechuanaland offered Rhodes the opportunity to test his ability to deal with Afrikaners of the frontier variety, and he exhibited great talent for it. There is the oft-quoted story of the encounter between Rhodes and a tough Afrikaner leader in Stellaland:

> It was morning and Big Adriaan, huge and grim, was frying chops over an open fire. He said nothing, and Rhodes sat down opposite him in silence. At last De la Rey looked up from the frying pan and with single-hearted trust in 'direct action' said, 'Blood must flow'. 'No', replied Rhodes, 'give me first breakfast and then we can talk about blood.'

Rhodes told his constituents that he stayed there a week, became godfather to De la Rey's child, and concluded a settlement.[39]

The crucial clause in the settlement recommended the recognition of land titles issued by the government of Stellaland.[40] Rhodes discovered to his delight that the frontier republicans were parish pumpers rather than staunch republicans. In a letter to Robinson in September 1884 he summed up his Bechuanaland experience with insight and succinctly:

> The people of Stellaland I believe to be for the most part animated by a sincere desire for the establishment of law and order in their midst upon a basis which could not be shaken. Annexation to the Colony is the dominating idea with which they were possessed, and I am of the opinion that the minority who manifest an inclination to cast in their lot with the Transvaal, do so not from deliberate preference, but from motives of distrust as to the intentions of H.M. Government. If sufficient assurances could but be obtained that the policy which led to the establishment of the protectorate would be preserved ... even those who are now malcontent would be reconciled to the present settlement, always provided that the

territory were not permanently kept under direct imperial Administration, but admitted to the privileges now enjoyed by the inhabitants of this Colony.[41]

There were more lessons for Rhodes in his Bechuanaland experience. In Goschen he encountered resistance from the settlers who were closely linked to the Transvaal and its expansive thrust, and his charm was of no avail.[42] Transvaal's involvement reached a climax in mid-September 1884 with the annexation of Goschen to the Transvaal.[43] This contravention of the London Convention by the Transvaal provided Rhodes with more challenges and opportunities which contributed to his appreciation of the complex regional system and to the evolution of his relations with the Afrikaner Bond in particular. It sharpened his awareness of the expansive, aggressive tendencies in the Transvaal and of the necessity to call in the imperial government, which on other occasions he proposed to exclude, in order to deal with republican intransigence and to thwart the potential for Transvaal–German collusion across the Kalahari. Indeed, Rhodes was one of those who, in the wake of the annexation of Goschen to the Transvaal, clamoured for the imperial intervention which resulted in the Warren expedition. This intervention, however, also alerted him to the havoc the imperial bull could cause in the South African china shop.

Direct military intervention was strongly criticised by the Bond, which also criticised the Transvaal for violating the London convention. The Bond supported instead Upington and Sprigg who went up to Bechuanaland on behalf of the Cape government to negotiate a peaceful annexation to the colony without imperial interference.[44] Rhodes faced the danger of losing the credit he had accumulated with Bondsmen in his previous dealings with the Stellaland settlers. In early November, the ZA viewed Rhodes as part of a jingoistic conspiracy:

> Does anyone doubt that between Rhodes in Stellaland and Merriman and Scanlen everything was concocted with the governor and that out of rage for their defeat in parliament they want to push the British government to take steps which will bring calamity to South Africa?[45]

Yet, by mid-December the newspaper saw in the appointment of Rhodes as deputy commissioner to Warren a good omen and a proof that the British government was ignoring Mackenzie's plans and wished to keep the peace. 'Rhodes', readers were reminded, 'has shown, in most cases, that he is not a bad colonist.'[46] However, Mackenzie was soon picked by General Warren as an assistant and the newspaper was disturbed by rumours that they and Rhodes had become a 'happy family', although it found contradictions between Mackenzie's claim of harmonious relations with Rhodes and the latter's condemnation of the former's policy 'in words and deeds'.[47] Only Rhodes's indignant resignation over Warren's

hostile attitude towards the Afrikaner settlers in the petty republics, and
his acrimonious break with him, cleared him from suspicion: 'A respectable Colonist – and we have always seen Rhodes as such – can hardly
co-operate with the man who praises Mackenzie as a "Christian gentleman".'[48] Rhodes used his quarrel with Warren in a further attempt to win
the Bond to his point of view. Addressing Parliament on 29 June 1885, he
presented himself as a champion of the Afrikaners:

> If a settlement of a portion of Her Majesty's dominions was to be based on
> a condition that no man of Dutch descent was to have land, what was the
> duty of this Colony, and what would be the position of colonists – they had
> better retire.

He also presented himself as the champion of the true empire which was
based on 'two cardinal axioms': 'One was that the word of the nation was
never known to be broken, and the other, that when other people came
under our rule there was no distinction as to race.' Warren, implied
Rhodes, had violated both axioms.[49] D.C. De Waal told parliament the
he had listened 'with great pleasure' to Rhodes's 'moderate' speech.[50]
Rhodes seems to have succeeded in establishing a measure of personal
credibility among Bondsmen.

In his 'moderate' speech, Rhodes, after warning of the negative consequences of the annexation of the interior by the Transvaal, outlined his
policy towards it quite clearly:

> The only possibility to avoid this was to place the Cape Colony in possession
> of the interior and to surround the Transvaal, and to deal with them as
> their own fellow-colonists, so that year by year, not by the rapid progress
> of Sir Bartle Frere ... they would prove to the Transvaal that the only
> solution of the future union of South Africa was to have a union with the
> Colony, and to have the terms of that union dictated by the Cape Colony.[51]

Rhodes was bitterly disappointed with the imperial intervention he had
precipitated. Warren, disregarding his settlement with the Stellalanders,
heeded Mackenzie's advice and was determined to use force in defence
of British prestige and paramountcy and African rights, ignoring the
need to secure the collaboration of Cape Afrikaners. The Warren
expedition seems to have pushed Rhodes further towards the strategy of
Cape sub-imperialism. As he wrote to a senior colonial official, he did
not believe that Britain would uphold its commitment in the interior in
the long run. The only alternative was to develop the Cape into a sub-
imperial agent.[52]

The Bechuanaland crisis in 1884–85 marked an interim period in the
relations between Rhodes and the Bond. From Rhodes's perspective the
record of the Afrikaners during the crisis was not altogether positive.

While managing well with the Afrikaner settlers in Stellaland, he was not convinced that Cape Bondsmen could be fully relied upon as local collaborators in his plans for imperial expansion. He had certainly made progress in establishing his credibility as a good colonist, and must also have been pleased to see that the Bond demonstrated its loyalty to the empire throughout the crisis. But although the Bondsmen were critical of the Transvaal for annexing Goschen and supported the assertion of imperial supremacy in Bechuanaland, he still believed, as he said in June 1885, that they would have preferred the Transvaal to have taken over Bechuanaland.[53]

Consequently, his attitude towards the Bond was marked by ambivalence. While courting it, Rhodes also voted against it on a number of occasions, during the 1884 parliamentary session, on issues ranging from the Dutch language, excise duty on Cape spirits and protection for Cape agricultural products to stock theft, the coal-field railway and duty on mules.[54] On an issue like protection, which was vital to the Bond, Rhodes was unequivocal in saying that he 'would oppose anything that pandered to Protection'.[55] His ambivalence was also manifested in his handling of the Bechuanaland crisis itself. On the one hand, he tried to please and appease the Bond, but on the other he also was among the founders of the jingoistic Imperial League[56] which agitated for imperial intervention and provoked rage and resentment among Cape Afrikaners.

This ambivalence was reflected in the bewilderment of Rhodes's English-speaking friends who could not figure out where exactly he stood politically. In December 1884 Merriman wrote to a mutual friend: 'I trust to you to keep Cecil Rhodes up to the mark; his wretched compromise with the Stellalanders was a bitter pill to swallow and surprised all those who looked on him as a strong Imperialist.'[57] In a letter to Merriman, Rhodes referred to himself as a member of the anti-Bond parliamentary group.[58] Merriman was, however, not convinced, and writing to a friend a few days later he complained: 'His proceedings under the Stellaland flag seem to me incomprehensible. Of course they are real jam to the Afrikaner party. Does he mean to serve the Baal or what?'[59] In March 1885 J.B. Curry suggested that 'Rhodes is playing for the premiership with their assistance', while Merriman himself added:

> I do not think so, but the temptation is a strong one. When I think that it was a cablegram from Rhodes and Leonard that started the whole affair [imperial intervention in Bechuanaland] going I am the more surprised and disgusted that things should have turned out so very badly.[60]

About a month later he replied to Curry who had written to him that Rhodes intended to enter into an alliance with Hofmeyr:

> I am very loath to believe any evil of a fellow whom I like so well, but really

his conduct lately has been ... inexplicable ... Yet according to you, he is prepared to sacrifice everything for the purpose of intriguing with the ignorant and anti-English section of the community.[61]

By September 1885, Merriman was more inclined to believe Dormer that a 'Hofmeyr–Scanlen–Rhodes combination' was probable.[62] All this points, if not to Rhodes's actual plans, at least to the confusion of his English friends in the face of his ambiguous behaviour during the Bechuanaland crisis.

MORE PERSISTENT COURTSHIP

Rhodes's friends were sensing a shift in his political strategy which would become much clearer and more definite during the 1886 parliamentary session. It seems that his involvement in Bechuanaland was largely responsible for it. In June 1887 Rhodes confessed to parliament that the road to the north was his 'Road to Damascus': 'As he had said, he himself had come down here as the most rabid Jingo ... but he had gained experience, and had been through the fire of Bechuanaland.'[63] It seems that between the parliamentary sessions of 1885 and 1886 Rhodes had, more or less, completed his strategic volte-face, becoming converted more clearly to Cape sub-imperialism. The road from Bechuanaland led directly to the Bond. Indeed, Cape sub-imperialism without the collaboration of the Bond was inconceivable. Consequently, he seems to have come to the 1886 session determined to get into the good books of the Bond, being prepared to pay a high price both in principles and in friends. In April, early in the session, Rhodes not only voted for, but also spoke in favour of, Hofmeyr's motion with regard to compulsory religious instruction in government schools. Aiming at the ears of Bondsmen, he declared that he favoured state education because 'in the education of this Colony lay their only hope of killing their race differences'.[64] Rhodes also supported the Bond against the operation of the Sunday 'pleasure' trains.[65] Moving from spiritual to material concerns, he displayed sympathy with the sheep farmers in the debate on the Scab Act, while voting with Hofmeyr against their representatives.[66]

Undoubtedly, the most significant shift towards the Bond was Rhodes's conversion from an avowed free trader to a devout protectionist. On 14 May 1886 he spoke and voted with the Bond for the abolition of the excise tax on Cape brandy which was major grievance in the wine districts in the west.[67] In a dinner held in Paarl to celebrate the repeal of the tax, Rhodes declared himself a protectionist, particularly with regard to the wine and grain farmers.[68] Clearly, this major change in his economic policy resulted from a conscious, concerted effort to win over Hofmeyr and other prominent leaders of the Bond from the western Cape. Indeed, the abolition of excise duty on brandy and protection against external competition were major demands of the wheat and wine farmers in this region. Rhodes also urged, in this speech, government assistance for an irrigation scheme to boost agricultural production.[69] He even began to make the right noises with regard to 'native' policy. In a debate on the Transkeian Territories Representation Bill, he said that he would have given the franchise to the whites 'and would leave all the others under purely personal rule'.[70] Earlier, at the beginning of 1886, Merriman complained of Rhodes's transformation:

> I remember when Rhodes used to propose to maintain British influence by using the native vote – now he descants on the theme of the integral race difference between black and white and I should not be surprised to find him an ardent advocate for the restriction of the franchise.'[71]

Indeed, the full extent of Rhodes's conversion came to light in late April 1887, during the debate on the Parliamentary Registration Bill through which Sprigg sought to limit the electoral power of the blacks by removing 'undeserving' Africans from the voters' list.[72] During the debate members of the Bond, who were careful not to display racial prejudice, argued for changes within the existing non-racial franchise. J. Joubert said that the Bond had never wished to introduce a 'colour franchise', while D.C. de Waal even saw fit to state that 'he was as strong a negrophilist as any of the members who had spoken in opposition to the Bill'.[73] Unlike Bondsmen, Rhodes, full of confidence and devoid of inhibitions, made a frontal attack on the Cape non-racial franchise:

> He preferred to call a spade a spade, and could not regard this as an interpretation of the Constitution Ordinance, but as a bold statement of the manner in which the government of this country, as far as related to the question of native franchise, should be carried on. (Hear, hear) The question was, did they say that the native population of this country should have the franchise, or that it should not have it?

He presented the 'native question' as the 'big test question for South Africa' which should determine party formation. He distanced himself, on this issue, from his colleagues from the opposition, implying that with regard to the most crucial question facing the country he belonged with the government and the Bond. Whereas, Rhodes claimed, the Constitution Ordinance granted the 'natives' the franchise on the basis of communal land tenure, he believed that 'as long as the natives remained in a state of barbarism we must treat them as a subject race and be lords over them ... There would be no injustice in refusing the franchise to the natives as a whole in the Colony ...'. He went as far as to argue that 'the natives did not want the franchise', and claimed that the 'native question' was the main obstacle to South African unification. He believed that the Cape would have to make concessions to her neighbours: 'This settlement would mean the readiness to take up an Indian despotism in dealing with the barbarism of South Africa. (Hear, hear)'.[74]Rhodes expressed, loudly and in broad daylight, Bondsmen's innermost hopes and desires on what they perceived as a vital issue affecting their survival.

During the parliamentary sessions of 1886 and 1887 Rhodes also showed understanding of the broader ethnic concerns of the Cape Afrikaners. The Transvaal and Bechuanaland crises had alerted Rhodes to the underlying solidarity of Cape Afrikaners towards their diaspora brethren. In a debate on the request by the republics to get a share of the customs duties collected at the Cape ports, Rhodes showed understanding towards the Transvaal, urging the accommodation of its legitimate claims.[75] He exploited this soft ethnic spot more thoroughly in his speech at the banquet in Paarl: 'I was told this morning that the last time a banquet was given in this hall was on the occasion of the visit of the Transvaal deputation. I believe there is a feeling or sentiment when I mention the name of the Transvaal.' He went on to criticise bitterly the government's unsympathetic response to the republics' reasonable requests. Presenting himself as more papist than the pope, he urged his audience to put pressure on their representatives to ensure that an appropriate policy towards the republics was adopted.[76] At the beginning of the 1887 parliamentary session, Rhodes criticised not only the government but also the Bond, for failing to respond appropriately during the previous session to the Transvaal's approaches: 'It was in the hands of those gentlemen at that time to take steps for the union of South Africa, but that union was not to be brought about by Bond meetings and after-dinner speeches.'[77]

Rhodes continued to bewilder and frustrate his friends from the opposition as he moved towards the Bond. T.E. Fuller, speaking after Rhodes in the debate on the Parliamentary Registration Bill, reminded his listeners that in the past 'no one in this House had more strongly insisted upon the registration of natives than the hon. member [Rhodes].' He also recalled that 'he could remember the time when that hon. member habitually depreciated the Bond'.[78] Merriman was tilting between hope and despair. In March 1886 he wrote to a friend about the forthcoming parliamentary session: 'pray ask Rhodes to come down soon ... We want everyone we can get or there will be wild work.'[79] By the close of the session he was exasperated:

> Rhodes's apostasis has made me feel sicker than a stuck hog. Here you have a feller [sic] with the birth, the manner, the feelings and the education of an English gentleman offering himself publicly for sale to a crew

composed of Venters and De Waals ... and doing it so clumsily that he has spoiled his own market. The idea of Rhodes, who used to quote manuals of political economy with all the zeal of a lad fresh from the Oxford schools, taking his stand on the platform of [an agricultural] protection [policy] whose sole *raison d'être* is extreme anti-British feeling![80]

Initially, the *ZA* was confused by Rhodes's conversion. While commending him for supporting the wine farmers' position in the debate on the excise duty, it reminded its readers that in his short spell as treasurer general in early 1884, Rhodes had included the excise in the budget. Just the same, the editor commended his 'colonial' political views which were much closer to the Bond-supported government than to 'the Scanlens, the Sauers, the Leonards and the Inneses'.[81] Two days later the editor thought it was unfair to ascribe to Rhodes wrong motives in his intention to vote for the abolition of the duty.[82] In inviting Rhodes to the banquet celebrating their victory, the Bond gave Rhodes full recognition for his support. Hofmeyr, in his speech, gave Rhodes broader credit: They must not forget, he said, that they had also been helped by English members, such as Mr Rhodes. There was a question of far greater importance than the Excise, which presented itself yearly. He meant that of nationality, and it was a mournful phenomenon, he continued that the separation between English and Dutch-speaking Afrikaners had not yet been cleared away. That must surely be the great aim of all who wished the Colony well. The two elements of the white population must be reconciled together, if they wanted to see true prosperity here. The men who contributed to this were benefactors, and therefore he praised Mr Rhodes.[83]

Rhodes, as we have seen, made use of the opportunity to court the wine growers who had a decisive influence in the Bond. C.W.H. Kohler recalled the impact of Rhodes on his audience:

> What a speech he made that day. Though he spoke in English, even the staunchest pro-Afrikaans farmer listened to him with rapt attention. I remember one old Boer patriot called Uys, who was sitting at the extreme end of a table, rising noiselessly and creeping nearer and nearer to Rhodes as he spoke. Like a bent ape, silently, the old fellow shuffled along ... Finally he crouched down right opposite Rhodes and sat there motionless, drinking in every word that was uttered, his eyes glued to the speaker's face ... I have always maintained that this great speech that Rhodes delivered that day in the heart of one of the principal wine-making districts of South Africa, indirectly and in some measure, helped to make him Prime Minister of the Cape.[84]

Rhodes also scored points with the Bond for his friendly attitude to the Transvaal and for inducing Cape politicians, including the Bond, to try to mend fences with it.[85] Following his exposition on 'native policy', he was hailed as the only opposition member to subscribe to the view that the colonists should be the dominant group.[86] In fact, the *ZA* presented Rhodes as more extreme in his 'native' policy than the Bond which sought to secure the colonist domination within the accepted framework of the Cape non-racial constitution.[87] The newspaper also highly commended Rhodes for sharing the Bond's broad policy combining full self-government and imperial defence.[88]

It is hardly surprising that the *ZA* soon began to view Rhodes as a potential political ally. In June 1886 it pointed out that there was nothing in Rhodes's parliamentary career which could prevent him from co-operating with the Bond.[89] In November, he was described as 'a man of British blood with whom the Afrikaner party could work'.[90] Similarly, in October 1887, he was depicted as 'the right ally of Afrikanerdom'. In early December, with a view to a prospective reshuffle in the government, the newspaper suggested Rhodes for the post of minister for public works, portraying him as 'a young man with great talent' who also enjoyed 'exceptionally good relations with Hofmeyr'.[91]

Rhodes's advances clearly struck a sensitive chord in the Cape Afrikaner heart. However, by the end of 1887, there had still been no formal understanding, let alone a political alliance, between them. While shamelessly courting the wine farmers in his speech in Paarl, Rhodes still presented himself as a member of the opposition.[92] The *ZA*, for its part, described the electoral victory of O'Leary, the representative of merchant interests in Kimberley and an arch-rival of Rhodes, as a victory for the Bond.[93] It was also critical of Rhodes's alleged attempt to thwart Transvaal's drive to link with Delagoa Bay in the adjacent Portuguese territory, by advancing the plan to extend the railway line from Kimberley across the Vaal River.[94] Indeed, the complexities and contradictions involved in the pull of the north had to be resolved before Rhodes and the Bond could come together. As we have seen, on the merits of their respective positions regarding intra-Cape and imperial issues, it seems that there was no obstacle in the way of an alliance between Rhodes and the Bond. For Rhodes, however, the Cape political base was a means rather than an ideal. For the price of an alliance with the Bond to be worthwhile, it had to serve his broader regional plans. Bondsmen were equally fully aware that Rhodes, as a potential ally and partner, was more than merely another parochial English-speaking politician. Before rushing into his outstretched arms, they would have to resolve the contradictions between their particular economic interests and their attachment to their republican ethnic brothers, and between this ethnic concern and their adherence to their imperial connection. These contradictions came to a head and were temporarily resolved during the years 1888–90.

THE BOND BETWEEN RHODES AND THE TRANSVAAL

Central to the resolution of these contradictions was the economic transformation of the South African economy during the 1880s. The depression which occurred in the early 1880s again highlighted the economic weakness of an economy based on primary products whose prices were subjected to the vicissitudes of the world markets. The discovery of diamonds in the late 1860s had created the illusion of a more sustainable economic prosperity. Indeed, the decline in the value of wool exports in the late 1870s was offset by the improved performance of the diamond industry. However, the depression of the 1880s flew in the face of those who might have believed that diamonds provided the Cape with an economic panacea. Despite the considerable contribution of the diamond industry to the economic development of the Cape, it was exposed, as a luxury product, to the fluctuations in demand and price in limited foreign markets. The Cape farmers, the backbone of the Afrikaner Bond, were severely affected by this slump.[95] Various local strategies – protection for local producers, railway extension, development of Cape coal and a spate of local mineral prospecting – failed to alleviate the economic plight of the farmers.[96]

Both the short- and the long-term economic salvation of the Cape lay in securing external markets for produce and capital. It was with this in mind that Hofmeyr tried to convince the British government, during the imperial conference in 1887, to grant preferential tariffs to the colonies. However, even if Britain was well disposed to Hofmeyr's protectionist proposals, it was bound by trade agreements with non-imperial trading partners. The British market might have offered a hope; it certainly did not provide a short-term respite. The only alternative that presented itself to the Cape was regional economic expansion. Economic interest beyond the borders of the colony had preceded the depression of the 1880s. During the boom of the 1870s Cape economic interests had stretched their tentacles in search of markets, labour supply, energy resources and profitable investment. In the forefront were merchant, financial and mining interests which possessed capital, initiative and a broad economic outlook. Cape Afrikaner farming interests were still too parochial to take an active interest in broad regional economic movements.

This expansive outlook was manifested in the opening of branches of Cape-based banks in the Transvaal during the 1870s, and in the completion of the telegraph line from Cape Town to Pretoria in 1880. The early gold discoveries in the eastern Transvaal inspired the author of the *Cape General Directory* of 1876 to make the following prophecy: 'The whole course of past, recent and passing events seem to indicate ... that

101

a few years, indeed, will see the Transvaal territory occupy a most important position in South Africa.'[97] However, the unstable financial and political conditions in the Transvaal, which culminated in its annexation in 1877, and the short life of the early gold mines discouraged any large-scale economic shift northwards. The stabilisation of the Transvaal in the early 1880s and the general South African depression, had stimulated a renewed interest in mineral prospecting in the Transvaal which culminated in the discovery of gold on the Rand in 1886. Capital accumulated in the Cape played an important role in this,[98] and Cape Afrikaners were also involved in the rush to the new Eldorado. In Paarl, the Paarl-Pretoria Goudmijn en Exploratie Maatschappij was formed with a capital of £60,000. Among its directors were prominent townsmen and Bondsmen such as S.J. du Toit and his brother, Oom Lokomotief.[99] Afrikaners were also involved in the Worcester Exploration and Gold Mining Company formed in 1886.[100]

The Bond was slow to grasp the implications of this regional economic shift, before the scope of the changes generated by the discovery of gold in the Rand became all too apparent. This was reflected clearly in their response to the challenge of Bechuanaland. When Rhodes alerted the dormant Cape polity to the need to stake a claim over Bechuanaland as a corridor to an alternative route for a northwards economic expansion, he was strongly opposed by the Bond. The Bond saw in Bechuanaland a legitimate sphere of expansion for their Transvaal ethnic brothers and believed that an amicable economic agreement with the Transvaal government could safeguard Cape interests. Their acceptance of the incorporation of Bechuanaland into the British empire was a show of political resignation rather than enthusiasm. However, Kruger and many Transvalers viewed the Cape Bondsmen as collaborators with British imperialism rather than ethnic brothers. Their animosity towards the Cape Bond was exacerbated by the fateful response of the Bond-controlled Cape government to Kruger's request, a few months before to the discovery of gold in the Rand, for a share in the customs duties collected by the Cape for goods destined for the Transvaal. This was a missed opportunity of enormous proportions. By positively responding to Transvaal's just and moderate request, the Cape could have obtained a customs union and railway connection with its republican hinterland. Rhodes, as we have seen, vehemently urged the government and parliament to respond positively to Kruger's request. It is astonishing that on such a subject no Bondsman took part in the debate in Parliament. On 20 May 1886, less than two months before the Rand gold rush began, the Cape parliament approved the prime minister's proposal which amounted to an insulting rebuff to the Transvaal.[101] Facing the contradiction between the call of ethnic blood and their immediate particular interests, Bondsmen succumbed to the latter. They also followed their parsimonious instinct instead of taking a broader and longer-term view of their regional economic interests.

In mitigation it should be borne in mind that the wealth of the Rand was not immediately and conclusively established. The *ZA*, in late August 1886, doubted that 'the pure gold, the gold of Ophir' would be found in the Transvaal. It predicted that, instead, many would lose money in speculations.[102] A month later there was still no sense of urgency, and while favouring, in principle, a South African customs union, it had reservations about allowing the import of tobacco which could adversely affect farmers in Oudtshoorn.[103] Tobacco, it should be emphasised, was marginal in the overall economic scheme of the Cape. Furthermore, the Bond press was at that time highly critical of the Transvaal regime and Kruger in particular. The *ZA* came out against Kruger as a candidate for the next presidential election, claiming that the Transvaal deserved a 'more capable' president.[104] Even the *Patriot*, with its traditional pan-Afrikaner orientation, began, after the estrangement between S.J. du Toit and Kruger, to attack the latter.[105]

Soon, however, the mineral wealth of the Rand became too apparent to be ignored. Johannesburg, the mining town, became the biggest potential South African market, especially for the highly depressed wine and brandy industry of the Cape. In January 1887, the *ZA*, which was particularly sensitive to the plight of the wine farmers in western Cape, began to preach more vigorously the gospel of South African free trade.[106] Soon after, the Cape Town branch of the Bond sent a delegation to urge the prime minister to negotiate with the Transvaal over free trade and railway extension.[107] In response, the Cape government sent the commissioner for Crown lands and public works, with D.C. de Waal as interpreter, to Pretoria to initiate such negotiations. In relation to the failure to respond appropriately to the request of the Transvaal in March 1886, the *ZA* conceded that the South African economic tables had been turned and that the Cape was becoming the weaker party. It was, it acknowledged, of utmost importance to facilitate the access of Cape wine and brandy to the Transvaal market.[108]

The Bond finally understood the economic shift and opted for the Transvaal as the destination of the economic movement northwards. The Transvaal, which was developing primarily as a mining economy, was a perfect complement to the agrarian interests represented by the Bond. The Cape, however, seems to have missed the train. By February 1887, it became apparent that the Transvaal was refusing to attend a conference to discuss a South African customs union.[109] Kruger never forgave the Bond for their rebuff in 1886 on the issue of his republic's share in the customs duties. Clearly, in the broad struggle between the two competing visions of South Africa – the colonial and the republican – Kruger and the Bond stood on different sides of the dividing line. Kruger and Transvaal Afrikaners more generally also did not follow instinctively the call of ethnicity. They also made the distinction between their ethnic core and their Afrikaner colonial diaspora, their political behaviour being equally core-motivated and oriented.

Thus, Kruger turned his back on the Cape, which was politically dominated by people of the same ethnic background as himself, and began to pursue more vigorously his independent Delagoa Bay option. As the minutes of meetings between Transvaal and Orange Free State delegations, in mid-1887, clearly indicate, Kruger made a great effort to convince the latter to disengage economically from the Cape and attach themselves to the northern economic system around the Transvaal.[110] When the Free State delegation tried to convince him that they had to come to an agreement with the Cape in order to get their share in the customs duties collected in the Cape, Kruger responded: 'Let them keep their money, and wait for us. Cut yourself loose from the south. We cannot enter a customs union while we are dependent on their ports or they will dictate terms to us.' Kruger even offered them a sum of £20,000 yearly for ten years, if they failed to secure a share in the customs from the colonies.[111]

From 1887 to 1890 the ZA carried numerous editorials and reports on the relations between the Cape and the Transvaal which gave expression to Bond members' and leaders' attitudes towards the latter. These tilted from hope to despair, from courting to rage. On the whole, relations between the Bond and the Transvaal deteriorated at the same time as Rhodes's courting of the Bond became more persistent and enthusiastic. Only the convergence of nadir and zenith in these parallel relations provides a satisfactory explanation to the fruition of the alliance between Rhodes and the Afrikaners in 1890.

In January 1887, D.C. de Waal reported that it was possible that the following session of the Transvaal *volksraad* would facilitate the importation of Cape wines and expressed his belief that the railway from the Cape would reach the Transvaal before the one from Delagoa Bay.[112] A fortnight later the ZA expressed disappointment and anger in the face of the Transvaal's hostile policy towards the Cape.[113] During March and April a sense of optimism set in again, as reports and assessments were indicating that the Cape delegation to Pretoria was well received and that the misunderstanding between the two governments had been replaced by a cordial understanding.[114] By August this optimism had given way to a painful awakening, the ZA conceding that the news from the Transvaal was a hard blow to Cape wine farmers. However, it continued to hope that a customs agreement would materialise in the end.[115] In November the *Patriot* complained that Cape Afrikaners were perceived, in the Transvaal, as enemies and interpreted the *rapprochement* between the Transvaal and the Orange Free State as being designed to exclude the Cape from the economic opportunities in the former.[116] In December the Transvaal government was blamed for sacrificing the interests of the Cape farmers to those of foreign states and Jewish distillers.[117]

Various approaches were employed by the Bond and its press in an attempt to lure the Transvaal government and to convince it to adopt more favourable policies towards the Cape. An appeal was made to national sympathy and the need for unity. Transvalers were reminded of the crucial assistance they had received from Cape Afrikaners in their struggle against the British. The Transvaal was also warned that disunity between Afrikaners would give *jingoism* a new chance to defeat the Afrikaners and pave the way for the victory of the English miners and speculators in the Transvaal. The Transvaal government, which was pushing for closer union with its sister republic, was told that the true guarantee for its independence should rest rather on an understanding with all the colonists, Transvalers being warned that the support of Cape Afrikaners could not be taken for granted. It was reported that even known friends of the Transvaal were condemning her. Special care was taken to court Kruger. Although the *ZA* had in the past advocated the replacement of Kruger with a more capable president, it now began to support his candidacy, stating that it had never opposed him.[118] The Paarl newspapers were torn between their pan-Afrikaner inclinations and their sympathies with the wine farmers they represented. They expressed deep disappointment with the Transvaal's hostile trade policies and even threatened the latter with the consequences of the inevitable alienation of Cape Afrikaners. On 16 September 1887, the *Patriot* was blunt, expressing disappointment at the thanklessness of the Transvaal and warning her that if she drove the Cape into bankruptcy the attitude towards her would change: 'Love for brothers is strong, but with most people the love for the pocket is stronger'.[119] The *Paarl* published a draft petition of wine farmers to Kruger, while the *Patriot* reminded Transvalers that 'we are one *volk*, we speak the same language, we have one church and ours is one blood', in an attempt to get free trade with the republic.[120] In September 1887 the Bond Cape Town branch made a direct appeal to Kruger, urging him to remove the obstacles to 'Afrikaner unity and reconciliation'.[121] Hofmeyr and D.C. de Waal urged parliament not to take hostile steps against the Transvaal, fearing the latter's retaliation.[122] The leader in the *ZA*'s Christmas edition repeated many of the above themes, expressing the hope that by Christmas 1888 the misunderstanding between the Cape and the Transvaal would belong to history.[123]

This hope was to remain unfulfilled. Christmas 1887 and New Year 1888 had come and gone and Kruger was no more forthcoming towards his hard-pressed ethnic brothers in the Cape. Kruger refused to attend the customs union conference which was convened in Cape Town on 30 January 1888, fearing that a customs union would undermine his efforts to complete the Delagoa Bay railway line.[124] The loyal Cape Afrikaners were still perceived as part of the colonial and imperial embrace he was trying desperately to evade. When in July 1888 the Cape government presented Parliament with a Bill proposing a railway extension from Kimberley northwards towards the Transvaal border, Kruger became conciliatory, using the Bond to thwart the construction of this line, apparently promising a free trade agreement in exchange. He also promised to exert influence on the Orange Free State to construct a railway line up to the Vaal river. The Bond reciprocated by opposing the Bill, which was nevertheless carried. By the end of the year, in the wake of the general election, the Bond had persuaded the government to postpone the construction of the line.[125] His goal achieved, Kruger failed to deliver the goods, and a free trade agreement was not signed. Kruger also refused to participate in the South African customs union conference which met in Bloemfontein at the end of March 1889, and in early March he signed a defence alliance with the Orange Free State. The latter also undertook not to extend the Cape–Orange Free State railway line beyond Bloemfontein, and on the eve of the Bloemfontein conference Kruger made it clear that he would not sanction the construction of a railway line beyond that city. Clearly, Kruger was trying to lure President Reitz, who was torn between south and north, away from the Cape, his republic's traditional trade partner.[126]

The Bond and its press continued to vacillate between hope and despair. They did not turn clearly against the Transvaal, despite increasing frustrations. This was not merely because of kinship ties and brotherly love. The wine growers in particular, who were so prominent in the Bond, could not easily give up even the flimsiest hope of gaining access to Johannesburg, which was inhabited by a 'thirsty race'.[127] For the Afrikaner farmers the future lay in the proven market of the Transvaal,[128] rather than in a prospective Eldorado further afield. They continued, however, to give vent to their frustrations against the Transvaal. 'Old Bondsman' stated that the Transvaal in its actions against Cape products 'transforms us into her bitterest enemies', while the ZA complained that the Transvaal preferred Natal's English traders to 'Afrikanerdom' and that 'while the farmer here is starving and languishing ... the Transvaal market is shut to him'.[129] They did not, however, cease to court the good will of Kruger, and their Transvaal brothers more generally, and to preach the gospel of unity.[130]

THE IMPACT OF RHODES'S NORTHERN EXPANSION ON HIS RELATIONS WITH THE BOND

During 1888 a barely perceptible process of change began in the Bond which was to culminate in the alliance with Rhodes in 1890. This shift was occasioned, indeed encouraged, by the gradual emergence of an alternative route and destination in the economic movement northwards – the fabulous land between the Limpopo and the Zambesi. Rhodes, of course, played a crucial role in opening up the new north. Having secured Bechuanaland, the 'Suez Canal' of the interior, he faced, in late 1887, a direct challenge to the region north of the Limpopo. He construed the Lobengula–Grobler agreement of July 1887 as transforming the kingdom into a vassal state of the Transvaal. A man like Rhodes, who had forestalled the Transvaal on the road to the north, was not likely to resign himself to its expansion to the north itself. He managed to convince the high commissioner to turn the Ndebele kingdom into a British sphere of influence, which was secured by the Moffat–Lobengula agreement of mid-February 1888.[131] Rhodes, who in courting the Bond was fully aware of the latters' ethnic sensitivities, conveniently kept secret his role in forestalling the Transvaal.

Rhodes's intervention transformed the north into an alternative space for a northward economic movement for the Cape's struggling economy and anxious Afrikaner farmers. It turned the future of the north into a subject of intense interest and debate in Bond circles. The region north of the Limpopo was presented as 'lands of fabulous wealth', Mashonaland being described as very rich in gold.[132] For Cape Afrikaner farmers, and particularly the wine farmers, who feared exclusion from the Transvaal market, the north was a great temptation. Nevertheless, their response to the challenge of the north was hesitant and ambivalent. This did not reflect simply the contradiction between blood and pocket, but was also informed by their cautious pragmatism which made them waver between the attraction of the proven wealth of the Rand and the assumed fabulosity of the north. It also stemmed, as we shall see, from their ambivalence towards British imperialism.

In March 1888, the agreement between Moffat and Lobengula caught the attention of the *ZA*. While justifying turning Lobengula's kingdom into a British sphere of influence as a step against intervention by foreign powers, it objected to it as a hostile act towards the Transvaal. The correct policy for the South African states was 'the extension of their control without disturbing one another, provided that the goal of colonization was the increase of power and well-being of the colonists as a whole'.[133] In June the *ZA* proposed that the railway line to the Zambesi should begin in Pretoria, while in July it stated that 'we are not happy that all the lands of Khama, Mashonaland and Matabeleland were exclusively under British influence primarily because we do not want to incur any injustice to ... the Transvaal'.[134] However, beyond this lip-service, the Bond took no action. There was no uproar and organised protest or active support, as there had been during the annexation crisis in the late 1870s and the early 1880s. There was not even the public outrage and concerted Bond opposition as in the Bechuanaland crisis of 1884–85. Merely-lip service. The ZA agreed with the *Patriot* that if the agreement had been signed a few years earlier the Bond would have condemned it unanimously: 'It has not happened now because of recent Transvaal attitude towards the Cape.'[135] It stated the reason quite specifically:

> Had the relations between the Transvalers and the Cape Afrikaners been better, it would not have been difficult to turn the behaviour of the British government into a grievance and organize a movement in support of Transvaal. There is no chance for this at this juncture.[136]

Arguably there was, with regard to the north, the potential for even more vigorous manifestations of solidarity than there had been on earlier occasions. Previously, it had been a pure manifestation of ethnic solidarity, as Cape Afrikaners could have expected no material gains from the impoverished Transvaal. In the late 1880s, a combination of ethnic solidarity and vital economic interests had a tremendous potential for political mobilisation and action among Cape Afrikaners. The ZA was candid when referring to Britain's desire to play an independent role in the north: 'Unity based on kinship and common interests would have neutralized this British tendency.'[137] Having been deprived of the economic motive, Cape Afrikaners responded to the contest over the north in accordance with a well-established pattern of political behaviour, namely resignation and acquiescence. The only difference was that now even the verbal manifestations of ethnic solidarity were much more muted.

Cape Afrikaner farmers could have expected to derive economic benefits from the development of the economic potential of the north under the aegis of their Queen. If they demonstrated no enthusiasm for such a prospect it was not primarily the result of either pan-Afrikaner solidarity or outright rejection of British imperialism. It rather reflected their ambivalence towards the imperial connection. While priding themselves on being loyal subjects of the Queen, Bondsmen had serious misgivings about imperial intervention in domestic and regional affairs. One of the few issues on which the ZA agreed with the *Patriot* was that 'direct imperial rule in the hinterland of South Africa could only have dire consequences for the colonists, because they favour the Natives and undermine the colonists'.[138] The choice in the north was clear:

The big question is whether the country will become India or Canada. Where Afrikaner Boers are, there can be no talk of a new India; it will be a country controlled by and for the colonists. If England is the master the opposite will happen.[139]

It is important to note that the alternative to a new India was a new Canada, an *opregte Boerenkolonie* (genuine Boer colony) and not a new republic.[140] The implication was clear: if the British opted for a new Canada, they could have expected unequivocal support from the Bond.

By elimination, a third option began to emerge in 1888 in Bond circles – Cape expansionism, or more precisely Cape sub-imperialism. It was believed, or hoped, that a 'new Cape' in the north could resolve the contradictions between Cape Afrikaners and the republican north on the one hand and between them and the British Empire on the other. Moreover, it offered a political and ideological garb for the vital economic movement northwards. It is important to emphasise, however, that, from a Cape Afrikaner viewpoint, Cape expansionism was not a predetermined consequence of economic forces. The Bond could have equally resigned itself to a Transvaal or direct British expansionism if certain political and economic prerequisites were respected.

The shift of the Bond towards the Cape's northwards expansion was manifested, in the second half of 1888, in the propagation of the annexation of Bechuanaland to the Cape.[141] Accepting British paramountcy north of the Cape as a *fait accompli*, and in view of the Transvaal's continuing economic hostility towards the Cape, the Bond's initiative made sense. Having advocated earlier the annexation of British Bechuanaland, it now recommended the annexation of the Bechuanaland Protectorate as well. Soon, the appetite increased and expansion to the Zambesi was contemplated and urged. By October 1888 it was stated clearly that in the long run the north must be incorporated in the Cape. Explaining to its readers this new expansionism, and also addressing the Transvaal gallery, the ZA presented the scramble for the north as a foregone conclusion. It argued that since a republican solution was not feasible, Cape expansionism was the lesser of two evils, the greater being direct imperial rule. It emphasised that the Cape should develop the north as a joint South African venture.[142] There were, however, also less altruistic motives. Bechuanaland was perceived as important, not only for its lands, but also as the trade route 'to the Zambesi and the gold fields north of the Transvaal'.[143] This supposedly gold-rich area was presented as a promising market for Cape products: 'We believe that many wine bottles from the Cape will find their way to the banks of the Zambesi.'[144]

It was, indeed, on the banks of the Zambesi that the paths of Rhodes and the Bond finally converged. In 1888, however, this was not yet a foregone conclusion. Rhodes, who during 1886 and 1887 had cultivated good will among Bondsmen, continued to court them. The support of the Bond in 1888 became more crucial than before as Rhodes's northern scheme was nearing a climax. In addition, in the same year Rhodes finally completed the amalgamation of the diamond industry. The amalgamated De Beers was not only a vital interest in its own right, but also the economic basis for Rhodes's southern African schemes. As such, it had to be consolidated, politically as well as economically, since the prosperity of the industry depended also on the state's attitude towards it. The latter could not be taken for granted. In Kimberley mercantile interests opposed the main thrusts of Rhodes, namely rationalisation and concentration of mining operations.[145] In the parliamentary elections of 1884 three of the four Kimberley seats were captured by representatives of these antagonistic interests and in a by-election in 1886 O'Leary, one of the bitterest opponents of the mining magnates, defeated J.B. Robinson, the candidate of the latter.[146] Upington, the prime minister from 1884 to 1886, was also clearly hostile to the mining interests.[147] In 1886 Rhodes had to negotiate a compromise with the Kimberley merchants regarding the compound system, for which he was strongly criticised by many of his colleagues.[148] As was shown by the debate on the Labourers' Wage Bill at the end of June 1886, in which O'Leary attacked the closed compound system, the mercantile interests of Kimberley elicited sympathy and support among Bond MPs. Representatives of hard-pressed farmers could identify with the small men of Kimberley struggling for survival against voracious capitalists. During the debate on the Bill, A.S. le Roex called for the abolition of the compound system. D.C. de Waal, who was to become one of Rhodes's staunchest supporters, 'wished to know what benefit the Colony derived from the Kimberley mines (Hear, hear)', arguing that the profit from the diamond industry 'went into the pockets of the shareholders who lived in Europe'. Even Hofmeyr, who vacillated, professed anti-monopolistic inclinations.[149]

Clearly, then, Rhodes's schemes still rested on shaky political ground. There is little doubt that his courting of the Bond in 1886–87 was not motivated only by his imperial expansion plans, but rather more broadly by the needs of all his operations in southern Africa. Besides seeking the good will of the Bond more generally, Rhodes also directed special lobbying efforts to securing support for his Kimberley interests. In 1886 he conveyed MPs to Kimberley to acquaint them with the mining industry. This effort paid off when J.A. de Wet, a Bondsman and a cabinet minister, who had been treated by Rhodes to a guided tour, supported the controversial compound system during the debate on the Labourers' Wages Bill.[150] However, at the beginning of the 1888 parliamentary session, Bondsmen still supported the taxation of the diamond industry,[151] which could have had a considerable adverse effect on the diamond industry as it progressed towards the final stages of amalgamation.

Consequently, Rhodes realised that more courting was needed to deepen and consolidate his inroads into Bondsmen's hearts and minds. Whereas in 1886 he gained their sympathy mainly by supporting the abolition of the excise duty on brandy and in 1887 he earned their admiration for subscribing to their 'native' policy, in 1888 he played the Transvaal card. Disappointed at the Transvaal's lack of co-operation in the sphere of free trade and railway extension, the Cape government submitted a Railway Extension Bill which included an extension from Kimberley northwards to the Vaal river. This fitted in very nicely with Rhodes's northern schemes. Rhodes, however, must have felt that before taking a definite initiative in the north, he had first to consolidate his Cape political and economic base. Thus, on 23 July 1888, he supported the amendment to the Bill by T.P. Theron which, in deference to the wishes of the Transvaal, called for the cancellation of the plan to construct a railway line from Kimberley to the Vaal. In this Rhodes not only lent support to the economic interests of Bondsmen who still hoped to secure access to the Transvaal market, but also showed respect for their ethnic feelings.

Having shown his colours, Rhodes used the opportunity to state his case for northern expansion, presenting himself as a Cape expansionist who only wished to promote Cape interests. He also gave expression to the view to which many Bondsmen would have subscribed:

> The position as to the interior expansion of the Cape Colony had changed entirely for the best both as to the English and the Dutch sentiment of this Colony. Instead of the feeling four years ago that the Transvaal should have the expansion of the interior and then we should join with them, honorary Members in this House now saw clearly that if they allowed the Transvaal to take the interior they would never join with us.[152]

This was certainly an attitude he wanted to reinforce among Bondsmen. The delay in the progress of the railway line northwards was a price worth paying.

The persistent courtship of the Bond was beginning to yield handsome dividends in Rhodes's improved standing in Bond circles. In July 1888 the *ZA* paid tribute to Rhodes for his support for the Afrikaner cause in parliament: 'British blood flows through Rhodes's veins, but he is no less a *Kapenaar* for that, seeing that as a member of the Cape parliament he proved himself more *Afrikaansch* than many colonists born and bred in South Africa'.[153] Rhodes, the 'full-blooded Englishman', who was particularly hailed for his support of Theron's amendment, was described as a man 'who knows the situation in the Transvaal'.[154] Indeed, the Transvaal card earned Rhodes handsome dividends. He was reported to hold the view that the interest of South Africa demands 'the strengthening of the republics'.[155] The *ZA* concluded from Rhodes's vote for Theron's amendment that he, like the Bond, wanted a *rapprochement* with the Transvaal.[156] On 23 August 1888 the government was urged to negotiate with the Transvaal on the basis of Rhodes's plans. This would, it was surmised, 'convince' the Transvaal that the Cape not only did not wish to obstruct the Delagoa Bay railway line, but, in fact, desired its speedy completion.[157] Ironic as it may sound, Rhodes was perceived as holding the keys to a better understanding between the Cape Afrikaners and the Transvaal.

Another indication, during the second half of 1888, of Rhodes's improved standing in Bond circles, was that the rationalisation of the *rapprochement* between him and the Bond was increasingly stated not simply in personalised terms. He emerged, much more clearly than before, as a representative of a class of colonists which shared economic interests with the Cape Afrikaner farmers. On 4 September, the *ZA* suggested a change in the class alliance in Cape politics:

> Whereas until now the farmers' party in the Cape had co-operated more with the merchant class than with the mining interests in the diamond fields, it is very possible that a change will soon come, and this change is persistently aimed at by the most powerful representative of the mine owners [Rhodes].

While stating that there was not a natural conflict between the 'farmers' party' and the 'merchants' party', it suggested that there were differences in outlook between them. The farmers preferred indirect taxation whereas the merchants preferred direct ones; while the farmers viewed the 'natives' as troublesome neighbours who could be transformed into good labourers, the merchants looked upon them as clients. On the other hand, the writer found little divergence of interests between farmers and mine owners: 'Both are owners of land and need labourers under proper supervision.'[158]

A month later these general observations began to take a more concrete political shape. Speaking of the forthcoming general election, the *ZA* related the 'very good chance' of changes in the political alliances in Griqualand West to the candidature of Barney Barnato, 'one of the wealthiest diamond people', for a Kimberley seat in the 1888 general election: 'It is not improbable that, in consequence, the Afrikaner party will cooperate with the mining companies rather than with the merchants and retailers in the city of Kimberley.'[159] Barnato was praised for his contribution to the indigenisation of the mining industry, a tribute which applied, of course, also to Rhodes. These members of the emerging national bourgeoisie, in contradistinction to the 'money wolves' who exported their profits abroad, were an asset to the farmers as well as to the colony as a whole: 'and to that extent the Colony as a whole benefits from the endeavour of Rhodes and Barnato not less than the diamond fields'.[160] Thus, it is hardly surprising that the *ZA*, which had viewed the election of O'Leary in 1886 as a victory, expressed satisfaction with the 1888 election results in Kimberley which brought a clear victory to the mining industry over the merchant interests.[161] This shifting class alliance had a more tangible manifestation when Hofmeyr delivered, in the 1888 parliamentary session, a most impressive speech against tax on diamonds which contributed to the withdrawal of the motion.[162]

Concurrently, Rhodes, whose rating in the eyes of Bondsmen was rising, was presented as a statesman by comparison with whom Merriman was a mere politician.[163] On 7 August 1888, in the wake of his support for the Theron amendment, it was reported, with a view to the possibility of a change of government, that Rhodes might be called to form a new one. His past record, his ability and his good relations with Kruger were elaborated upon in this context. Four days later, it was predicted that he was going to be assigned a prominent role in the affairs of South Africa, and on 21 August it was stated that, with the exception of Upington and Sprigg, the only English-speaking MP of 'ability and consequence' was Rhodes. On 23 August he was included among the few Englishmen who could, together with prominent Bond leaders, lead a genuine colonial party.[164] In early October, with a reshuffle in the cabinet a possibility, the *ZA* asked that Rhodes not be forgotten, particularly in view of his ability to promote co-operation with the Transvaal.[165] More generally, the newspaper believed that 'only where Rhodes and ... Hofmeyr work together will there be success'.[166] In an election speech in Stellenbosch on 3 November 1888, Hofmeyr gave official party sanction to the pro-Rhodes campaign of the main Bond mouthpiece. He said that the Bond would never be a truly national party unless it secured the confidence and co-operation of 'enlightened Englishmen who are prepared to rally on our side'. Therefore, he said, he was glad 'in the friendship and support of men like Sivewright and Rhodes'. J. Sivewright, Rhodes's friend and close collaborator, had officially joined the Bond. Hofmeyr, referring to Rhodes as a man 'of European fame', told his audience that their friendship dated back to Rhodes's first days in Parliament. He described Rhodes as a man who had 'a heart for the colonial farmer' and said that in his attitude towards the Theron amendment he exhibited a broad outlook on South Africa and its future.[167]

It seems, indeed, that the 1888 general election occasioned a further political *rapprochement* between Rhodes and the Bond, and Hofmeyr in particular. In October 1888 D.C de Waal wrote to Rhodes: 'I read your speech with interest and fully endorse contents of same.'[168] There seems

113

to have been an unofficial electoral alliance between Rhodes and the Bond. Sivewright seems to have played an important role as a link between the Bond and Rhodes.[169] In a letter to Rhodes, Hofmeyr himself reported on his efforts to get his people elected in various constituencies, ending thus: 'However, do your [part?] and I'll do mine.' While not expressing personal opposition to Rhodes's plans for northern expansion, Hofmeyr advised him that he 'doubted very much whether he would find the "National Party" [the Bond] as a whole endorsing, as one to be carried into *immediate* effect'.[170] The letter definitely conveys the existence of political intimacy between the two politicians. It also indicates that Hofmeyr was privy to Rhodes's expansion plans. While not personalising the Bond's attitude towards Rhodes, there is no doubt that the latter, while courting the Bond, devoted particular attention to Hofmeyr, and that the close relations between the two greatly improved Rhodes's standing among Bondsmen. On 5 January 1889, while referring to a possible rift between the Bond and the government, the *ZA* posed a rhetorical question: 'What can we get then if not a combination between Hofmeyr and Rhodes.' It emphasised that Rhodes believed in the necessity of a northward expansion of the Cape even more strongly than Sprigg.[171]

Indeed, the much improved standing of Rhodes among Bondsmen served him well when the nature of his direct involvement in the north began to unfold. Thus, on 27 November 1888, the *ZA* reported favourably on the Rudd concession, noting that behind it were Rhodes and Barnato, 'colonists who chose South Africa as their homeland'. In fact, it presented the concession holders as saviours of the north from competing 'native lovers'.[172] A few days later Rhodes's endeavour in the north was defended on the grounds that he would co-operate with his neighbours, including the Transvaal and that he would not repeat the 'follies and one-sidedness' of Warren, Mackenzie and the like.[173] In early April 1889, the *Cape Argus* reported on Rhodes's plans for the north – the annexation of Bechuanaland to the Cape, the non-interference of the Transvaal in the area north of the Limpopo, the annexation of Swaziland as compensation to the latter, and the treatment of the rights of concession holders in Lobengula's kingdom within the framework of a royal charter. While expressing reservation about the feasibility of such a plan, the *ZA* stated that if gold mining in the north was to be regulated by a royal charter 'then we shall always prefer to see it happening under the influence of Rhodes than under that of English capitalists who cherish no sympathy towards the settler population of South Africa'.[174] This, however, reflected a preference for Rhodes rather than for a royal charter.

Indeed, as the implications of the struggle for the north became more apparent, vacillation and unease set in. There was a definite opposition to British rule, seen as inimical to settlers' interests in the north. Support was given to Portugal's counter claim to Mashonaland where Boer settlement under the Portuguese flag was presented as the best solution. In early April 1889, in response to a report that the exploitation of Matabeleland would be in the hands of a London-based company, sharp disapproval was expressed.[175] It was against this background that a British chartered company controlled by Rhodes seemed preferable to unknown greedy British capitalists. This did not, however, represent a definite shift in favour of Rhodes's northern plans. Bondsmen were still torn by the contradictory pull of the two northern options. Rhodes would have to be perceived by them as the promoter of a genuine Cape colonial expansion before they could lend him unequivocal support. This appeared on the surface only in November 1889. Until then, they vacillated between their interest, indeed desire, to gain access to the proven, expanding Transvaal market, and the prospect of a possible alternative one north of the Limpopo offered by Rhodes. A definite shift towards the Rhodesian option resulted primarily, not from the great promise of the latter, or even from the attraction of its promoter, but rather from a loss of hope in the preferable Transvaal option. Essentially, the Rhodesian option was a second best; it was also perceived, somewhat less optimistically, as the lesser of two evils. The complex, loaded relationship between Cape Afrikaners and the Transvaal was a major determinant of this shift.

There is little doubt that the Bond preferred the Transvaal option and still hoped that it could materialise. For that end, despite past frustrations, they continued to court the good will of Kruger and the Transvaal. D.C. de Waal, addressing a Bond congress dinner, even presented himself as a 'genuine republican' who had a liking for a united states of South Africa under one flag.[176] The ZA, while paying tribute to Rhodes and his plans to exploit the north, stated categorically that it did not pay to sacrifice the benefits of the connection with the Transvaal even for the prospect of controlling all the lands up to the Nile river.[177] Consequently, as soon as it became clear that Rhodes's plans in the north were in conflict with the requisites of cultivating the Transvaal option, the attitude towards the former changed. Opposition towards Rhodes's plans surfaced as it became known that he intended to build a railway line from Kimberley northwards, his vote against which had earned him so much credit in 1888. In mid-May 1889 such a railway line was perceived as most detrimental:

> Not only will the Cape lose all the fruits of the wise policy it had adopted towards the republics, but, even worse, it will place a barrier on the way to co-operation between the different states which is essential for the natural development of our region.

Kruger was urged to grant free trade to the Cape in order to strengthen the Bond in its opposition to such a plan,[178] and Rhodes was taken to task for reversing his policy: 'We are sad to see a man whom we view as a friend of South Africa follow the path of our country's enemies.' Prophetically the writer added: 'We know that Rhodes, having so much power, can cause equally much good and much evil.' He also expressed the hope that the government and parliament would see to it that 'the interests of the country would prevail over those of Rhodes in case of a contradiction between them'.[179]

The Transvaal was not, however, impressed by such gestures and the *Volksraad*, which was supposed to deal with free imports from the Cape, procrastinated. After the signing of the customs convention between the Cape and the Orange Free State in March 1889, Hofmeyr attempted again to prevent a rift with the Transvaal. In April 1889 he tried to do it through the mediation of F.W. Reitz, president of the Orange Free State.[180] When this failed, Hofmeyr sent Kruger a long letter urging him to concede to the Cape's request for free trade and for the extension of the Orange Free State railway line into the Transvaal. He argued that this was in the best economic interests of the Transvaal and would also 'lay a strong bond between your burghers and their kinsfolk in the Free State and the Cape Colony.' While the Transvaal government's belated reply of 19 July was only partially satisfactory, it gave some hope.[181] It was, however, to no avail since the issue was in the hands of the *Volksraad*. At the end of June, the *ZA* complained that the *Volksraad*, which had been in session for two and a half months, had not yet dealt with the issue.

The ensuing frustration at the inaction of the *Volksraad* brought to the fore Rhodes's railway northwards as a viable option or, at least as a threat to the Transvaal.[182] On 30 July, *ZA* warned that rejection of the Cape's request would be a very serious setback to the Cape farmers and would considerably exacerbate the alienation between the two states.[183] In fact, a day earlier the *Volksraad* had not only turned down Kruger's request that the Cape be granted free trade, but had also expressed contempt for the Cape and sympathy for Natal. In their desire to avoid competition from Cape farmers, argued the *ZA*, Transvalers had forgone the opportunity to expand northwards in collaboration with the Cape 'without the influence of British companies and British ideas'. It stated that while the Bond still favoured co-operation with the republics, it would be difficult to organise effective opposition to a prospective chartered company in the north.[184]

Despite the deep disappointment at the Transvaal's overt hostility towards the vital interests of Cape Afrikaner farmers, the pages of the *ZA* continued to reflect ambivalence over the northern expansion. The option of Transvaal's rule in the north was still presented as preferable to the rule of either Britain or a British company.[185] All this time, while Rhodes was negotiating a royal charter in England, the exact nature of his plans was unknown. The news which filtered through during August 1889 regarding his intentions certainly did not meet with enthusiasm. Even reports that the company would have £70 million at its disposal did not impress the Bond's mouthpiece. In fact, such power in the hand of Rhodes was perceived as inimical to the ideal of 'an independent politics of the Cape in the north in consultation with the Transvaal'. It was presented, rather, as a victory for England.[186] In response to reports that Rhodes had succeeded in his endeavours in London, it was suggested that a company with 'British nobles of the highest rank' at its head posed a threat to 'the colonist states of South Africa'.[187] Two days later the full extent of the dilemma and ambivalence of the Bond, as it approached its Rubicon, was echoed in the ZA. It was torn between its suspicion of British capitalists and its appreciation of Rhodes as a national capitalist; it viewed imperial support for the chartered company as both beneficial and detrimental; it still desired to gain the benefits of improved relations with the Transvaal, but at the same time laid claim to the riches of the north; while expressing preference for a struggle against a 'British company' under the slogan of 'South Africa for the colonists', it also lamented that the attitude of the Transvaal towards the Cape made that impossible.[188]

While by 10 September, with Rhodes back in the Cape, the content of the charter was still unknown,[189] his return definitely sharpened the vacillation in the Bond. On that day, after a spell of bad press and with the nature of his charter still not clear, Rhodes was praised for his constant support for Cape expansion through Bechuanaland to the Zambesi and for his desire to co-operate with the republics. In the same breath, it was stated that because of the 'pettiness of the Transvaal farmers', Cape farmers had no reason to oppose the construction of the railway line from Kimberley northward.[190] However, on the nineteenth a counter argument was produced, namely that there was a place only for one line northwards and that the Orange Free State one was preferable 'because then we shall reach the north independent of English influence.'[191]

By then, with Rhodes back on the scene, political bargaining replaced public discourse, pushing the matter to a head. Rhodes must have returned to the Cape in early September. After a short stay in Cape Town he left for Kimberley to meet Hofmeyr, who was there on a visit.[192] It was there that Rhodes took Hofmeyr into his confidence and sought his and the Bond's support for his northern plans and for the charter he expected to be approved.[193] As Rhodes needed a solid Cape political base for his northern expansion, he knew that without the support of the Bond all his plans would be in jeopardy. In particular, he needed the support of Parliament and the government for the extension of the railway line from Kimberley northwards, which was a condition for obtaining the royal charter. The time had come to collect dividends on his extensive political investment in the Bond. The nature of the discussion between Rhodes and Hofmeyr emerges from a letter Rhodes sent Hofmeyr on 20 September. Two main issues must have been discussed between the two men. The first was the northern railway extension, which Rhodes also discussed with Sivewright, who was, according to the former, 'heart and soul' behind the extension plan. The second issue was the proposed local board for the charter. Rhodes also referred to a common electoral strategy. Hofmeyr's reply on 26 September implied that he had no reservations as to the content of Rhodes's letter. He only advised Rhodes to suspend, 'in his own interest', the construction of the railway and to consult Sprigg.[194] Rhodes reaped the first tangible fruit of his keen courting of the Bond. On the same day, 29 October 1889, that the British South Africa Company received a royal charter, it signed an agreement with the Cape government providing for the construction of the railway line from Kimberley to Vryburg.[195]

It was more than a month before the understanding between Rhodes and Hofmeyr was announced to the Cape Afrikaner public. In late September the ZA rejected the allegation that it supported the construction of the railway line from Kimberley. However, on the same occasion, as if to prepare its readers, it also stated that 'as things stand now we don't know whether the victory of Mr Rhodes is not the lesser of two evils'.[196] Twice more during October the 'lesser of two evils' argument was repeated, Rhodes being presented as preferable to 'Shippard or another product of Mackenzie's party', or to 'other British schemers' in developing the north.[197]

In early November 1889 a definite shift in favour of Rhodes's northern enterprise began to emerge. The time came when choices had to be made with regard to the contradictory considerations, motives, goals and political actors involved in the movement northwards. The nature of the choice was informed by a vital characteristic of the Cape Afrikaner political culture, namely resignation and the acceptance of *fait accompli*: 'It is known that we would have liked things to develop differently, but one cannot always get what one wants.' Clearly their preference for collaboration with the Transvaal in the occupation of the north was no more possible. The alternative to the politics of the desirable was the full exploitation of the politics of the possible. The rationalising effort was directed towards presenting the Rhodesian option not as a lesser evil but rather as second best and towards minimising the potential damage that might have resulted from a clear choice. It was argued that Rhodes would implement his plan 'as much as possible in a colonial spirit': 'A colonial government supported by the Afrikaners ... seem to be marching together with a company whose head enjoys the best relations with the Afrikaner party.' Rhodes's plans were also praised as possible and practical. The conviction was expressed that the incorporation of the new areas in the Cape was 'only a matter of time', and it was taken for granted that Rhodes saw the Afrikaner farmer as the best agent for colonising the northern highlands. Furthermore, the belief, indeed the conviction, was articulated that Rhodes's control of the north would usher in co-operation with Transvaal:

> The relations between the British government in the north and the Transvaal government will immediately change their nature when the company will establish its rule in collaboration with the Cape ... We think that it is a clear interest of the company to cultivate good relations with the Transvaal and consequently we think that co-operation between the company and the Transvaal is not chimerical and could be achieved in a very nice way.

To sweeten the pill, it was suggested that support for the annexation of Swaziland to Transvaal be announced[198] – this had been Rhodes's idea for some time. A reflection of the Cape-centricism of the Cape Afrikaners was their insensitivity to the anxieties of Transvaal Afrikaners, who saw in Rhodes their arch-enemy.

From that point on, there remained very little of the past vacillation, the themes of early November being repeated, elaborated and improved upon. The success of the charter was repeatedly presented as a vital interest of the Cape, Rhodes's enterprise being hailed as colonial and South African, rather than British.[199] At the same time it was believed that the establishment of Rhodes's company, with the support and collaboration of the Cape government, would strengthen considerably the bond between the colony and England.[200] By January 1890, all inhibitions were shed: 'Under the British flag and with the help of British capital we are marching to the north.'[201]

The Bond congress, in March 1890, presented a crucial test for Rhodes's northern plans. From November 1889 it was the *ZA* which carried the main burden in defending the chartered company. Even Hofmeyr, who was privy to Rhodes's plans, was reticent, and the newspaper had to explain why he had not mentioned this subject in a speech in Graaff Reinet.[202] D.C. de Waal, who had in the past strongly opposed the railway extension from Kimberley, was known to have been won over to Rhodes's plans.[203] However, antagonistic views were also aired. The *Patriot* constantly criticised and attacked Rhodes and his charter from the wings, forcing the *ZA* into a defensive position.[204] The latter had also to ward off attacks by Bond leaders. I.J. van der Walt criticised government support for the railway line extension from Kimberley northwards.[205] More serious was the attack by T.P. Theron who argued, in a meeting with his constituents, that the chartered company robbed South African settlers of their inheritance.[206] In response to the *Patriot*'s criticism, the *ZA* argued that, if the Bond followed Hofmeyr, all would be well.[207] It knew well what Hofmeyr's position was and articulated it ably. In response to Theron's criticism it was surmised that before the forthcoming parliamentary session the affairs of the chartered company would undergo such a turn that men like Van der Walt, Theron and others would change their attitude towards it.[208] There were indications that such a change of heart had already taken place before the Bond congress. In early March 1890 it seemed that even the more radical *Patriot* succumbed to the prevailing air of resignation. The newspaper, which in November 1889 had called on the Transvaal to fulfil its destiny by heading 'a true Afrikaner movement', became surprisingly acquiescent:

> Our readers know that we are against the company. However, it exists and there is nothing we can do about it. If the company will promote the interests of the Afrikaners, we will be able to collaborate with it. In any event, Rhodes, who is familiar with the conditions of the country, is a man with whom we can get along. It is to be expected that we could come to an understanding with a man like this.[209]

There is little doubt that the Transvaal was Rhodes's most useful ally in fulfilling his vision of northern expansion. Before he knew anything about the charter Hofmeyr had told Parliament: 'The sympathy of many people in that House and in the country with President Kruger had waned of late'.[210] D.C. de Waal, a staunch supporter of closer relations with the Transvaal and also a bitter opponent of the Kimberley extension, had expressed, as early as 1 August 1889, a transformation rooted in deep frustration:

> ... he felt aggrieved. It was a disappointment not only to him but to many other members of the House. It was promised to the House that they would get free trade if they did not extend the line from Kimberley. He felt in duty bound to change his mind ... He hoped the Government, if they saw that they could not come to terms with the Transvaal, would take decided steps about the extension from Kimberley to the Vaal River. The Bond party had sacrificed time and money in this matter, and they should see that money and time was not wasted.[211]

The *ZA* continued to put the blame on the Transvaal for the deteriorating relations between the latter and the Cape.[212] Even the *Patriot* condemned the Transvaal for its selfishness.[213] The disenchantment with it was also manifested in a critical attitude towards the monopolistic practices of its government.[214] This anti-Transvaal mood influenced the political discourse in the Bond, and the adoption of critical and hostile attitudes towards the republic even came to be perceived as an electoral asset. In a Bond election meeting in early March 1890, W.A. Krige spoke of the despicable way in which Kruger had reneged on his promises and declared his support for the construction of the railway line northwards.[215] The most blatant manifestation of anger and hostility towards the Transvaal occurred, not surprisingly, in Paarl, a major centre of the wine industry. In a public meeting, held shortly before the Bond congress, J.I. de Villiers, a Bond leader and MP, called on the high commissioner not to hand Swaziland over to Transvaal while it did not grant the Cape free trade. More surprisingly, it was D.F. du Toit, the editor of the *Patriot* and a champion of the Transvaal, who proposed a resolution in this spirit. Significantly De Villiers was of the opinion that it was desirable to send a copy of the resolution to Rhodes 'since, with his influence, he could do a lot for us'.[216] On the eve of the congress, R.P. Botha, the Bond's chairman, said that although he was not familiar with Rhodes's company, his feeling was that the enterprise was most beneficial to South Africa as a whole and especially to the farmers. His audience thundered its applause.[217] Speaking retrospectively, Hofmeyr was very candid about the role of the Transvaal in the making of the alliance with Rhodes: 'Had Kruger fulfilled my expectations, and fallen in with my advice, then Rhodes and I might have agreed to differ.'[218]

The Bond congress in March 1890, which was scheduled to debate the charter, was too important for Rhodes to leave to chance. Consequently, he was involved in intensive lobbying of congress delegates. A.S. le Roex, who was by no means a prominent leader, told the congress that he discussed the charter with Rhodes for two days.[219] Rhodes probably applied the same treatment to many other Bond leaders. According to Le Roex, Rhodes told him that 'he wanted to develop the country for the Afrikaners'. T.P. Theron subsequently told of a meeting he had, in 1889, with Rhodes who was very angry with him for saying that he opposed the charter because the north was the birthright of the Afrikaners. Rhodes told him that all he did was for the Afrikaners.[220] This line of argument had an appeal among delegates representing a farming population which craved new settlement spaces and new markets. A commentator remarked that although the congress's decision was to wait and see, there was a 'clear tendency to see the bright side of the affair.'[221]

Rhodes's efforts to secure Bond support for his charter were not confined to verbal persuasion. He had been busy, for some time, distributing patronage in his campaign to consolidate his local power base. In early December 1889 he wrote to Cawston in London: 'Please tell Beit that I want at least £20,000 of subscriptions for colonial people of political position who will help us as against the Transvaal.'[222] Michell wrote that in February 1890, Rhodes was in Cape Town, 'busy with the allotment of 25,000 shares in the British South African Company, which at his request, had been reserved to Colonial applicants'. He added: 'It was reported at the time, and probably with some truth, that he had shrewdly allocated the bulk of these shares to members or friends of the Afrikaner Bond, whose identification with the Company's work was eminently desirable.'[223] It was, indeed, about the same time that James Rose Innes refused to accept shares offered to him in a 'circular'.[224] On 24 April Merriman wrote that 'shares are being plentifully distributed to members of Parlt., even very obscure ones coming in for a share'.[225] Innes wrote in his autobiography: 'the body politic was virgin soil for the new infection to which in 1889 Rhodes subjected it'.[226]

As a list of shareholders from December 1890 shows, Michell was wrong, most of the South African shareholders being English rather than Afrikaners. However, a handful of Bond leaders received far more shares than the average local shareholder. Notable among them was Hofmeyr's brother who possessed 1,000 old shares and 2,000 new ones. There is evidence that Hofmeyr was directly linked to this transaction. On 5 November 1890 he wrote the following to Dr Harris, the secretary of the chartered company:

> Mr. Rhodes has handed me your letter of the 30th October with reference to the 1,000 fully paid and the 2,000 3/-shares standing in my name. I now beg to enclose my official power of attorney authorising you to ... the Trust Deed of the Co in my behalf, as well as a draft of the Standard Bank for 1,300 pound'.[227]

D.C. de Waal held 1,500 old and 1,000 new shares, while David de Villiers Graaff possessed 750 shares. The preference accorded to these Afrikaner beneficiaries stands out when compared with the 200 shares held by T.E. Fuller, MP and Rhodes's friend, most South African subscribers possessing even fewer.[228] The shares, it should be added, were subscribed 'at par' when they were 'then standing at a considerable premium'.[229] In early 1889 Rhodes engaged D.C. de Waal in a large business transaction for which he offered him 'an additional 20,000 pounds in fully paid one pound shares in the Company to be formed'.[230]

This evidence certainly proves that Rhodes used patronage liberally and unscrupulously to secure support for his schemes. It does not, however, provide sufficient proof that, at that stage, this was a crucial determinant in the Bond's support for him, De Beers and the chartered company. His investment in Hofmeyr and his Cape Town coterie was certainly designed to elicit the desired attitude from the Bond. Rhodes, as we have seen, viewed the Bond as a disciplined political phalanx commanded by Hofmeyr. Rhodes, however, may have exaggerated Hofmeyr's influence in his party. When asked by Molteno why he would not form a ministry, Hofmeyr replied candidly: 'I know my countrymen better than you, some of them would be the first to drag me down from the office of P.M.'[231] Furthermore, the three Afrikaner recipients were from Cape Town, whereas the main support of the Bond came from the Midlands and the east. As we have seen, the Bondsmen's support for the chartered company, and for Rhodes personally, was much more deeply rooted. Smuts referred, in retrospect, to 'squaring' by Rhodes as the main reason for the Bond's support for him:

> To say that this was the result of indirect bribery and corruption is ludicrously unjust. Some Dutch members of Parliament and some influential people may have materially benefited from Rhodes's friendship; but a people cannot be bribed in the vulgar sense.[232]

Even in the case of Hofmeyr it is hard to accept that his motive in collaborating with Rhodes was primarily mercenary. His *rapprochement* with Rhodes, which had developed gradually, rested on both personal friendship and perceived common interests and outlook. In his case, the material benefit was more likely the lubricant than the engine.

It is significant that the resolution adopted by the Bond congress was proposed by T.P. Theron who had shortly before been highly critical of the charter:

> This gathering is not in a position, without further information, to pass a definite judgement on the chartered Company, and expects from the Bond members in Parliament to institute a thorough investigation and act according to their findings; and in any event, the gathering hopes that the Company will so manage its operation that Afrikaners in general will have the opportunity to take part in the exploitation of the land south of the Zambesi.

The resolution was adopted unanimously.[233] This resolution was as good as Rhodes could have hoped for. The judgement of the parliamentary caucus, which was under the influence of Hofmeyr, could only be a foregone conclusion. The position adopted by the congress seems to have had the desired effect on Bondsmen. In mid-April 1890 it was reported that I.J. van der Walt, 'one of the most respected and independent farmers in the House', who had previously criticised the government for its positive attitude towards Rhodes's company, declared in public that, after reconsidering his position, he had come to the conclusion that, if he acted against Rhodes, he would have acted against the interests of the Cape.[234]

By the end of May, as the railway line from Kimberley to Vryburg, the first tangible thrust of Rhodes's northwards push, was completed with the support of the government, the main opponents of the project became its supporters. Resignation and the pursuit of the politics of the possible were again shaping the political behaviour of Bondsmen. The reason for their change of heart was, according to the *ZA*, 'because they realize that under the circumstances it is better to work enthusiastically with the plans involving the North than either to offer resistance or to adopt an attitude of indifference'.[235] Only the *Patriot*, which had had a moment of grace before the congress, reverted to its previous opposition to the charter,[236] but not for long. By early June it joined the bandwagon, concluding that the correct approach was not to resist Rhodes's plans but rather to see to it that they benefited the Cape.[237] The victory of Cape-centricism suited Rhodes well; he had been preaching it all along.

The distance between the Bond's adoption of Rhodes's northern scheme and his assumption of the premiership, in alliance with the former, was short both logically and chronologically. The alliance with Sprigg had served the Bond well. Within the framework of their symbiotic strategy Sprigg and his government earned the Bond's support. While there was neither much love lost nor full convergence of interests between them, Sprigg was the best English-speaking premier available. For the Bond leaders, whose conception of politics was conservative and pragmatic, he was good enough. Indeed, praise for Sprigg and his government was strictly within the confines of the politics of the possible, and there was also the occasional criticism.[238] From 1888, the relationship between the government and the Bond came under increasing strain. In his policy and attitude towards the Transvaal Sprigg betrayed a lack of sensitivity to both the economic interests and the ethnic concerns of his allies. During the 1889 parliamentary session, when an English-speaking minister resigned, it was perhaps not surprising that Hofmeyr refused to fill the post. Yet the fact, that even Sivewright, 'the Afrikaner from Aberdeen', turned down the invitation to join the government was not a good omen for Sprigg. To make a bad situation worse, Sprigg filled the post with H.W. Pearson, who was not particularly liked by Bondsmen.[239] At the beginning of June 1890, on the eve of Sprigg's fall, J.A. de Wet, the Bond's only representative in the government, resigned to take up the post of political representative in Pretoria.[240] Then came Sprigg's grandiose railway scheme which served as the last nail in his political coffin.[241] In proposing his railway scheme, at the cost of more than £7 million, Sprigg exhibited a gross insensitivity to one of the major concerns of the Bond, namely *bezuiniging* (economy, retrenchment). When Rhodes rushed down from Kimberley to join forces with the Bond in opposition to the scheme Sprigg's fate was sealed.

As the *ZA* had written on a different occasion, 'the best is the enemy of the good'. In the case of Sprigg's demise, the desirable was the enemy of the possible. The desirable was, of course, Rhodes. It is not that Bondsmen became radical politicians striving for the desirable. In 1890 Rhodes was a desirable possibility, an alternative to Sprigg who began to forget to whom he owed his premiership. On most, if not all, Cape-centred issues there appeared to be full convergence of views and interests between them. Once the Bond had opted for the Rhodesian expansion, the last obstacle to an alliance between them and Rhodes had disappeared. It is not suggested that the Bond intentionally precipitated the fall of Sprigg in order to crown Rhodes in his stead. They were too cautious and pragmatic for such manipulation. But Sprigg's folly forced them to think seriously about the desirable. It is suggested, however, that had the desirable not been within easy reach, the Bond might have thought twice before bringing the railway scheme crisis to a head. On the day Sprigg resigned the *ZA* wished that the crisis had not erupted: 'The failure of the railway scheme would not have occurred if there were in the government men who knew the people. If de Wet was in the government it would not have happened.' As this statement was made in the context of the imminent resignation of the government the writer added, almost instinctively, that Rhodes was the only alternative. A coalition between Rhodes and Sprigg was considered as a first priority. This, however, was made impossible by Sprigg's opposition to Rhodes's dual position as premier and head of the chartered company.[242]

It was hardly surprising that when J.W. Sauer, the head of the opposition, was called to the governor, he recommended that the task of forming the new government be entrusted to Rhodes. Rhodes himself, according to a telegram he sent to Hofmeyr who was in Pretoria, preferred serving in a government under the latter. Alternatively, he wanted a guarantee that Hofmeyr would join his ministry. Hofmeyr replied:

> Glad you are at the head of Ministry, thanks for your kind offer. Innes knows why I can't take office. Of course, I shall support your Ministry, more particularly so long as the views, with which the names of Rhodes, Sivewright and Marais are identified, are kept in view by them.[243]

Hofmeyr, in Pretoria, was fulfilling a mission which was in line with his increasing identification with the British empire and with Rhodes. He negotiated, on behalf of the British government, the Swaziland Convention with the Transvaal government which also served Rhodes. In article 10 of the convention the Transvaal government undertook to refrain from expansion and involvement in the sphere of Rhodes's chartered company.[244] For his service he was highly praised by the high commissioner and the British secretary of state for colonies.[245] While in

Pretoria Hofmeyr also performed a private service for Rhodes, passing to him information regarding the activities of one of his arch-rivals in the north.[246] To appreciate the extent of Hofmeyr's and the Bond's commitment to the British imperial cause and to Rhodes, a Transvaal perspective on his Swaziland mission is instructive. A Pretoria newspaper commented:

> It cannot be pleasant for Mr. Hofmeyr to contemplate the handiwork of himself and that humble political organization, of which he is at the head, the Africander Bond, because though they have jointly succeeded in carrying out their vile machinations against this Republic, and in preventing any expansion of our people to the sea, they have put a nail into the coffin of their own independence, and have become nothing more nor less than the tools of British diplomatists. If there is a touch of shame left in them, they must blush for the foul work, which they have accomplished.

Kruger, giving vent to his frustration and anger, told Hofmeyr: 'You are a traitor, a traitor to the Africander cause.'[247]

Before Rhodes accepted the premiership he asked R.P. Botha, the Bond's chairman, to convene the Bond Members of Parliament. The meeting was held on 16 July in the Parliament building. According to Botha:

> he met us and presented his programme. He said that if the Bond would give him a chance he would go [to the governor] with the approval of the Bond; otherwise he would not. His government will be *Afrikaans*. The 'Native' policy will be his policy and a minister who will not go along with him will be out. He acknowledges that it is impossible to maintain a government without the Bond. Hofmeyr goes with him.[248]

The most detailed account of the meeting appeared in the *Johannesburg Star*. In addressing the caucus Rhodes said that the parliamentary proceedings over the last eight years offered a proof of his sympathy with the Bond. While mentioning his support for the abolition of excise tax on brandy, for the protection of local industries and for the development of local resources, he emphasised that 'on the most important question I am at one with the Bond'. He referred to his support for corporal punishment and for the Bond's franchise proposals. He also promised two Bond ministers in his cabinet. Responding to T.P. Theron's question regarding the contradiction between his position in the chartered company and as premier, Rhodes argued that he had saved the north for the Cape from Germany, Portugal and British humanitarian imperialism, and promised that it would be developed for the Cape and by the Cape without any cost. In promising to follow a 'genuine South African policy' and opposing 'unnecessary expenses', he exhibited great sensitivity to two main Bondsmen's concerns – their broad ethnic connection and their obsession with economic retrenchment. Rhodes exploited the latter, in particular, in cementing his alliance with the Bond: 'The entrenched interests he had in South Africa were the best guarantee that he would always co-operate with the farmers, because he knew that they, together, would have to pay for these reckless expenditures.' Rhodes asked for 'fair play' for his government, urging the caucus to judge it by its performance.[249]

According to the minutes of the meeting the following resolution, proposed by Theron, the Bond's secretary, was accepted unanimously: 'This meeting is of opinion, that Mr. Rhodes and his Government should be given "fair play" in the administration of the country and its interests.' A second resolution approved Hofmeyr as a local director of the chartered company.[250] A local board of the chartered company headed by a prominent Afrikaner was another means through which Rhodes sought to secure the Bond's support for it. He offered it to Hofmeyr after Chief Justice J.H. de Villiers had declined.[251] In the wake of the caucus meeting with Rhodes, even the *Patriot* informed its readers, on 17 July, in a spirit of resignation over its change of mind: 'Although in the last week we said that we did not see Rhodes as suitable for membership in the government, it is possible that things are different from the way we have seen them.'[252] Rhodes definitely had it all his way.

Rhodes was accepted as prime minister unanimously and unreservedly because the conditions for an alliance between Rhodes and the Bond were at their best at the beginning of the 1890s. On intra-colonial issues there seemed to be full convergence between the two allies. Rhodes appeared to have fully converted to the Bond's point of view on vital issues affecting it, like agricultural protection and 'native' policy. Rhodes also cultivated good personal relations with Bond leaders, and with Hofmeyr in particular. The relevant external conditions also appeared very congenial. The lure of the two external forces which could have pull the two partners away from the colonial common ground was at its weakest. For Rhodes, there was at that stage no incongruity between the call of the empire and his Cape-centric strategy. The days of aggressive imperial intervention which caused havoc in South Africa in the late 1870s and the first half of the 1880s seemed a thing of the past. Salisbury's Conservative government adopted a policy of indirect imperialism through Cape sub-imperialism which Rhodes advocated so ably. On the other hand, Transvaal's hostile trade policies towards the Cape weakened the pull of the call of ethnicity among Bondsmen and encouraged them to pursue a Cape-centric course which also incorporated Rhodes's northern sub-imperialism. The Bond and Rhodes were left free to exploit their colonial common ground to its fullest.

NOTES

1. Williams, *Cecil Rhodes*, p. 57.
2. Dormer, *Vengeance as Policy in Afrikanerland*, pp. 241–4.
3. Davenport, *Afrikaner Bond*, p. 62; Hofmeyr, *Hofmeyr*, p. 202.
4. Vindex, *Cecil Rhodes*, p. 218.
5. Michell, *Cecil Rhodes*, Vol. i, p. 94.
6. McCracken, *Cape Parliament*, pp. 105–9.
7 P. Lewsen (ed.), *Selections from the Correspondence of John X. Merriman* (Cape Town, 1960), Vol. i, p. 209.
8. Michell, *Cecil Rhodes*, Vol. i, p. 94.
9. B.A. Tindall (ed.), *James Rose Innes: an Autobiography* (Cape Town, London New York, 1949), p. 58. The White House was considered to be the head-quarters of the Bond.
10. Lewsen, *Selections*, Vol. i, p. 177, Merriman to Currey, 15 May 1884.
11. 'Imperialist', *Cecil Rhodes*, p. 395.
12. Fuller, *Rhodes*, p. 30.
13. Lewsen, *Selections*, Vol. i, p. 111, Merriman to Mill, 3 Aug. 1882; p. 197, Merriman to Currey, 27 April 1885.
14. Hofmeyr, *Hofmeyr*, p. 202.
15. *Cape Times* (*CT*), 23 Aug. 1892.
16. Michell, *Cecil Rhodes*, Vol. i, p. 94.
17. Vindex, *Cecil Rhodes*, p. 52.
18. *CT*, 20 July 1883.
19. J.G. McDonald, *Rhodes: a Life* (London, 1941), pp. 52–3.
20. Michell, *Cecil Rhodes*, Vol. i, p. 93.
21. Rotberg, *The Founder*, pp. 134–5.
22. Michell, *Cecil Rhodes*, Vol. i, p. 99.
23. Vindex, *Cecil Rhodes*, p. 48.
24. Michell, *Cecil Rhodes*, Vol. i, p. 151; *CT*, 8 April 1882.
25. *CT*, 14 July 1883; Vindex, *Cecil Rhodes*, pp. 44–53 and 58.
26. On this crisis see, Schreuder, *The Scramble for Southern Africa*, pp. 158–72.
27. *ZA*, 21 July 1883.
28. Rotberg, *The Founder*, pp. 154–7.
29. Vindex, *Cecil Rhodes*, pp. 64–8.
30. *CT*, 17 Aug. 1883.
31. *ZA*, 18 Aug. 1883.
32. J.A.I. Agar-Hamilton, *The Road to the North: South Africa 1852–1886* (London, New York and Toronto, 1937), p. 321.
33. Hofmeyr, *Hofmeyr*, p. 255.
34. *Hansard*, 15 July 1884, pp. 345–7.
35. *ZA*, 2 Aug. 1884.
36. *ZA*, 30 Aug. 1884.
37. *BPP*, Africa, 38, Transvaal, sessions 1884–85, p. 533, Rhodes to High Commissioner (1884).
38. Ibid., p. 763, Rhodes to Van Niekerk, 3 Dec. 1884.
39. Agar-Hamilton, *The Road to the North*, p. 336.
40. *BPP*, Africa, 44, Botswana (Bechuanaland) sessions 1883–88, p. 82.
41. *BPP*, Africa, 38, Transvaal sessions 1884–85, p. 602, Rhodes to Sir Hercules Robinson, 20 Sept. 1884.
42. Rotberg, *The Founder*, p. 166.

43. Hofmeyr, *Hofmeyr*, p. 256.
44. *ZA*, 20 and 25 Sept. 1884, 11 and 28 Oct. 1884, 6 Nov. 1884, 4 and 14 Dec. 1884.
45. *ZA*, 1 Nov. 1884.
46. Ibid., 14 Dec. 1884.
47. Ibid., 29 Jan. 1885 and 3 Feb. 1885.
48. Ibid., 19 Feb. 1885.
49. *Hansard*, 29 June 1885, pp. 270–4.
50. Ibid., 1 July 1885, p. 320.
51. Ibid., 29 June 1885, p. 271.
52. Rademeyer, *Die Land Noord van die Limpopo*, p. 153.
53. *Hansard*, 29 June 1885, p. 271.
54. Ibid., 12 June 1884, p. 169; 16 June 1884, p. 182; 19 June 1884, p. 220; 30 June 1884, p. 265; 1 July 1884, p. 274; 2 July 1884, pp. 277–9.
55. Ibid., 23 June 1884, p. 217.
56. H.M. Wright,(ed.), *Sir James Rose Innes: Selected Correspondence (1884–1905)* (Cape Town, 1972), p. 36.
57. Lewsen, *Selections*, Vol. i, p. 184, Merriman to J.B. Curry, 20 Dec. 1884.
58. Ibid., p. 188, Rhodes to Merriman, 13 Jan. 1885.
59. Ibid., p. 189, Merriman to J.B. Curry, 17 Jan. 1885.
60. Ibid., p. 196, Merriman to A. Merriman, 31 March 1885.
61. Ibid., p. 197, Merriman to J.B. Curry, 27 April 1885.
62. Ibid., p. 202, Merriman to J.B. Curry, 24 Sept. 1885.
63. *Hansard*, 23 June 1887, p. 102.
64. Ibid., 30 April 1886, p. 113.
65. Lewsen, *Selections*, Vol. i, p. 211.
66. *Hansard*, 7 May 1886, p. 165–6.
67. Ibid., 14 May 1886, pp. 221–2.
68. Vindex, *Cecil Rhodes*, pp. 137–140.
69. Ibid, pp. 141–4.
70. *Hansard*, 15 June 1886, pp. 399–400.
71. Lewsen, *Selections*, Vol. i, p. 205, Merriman to A. Merriman, 16 Jan. 1886.
72. J. van Huysteen, 'The Non-European Franchise, 1872–1892', (MA thesis, University of Cape Town, 1952), pp. 52–3.
73. *Hansard*, 27 June 1887, pp. 115–8.
74. Ibid., 23 June 1887, pp. 101–4.
75. *Hansard*, 20 May 1886, p. 265.
76. Vindex, *Cecil Rhodes*, pp. 139–140; Rhodes was referring to the Transvaal delegation which had solicited help in the Cape during the 1881–2 crisis.
77. *Hansard*, 22 June 1887, pp. 88–9.
78. Ibid., 23 June 1887, p. 105.
79. Lewsen, *Selections*, p. 209, Merriman to Curry, 24 March 1886.
80. Ibid., p. 217, Merriman to Curry, 8 July 1886.
81. *ZA*, 13 May 1886.
82. Ibid., 15 May 1886.
83. Hofmeyr, *Hofmeyr*, p. 281.
84. A. Joelson, *The Memoirs of Kohler of the K.W.V* (London, 1946), pp. 48–9.
85. *ZA*, 22 May 1886, 3 March 1887, 17 March 1887.
86. Ibid., 2 July 1887.
87. Ibid., 9 July 1887.
88. Ibid., 1 Oct. 1887.
89. Ibid., 29 June 1886.

90. Ibid., 30 Nov. 1886.
91. Ibid., 7 Dec. 1886.
92. Vindex, *Cecil Rhodes*, p. 138.
93. *ZA*, 31 Aug. 1886.
94. Ibid., 9 July 1887.
95. Mabin, 'The making of colonial capitalism', p. 220.
96. Ibid., pp. 221–8.
97. Ibid., p. 215.
98. Ibid., pp. 229–38.
99. Scholtz, 'Ds. S.J. du Toit as kerkman en kultuurleier', p. 184.
100. T. Vienings, 'Stratification and proletarianization: the rural political economy of the Worcester District, 1875–1910', (BA Honours thesis, University of Cape Town, 1986), p. 23.
101. *Hansard*, 20 May 1886, pp. 260–6.
102. *ZA*, 31 Aug. 1886.
103. Ibid., 30 Sept. 1886.
104. Ibid., 25 and 28 Sept. 1886, 14 and 28 Oct. 1886.
105. Ibid., 23 and 26 Oct. 1886.
106. Ibid., 18 Jan. 1887.
107. Ibid., 22 Jan. 1887.
108. Ibid., 25 Jan. 1887.
109. Ibid., 18 and 25 Jan. 1887.
110. Fraser, *Episodes in my Life*, pp. 82–127 and 134–42.
111. Van der Poel, *Railway and Customs Policy*, pp. 28–9.
112. *ZA*, 22 Jan. 1887.
113. Ibid., 3 Feb. 1887.
114. Ibid., 19 and 22 March 1887, 26 and 28 April 1887.
115. Ibid., 6 Aug. 1887.
116. *Patriot*, 4 Nov. 1887.
117. *ZA*, 20 Dec. 1887.
118. Ibid., 3 Feb. 1887, 6 and 9 Aug. 1887, 1, 10, 15 and 24 Nov. 1887 and 8 Dec. 1887; *Patriot*, 16 Sept. 1887.
119. Ibid., 16 Sept. 1887; see also 6 May 1887 and 26 Aug. 1887; *Paarl*, 17 Aug 1887 and 3 Sept. 1887.
120. Ibid., 14 Sept. 1887; *Patriot*, 1 April 1887.
121. *ZA*, 15 Sept. 1887.
122. Ibid., 6 Aug. 1887.
123. Ibid., 24 Dec. 1887.
124. Van der Poel, *Railway and Customs Policy*, p. 33.
125. *Hansard*, 18 July 1888, pp. 302–3 and 310–11 and 23 July 1888, pp. 329–41; van der Poel, *Railway and Customs Policy*, pp. 38–9.
126. Ibid., pp. 40–1.
127. *ZA*, 2 Feb. 1889.
128. Ibid., 13 Dec. 1888.
129. Ibid., 27 Feb. 1888, 19 April 1888 and 30 Aug. 1888.
130. See for example, ibid., 28 Jan. 1888, 7 Feb. 1888, 26 April 1888, 5 June 1888, 28 July 1888, 18 and 28 Aug. 1888, 25 Oct. 1888, 25 Dec. 1888 and 8 Jan. 1889.
131. Rotberg, *The Founder*, pp. 248–9.
132. *ZA*, 9 June 1888 and 7 Aug. 1888.
133. Ibid., 10 March 1888; see also 26 April 1888.
134. Ibid., 23 June 1888 and 28 July 1888.

135. Ibid., 10 May 1888.
136. Ibid., 1 May 1888.
137. Ibid., 16 Aug. 1888.
138. Ibid., 10 May 1888; see also 26 April 1888.
139. Ibid., 27 Sept. 1888.
140. Ibid., 27 Sept. 1888.
141. Ibid., 15 Sept. 1888, 9 Oct. 1888.
142. Ibid., 9 Oct. 1888.
143. Ibid., 17 Nov. 1888.
144. Ibid., 25 Oct. 1888.
145. On the clash between mining and mercantile interests see W.H. Worger, 'The making of monopoly: Kimberley and the South African diamond industry, 1870–1895' (PhD thesis, Yale University, 1982), pp. 236–310.
146. Ibid., pp. 262–4.
147. Ibid., pp. 259–61.
148. Ibid., pp. 268–75.
149. *Hansard*, 29 June 1887, pp. 126–30.
150. Ibid., 29 June 1887, pp. 127–8.
151. Ibid., 12 June 1888, pp. 84–90.
152. Ibid., 23 July 1888, pp. 337–8.
153. *ZA*, 12 July 1888.
154. Ibid., 26 July 1888.
155. Ibid., 4 Aug. 1888.
156. Ibid., 25 Aug. 1888.
157. Ibid., 23 Aug. 1888.
158. Ibid., 4 Sept. 1888.
159. Ibid., 2 Oct. 1888.
160. Ibid., 3 Nov. 1888.
161. Ibid., 27 Nov. 1888.
162. Hofmeyr, *Hofmeyr*, pp. 314–15.
163. *ZA*, 4 Oct. 1888.
164. Ibid., 7, 11, 21 and 23 Aug. 1888.
165. Ibid., 2 Oct. 1888.
166. Ibid., 23 Aug. 1888.
167. Ibid., 3 Nov. 1888.
168. Rhodes Papers, Mss. Afr. C26, No.23, D.C. de Waal to Rhodes, 12 Oct. 1888. He must have been referring to Rhodes's election speech on 28 September 1888, in which he unravelled the full extent of his regional plans; see Vindex, *Cecil Rhodes*, pp. 208–226.
169. Rhodes Papers, Mss. Afr. C26, No.24, Sivewright to Rhodes, [c. October 1888].
170. Ibid., No.7, Hofmeyr to Rhodes, 3 Oct. 1888.
171. *ZA*, 5 Jan. 1888.
172. Ibid., 27 Nov. 1888; the concession obtained by Rudd from Lobengula gave Rhodes exclusive right to prospect for minerals. It was interpreted by Rhodes as giving him the right to rule and settle future Rhodesia.
173. Ibid., 1 Dec. 1888.
174. Ibid., 9 April 1889.
175. Ibid., 4 April 1889; see also 9 Feb. 1889 and 14 March 1889.
176. Ibid., 16 March 1889.
177. Ibid., 22 June 1889.
178. Ibid., 14 May 1889.

179. Ibid., 11 May 1889; see also 15 and 18 June 1889.
180. Hofmeyr Papers, Reitz to Hofmeyr, 27 April 1889; Hofmeyr to Reitz, 28 April 1889; Hofmeyr, *Hofmeyr*, p. 355.
181. Ibid., pp. 355–7.
182. *ZA*, 27 June 1889; see also 2 and 13 July 1889.
183. Ibid., 30 July 1889.
184. Davenport, *Afrikaner Bond*, p. 128; *ZA*, 1 Aug. 1889.
185. Ibid., 8 Aug. 1889.
186. Ibid., 13 Aug. 1889.
187. Ibid., 22 Aug. 1889.
188. Ibid., 24. Aug. 1889; see also 10 Sept. 1889.
189. Ibid., 29 Aug. 1889 and 10 Sept. 1889.
190. Ibid., 10 Sept. 1889.
191. Ibid., 19 Sept. 1889.
192. Ibid., 10 Sept. 1889.
193. Hofmeyr, *Hofmeyr*, p. 384.
194. Hofmeyr Papers, Rhodes to Hofmeyr, 20 Sept. 1889; the main thrust of Hofmeyr's reply was inscribed on Rhodes's letter.
195. Rotberg, *The Founder*, p. 285; Davenport, *Afrikaner Bond*, p. 129.
196. *ZA*, 24 Sept. 1889.
197. Ibid., 17 and 31 Oct. 1889.
198. Ibid., 2 and 5 Nov. 1889.
199. Ibid., 12, 14, 23 and 30 Nov. 1889, 19 and 24 Dec. 1889, 9 and 18 Jan. 1890 and 6 March 1890.
200. Ibid., 14 Nov. 1889.
201. Ibid., 23 Jan. 1890.
202. Ibid., 23 Nov. 1889.
203. Ibid., 26 Nov. 1889.
204. *Patriot*, 2, 14 and 28 Nov. 1889; *ZA*, 26 Nov. 1889, 18 Jan. 1890, 8 Feb. 1890; *CA*, 13 Sept. 1889 and 23 Nov. 1889.
205. *ZA*, 26 Nov. 1889.
206. Ibid., 19 Dec. 1889.
207. Ibid., 26 Nov. 1889.
208. Ibid., 24 Dec. 1889.
209. *Patriot*, 6 March 1890.
210. Hofmeyr, *Hofmeyr*, p. 384.
211. *Hansard*, 1 Sept. 1889, p. 416.
212. *ZA*, 6 March 1890.
213. *Patriot*, 21 Nov. 1889.
214. *ZA*, 8 Feb. 1890.
215. *CT*, 7 March 1890.
216. *ZA*, 13 March 1890.
217. Ibid., 18 March 1890.
218. Hofmeyr, *Hofmeyr*, p. 383.
219. *ZA*, 22 March 1890.
220. *Graaff Reinetter (GR)*, 23 March 1896.
221. *ZA*, 22 March 1890.
222. British South Africa Company Papers, Vol. i, 1888–1890, No. 205, Rhodes to Cawston, 4 Dec. 1889.
223. Michell, *Rhodes*, Vol. i, p. 276.
224. Wright, *Innes, Selected Correspondence*, Innes to Rhodes, 14 Feb. 1890.

225. Davenport, *Afrikaner Bond*, p. 356.
226. Tindall, *Innes*, p. 87.
227. Hofmeyr Papers, 16C, J.H. Hofmeyr to Harris, 5 Nov. 1890.
228. Rhodes Papers, C/A, Second list of allotments in South Africa, 8 Dec. 1890.
229. Tindall, *Innes*, p. 87.
230. Rhodes Papers, Afr. t.5, Rhodes to D.C. de Waal, 8 Feb. 1889.
231. Molteno, *The Dominion of Afrikanerdom*, p. 27.
232. Hancock and van der Poel, *Selection from Jan Smuts Papers*, Vol. i, p. 173.
233. *ZA*, 22 March 1890.
234. Ibid., 15 April 1890.
235. Ibid., 29 May 1890.
236. Ibid., 6 May 1890.
237. Ibid., 7 June 1890.
238. See, for example, ibid., 15 Jan. 1887, 14 June 1887, 18 and 27 Sept. 1888, 2 and 16 Oct. 1888 and 18 June 1889.
239. Hofmeyr, *Hofmeyr*, pp. 386–7.
240. *ZA*, 3 June 1890.
241. Vanstone, 'Sprigg', pp. 290–6.
242. *ZA*, 10 July 1890.
243. Hofmeyr, *Hofmeyr*, pp. 388–9.
244. *BPP*, C.6217, South Africa, A convention between Her Majesty and the South African Republic for the settlement of the affairs of Swaziland, 1890, p. 8.
245. Hofmeyr Papers, 7/C, government publications–affairs of Swaziland, Loch to Lord Knutsford, received 1 Sept. 1890, p. 16; G. Bower to Hofmeyr, 28 Nov. 1890.
246. Rhodes Papers, Mss. Afr. CA/7, Secretary to Imperial secretary, Cape Town, 12 July 1890. Hofmeyr asked that a letter he had received from Lippert be shown to Rhodes.
247. Hofmeyr, *Hofmeyr*, pp. 405–6.
248. Te Water Papers, R.P. Botha to Te Water, 14 July 1890.
249. Quoted by the *GR*, 2 June 1892.
250. Hofmeyr, *Hofmeyr*, p. 388.
251. Williams, *Cecil Rhodes*, p. 141; the plan to form a local board did not materialise.
252. *Patriot*, 17 July 1890.

3

The marriage, 1890–95

Rhodes's assumption of the premiership of the Cape Colony in mid-July 1890 was the culmination of long political courting by him, which had been eliciting an increasingly enthusiastic response from the Afrikaner Bond. As we have seen, the political *rapprochement* between Rhodes and the Bond was premised on perceived convergence of outlook and interests. It was enhanced by personal relationships, particularly between Rhodes and Hofmeyr, which were also lubricated by material benefits, actual and/or expected. It had the makings of at least a stable and solid political marriage. For Rhodes, the cultivation of the Bond's support for his government was very important. His pious protestations notwithstanding, Rhodes was not a reluctant prime minister. As his southern African project was nearing consummation, a firm control of his Cape political power base was vital. The Bond's attitude toward Rhodes's premiership was symmetrical. For the first time they had a prime minister who appeared to share not only their interests and vision, but also their prejudices.

The dramatic way in which the marriage broke up, in the wake of the Jameson raid, did not reflect on its soundness. There was nothing in the apparent bilateral relations between the two which could either explain or justify the raid. There was no indication that the betrayed Bond either suspected or expected such an act of perfidious transgression on the part of their admired ally. At the level of public knowledge there was nothing in Rhodes's behaviour which could have portended it. Yet the end of the alliance was not incongruent with its deep undercurrents. The full convergence of interests and outlook was only in the realm of perception or illusion.

Underneath the solid crust of the alliance there was a threatening gulf between the Cape-centricism of the Bond and the aggressive imperialism of Rhodes. Only the Cape-centric disguise of Rhodes's imperial vision lured the Bond into the alliance. For Rhodes, however, the alliance was essentially worth maintaining only as long as it was instrumental to the implementation of this vision. To the extent that this involved not only expansion to the north, but also the coercion of the Boer republics into the British empire, it was anathema to the Bond. It was so, not only because it went much beyond its Cape-centric conception, but also because it represented a serious infringement of an ethnic taboo.

On the surface the alliance was stable and the Rhodes government enjoyed the firm support of the Bond leadership and MPs. Yet the political space carved out by the alliance was not a happy political valley for the Bond. On the contrary, it was a highly contested territory, the supporters of the alliance being constantly challenged and condemned. This reflected the tension between the inherent contradiction between the two parties and the illusion of convergence. It was exacerbated by the nature of the Bond as a political party.

The Bond was a relative novice on the political scene, resting on a social base whose political consciousness and experience were of recent origin. Contrary to Rhodes's early impression, and to the views of other English contemporaries,[1] it was not a cohesive, effective political party. Political parties, in the modern sense, were non-existent in the nineteenth century Cape. During the election campaign of 1888 Hofmeyr complained:

> There is too much narrow localism and personal feeling in the Afrikaner ranks ... I now only advise my friends to vote for men with good sound Africander views and independent of feeling who will not pin their faith to either opposition or ministry, but judge for themselves.[2]

The constitution adopted by the following Bond congress in 1889 tried to deal with this state of affairs by instituting the Commissie van Toetzicht op Eleksie (Election Supervision Committee) to control the process of selecting parliamentary election candidates.[3] However, as the election campaign of 1894 showed, the committee's attempt to exert influence only highlighted the inherent weakness of the Bond. It lacked a permanent, effective central organisation and had little control over its branches. Hofmeyr, the undisputed leader of the party, did not even hold a formal position in the party organisation.

The only functioning central institution, with the exception of the Commissie, was the annual congress which conveyed its resolutions to the party's MPs as directives. As we have seen, on the important issue of the charter, the 1890 congress entrusted the caucus with the final decision. Indeed, the parliamentary session was the only occasion when prominent Bond leaders from all over the Colony were assembled together for any length of time. Even Parliament, however, was in session only for a period of some two to three months in a year. Furthermore, the political clout of the Bond in Parliament did not rest on a large tightly controlled caucus. In March 1892, *Ons Land* (*OL*), the new Bond's mouthpiece, gave a clue as to the source of power of the party. It claimed that only 19 of the 76 members of the legislative assembly were full Bond members

135

subjected to its discipline. The Bond's influence was exerted through the informal Afrikaander Nationale Partij, which included, in addition to the above, seven who were Bond members but had not been elected by it, and 11 who were neither Bond members nor elected by it, but who, on most issues, agreed with it and voted with it (among whom Rhodes was also listed). The success of 'Afrikanderisme' rested on the Bond's patience and its knowledge 'how to operate'.[4] In other words, the Bond's influence rested on constant bargaining rather than on a compact, regimented caucus and party discipline. In fact, a close scrutiny of voting patterns in Parliament reveals that not only members of the 'Afrikaner National Party', but also Bond members, were often guided by constituency interests or personal preference and outlook, rather than by party directives and discipline.[5]

When the Bond entered into formal alliance with Rhodes, it was still in a state of flux, not only organisationally but also ideologically. As we have seen, the Bond evolved a pragmatic, conservative, Cape-centric political outlook which reflected the colonial experience of the Afrikaner land-owning farming community which formed its social base. Such an outlook could flourish under conditions of Cape isolationism. However, the cosy colonial world which gave rise to this outlook began to disappear as soon as the Bond came into being. The British annexation of the Transvaal in 1877, the German occupation of South West Africa in 1884 which signalled the beginning of the scramble for southern Africa and the discovery of gold in the Rand in 1886 considerably broadened the economic and political horizons of the Cape. Indeed, Cape politics during the formative years of the Bond were engulfed by violent movements of international diplomacy, power and capital in the Cape's hinterland. The parochial colonial environment which shaped the Bond's dominant political outlook hardly prepared Bondsmen to deal with their new world.

The turbulent winds of change blew violently on the young, fragile plants in the Cape Afrikaners' political, ideological garden. Conventional wisdoms, ideological premises and political strategies were constantly challenged and contested by recurring crises and old and new actors. As we have seen, the impact of the changed environment, during the 1880s, tended to reinforce the existing world outlook of the Bond. Ideological and political harmony was preserved and contradictions contained, partly because the Bond, while supporting the government, kept a safe distance from it, and partly because critical choices had yet to be made. During 1889–90, in its support for the chartered company and its alliance with Rhodes, the Bond came much closer to both critical choices and intimate association with the government. Rhodes was not merely a product of the new forces which radically changed the southern African environment; he was their sharp edge. As we have seen, the Bond was attracted to Rhodes because he was perceived as the one who would enable Cape Afrikaners to maintain their cosy, imagined ideological and political harmony in a fast changing world. They failed to grasp the sharp contradiction between their world outlook and interests and his, that between the pursuit of immediate interests, and the politics of the possible, and the quest for visionary goals. Rhodes intended to carry the Afrikaners with him beyond the frontiers of the possible; by instinct and temperament their desire was to stay well within their confines. Fuller recalled a conversation between Hofmeyr and Rhodes in the early 1890s: 'You have got hold of the interior, now be generous. Let us down gently.' Rhodes's reply was portentous: 'I will not let you down, I will take you with me.'[6]

It is hardly surprising, then, that the stable political marriage between the Bond and Rhodes was not as peaceful and uneventful as the average conservative, pragmatic Bondsman would have wished. Inhabiting, through their alliance with Rhodes, the frontier between the possible and the desirable, they were constantly involved in ideological and political skirmishes. This frontier, unlike a geopolitical one, was not on the periphery of the Cape Afrikaner territory; it ran through the heart of their domain. Rhodes, far from exercising a harmonising effect on Cape Afrikaners, exacerbated their divisions and their internal debate. In fact, the relations with Rhodes were at the centre of an intensifying contestation on the essence of 'Afrikanerdom'. This was so not simply because Rhodes dragged the Bond to the habitually contentious frontier zone. Perhaps not less importantly, it was so also because, through its intimate association with Rhodes, the Bond came much closer to effective political power and responsibility. The Bond, as a manifestation of Cape Afrikaner political assertion, strove to shape the Cape in accordance with their interests, perceptions and goals. Because between the Bond and previous prime ministers there was only partial convergence of interests and political outlook, it could only expect partial improvement. With Rhodes it was different. At the time the Bond struck the alliance with him, he was perceived by it, not only as a leader, but as a virtual Moses who could turn the Cape and the broader southern African environment into a promised land. For the first time, through its association with Rhodes, there emerged the possibility, the expectation, or at least the hope, of constructing an ideal Afrikaner order in the Cape and beyond. This prospect tended to sharpen the internal debate, and to push for a constant evaluation of the alliance and its balance sheet.

The essence of the prospective order was the focus of an unfolding discourse. In fact, under the umbrella of an Afrikaner order, a variety of orders were at the centre of this discourse. There was the economic order related to the material needs of Cape Afrikaner farmers; there was the Cape colonial political order; there was the ethnic pan-Afrikaner order; there was the South African and the broader southern African order; and there was, finally, the imperial order. All these particular orders were interrelated and intertwined to produce an overall appropriate Afrikaner order. The appropriateness of this order was premised not only on the satisfaction of immediate material and other interests. Above all it was underpinned by an assumed appropriate moral order. This discourse, stimulated by the alliance between the Bond and Rhodes, was not restricted to the confines of this party. In fact, its intensity was partly the result of frequent and challenging inputs from external actors. There were inputs from non-Bond Cape Afrikaners, from non-Afrikaner Cape colonists, from non-Cape Afrikaners and from imperial quarters. Rhodes, himself, was not merely the object and focus of this discourse; he was also a very active contributor thereto.

The balance of the discourse was critical to the prospect of the alliance. From a Bond perspective, the alliance was sustainable as long as it was perceived as contributing to an appropriate Afrikaner order. Rhodes, on his part, had constantly to prove his usefulness. This introduced to the relations between Rhodes and the Bond an underlying tension. The Bond had to legitimise Rhodes's imperialist thrusts in terms of Cape Afrikaner interests, while Rhodes had to disguise his imperial designs under the veil of 'colonialism'. The tension was exacerbated by the Bond's need to justify Rhodes's extra-Cape pursuits in terms of broad ethnic interests, and by Rhodes's need to satisfy colonial as well as imperial metropolitan constituencies. The purpose of this chapter is not only to analyse the discourse and to uncover the overt and underlying tensions, but also to account for the resilience of the alliance right through to the Jameson raid.

RHODES'S FIRST MINISTRY

Rhodes did not enjoy even a week of grace. Immediately after the government was sworn in, an English-speaking member moved in Parliament that it was undesirable that Rhodes should maintain his dual position as prime minister and the head of the chartered company. In elaborating on his motion, J. Laing clearly tried to drive a wedge between Rhodes and the Bond:

> it is well known that the interests of the Chartered Company are Imperial interests and consequently their objects are Imperial objects, as, on the other hand, the objects of this colony are strictly the interests of South Africa.[7]

138

In defending his dual position, Rhodes clearly addressed almost exclusively the Bond gallery, taking special care to establish his colonial credentials. To make a dual position triple he reminded MPs that 'I represent a company [de Beers] whose wealth is equal to a quarter of that of the whole of the Cape Colony, and which is situated in and under the government of the Cape colony'. He described his northern expansion as a pure Cape project: 'I have interfered in the interior because I wished the movement to be conducted as an expansion of the Cape Colony ... I have worked with the idea that eventually the country right up to the Zambesi should also belong to the Cape Colony.' He presented the north as his free gift to the Cape, and emphasised his choice of 'Colonists' as the colonisers of the north 'because I thought they were most fitted to open up a new country'.[8]

Rhodes chose his words carefully so as to influence Bondsmen. He must have been pleased with the support he received from A.S le Roex and D.C. de Waal who hailed Rhodes as a champion of an appropriate South African order. The former said: 'There was no better man to promote the union of South Africa than the Premier, and he was now in the best position to work for that union. In England people were afraid that the Premier would work for the interests of South Africa.' He probably was less pleased with the contribution of two other prominent Bondsmen. I.J. van der Walt was prepared to give Rhodes a chance but 'doubted whether the Premier had the time to attend to all these different duties'. More perturbing was the short speech by T.P. Theron who supported, in essence, Laing's motion, arguing that 'not a shilling of the Chartered Company would be invested in the Colony without the Colony having to repay it ultimately'. He stated categorically: 'The great point was that no one could serve two masters. Money was the object of the company, and there might occur circumstances in which the interests of the Colony and the company might clash.'[9] Laing's motion was rejected by a large majority.

Rhodes and his north were again a subject of debate in Parliament a week later, when the allocation of money for the construction of the railway from Kimberley northwards on the basis of the agreement reached between Rhodes and Sprigg in 1889 was discussed. This debate also highlighted the tension among Afrikaner MPs between their instinctive parish pump inclinations and the dramatic movement northwards into which they were drawn by Rhodes. J.S. Marais from Paarl was not impressed by the argument that the railway line would give the Colony access to the north. He saw no value in the north 'unless some great riches were discovered beyond what he saw when he went over the land', implicitly objecting to the Cape paying for Rhodes's fancy. I.J. van der Walt, who doubted the profitability of the line and declared his intention to vote against the motion, argued for the traditional Afrikaner way of doing things: 'A country should first be cultivated before a railway was built.' B.J. Keyter, a member of the 'Afrikaner National Party', claimed that 'on principle he could not vote for this line'. His 'principle' epitomised the Cape-centric, parochial inclination of Afrikaner politics: 'A Government was not appointed to work outside the colony.' He complained about building railway lines outside the colony when 'within this colony there was a loud cry for railways, and they could not get them ... He would like them to compare Oudtshoorn with Vryburg [in Bechuanaland].' Oudtshoorn, needless to say, was his own constituency. He actually stated that the government deserved to fall on this issue. Even A.S. le Roex, who had strongly supported Rhodes on the previous motion, 'did not approve of this large expense having been incurred without the consent of parliament'.[10]

Clearly, the Bond could not be taken for granted, and more courting was required. This may have motivated Rhodes in voting for the Masters and Servants Amendment Bill (the Strop Bill) which allowed the flogging of black servants. Implicit in his support was a bargain – support of the Bond for his imperial expansion in exchange for his support for an appropriate Afrikaner order in the Cape. Rhodes and Sivewright, his Bondsman friend, were the only Englishmen who supported the amendment. Significantly, even a few Bondsmen voted against the motion, contributing to its defeat.[11] Shortly after the end of the session Rhodes had another opportunity to fertilise his Afrikaner field. Addressing a banquet in his honour in Kimberley, he justified his understanding with the Bond, saying that he thought that 'if more pains were taken to explain matters to the members of the Bond Party many of the cobwebs would be swept away and a much better understanding would exist between the different parties than at present'. He postulated a vision of South Africa corresponding to the Bond's perception of an appropriate South African order – a settlement of the Swaziland question to the satisfaction of the Transvaal, the promotion of economic co-operation, and progress towards South African unity without forcing the British flag on the reluctant republics.[12] It is possible that the large transaction in charter shares in October 1890, in which Hofmeyr was involved,[13] was intended as additional lubrication. Rhodes was probably similarly motivated in taking two Afrikaner Bond MPs, D.C. de Waal and M.M. Venter, along with him on his first visit to Mashonaland in 1890.[14]

If Rhodes wished his Kimberley speech to make a favourable impression on Afrikaner opinion he could derive satisfaction from the positive response in the Dutch press.[15] Indeed, much of the Cape Afrikaner discourse focusing on the alliance between Rhodes and the Bond took place in the Dutch and Afrikaans press. Unlike the short parliamentary session, the newspapers were a permanent arena for public debate. At first, the response of the Afrikaner press to Rhodes's premiership was hesitant and reserved. The *BG* advised caution with reference to reports that Rhodes would subject the interests of the Cape to his chartered company.[16] The *GR*, before the formation of the new government, wished that Sprigg would maintain his position and predicted that a government headed by Rhodes would not last long.[17] The *Volksbode*, representing sections of the DRC, which was at loggerheads with the Bond over 'native' policy, pointed out that Rhodes could either bring the Cape glory, or drive her to her grave.[18] The *ZA* thought that, because of Rhodes's dual position, the best way out of the government crisis was a temporary Rhodes government, and a speedy handover of the premiership to Sprigg.[19] The newspaper also published a letter to the editor urging the resumption of office by Sprigg.[20] *Patriot*, too, while committing itself to 'fair play', published a letter criticizing Rhodes and his government, and threatened the Bond leaders with the defection of their followers.[21]

Soon, however, the muses began to sing Rhodes's praise. Supporting Rhodes's dual position, the *BG* predicted that if Rhodes succeeded as premier, as he had as the head of the chartered company, the country would 'never regret the assumption of power by this government'.[22] Similarly, judging by the energetic way in which Rhodes had pursued his different undertakings, the *GR* expected that the next parliamentary session would be 'one of the most important' that the Cape had ever experienced.[23] The *BG* commended Rhodes mainly for promoting an appropriate South African order, namely unity with the republics, which was, of course, also an important component of a favourable economic order for the Cape.[24] It was, however, the development of a new regional order in the north that earned Rhodes the greatest credit. The verdict of the *GR* was that Rhodes was doing a lot of good for the Afrikaners by his work in the north.[25] The *Volksbode* asserted that the opening of the road to the north was more important for the future of South Africa than the diamond mines of Kimberley or the gold mines in the Transvaal. Rhodes was also hailed for his ability to exert influence in the international arena for the protection of the Afrikaner regional interests against foreign encroachment.[26]

The *ZA*, which was closely associated with Hofmeyr, presented Rhodes's project in the north as the centre-piece of a glorious Afrikaner order. To begin with, the north was a solution to the dire economic problems in the Cape. The arrival of the Pioneers Column at its destination was a cause for special joy. Referring to the collapse of two Cape banks, which caused confusion in the Cape economy, the *ZA* sought consolation in the exploitation of the new riches in the north which 'would overcome the difficulties in the not distant future'.[27] With a view to securing a market for Cape wines, the ZA suggested sending to the north a DRC predikant who would not object to the consumption of liquor.[28] Equally important was the fact that the north was perceived as a new frontier of settlement for the increasing number of land-hungry Cape Afrikaner farmers. The ZA reported a *treklust* [trek drive], especially among the stock farmers in the northern regions of the Cape. Mashonaland was presented as an ideal settlement zone, and preferable to other settlement opportunities like Bechuanaland and Great Namaqualand. It possessed two vital ingredients, namely fertile land and ample markets among the miners. The Afrikaner farmers would be a third ingredient, contributing to the development of the north.[29]

Furthermore, because of Rhodes, Mashonaland had the makings of an ideal colony. Its future seemed bright because Rhodes was expected to provide the fourth essential component for ideal colonisation: 'Rhodes and his advisers must know that when there is a crop there is a need for workers.'[30] Rhodes, it was believed, had the right approach to the labour problem:

> Rhodes does not see any blessing in uplifting the Natives beyond what they should be, namely, a race of workers and servants ... It is a disastrous policy to allow the Natives land rights ... In the Cape we believe, justifiably, that Rhodes upholds these views.[31]

Indeed, the provision of labour in Mashonaland was expected to be better than that in either the Cape or the Transvaal.[32]

Rhodes was perceived, more broadly, as a promoter of appropriate race relations: 'this is another experiment, a very important experiment, how in the ... highlands suitable for European colonization ... appropriate relations between races are obtained'.[33] From this perspective, this experiment was elevated to an Afrikaner version of the civilising mission. Responding to an allegation that the cause of civilisation was not being advanced in Mashonaland, the ZA put forward a counter argument:

> Here we see it differently ... we expect to see there a settlement under which English and Dutch Afrikaner settlers, as well as the Natives, will be given their appropriate place, and so they will show the world what can be made of a country where an appropriate distinction between superiors and inferiors is maintained.[34]

The north was promoted not merely as an ideal European settlement, an Eldorado cum Utopia; it was also seen as the foundation stone for a more appropriate Afrikaner regional order. In the first place, Rhodes was an agent of a South African, rather than an imperial order. The chartered company was perceived to have an interest in the exclusion of

British imperialism, as much as anybody else in South Africa.[35] Rhodes saved the north from the influence of the dangerous combination of Chamberlain and Mackenzie, from the 'follies perpetrated under the British flag'.[36] He was a bulwark against those in England who dreamed of Mashonaland as a strictly British settlement country which would, in turn, control the rest of South Africa.[37] Beyond that he was hailed as the agent of the Bond in its forward policy of expanding and consolidating the power of the settlers.[38] Cape colonists were urged to settle in Mashonaland to facilitate its transformation into a genuine settlers' colony to be joined with the Cape.[39]

Beyond that, the settlement of Mashonaland was presented as a South African project: 'What Rhodes says has a genuine South African flavour. For whom does he want to develop the country? For his fellow South African citizens without regard to the country they belong.'[40] Indeed, for the *ZA*, 'an alliance, between Rhodes's Company and not only the Afrikaner party, but also the Republics, seems very natural.'[41] Referring to the north, it saw the prospect 'not only of gaining riches, not only of the rise of the Colony of which we are citizens ... but also of approaching a solution of the great problems of our region.' The establishment of the ideal settler state in the north was perceived as a launching pad for the construction of an ideal Afrikaner South African order with Britain being forced to submit to the wishes of the colonists.[42]

Little wonder that Cape Afrikaners, borrowing from the historical myths of their republican brothers, depicted Rhodes's pioneers as *Voortrekkers*. Little wonder that, inspired by love for the Old Testament, the *ZA* became carried away: 'As Canaan was for the Israelites so the interior is the inheritance of the Afrikaner farmers.'[43] Little wonder that Rhodes was depicted as Moses leading the Afrikaners to the promised land.[44] Cape sub-imperialism acquired a comprehensive legitimising ideology, inspired by immediate economic interests, by the requisites of a South African order and by a vision of an Afrikaner moral (or, in some respects at least, immoral) order.

The conversion of S.J. du Toit

By the end of 1890, the *Patriot* from Paarl, the capital of 'Afrikanerdom', edited by D.F. du Toit ('Oom Lokomotief') had not joined Rhodes's bandwagon. While granting Rhodes 'fair play', it remained sceptical about his exploits in the north. This attitude was manifested in a leader article entitled 'the new Land of Canaan'.[45] The Du Toit brothers also published a Dutch newspaper, *De Paarl*. Having the Mecca of 'Afrikanerdom' as a focus of opposition could have proved embarrassing to Rhodes. However, by April 1891, when S.J. du Toit, back from some eight years in the

Transvaal, took over the editorship of both newspapers, the horizons of Paarl brightened up for Rhodes, the town and its press becoming his staunch supporters. This volte-face, by the father of 'Afrikaner nationalism' and Afrikaner cultural revival, is a fascinating episode in the evolution of Cape Afrikaner politics which still awaits a conclusive account and interpretation. Claims that he was 'squared' by Rhodes seem to be corroborated by his dire economic position, his speculations in the Transvaal having come to an end in a scandalous bankruptcy. At the end of 1891 there were accusations that Rhodes gave him 6,000 chartered company shares.[46] However, there is no evidence in the Rhodes Papers of such transaction. His son and biographer denied that his father ever received money from Rhodes, invoking the family's poverty in support of his claim.[47] In 1906 S.J. du Toit himself denied that Rhodes ever tried to exert influence on his opinion and his writing.[48]

In the absence of clear evidence of sordid motives, one has to look elsewhere for an explanation. It is very likely that at the root of his change of political course lay his disappointing financial, as well as political, experience in the Transvaal. The reality of the Transvaal was not as heroic and glamorous as the romantic ethno-cultural nationalist, in the wake of the anti-imperialist war of liberation, had expected. The lure of material wealth, in the wake of the gold discovery, proved so strong that even the idealist Du Toit succumbed to the temptation of the glittering metal. In addition, the monopolistic, corrupt practices of the Transvaal bureaucracy, his confrontation with the 'Hollander kliek' which surrounded Kruger, and his volatile relations with the latter, dimmed the aura of Afrikaner republicanism in the eyes of the nationalist dreamer from Paarl.

It seems that these experiences, coupled with his economic misfortunes, precipitated a process of ideological, and subsequently physical, withdrawal back to his Cape political womb. As early as 1888, in view of Kruger's antagonistic economic policies against the Cape, S.J. du Toit manifested a clear anti-Kruger attitude. In August 1888, he wrote to Hofmeyr:

> You really must believe me, we are not doing this out of a desire to be awkward. But until the neck of Kruger's policy is broken all your beautiful plans are so many soap bubbles. Sprigg's policy will undermine Kruger's; but the policy now followed among our people gives Kruger and his Hollanders a dictatorship not only over the Transvaal but over the whole of South Africa.[49]

In April 1890, while on a visit in Europe, and intending to return to the Transvaal to take up a government appointment, Du Toit gave an interview to the *Pall Mall Gazette* in which he claimed that his original goal of 'united South Africa under its own flag' had been merely a slogan designed to enthuse the Bond upon its establishment. He also predicted that within a few years Transvaal would have an English-speaking president.[50] In his book *Afrika het Land van de Toekomst*, published in 1890, Du Toit stated that his goal was 'a united South Africa with British coast protection'. Not much of his past fiery stuff seem to have survived.

With regard to the development of the region, he was originally opposed to the opening up of the interior through military campaigns and chartered companies, preferring to see it done in the old *Voortrekker* tradition.[51] Du Toit seems to have sorted out his differences with Rhodes with regard to the north in a meeting they had when the latter visited Pretoria in November 1890 on his way to Mashonaland. Subsequently, addressing a Bond meeting in Paarl, S.J. du Toit said that, in their meeting in Pretoria, he asked Rhodes 'whether he would like to see the country opened up by Afrikaners or by Europeans only'. Rhodes replied, to his satisfaction, that 'he would like to have Afrikaners also in the country as they were the best pioneers'.[52] The two men struck up some degree of understanding at that meeting.

Towards the end of 1890, upon returning to the Cape to resume his political and journalistic career, S.J. du Toit found Rhodes, not only prime minister, but also the hero of the Bond. Joining the bandwagon was not incongruent with his past experiences and current change of political heart. His idealism dimmed, Du Toit discovered his innate Cape Afrikaner pragmatism. Responding to a question by the *Cape Argus*, in mid-April 1891, as to whether he had changed his views about 'united South Africa under its own flag', he said: 'Well, I have somewhat modified that policy. Circumstances have altered since the time that my opinions were first formed, and one must march with the times, and not remain behind.'[53]

If personal material benefits were transferred, they were the icing rather than the cake. What is absolutely clear, is that S.J. du Toit became an admirer of Rhodes. At the annual Bond congress in March 1891 Du Toit employed his scheming mind in Rhodes's service.[54] Back in Paarl Du Toit sought to enlist Rhodes's support for his pet public schemes. While in Kimberley for the Bond congress, Rhodes invited Du Toit to meet him in Cape Town. Before the meeting, Du Toit wrote to Rhodes listing proposed topics for discussion. One concerned the Bond congress's resolution regarding the establishment of a national bank. He attached a lengthy memorandum, drawn up by A.B. de Villiers and himself, on the subject and sought to know 'your wish and have your advice as to further steps'. Another topic was: 'A Press Union as one of the great factors in preparing a United South Africa, has long been my idea.' D.C. de Waal, by then a close friend of Rhodes, had apparently advised Du Toit to discuss the matter with him. Du Toit claimed: 'I do not see any difficulty in arranging a Press Union throughout South Africa advocating our principles.' He gently broached the possibility of financial support for this particular scheme.[55] From a subsequent letter we learn that when the two had discussed the subject, Rhodes advised Du Toit to approach D. de Villiers Graaff, a wealthy Cape Town Bondsman. Rhodes was apparently involved in further examination of the 'Press scheme'.[56]

The return of S.J. du Toit, who became very active in the Bond, proved most beneficial to Rhodes's cause. By April 1891 he had taken over the editorship of both the *Patriot* and the *Paarl* from his brother Oom Lokomotief, who had been hostile to Rhodes. The latter, disappointed with his brother's change of heart and with the Bond more generally, left the Cape to settle in the Orange Free State. The radical margins of the Bond were seriously eroded by his withdrawal and by the change in the Paarl press. Under S.J. du Toit the Paarl newspapers became arch-defenders and articulators of the alliance between Rhodes and the Bond.

The alliance between the Bond and Rhodes under attack

This improvement in fortunes did not guarantee smooth sailing for the Bond–Rhodes alliance, which, in fact, soon came under fire. The challenge to the Rhodes-centric ideology of Afrikaner order was initiated by the Transvaal press. The Transvaal Afrikaners could not sing hymns to Rhodes, the new messiah of their Cape brethren. As far back as the mid-1880s, after meeting Rhodes for the first time during the Bechuanaland crisis, Kruger was reported to have said: 'That young man will cause me trouble if he does not leave politics alone and turn to something else.' For the Transvalers, Rhodes was the arch-imperialist that he was, and an enemy of the well-being and independence of their republic. One could hardly have expected Transvalers to be converted to the new gospel emanating from the Cape at a time when the alliance was manifested in another attempt to forestall the Transvaal's expansion. In August 1890 Hofmeyr and the Bond were condemned by the press for working for imperial domination throughout South Africa.[57] It was then that Kruger condemned Hofmeyr as a traitor. In October Rhodes was accused of wishing to remove Kruger who was an obstacle to his plans.

Bond newspapers rallied to refute these accusations. The *ZA* responded that 'no one who knows him can suspect that he harbours plans against Kruger. On the contrary, if there are two people in South Africa who can understand one another and co-operate cordially they are Kruger and our prime minister.'[58] The *BG* was even more positive: 'Therefore we feel confident that Mr. Rhodes and President Kruger will work harmoniously together for the good of South Africa.'[59] It is very doubtful that this interpretation had any impact on Afrikaner public opinion across the *Vaal*. The raving about a friendly meeting between Kruger and Rhodes in Pretoria[60] was a manifestation of wishful thinking rather than a reflection of the actual relations between these antagonists.

These were only light skirmishes. A major confrontation was, however, already looming large. It related to the essence of the new order, and touched upon past myths, current interests and future goals. It concerned the north, the centre-piece of Rhodes's southern African project. In 1890 two Transvalers, Adendorff and Vorster, organised a trek to settle Banyailand, an area claimed by the British government as a sphere of influence and by the chartered company as a sphere of operation. They based their claim to the area on an agreement with Chibi, a local chief. On his way back from the north to Pretoria in November 1890, Rhodes met the leaders of the trek in Pietersberg. He rejected their claim, which they apparently used to try to extract compensation from him.[61] In November, the *ZA* expressed the hope that Rhodes would accommodate the trekkers and allow them to settle in that area.[62] The issue was left in abeyance until the eve of the Bond congress which assembled in Kimberley at the end of March 1891. Rhodes was, at that time, approaching the shores of South Africa, on his way back from a trip to England. On 24 March, Adendorff issued in Pretoria an open letter formally announcing his intention to launch the trek and calling on Afrikaners from all over South Africa to join it. This pan-Afrikaner initiative, drawing on the *Voortrekkers'* traditions and myths, was a serious challenge to the Bond's Cape-centric conception of expansion to the north under the aegis of Rhodes. Worse still, among the leaders of the trek, listed in the letter, were a few Cape Afrikaners, including Oom Lokomotief, the editor from Paarl.[63]

This was the situation which Rhodes encountered when he disembarked in Cape Town at the end of March. The challenge from Adendorff was most embarrassing, because of the potential for a confrontation with the Transvaal, and for a bloody collision with Afrikaner trekkers, possibly also from the Cape, at a time when the settlement of the north was at an initial and fragile stage. This could have been disastrous for a company courting private investment and South African settlers. This was the background to Rhodes's hasty departure to Kimberley where the Bond congress was in progress. Rhodes told the congress that he came straight to Kimberley because 'he had a strong urge to meet the representatives of most agricultural interests in the Cape'.[64] These representatives were, of course, the political base for his various enterprises and projects, and he could not afford to lose them.

Rhodes was eager to meet them, not only because of his concern for the north. At stake was also the future of De Beers, the economic

147

foundation of his entire project. From Rhodes's perspective, March 1891 was not an ideal time for holding a Bond congress in Kimberley. The amalgamation of the diamond industry in 1888 had not brought economic salvation to the diamond fields. The price of diamonds continued to decline and by mid-1891 the prospects of De Beers were grim. As the company tried to combat declining profitability by cutting costs and salaries, reducing its labour force, using convict labour, and tightening up the compound system for its black workers, the diamond fields sunk into a deep slump. Business was depressed, unemployment was rife, and white poverty and destitution were the order of the day. A ray of hope pierced through the black clouds of hopelessness when, in February 1891, news of the discovery of diamonds in the Wesselton mine precipitated a local rush. This seriously threatened De Beers's monopoly at a time when the company's position was very precarious. Rhodes's government, conveniently, refused to proclaim the mine a public digging, or to sanction the diggers' claims. This provoked, in late February and early March 1891, widespread protest in Kimberley and Beaconsfield.[65] In early March the local Bond branch unanimously adopted a resolution urging the opening up of newly-discovered mines.[66] In mid-March it was reported from Kimberley that the forthcoming Bond congress was awaited with expectation and hope.[67] As the opening of the congress approached, interested parties in Kimberley were busy organising a colony-wide movement for the opening up of Wesselton mine.[68] This was hardly a congenial backdrop for the first Bond congress after the alliance with Rhodes had been struck.

It is probable that on his way to Kimberley, the gathering storm on the horizons of De Beers worried Rhodes more than the Adendorff egg which had hardly been laid.[69] However, by the time he got to Kimberley the stage was set for a successful conclusion of the issue. On 27 March, the day Rhodes arrived in Cape Town, congress delegates paid a visit to de Beers mines which culminated in a lavish dinner hosted by the deputy chairman of the company.[70] Beside him, at the head table, were the chairman, the assistant secretary and the secretary of the Bond, and S.J. du Toit. The deputy chairman of De Beers presented the case for his company, exonerating it from responsibility for the economic depression in Kimberley and highlighting its contribution to the welfare of the town and the colony. N.F. de Waal, the assistant secretary, responding on behalf of the Bond, said 'now that they had seen, they would be in a better position to do full justice to its [De Beers's] claims and when they saw how successfully Mr Rhodes had administrated this Company and his own affairs, they could also safely entrust the Government to him'. In proposing a toast to 'the Company', S.J. du Toit, in his new garb, out-performed De Beers's man in pouring praises on this company, the chartered company and Rhodes. With regard to the controversy, he said that they would hear both sides carefully, and give a good and righteous judgement.[71]

Three days later, in the presence of Rhodes, the congress sat in judgement. After a deputation of the Wesselton Claimholders' Protection Association presented its case for the opening up of the mine, P.J. Marais, a delegate from the Kimberley branch of the Bond, proposed that a law be passed 'making provision that all property containing metals and precious stones in payable quantity should be proclaimed and worked to the advantage of the country and people'. S.J. du Toit stepped in to render a service to Rhodes. Arguing that the matter was too serious to be resolved by a 'superficial resolution', he proposed the appointment of a committee of three to investigate the issue and report to the next congress. As members, he proposed, besides Marais, D.C. de Waal and himself.[72] In a subsequent letter to Rhodes he presented it as a tactic to prevent 'a premature resolution'.[73]

On 30 March, the congress was concluded with the traditional banquet, at which Rhodes was the guest of honour. Presenting the toast for the government, D.C. de Waal assured Rhodes of the support of the entire Bond 'because the Premier's Northwards politics was also the politics of every upright Afrikaner (hear, hear)'.[74] In responding on behalf of the government, Rhodes courted Bondsmen by showing concern for their immediate economic interests. This was, however, only the starter, the main course being reserved for his speech upon presenting a toast to the Bond. He flattered their collective ego by confiding to them that he, who had the confidence of the British leaders and the Queen, fully identified with them: 'Your ideas are the same as mine.' He also presented himself as their humble ambassador and crusader. He showed sensitivity to their ethnic concerns by exhibiting respect for the independence of the republics. Then he thrust upon them his grand ideas of South African and imperial unity, taking special care to present his northern project as theirs: 'I have undertaken that northern development as a Cape colonist. If there was anything that induced me to take the position of Prime Minister, it was the fact that I was resolved in my mind that we should extend to the Zambesi.'[75]

Rhodes must have been pleased with the performance of the congress. The attempt to get the Bond's support for undermining De Beers's vital interests had been thwarted. The challenge to the north by the Adendorff trekkers was not even discussed. Furthermore, he was given a platform to preach his gospel to Bond leaders from all over the colony and to rally their support.

It was, however, the winning of a battle rather than the war. In Kimberley the first shots were fired in a long political struggle. The two issues which had hastened Rhodes's departure to Kimberley continued to beset him, the Bond and the relations between them. Of the two, the Adendorff trek was the more threatening. The suffering of townsmen in Kimberley, many of whom were English speaking, did not elicit wide, active sympathy among Afrikaner farmers, the backbone of the Bond. The townsmen certainly did not draw support from the progressive leadership of the Bond which articulated and practised an alliance between Afrikaner farmers and mining capital. The Adendorff trek had much greater resonance, because it raised critical issues related to the essence of 'Afrikanerdom', and to their solidarity with their republican brothers. The two issues, however, combined together to feed an opposition to Rhodes and to the Bond's alliance with him.

The challenge to the dominant Bond position on these two issues was taken up by J.E. McCusker, the editor of the *GR* and a Bondsman, soon after the Kimberley congress. On 14 April 1891, he launched a frontal attack on De Beers and the Bond's support for it, writing about bare-foot white children and men without work: 'And all this is so because of De Beers, which, in a dinner over champagne, told the Bond that it provided work and planted trees!' He attacked the monopoly, convict labour and the compound system which impoverished local whites for the sake of shareholders living in England, complaining that 'despite all this the Bond support it'.[76]

McCusker's attitude to the Adendorff trek evolved more slowly and hesitantly. On 6 April 1891, he responded most favourably to Rhodes's speech at the congress, presenting him as a crusader for Afrikaner interests in the north.[77] Three days later he warned Rhodes that if he did not remain neutral, with regard to the trek, he would lose his popularity in the Bond.[78] However, until mid-May he kept a safe distance from the brewing confrontation in the north and even supported Rhodes's position, advising the trekkers to negotiate with him and settle under his company.[79] By then others had taken initiatives on the evolving crisis. On 2 April, the *Patriot* reported that the trekkers intended to establish a new republic modelled on the 1858 Transvaal constitution. In his last contribution as an editor, before his brother took over from him, Oom Lokomotief urged Rhodes to accommodate the trekkers and allow them to settle under their own government.[80] On 7 April, the *ZA* supported Rhodes's right to settle Mashonaland, depicting Adendorff as dangerous.[81] Two days later S.J. du Toit, as the new editor of the *Patriot*, lent support to Rhodes and declared himself against the trek. He reported that Rhodes intended to give the trekkers land under the best conditions and was prepared to finance a deputation to investigate the country.[82]

The challenge of Adendorff forced Rhodes and his Bond allies to take the initiative to enhance their case. S.J. du Toit, unwavering in his conversion, took the lead. He attempted, through contacts in Pretoria, to facilitate a settlement between the two, on the basis of the trekkers settling under Rhodes. At the same time, he schemed to undermine the trek by offering an alternative one. At the Kimberley congress he had discussed with Rhodes the idea of sending a deputation to Mashonaland 'to inspect and report upon the country'. 'Before, however, going any further', he wrote to Rhodes, 'I should like to know exactly what your wishes are, so that I may be able to carry them out.'[83] Du Toit was not only subservient to his new master, but also determined and efficient. Ten days later, a meeting in Paarl launched the Bond's settlement initiative. After hearing a report on the Adendorff trek and the suitability of Mashonaland for settlement, the issue was debated. G.J. Malherbe, an old member of the language movement, supported Adendorff's case and claimed to be his representative. He was followed by S.J. du Toit who again rendered Rhodes a very useful service, persuading the meeting to set up a committee to select men for a deputation to inspect Mashonaland and make contact with Rhodes with a view to expediting their departure. Du Toit concluded his speech by saying that 'it will be a good country for your children', and that the intention was to send a trek the following year.[84] A letter sent by Du Toit to Rhodes, the day after the meeting, reveals the extent of collusion between Rhodes and the Bond leaders. After reporting on the Paarl meeting and the propagation of an alternative trek, he wrote: 'I write to Hofmeyr and De Waal on the subject, so it will be sufficient to give one of them a hint as to your wishes.'[85] Having been the Mecca of 'Afrikanerdom', Paarl was being transformed into a temple of Rhodes.

About a week later, a second meeting was held in Cape Town under the chairmanship of Hofmeyr, in which a letter from Rhodes was submitted specifying the terms for granting land to settlers from South Africa as a whole. Rhodes also stated his determination to resist the Adendorff trekkers and his commitment to resign his premiership should a conflict of interests between his two positions arise.[86] From this meeting emanated a circular letter to the different Bond branches, signed by Hofmeyr and the Cape Town branch secretary, and entitled 'The Afrikaner Bond and the threatening conflict in the North'. Clearly taking Rhodes's side in the conflict, the circular came out squarely against the Adendorff trek in the name of the well-being of South Africa. It also included three resolutions adopted by the Cape Town branch – expressing satisfaction with Rhodes's intention to open up the north for occupation, and calling on those wishing to settle there to contact the chartered company; pointing to the sad results of a trek in conflict with Rhodes, and appealing to Bondsmen to do all they could to prevent such conflict; and applauding the plan to send a deputation of farmers and expressing the hope that their negotiations with the Adendorff trekkers and with the company would avert the conflict. Rhodes's letter was attached to the circular.[87]

On 24 April, Rhodes and P.H. Faure, his Minister for Native Affairs, were the guests of honour at a dinner in Paarl. In his toast to the government and the guests, S.J. du Toit paved the way for Rhodes by presenting his enterprise in the north as most beneficial to the Cape.[88] Rhodes was received with 'prolonged thundering applause'. After craftily appealing to the audience's pocket and heart, he presented his endeavour in the north as a selfless service to the Cape, listing all the benefits that would accrue to the colonists and their sons therefrom. He presented Adendorff and his friends as swindlers who wished to deprive the Cape colonists of their birthright, and showed no inclination to concede to them.[89] Faure who followed Rhodes described him as 'an Englishmen with an Afrikaner heart'.[90] On 30 April, S.J. du Toit wrote a long open letter to his 'Transvaal friends who favour the Banyailand Trek', urging them not to take action before the arrival of the deputation from the Cape.[91] Having consolidated their position in the bastions of the Bond in the west, the anti-Adendorff, pro-charter Bond leaders followed up the Cape Town branch circular by organising meetings across the colony. Some of these, which lent support to the pro-charter position, were attended by leading Bondsmen from Paarl.[92] In the background, the ZA published a travel journal by two DRC clergymen who had toured Mashonaland under Rhodes's auspices.[93] And at the end of May, it was reported that Van der Byl, a prominent, though bankrupt farmer, was recruiting young farmers for settling in Mashonaland.[94] Towards the end of June he set out to the north at the head of a group of 25 men.[95]

This orchestrated campaign did not remain unchallenged for long. The lead was again provided by the republican press. On 23 April 1891, the *Volkstem* from Pretoria sadly noted, and bitterly attacked, the Bond's support for Rhodes on the issue of the Adendorff trek: 'Have the Afrikaners become lifeless puppets, allowing themselves to be governed by Rhodes's will?'[96] The *Express* from Bloemfontein was even more bitter, deploring the conversion of S.J. du Toit and attacking the Bond meetings which had condemned the Adendorff trek.[97] Responding to the Cape Town branch circular, the editor fulminated:

> To whatever depth the Bond may descend in furthering Mr. Rhodes's personal schemes or hobbies of imperial expansion and influence is a matter that concerns those responsible for the Bond's action. But there is a limit to the Bond's admissible agitation, and that limit has been reached.[98]

On 12 May it praised the *GR* for turning against the Bond and Rhodes.[99]

The *GR* editor may have indeed have been inspired by his republican counterparts. On 30 April, he still supported Rhodes's position; by mid-May he had begun to turn his pen against Rhodes and the Bond and for the Adendorff trekkers.[100] McCusker, who was soon to resign from the Bond, became a veritable anti-Rhodes, anti-Bond crusader with his aversion to both De Beers and the chartered company fuelling his zeal and determination. He vehemently repudiated Rhodes as 'the great whale' for his position with regard to Adendorff, condemned him as the enemy of the republics, called for his resignation as prime minister, and sent him alternately to hell and Timbuctoo.[101] The Bond and its leaders were subjected to a barrage of fierce criticism and condemnation for their position towards the trek, and for worshipping Rhodes, 'the Mahdi'.[102] In connection with Rhodes's attitude towards the trekkers, the *GR* called on the Bond to put pressure on him to resign his premiership. For his role in the diamond fields Rhodes was labelled 'Octopus'.[103] The *GR* supported Upington's motion to appoint a commission of inquiry to investigate the situation in Griqualand West and favoured taxation of diamonds, claiming that the Cape did not benefit from De Beers' excessive profits.[104]

McCusker was not a lone crusader in the campaign against the Bond and Rhodes on these issues. Thus, the *GR* published a letter from two Afrikaners, from the Kimberley area, asking why the government did not buy the Wesselton mine and open it up for exploitation.[105] As could have been expected, the Adendorff trek controversy attracted much wider interest and involvement. In a letter to the *GR*, a correspondent from the Midlands expressed the feelings of fellow Bondsmen from his area towards the leaders of the party, complaining that the spirit of the Bond was not what it used to be. He claimed that the trekkers enjoyed wide support in his area (Aberdeen) and that they would not be neglected, even if 'a dozen of Hofmeyrs, Bothas and more of their kind sit on the platform in Bond's congresses'.[106] The *ZA* published a letter by a Bondsman, who had emigrated to the Transvaal, depicting Rhodes as an imperialist using the Afrikaners as cannon fodder in the conquest of the north, and condemning the Bond for lending him support.[107] D.P. van den Heever singled out S.J. du Toit for his involvement in the conflict in the north, ending up with a prophetic warning:

> I urge you, do not take part in the trek [the Bond trek] and do not involve yourselves in the affairs of the Charter. You may soon reap fruits from the Charter, but the smell which will be left over will be smelled by the next generation.[108]

Van den Heever became one of the leading opponents of Rhodes and the Bond–Rhodes alliance. Another correspondent predicted that it would

153

be hardly surprising if all the patriots were soon to say: 'Farewell Afrikaner Bond with your Rhodes politics.'[109]

Indeed, the opposition to the alliance was soon taken up by Bond branches. In a Bond meeting convened in Worcester there was strong opposition to a resolution in support of the Cape Town branch circular. Many left the meeting in protest and the resolution was adopted with 14 in favour and 11 against.[110] At a meeting of the Graaff Reinet district branch executive, the congress's treatment of the Wesselton mine issue came under fire,[111] and at a public meeting in the same town the Bond chairman, R.P. Botha, was asked embarrassing questions on the trek and his relations with Rhodes.[112] Indeed, the opposition to the Bond–Rhodes alliance was centred in the Midlands. In a letter to the editor of the *GR*, a correspondent, purporting to represent his Bond branch, called on Rhodes to either resign his position in the chartered company or relinquish his premiership: 'He is the head of De Beers and consequently the Wesselton Mine cannot be opened; he is the head of the Charter and consequently the trekkers cannot settle in Mashonaland.'[113] In mid-July the *GR* reported that meetings were being held 'everywhere', manifesting sympathy for the trekkers and trying to exert influence on Rhodes through the Bond and in other ways.[114] From September to November 1891, there were reports of numerous meetings, in the Midlands and elsewhere, supporting the trekkers and the *GR* and condemning the Bond for its support for Rhodes.[115]

In the Midlands the controversy created a serious rift between the leadership, particularly R.P. Botha and Dr T.N.G. Te Water, and the supporters of the trekkers and the *GR*.[116] This led to the establishment of the *Onze Courant* (*OC*), as the Bond organ in the Midlands.[117] R.P. Botha must have viewed the challenge of the *GR* in a serious manner. In supporting the idea of an alternative newspaper he even appealed to the Afrikaners' aversion to Catholicism,[118] calling on the protestants to set up their own paper. It is difficult accurately to assess the balance of support between the Bond's establishment, which supported Rhodes, and its challengers, mainly from the Midlands and the east. The *GR*, naturally, claimed that an investigation would reveal more sympathy for the trekkers than for either Rhodes or the Bond.[119] It claimed that while losing 17 subscribers, it had gained 46 new ones.[120] But even S.J. du Toit, who assured Rhodes that they were able to keep the pro-trekkers sentiment down, conceded that 'there is certainly a strong feeling in their favour especially amongst the *Patriot* and Bond party'.[121]

The intensifying controversy was further fed by external, republican inputs. On 22 June 1891, the *GR* published an open letter to 'the Afrikaners' by Revd A.A. van der Lingen, a DRC clergyman from Harrismith in the Orange Free State. Criticising the Bond press and leaders for their position regarding the Adendorff trek and for supporting Rhodes, the enemy of the republics, he called on Cape Afrikaners to set up committees, elect leaders and sign petitions to be sent to the British government and the British press.[122] At the beginning of August he issued another circular letter urging *rechtzinnige Afrikaners* (orthodox Afrikaners) in the colonies as well as the republics to form a movement to oppose the expansion of imperialism in South Africa. He claimed that 'in Cape Town and its surroundings' the leaders of the Afrikaners had defected to the imperialist camp, and called for the formation of an Afrikaner Unie.[123] The call was echoed in a letter to the editor which suggested that the time was not far off when 'we will establish a new Bond, composed only of upright Afrikaners, because upright Afrikaners do not feel at home with Rhodes's riff raffs'.[124] On 17th July, a meeting had been convened to establish a new Bond, the slogan of which was to be 'Africa for the Afrikaners'.[125] The *GR* apparently preferred to purify the Bond from 'undesirable leaders' who used the Bond for the promotion of Rhodes's imperialism.[126] The tension in the Midlands Bond rose sharply in September–October 1891. Botha and Te Water, who rushed to Aberdeen, failed to convince Bondsmen assembled there on 25 September. The meeting expressed no confidence in Botha and asked him to vacate his seat in the Legislative Council. The meeting expressed support for the editor of the *GR* and opposed the establishment of a new newspaper.[127] There was also an attempt to tar and feather Dr Te Water,[128] a treatment reserved for traitors. Botha was criticised and condemned in meetings of other branches as well.[129] In October, the chairman of the Bond in Murraysburg district resigned in protest at the intention to set up a new newspaper in competition with the *GR*.[130] A correspondent approved of his step 'because Rhodes's Bond has become intolerable to us, the farmers, and I think to follow in his footsteps'.[131]

Clearly, there were many Bondsmen who were unhappy with their party's alliance with Rhodes. Because of the diffused nature of the Bond it is difficult to assess the size of the popular base of the anti-Rhodes elements within the party. What can be established is that the alliance was objectionable to many Bondsmen on two main issues which were central to the Cape Afrikaners' political consciousness. The anti-De Beers thrust touched upon one of the main components of the common ground on which the alliance rested. While the leadership of the party articulated and practised an alliance between Afrikaner farmers and representatives of mining capital, the opposition to this alliance was inspired by an anti-capitalist, populist disposition which upheld the rights of the small man. This disposition was fed not only by the encounter of Cape Afrikaner farmers with the diamond fields capitalists, but also by the long rivalry between them and merchant capital which was reinforced

155

by its ethno-cultural dimension, the capitalists being predominantly English-speaking. Thus, this anti-Rhodes, anti-alliance thrust rested on one of the main foundations of Cape Afrikaner colonial experience. The second pro-Adendorff, anti-north drive touched upon sensitive pan-ethnic nerves and traditional suspicion of, if not hostility to, direct imperial meddling in South African affairs. Even if the anti-alliance campaign did not have much resonance in the leadership of the Bond, it had at least a potential for widespread popular support. It was a challenge that the Bond leadership could not ignore.

The response of the alliance

Clearly, tough talk and threats of use of force against the trekkers[132] were only counter-productive. The alliance had to do more to win the battle with the trekkers and for the hearts and minds of Cape Afrikaners. Rhodes, as we have seen, did his best, at the Paarl meeting, to maximise his appeal among Cape Afrikaners. He also did his share during the 1891 parliamentary session. In view of the difficulties being encountered in exporting wine and brandy to the Transvaal, Rhodes elaborated extensively on his efforts to secure preferential tariffs for Cape wines in Britain.[133] Supporting protection for Cape wheat, he stated that he had always been for a moderate protection for foodstuffs which could be produced in the Cape.[134] As a contribution to the very sore labour problem, Rhodes again lent his support to the Masters and Servants Bill.[135] He also voted with the Bond in opposition to the Ballot Bill,[136] and to please Bondsmen he proclaimed in parliament that democracy was a failure. The ZA praised Rhodes for being free from the democratic spirit: 'Thus, his partnership with the Bond is not coincidental; it stems from the nature of the matter and from Rhodes's nature.'[137] Responding to Sprigg's attack on the chartered company, Rhodes elaborated on the benefits the Cape derived from the north.[138] This was sweet music to the ears of the converted; it failed to convince opponents.

The Bond press was also mobilised in defence of Rhodes and the alliance. Rhodes was presented most favourably and the alliance was constantly rationalised and legitimised. Since the controversy was centred on the north, a special effort was made to portray its prospects and its benefits for Cape Afrikaners in a most favourable light. As the key to the development of the north lay in the discovery of substantial gold deposits, the press reported very optimistically about the mineral wealth of the country, even suggesting that Mashonaland was as rich in gold as the Rand.[139] Enthusiastic reports about the prospects of the other crucial pillar of the new Eldorado, namely, agriculture, also appeared. In his travel journal, Revd Adriaan Hofmeyr, who had gone on a tour to Mashonaland under Rhodes's auspices, presented an appetising description of fertile valleys, grassy meadows and flowing streams.[140] On his return he lectured to the Afrikaner public on his expedition, raving about the fertility of the country and describing it as the 'future for their sons and daughters'.[141] The *Paarl* and the *ZA* also published in serial form the travel journal of the Paarl Mashonaland deputation,[142] whose report was very positive. S.J. du Toit concluded from the report, and from his own experience in the Transvaal, that Mashonaland was even more suitable for viticulture than the western Cape. Referring to the devastation caused by the phylloxera to vines across the world, he concluded: 'Will a new country not have to be opened for the vines on the healthy plateaus to replenish our empty cellars?'[143] The north was presented not only as an ideal economic space for the 'crowded' Cape, but also, on the same lines described earlier, as a potential space for an appropriately Rhodes–Afrikaner social and political order.[144] It is hardly surprising that the agency for turning this dream into reality was a *groot trek*.[145]

Thus, both Rhodes and the Bond press were busy constructing a congenial backdrop. This, however, did not obviate the need to deal with the main theme of the drama. The Adendorff trekkers could not be wished away, and they continued to be a grave source of trouble in Cape Afrikaner politics. On 24 June 1891, some 112 trekkers, who had arrived at the banks of the Limpopo, were turned back by Dr Jameson.[146] The trekkers went back home, but were not deterred from pursuing their cause, only shifting the focus of their enterprise from the Transvaal to the Orange Free State. S.J. du Toit, who had gone up to the Transvaal, reported to Rhodes on this shift in the trekkers' strategy, which included holding meetings around the country to arouse 'popular sentiment'.[147] On 8 September, it was reported that attempts were being made in the Orange Free State to revive the trek.[148]

The trekkers had to be constructively engaged if a most embarrassing and damaging collision was to be averted. S.J. du Toit again proved himself a very useful ally. In early September he facilitated a meeting in Cape Town which was attended by D.J. Malan, one of the two holders of the Banyailand concession, Rhodes, Hofmeyr, D.C. de Waal and himself. The two sides agreed to submit their dispute to the arbitration of the Chief Justices of the Cape and the Orange Free State, and Rhodes undertook to abide by the decision of the arbitrators.[149] Malan proceeded to Paarl where he expressed satisfaction with the terms of the arbitration in the presence of two prominent members of the du Toit family. It seems that a third member of the family, Oom Lokomotief, had persuaded him to reject them.[150]

Within about a week of concluding the agreement, Malan, now back in Bloemfontein, withdrew his consent and handed the matter over to a

Trek Committee. In a letter to Rhodes, on 21 September, J. van Soelen, the committee's chairman, distanced it from the agreement. The committee agreed to arbitration provided it also included, among its terms of reference, the validity of the British sphere of influence in the north. It also demanded that each side appoint an arbitrator. If Adendorff was originally interested in compensation, Van Soelen presented himself as the representative of the 'Afrikaner Nation'.[151] In early October, the Trek Committee issued a manifesto to 'Men, Brothers, Kinsmen, Fellow-believers', entitled 'the Mashonaland Question, or Imperialism versus Afrikanderism'.[152] The *GR* reported on meetings, held 'everywhere', to discuss the trek and to combat the 'negative influence' of certain Bond branches. It claimed that 'thousands of Afrikaners are determined to force the Bond to submit the conflict to arbitration and to demand that Britain ... recognize the trek's rights if they were well grounded'.[153]

The Bond responded with a meeting convened in Paarl to hear and discuss the report of the Mashonaland Commission. Members of the deputation who had returned from their inspection tour reported most favourably on the agricultural potential of the area. The meeting thanked the deputation and the Commission for their sacrifice and work, and resolved, with only two dissensions, to leave the implementation of the report in the hands of the Commission – which was composed mainly of Rhodes's friends. The ensuing debate revolved not on the report but on the conflict between Rhodes and the trekkers. Hofmeyr delivered the main speech, strongly defending Rhodes and the chartered company.[154] The outcome of the meeting was hardly surprising since, by then, Paarl, and western Cape in general, were the bastion of the Bond–Rhodes alliance.

The Paarl meeting, however, could not resolve the conflict between Rhodes and the trekkers. Neither could it avert the escalating strife within the ranks of the Bond, since the centre of the support for the trek and of the opposition to the alliance was in the Midlands and the east. In fact, the affirmation of the alliance and the Bond's attitude to the trek only exacerbated the intra-Bond tension. In order to avert a split in the Bond and to reaffirm its unity, a special Bond mini-congress was convened in Burgersdorp on 4 November, 1891. According to the *CA* 'strenuous efforts were made ... to patch up the split which is imminent in the Bond camp'. Indeed, intensive lobbying took place, on the eve of the congress, to pave the way for its success. Oom Lokomotief and D.P. van den Heever represented the pro-trek faction, while Hofmeyr and S.J. du Toit stood for the Bond leadership. Van Soelen, the chairman of the trek, also attended the congress.[155] The resolution, which was unanimously accepted by the congress, was a compromise, with the trekkers getting their way with regard to the terms of reference of the inquiry, while conceding imperial arbitration.[156]

On 16 November the 'Burgersdorp Committee', comprising Hofmeyr, Van Soelen, Oom Lokomotief and his brother S.J. du Toit, officially submitted, to the Governor, the resolution of the congress.[157] Yet, by late November it appeared that the Trek Committee objected to British insistence that Banyailand be recognised as a British sphere, and blamed the Bond leadership for manipulating them.[158] The trek wound proved hard to heal. In the same month a meeting in Ventersdorp, attended by Van Soelen and Oom Lokomotief, elected a committee to collaborate with the Trek Committee.[159] In May 1892, the *GR* still expressed dissatisfaction with the British government's insistence that Banyailand was under British sovereignty.[160] D.P. van den Heever made the occasional reference to his support for the trekkers, criticising the Bond for its support for the chartered company, and the *GR* reminded its readers that the trekkers still enjoyed the support of their countrymen.[162] The trek, however, was dead and almost ceased to feature in the political debate of the Cape Afrikaners.

The supporters of the trek now directed their efforts against the Bond and Rhodes's attempts to encourage settlement in the north. In February 1892, Revd van der Lingen, the anti-charter apostle from the Orange Free State, issued another epistle warning fellow Afrikaners against settling in Mashonaland.[163] Van den Heever, who supported the trekkers' project, discovered that there was an abundance of fertile lands in the Cape and argued that there was no logic in emigrating to the north.[164] The *GR* countered a call by the Paarl press to trek northward, warning against settling in the unhealthy country of a bankrupt company: 'Do not listen to the nice offers of Mr Rhodes and Revd S.J. du Toit and do not go to the North.'[165] Interest among Cape farmers in emigrating to Charterland seemed to grow just the same.[166]

The waning of the trek from the public arena did not augur an end to the troubles within the Bond on account of their alliance with Rhodes. The chartered company and Rhodes's dual position continued to be the targets of the opponents of the Bond–Rhodes alliance.[167] Van den Heever, becoming the arch opponent of the government and of the Bond–Rhodes alliance, led the attack on a broad front of issues.[168] In late February he came out strongly for the trekkers, for the Wesselton miners and condemned the cordial co-operation between the Bond and the chartered company.[169] Another leading opponent, I.J. van der Walt, who was described by the *ZA* as 'one of the most respectable Bond members', spoke bitterly against Rhodes's dual position as premier and head of De Beers, and demanded the opening up of the Wesselton Mine.[170] On another occasion he criticized Rhodes's dual position as premier and head of the chartered company:

159

He is head of two Governments, and no man can look after two countries' interests at one time. The Chartered Company is a money-making concern, and what man can be so perfect as to be able to promote the interests of such a concern and look after our affairs conscientiously at the same time?[171]

The focus, however, was diverted from the external northern scene to the local, De Beers one.

De Beers under assault

The issue of De Beers and the state of diamond mining was one of the most controversial issues dealt with by the Bond congress of 1892. S.J. du Toit, who in the previous congress proposed a De Beers-inclined committee to report to the next congress on the state of diamond mining, failed to follow up his initiative. He, in fact, instructed the chairman of the Kimberley branch to appoint a local committee to compile the report. The task was given to P.J. Marais and H.D. Stiglingh, arch-opponents of De Beers, who had a personal interest in the matter. These two also submitted the report to the congress as delegates of their branch.[172] S.J. du Toit rendered great disservice to Rhodes in soliciting the report, which bitterly attacked De Beers's monopoly and Rhodes personally. The monopoly, the compound and its concomitant truck system, the construction of Kenilworth as a town for white employees, and the employment of 'bandits', were presented as the causes of the severe depression not only in the diamond fields but also in the colony as a whole. The report recommended the abolition of the monopoly and the other malpractices of De Beers and a return to the pre-monopoly system of competitive mining. Rhodes was explicitly accused of dishonesty and of using his position as premier to promote his private interests.[173]

Not having elicited in the congress the support they might have expected, or at least hoped for, the opponents of De Beers continued their attack. The *GR* again gave the lead in the frontal assault on De Beers and the Bond's support for Rhodes. In October 1892 the editor visited the diamond fields to replenish his arguments and enthusiasm for his ongoing crusade. He described in great detail the effects of De Beers's monopoly and other malpractices and exposed government complicity. He depicted Rhodes as 'the most successful fortune seeker that South Africa has ever created', arguing that he could not serve concurrently as premier and as head of De Beers. Listing all his transgressions against the welfare of the diamond fields, he concluded that Rhodes brought no benefit to the country. And, yet, Rhodes enjoyed the support of the servile Bond whose leaders viewed him as an exceptional manifestation of patriotism, as a man 'in whose leadership the Bond can be proud'. Thousands of people were suffering from Rhodes's disastrous ventures while most Bond leaders were bowing to the 'golden calf': 'The Bond which had to promote the welfare of the public ... which had opposed the monopolistic system, became the servant of the same system.' He mourned that while the eyes of the people were opened to the detrimental impact of Rhodes, the opposition to him lacked leadership because the natural leaders of the Bond followed him.[174] In early November, McCusker prophesied the end of Kimberley:

> Poor Kimberley! And all this is thanks to Rhodes – the man who, like Cholera, brings with him everywhere misery and grief. Woe woe! The Bond has got a lot to answer for, for they support the unholy politics of such a man.[175]

Politically, Griqualand West, the locus of the diamond fields, and Rhodes's economic and immediate political base, was the arena where the battle against De Beers and its head was waged. At a meeting of the Kimberley branch of the Bond, Stiglingh attacked the compound system which brought no benefit to the country.[176] On 15 October 1892 the Bond held a public meeting in Herbert District, Griqualand West. Dr J.M. Hoffman and S.J. du Toit from Paarl, who were the main speakers, addressed general ethno-cultural issues, not even mentioning the burning local issue, namely De Beers. The local contribution to the debate was, however, almost exclusively focused on that question. De Kock argued that in the last congress the Bond lent support to Rhodes with regard to the Wesselton mine, causing damage to Griqualand West. He listed all the negative ramifications of De Beers's practices and called for the break-up of the bond between Rhodes and Hofmeyr. The indefatigable Stiglingh was also there attacking De Beers and Rhodes, and claiming that the government, which did not promote the welfare of the country, enjoyed no support in Griqualand West.[177] Reporting on the meeting, the *GR* surmised, happily, that Bondsmen in the Kimberley area were waking up and struggling against Rhodes and his 'slavish system'.[178] In early November Stiglingh congratulated McCusker for his description of the conditions in this region. He also attached a letter addressed by himself and Marais to the Kimberley Bond branch on the predicament of the inhabitants of the diamond fields.[179]

In the by-election in Kimberley, in November 1892, Rhodes and De Beers were at the centre of the campaign. *OL* gave mild support to the candidate fielded by Rhodes and De Beers, while the *GR*, expectedly, supported his opponent. *OL* conceded that the latter represented a substantial coalition of forces.[180] The *GR* condemned *OL* for supporting De Beers's candidate and pursuing Stiglingh 'for standing against the candidate of the selfish, wretched De Beers'.[181] It was incensed that De

Beers's candidate, who overwhelmingly beat the local Bond candidate, was supported by the Bond press. It lamented that all Kimberley's four Members of Parliament represented De Beers and called on Bondsmen to support Stiglingh and Marais, Rhodes's foremost opponents, as candidates in the forthcoming general election.[182] In January 1893, a conference in Griquastad, which was also attended by C.W.H. Kohler and S.J. du Toit from Paarl, discussed again the situation in the diamond fields. A resolution adopted by the conference expressed criticism of some of De Beers' practices.[183] In the Bond congress in Queenstown in early March 1893, issues relating to De Beers were again on the agenda.

As in the case of the Adendorff trek, the assault on De Beers, and the Bond's support for it and for its head, did not penetrate the bastion of the Bond–Rhodes alliance. At the Bond congress in Stellenbosch in 1892 Stinglingh's resolution to impose the opening up of all mines and the abolition of the compound system was defeated by a large majority. An alternative resolution submitted by two of the most prominent leaders of the party was very vague, committing neither the government nor the Bond. T.P. Theron regretted that Stiglingh dragged Rhodes's person into the debate, while A.S. le Roex, who said that it was 'scandalous to hold Rhodes under the thumb', was received with continuing applause.[184] Stiglingh and his supporters did not enjoy much support in the 1893 congress either. On the issues of convict labour and compound trading, the congress merely reaffirmed the previous year's resolution.[185] With regard to convict labour a correspondent from Griqualand West was astonished that Stiglingh, who raised the issue in the congress, did not enjoy much support.[186] The GR was disappointed that the congress rejected the proposal to impose taxation on diamonds, despite having supported it in the past.[187] The press associated with the Bond supported De Beers against its critics. The ZA justified De Beers's monopoly and saw no danger in its operation. Both it and OL preferred De Beers's non-Bond candidate in the Kimberley by-election to Stiglingh, the local Bond leader.[188]

The political and ideological impact of the controversy on the Bond

While the Bond's leadership defended their position on issues linking them closely to Rhodes, the challenge to the alliance caused severe tensions within the party. These were particularly disturbing because the party had not yet been galvanised into a compact and cohesive body, ideologically and organisationally. While the Western Cape provided a solid base for the leadership, the alliance exacerbated tensions and conflict between the leadership and the party's periphery in the Midlands, the east and Griqualand West. It also intensified conflicts within the different regions. This was particularly so in the Midlands, where the Bond, according to the *GR*, interfered in the functioning of local bodies, politicised them and exacerbated local divisions.[189] It blamed the Bond for exerting influence on the Aberdeen Divisional Council to disqualify its tender for printing jobs.[190] Even an agricultural show became a bone of political contention between the Bond district leadership and its opponents.[191] The *GR* even blamed the Bond for dividing families.[192] In the Midlands, in particular, but also in the east and Griqualand West, there were divisions within branches and between branches and district leaderships.[193]

The *GR* continued to call for the formation of a new Bond. At the end of February 1892, it reported again Revd. van der Lingen's call for the foundation of an 'Afrikaner Union' and promised to furnish details and to deal with the question of the establishment of a local branch of the 'Union' in Graaff Reinet.[194] In early March D.P. van den Heever considered reforming the Bond, rather than forming a new one: 'I call on the independents, let's reform the Bond, let's form a new Bond from the remnants of the old one.'[195] In early October the *GR* reported that there was an intention to convene a conference to consider ways of improving the state of affairs in the Bond.[196] While this intention never materialised, there were local manifestations of active dissent. Thus, Van den Heever supported an opposition candidate against a Bond candidate in a by-election in the east.[197]

Although the leadership managed to control the congresses and shape their course and outcome, the challenges of the periphery worried them. The western Cape which was the solid base of the leadership and its alliance with Rhodes, included only some seven out of 60 branches.[198] The escalation of the internal conflict could seriously erode the party's power base. The Bond leadership responded to this threat by convening the Burgersdorp congress in November 1891, and by sending Rhodes supporters from Paarl to address meetings in Griqualand West.

Another response was the establishment of new newspapers loyal to the pro-Rhodes leadership. As we have seen, in 1891 S.J. du Toit had proposed to set up a 'Press Union advocating our principles',[199] believing that 'The press ... is the greatest power and strongest factor in politics. And we have the chance to get the press of the Colony in our hands to such an extent that we can dominate public opinion.'[200] In 1891–2, within a year, five new newspapers were established or transformed – *Ons Land* (*OL*), *De Paarl*, *Onze Courant*, *Philipstownsche Weekblad*, and *Het Oosten*. According to the Stellenbosch congress in 1892, these newspapers 'alone have declared themselves to be based on our Programme of Principles'.[201] *OC* in Graaff Reinet was established by the R.P. Botha 'loyalist' faction in the Midlands to counteract the vicious anti-Bond campaign of the *GR*. *Het Oosten* and the *Philipstownsche Weekblad* were to service the east and the Karoo. *De Paarl* provided the Paarl area with a Dutch, as distinct from Afrikaans, newspaper. It was the establishment of *OL* in Cape Town which betrayed the leadership's eagerness to secure the strict loyalty of its press. The *ZA* was certainly not a rebel newspaper. The editor, Dr J.W.G. van Oordt,[202] who was a member of the local Bond branch, supported the Bond and its alliance with Rhodes. Yet it was too independent for the taste of the leaders at a time they were under increasing pressure from below.[203] A correspondent to the *GR* described the new newspapers as "Rhodes papers, masquerading in Bond garb'.[204] There is no evidence of Rhodes's direct involvement in establishing or financing these newspapers. There is clear evidence that in the case of *OC*, money from Cape Town was invested in the Graaff Reinet newspaper.[205]

The establishment of a loyal press was a major initiative which was definitely precipitated by the assault on the Bond–Rhodes alliance. It represented an effort by the pro-Rhodes leadership to win the battle for the hearts and minds of Cape Afrikaners. This battle was crucial because the assault on the alliance did not reflect merely personal likes and dislikes, and divergent regional and class interests. It touched upon the essence of 'Afrikanerdom', upon the appropriate Afrikaner order and its moral underpinning. An effective agency for the propagation of the leadership position and perspectives was particularly important, because 'Afrikanerdom' was ideologically and morally a highly contested territory. Indeed, the debate between the pro-Rhodes leadership and its challengers was not merely over interests; it was at least as much a debate over ideology and morality. It was from this vantage point that Rhodes played a vital role in the evolution of Cape Afrikaner political consciousness and outlook.

The crisis in the diamond fields which was highlighted and sharpened in 1891 in the wake of the discovery of diamonds in the Wesselton mine was obviously about material interests of specifically affected groups. It was not coincidental that the focus and the main arena of the controversy was Griqualand West. The main contenders were De Beers which profited immensely from the amalgamation, and a variety of individuals and groups who greatly suffered from it – the individual prospectors, the retailers, the property owners and the workers. It is hardly surprising that within the Bond the main antagonist was Stiglingh, a diamond prospector of substantial means with 18 years' experience in the diamond fields, who was threatened by De Beers's monopoly.[206] He had the experience, confidence and the means to dedicate himself to the struggle against those responsible for his plight. The other major centre of agitation was Graaff Reinet which was directly affected by the shrinking of the economic volume in Kimberley. However, beyond these immediate sectorial interests, the controversy over De Beers touched upon the core issue of the appropriate economic and social order and its moral basis.

From the perspective of the challengers to De Beers's position, the struggle was inspired by a clear populist outlook. The main motive of a protest meeting in Kimberley, on the eve of the 1891 Bond congress, was the struggle of the small man against the wealthy monopolists.[207] The diamond fields, moving from the era of pioneering, adventurous and individualistic economic frontier, into one of monopoly and economic rationalisation in which the small man was being squeezed out, were ideal breeding grounds for such conflict of interests and outlooks. Moreover, the Cape as a whole, with its individualistic, conservative pre-industrial farmers engulfed by powerful capitalist forces, offered a congenial backdrop for the confrontation in Kimberley. The cause of the small man, languishing under the pressure of powerful alien economic forces, had a potential for considerable resonance among Bondsmen. It concerned the core of Afrikaner perception of the appropriate moral, economic and social order. In the past, before S.J. du Toit's conversion, the *Patriot* would have undoubtedly taken up such a populist cause. In its early days the *Patriot*, in its struggle against the imperial banks and for local banks and farmers' co-operatives stores, pioneered this socio-economic outlook. In the early 1890s, S.J. du Toit, while still fighting for a national bank,[208] seems to have forgotten and forsaken the small man. Perhaps his experience of high speculative capitalism in the Transvaal had cured him of this childhood ideological disease. The broad socio-economic conditions in the early 1890s were conducive to the evolution and propagation of such an outlook. At a time when rural impoverishment swelled the ranks of the 'poor whites' to alarming proportions, the small Afrikaner man needed both compassion and protection more than ever before. It is not surprising that, among the leaders who supported the small man's cause, we find D.P. van den Heever from Burgersdorp and I.J. van der Walt from Colesberg, representatives and champions of the more marginal and vulnerable sheep farmers.

With S.J. du Toit and the *Patriot* having folded old flags and acquiring new colours, it was the *GR* which, shortly before the 1891 Bond congress, picked up the cudgel, articulating and propagating the populist perspective and urging supporters and zealots on. In a long leader article we find an important element of the populist outlook, namely the golden age of the small man. The writer raved about the good old days when diamond digging provided livelihood to thousands of individual diggers who contributed to the flourishing of the Cape economy as a whole.[209] This was a recurrent theme among propagandists and crusaders. Van den Heever asked a public meeting in Hanover: 'When was Kimberley flourishing?' His answer was short: 'When every man exploited his own concession.'[210]

The report of the Kimberley branch to the 1892 Bond congress was, befittingly, more elaborate:

> Before the Amalgamation, when the mines were worked by different companies and individual persons, everything was flourishing, not only the Diamond fields, but South Africa as a whole. Through competition we had a market for all sort of products, which had been transported from all over the country by thousands of freighter carriages, and which fetched good prices. And although the diamonds, at that time, were sold for a small sum ... and we paid expensively for everything, everyone had enough to live, and to save, because the money was in circulation.[211]

Stiglingh added a human touch when addressing the conference in Griquastad: 'We were in a flourishing state. The diamond miner was surely, not a rich man, but by Saturday he always had 2 to 3 pound sterling in his pocket.'[212] A correspondent depicted the previous era in the diamond fields as a golden era with thousands of miners and others living in honour and happiness.[213] A miner, who had worked in the diamond fields for 22 years as an independent digger and as company manager, hailed the principle of competition. He preferred a situation in which some 20,000 miners earned about £100 a year. He wrote thus on the good old days: 'I had worked 17 years in the diamond fields prior to the amalgamation and we were always happy if by the end of the year we had more or less 100 pound, and the colony and the beach in Somerset West were full of miners and businessmen from the diamond fields.'[214] Old Kimberley was a small man's paradise.

Then came the fall: 'When did the flourishing stop?' asked Van den Heever: 'From the moment compounds were established, and De Beers acquired monopoly.' Van der Walt was short but expressive in stating his position: 'I loath the principle of monopoly.'[215] The amalgamation marked the victory of profit and rationalisation over the free-for-all economic frontier. It was a victory of the economic power of the rich over the economic hope of the small man. According to Stiglingh the decline of the diamond fields occurred when Rhodes came and said: '10,000 pounds a year is too little for me, I must have 60,000 or 70,000 pounds, and that is the cause of amalgamation.'[216] The enrichment of the few was at the expense of the many who had scratched a living and dreamt of better days: 'Now that the Amalgamation is through, and the diamonds are sold for a high price ... everything is in a languishing state.' The impact on the small man, as stated by the report of the Kimberley Bond branch, was devastating: 'Businesses are closed in great numbers, hundreds of houses are demolished, the poverty grows alarmingly, workers walk around hungry looking for work and yet can earn nothing ... The monopoly of the Beers is responsible for all this.'[217] The monopoly had a devastating impact on the farmers of Griqualand West as well. As De Kock complained, the farmer was unable to sell horses to the company, as much of the work was performed by machines; he was unable to find markets for his grain because the company began sowing its own grain to save expense; he had to pay much more for wood because of the large-scale demand for wood by De Beers.'[218] Economic progress definitely had its ugly face.

The crusaders for the small man did not accept the advent of monopoly dispassionately, as an inevitable, if undesirable, outcome of the laws of macro-economics, and the suffering of the common man as the pangs of economic development. For them it was a contest between the profits of the rich and the justice of the small man. It was morally a highly charged contest. The editor of the *GR* gave a succinct description of this moral dimension, arguing that the cause of the small man was deserving 'because it is a struggle between capital and labour, between monopoly and free trade, between tyranny and freedom, between the rich companies, which want to become richer, and the poor who also want to live'.[219] The moral indignation was fed by the fact that the wealth in the diamond fields was concentrated in the hands of foreigners. Thus, the past, when mining had been in the hands of 'individual miners who had made a living by the sweat of their brow' and the present, with the diamond fields in the hands of 'a lot of English capitalists' were morally juxtaposed.[220] Stiglingh told a Bond meeting at Kimberley that he failed to understand 'why European capitalists must be made millionaires through the compound system from which the country derives no benefit'.[221] The capitalists' profits were presented as excessive, and by implication illegitimate.

Rhodes was portrayed as the epitome of capitalist immorality: 'In short he is a model of selfishness. As long as he can fill his coffers and achieve his goals he cares nothing about the land and the people.'[222] He was pursuing his private interests with great determination without regard to the 'losses and calamities he has caused to people and villages, and consequently to the whole colony'.[223] The attitude towards Rhodes among the crusaders had a definite element of populist moral judgement and outrage: 'Let Rhodes with his unholy influence go to hell. *Vox populi, vox dei*, let the voice of the people prevail, and away with Rhodes, the ambitious and rich Dictator. Long live uprightness among our *volk*.'[224]

The struggle for the opening up of newly discovered diamond mines for public digging was one against the injuries and injustices perpetrated by a monopolistic De Beers, and for the re-creation of the lost paradise, of a morally appropriate economic and social space which would allow the small man to scratch a living independently and to cherish the hope of a big fortune and a respectable position in society.

From the point of view of the populists, the struggle between the Rhodes and the Banyailand trekkers had a similar moral-ideological dimension. The ordinary trekkers seeking land for settlement for themselves and their children were being frustrated by another company headed by the same 'octopus'. This dimension of the conflict provided the challengers with more ammunition in their battle for the high economic and social moral ground which was mainly waged in the mining fields of Griqualand West.

The struggle in the north, however, also had broader and deeper dimensions which fed the ideological-moral contest within Cape 'Afrikanerdom'. From a challenger, populist perspective, the controversy over the Banyailand trek brought to the fore issues related to the core and essence of the Afrikaner settler ethos and tradition in South Africa. For the opponents of the chartered company supporting the trekkers, it represented the struggle between *Afrikanderisme* and imperialism, the two contending traditions and practices in the expansion of European frontiers in South Africa. It was a contest between the internal expanding dynamic of indigenised European settlers towards the vast expanses of the interior, which was manifested in the micro, gradual, incessant endeavours of the *trek boer* in the Cape, and in the more determined and organised effort of the *Voortrekkers* in the Great Trek, on the one hand, and the macro, external imperial intervention, on the other. In the Cape, the indigenous Afrikaner settling tradition was fed by two sources. The one flowed from the Midlands and the east, the domain of the *trek boers* and the springboard for the *Voortrekkers*. The *GR*, enthusing about the supposed victory of the 'free trekkers' in the Burgersdorp conference in November 1891, mirrored this tradition:

> The more one moves away from Cape Town, the less there are people who are bewitched by Rhodes. The more one approaches the republics the heart beats more warmly for the free trekkers. It is not coincidental that Burgersdorp is the place where the trekkers have obtained a moral victory. Since the old times this place has been the focus of a genuine uncontaminated independent Afrikaner disposition.[225]

The second source was the Paarl 'patriotic' tradition manifested in the Association of Genuine Afrikaners and the *Patriot*. It was in the 'History of our Land in the Language of our People', that the Paarl zealots, particularly S.J. du Toit, laid the historiographical foundations for a nationalist mythology which highlighted and elevated the Great Trek.[226] While S.J. du Toit 'changed with the time', his brother, Oom Lokomotief, continued to carry the flame. On 14 October 1891, he wrote to his brother: 'When will you stop fulfilling the role of a *misleider* (misleader) in the Mashonaland question?'[227] It was another Paarlite, one of the founders of the Association, who, in a private letter to a cabinet minister, emotionally confirmed that the local 'patriotic' tradition had not been totally extinguished:

> I am ... an Africander and have a heart within me which beats for my fellow colonists (*stamverwantes*) who have suffered a century by imperialism. You know me and are aware that I mean it seriously when I solemnly declare that sooner may my right hand forget its cunning than that I can forget the Kaffer-Hottentot and slave questions which caused the tragedy of Slagters Nek and the suffering at the hands of Mzilikazi, Dingaan ....

Complaining that Africans and Hottentots were allowed to trek to wherever they wished he continued: 'It is a crying shame that it is only to the Africander boer this is prohibited by ... England.' Another member of the Association, D.J. Malan, was one of the leaders of the trek.[228]

After the *Patriot* defected to Rhodes's camp, the *GR* provided the flagship for the bearers of this tradition. It is hardly surprising that in the midst of the trek crisis it ran a long account of the *Voortrekkers* of the Great Trek and dedicated a long article to the Paardekraal ceremony.[229] The supporters of the Banyailand trekkers were inspired not only by historical tradition but also by contemporary republicanism. The *GR* published the appeal of Revd. van der Lingen from the Orange Free State to support the trekkers.[230] It also took over from the *Express* from Bloemfontein a long emotional poem on the trek to the north.[231] On the same day that these republican contributions were published, the editor proclaimed: 'Long live the Trekkers, the true reclaimers of the land.'[232] On another occasion he pinned his hope on this trekking tradition: 'We declare frankly that we sincerely hope that the Trekkers may win, because the Afrikaners have been up to now the *Voortrekkers* of South Africa, and more qualified men can not be found.'[233] The struggle in the north was presented as one 'between the representatives of the true Afrikaner Nationality and Imperialism'.[234] Subsequently, the editor called on D.P. van den Heever to lead a movement 'to save *Afrikanderisme* from the hands of imperialism'.[235]

If in the case of the diamond fields Rhodes performed the role of the arch-capitalist, in the Banyailand drama he was presented also as the epitome of aggressive imperialism. After a period of decline in the fortunes of imperialism which culminated in Sir Hercules Robinson's farewell speech, the ascendance of Rhodes marked an imperialist resurgence.[236] The chartered company was portrayed as a pure imperialist project, and Rhodes as 'an adventurer of the first degree' who 'cares nothing about our land and our people as long as he can promote his Charter'.[237] He abused his influence 'not to exploit our resources, but to exploit the resources of Zambesia and to promote De Beers' monopoly'. Rhodes, 'who oppressed our brothers the trekkers for the sake of imperialism and his self interest', wanted the Afrikaners to conquer the wilderness for him.[238] A correspondent revealed, and condemned, the linkage between Kimberley and the north: 'There is here a diamond monopoly which is injurious to the colony and whose profits are being used for the acquisition of countries like Mashonaland and Matabeleland for the sake of expanding imperialism … and for infringement on the independence of the Transvaal and the Orange Free State.'[239] The 'octopus' stretched his tentacles to grab, not only diamonds, but also lands.[240] Both the diamond fields and the north were the birthright of the sons of the land.

It is hardly surprising that, as in the former case, the assault on the chartered company and its head had a clear moral dimension. Thus, with reference to his venture in the north Rhodes was labelled 'Cecil the Mammon'.[241] On another occasion, while hailing the trekkers, the *GR* added: 'away with all the intrigue. Let right and justice prevail.'[242] Little wonder that there was, among the challengers, strong opposition to Rhodes's dual position, as premier and head of the chartered company. Expressing a hope for his speedy downfall the editor wrote: 'That Mr. Rhodes has a mind of wonderful capacity we admit, but looking upon his gigantic speculations, connected as he is with this colony as head of our Government, we cannot but fear and tremble.'[243]

The Bond was guilty by association. Since its prominent leaders were closely associated with Rhodes and his government, and since they also supported his ventures in the diamond fields and in the north, they also became a target of the moral crusade. In articulating the unnatural, immoral alliance between the Bond and Rhodes, the challengers resorted, as in the case of the diamond fields, to the cycle of golden era and decay, of paradise and fall. The glorious past of the Bond and its decay, corresponded to, and were the cause of, the flourishing and decay in Griqualand West and the colony as a whole. The socio-economic decay resulted not from the thrust of amoral economic forces, but rather from the fall of immoral politicians. Likewise, the misfortunes of the Banyailand trekkers were caused, primarily, not by violent intervention of external forces, but rather by immoral local choices. The populist cure to the present ills was a return to the healthy past. Since, however, the ills were moral, rather than physical, what was urgently needed was not a medical practitioner, but rather a moral crusader who could resurrect the past.

A correspondent from Aberdeen, in the midlands, conveying the sentiments of Bondsmen in his area, stated that the 'spirit of the Bond is not what it used to be in the past'.[244] Van den Heever told a public meeting that the Bond 'is not what it ought to be and what it could have been'. 'Is the Bond still carrying its flags?' he asked rhetorically. Liebenberg, another Bondsman, reinforced this assertion: 'The Bond has lost its true original colours.'[245] Reflecting on current decay, the latter said in a previous meeting: 'The Bond is one of the greatest and most worthwhile things to be created in the country. It was established in honour and honesty and so it was managed for a long time.'[246] Indeed the glorious past was rooted in its moral qualities. The *GR*, referring to members' attitudes towards the Bond, added another moral quality to the golden era: 'The Bond, when it was small and hated by everybody, was dearer to them than now that it is respectable and praised. Then the Bond was despised from without, but inside a strong patriotism prevailed.'[247] Modesty, honour, honesty and patriotism were the moral pillars of Cape Afrikaner populist political paradise. This morally purist approach to politics was oblivious to the requisites of the politics of power. The political morality of the challengers was congruent with their predominantly peripheral support base.

Facing the onslaught of huge waves of new economic and political forces which transformed the scale and scope of Cape politics, rendering it far more complex than ever before, the moral purists did not accept the new politics of the Bond, and particularly its alliance with Rhodes, as a necessary adaptation to new actors and new circumstances. Rather, they presented it as a manifestation of the moral decline of the leadership. Indeed, the personalisation and moralisation of the critique of the Bond–Rhodes alliance was a haven to many who could not grasp, and come to terms with, the dramatic changes in the scale and intensity in both economy and politics. It was easier, and morally satisfying, to brand the Bond–Rhodes alliance as 'unholy', as van den Heever and the editor of the *GR* did,[248] than to accept responsibility for the messiness of the kitchen of the politics of power. It was easier, and more personally gratifying, to depict Bond leaders as corrupt self-seekers, than to sympathise, or at least empathise, with their dilemmas.

Indeed, Bond leaders were subjected to a barrage of unsavoury characterisations. They were 'traitors, imperialists and turncoats'; they were 'ambitious, self-seekers, tyrants'; they were modern false prophets worshipping Rhodes's gold sacks; they were Bondits (bandits) worshipping Cecil the Mammon; they showed devotion to the 'octopus'; they believed that might was right.[249] Forgetting their early humility they indulged in self-glorification and viewed the world 'through the glasses of the big men'.[250] The biblical metaphor was that the innocent leaders who had inhabited the political paradise were seduced by the modern snakes and ate the proverbial apple. The *GR* suggested that the agents of seduction were shares in De Beers and the chartered company and other material benefits received by Bond leaders.[251] That S.J. du Toit, 'who ignores logic, justice and honesty', was singled out for special treatment is understandable, as he was the epitome of the fallen Afrikaner. He was the father of all that the challengers cherished and, yet, he had become an arch supporter of Rhodes. For that he earned himself the role of Judas Iscariot disguised as a patriot.[252] Hofmeyr was not spared either,[253] while R.P. Botha, the most prominent Bond leader in the midlands, was the local scapegoat.[254]

It is hardly surprising that in the eyes of the challengers the Bond leaders shirked their responsibility and neglected their calling. In criticising the behaviour of the Bond and its leaders the populist inspiration is all too apparent. Thus, the Bond leaders 'lost the sympathy for their poor brothers, instead of offering them a helping hand'. With reference to the two burning issues Bond leaders were condemned for not acting 'in accordance with the voice of the people' and showing no sympathy 'for their brothers [the trekkers] or for the poor in Kimberley'. In worshipping Rhodes they 'have forgotten their promises to the burghers'. They 'sealed their ears to the supplications of the sons of the land'. Referring to the 1893 Bond congress, the *GR* complained that the Bond 'plays the imperial game more enthusiastically than ever before', and that instead of checking imperial influences it served as a conduit thereto.[255] A correspondent blamed Hofmeyr for supporting a government which was the enemy of the Afrikaners.[256] The conclusion was highly congruent with the criticism: 'We are convinced that the Bond, in the way it operates today, does not serve the interests of the country, on the contrary, it brings more harm than good.'[257]

Clearly, from the point of view of the challengers, the leaders of the Bond forfeited the right to lead, because they betrayed the cause of 'Afrikanerdom'. Indeed, the assault on the leadership also raised the question of who was the true Afrikaner. With regard to the *Patriot*, the *GR* argued that it was no longer an Afrikaner newspaper.[258] Referring to the supporters of R.P. Botha, it was argued that they 'could not be genuine Afrikaners, because no true Afrikaner could be a Rhodes's proselyte'.[259] The trekkers, it was suggested, 'could now appeal only to independent Afrikaners and a few upright Afrikaners'.[260] 'An upright Afrikaner' was the 'genuine, honest' one who was enraged by injustices perpetrated against fellow Afrikaners.[261] He was 'the ordinary Bondsman who does not entertain in his head crafty schemes'. An upright Afrikaner was also a lover of truth. The concept of the upright Afrikaner was distinctly populist. These qualities are more usually found in utopian sects, or in lost paradises, than among real politicians. From the challengers' perspective the *GR* question 'is there a need for the Bond?',[262] was rhetorical. The predicament of 'Afrikanerdom' demanded that the Bond 'be led by men of conscience who would perform the role that it had performed in the past'. A moral leadership would lead the Bond to the golden past. With a view to the need to replace Hofmeyr as leader of the

Bond, it was clearly stated that sincerity was a more important leadership quality than ability.[263]

The Bond leadership faced a serious moral, ideological and political challenge. Its seriousness stemmed not from the political-institutional strength of the challengers. As we have seen, the Bond leadership easily thwarted the challenges from these quarters within the party, and within the parliamentary caucus they enjoyed overwhelming support. However, the Bond, as we have seen, was rather ineffectual as a political party. Its electoral success and parliamentary influence stemmed more from being perceived as the vanguard of 'Afrikanerdom' than from effective leadership and party discipline. Despite constant attacks on the mouthpiece of the challengers, and the establishment of a Bond newspaper in Graaff Reinet, the *GR* was able to survive without diluting its message. Another reason that the challenge could not be ignored was that its moral and ideological content was rooted in Afrikaner sensitivities and the Afrikaner belief system, namely moderate anti-imperialism and concern for the small man engulfed by the forces of international capitalism. Furthermore, the assault of the challengers within the Cape was constantly supported by moral and ideological artillery fire from the republics.[264] The challenge had to be faced, not only in party congresses and parliamentary caucuses, but also in the moral and ideological battle fields.

The response of the Bond to the ideological and moral assault on its alliance with Rhodes

Whereas the challengers resorted mainly to ideological and moral arguments, the Bond, as a political party closely associated with the government, responded on a broader front. Its response covered almost the whole spectrum of the appropriate Afrikaner order. It touched upon material interests, foreign relations, political strategy, ideological vision and moral basis. In responding to the challenge to the alliance with Rhodes, the Bond mostly sharpened old weapons rather than produced new ones. It picked up, and further articulated, concepts and arguments it had been using since it first 'discovered' Rhodes in about 1886.

With regard to De Beers, a range of arguments were employed in defence of the Bond's support of the company's monopoly, and against the Wesselton miners, the proposed export tax on diamonds and the demand for ballot in the Kimberley elections. In defence of the monopoly the law of supply and demand in a limited market was mobilised, the argument being that unless the price of diamonds was kept high mining would not be profitable.[265] The monopoly was to be supported, despite opposition in principle, because De Beers was a 'colonial' company, the operations of which benefited not only the Cape but also South Africa as a whole.[266] Then there was the class alliance argument. The interests of the farmers and mining capital were the same and capitalists like Rhodes and Barnato understood this, despite being English. De Beers was a bulwark against the other, threatening Kimberley – swarming radical types, agitators and rioters. It was in the 'other Kimberley' that the 'natural' class enemies of 'Afrikanerdom' were to be found – the traders who wanted to improve the standard of living of their potential 'native' clients, and the 'have nots' who harboured jealousy and contempt towards the Afrikaner landowners and desired to beat the 'haves'. Rhodes's opposition to the ballot in Kimberley was justified on the grounds that its proponents wanted to use it for the introduction of workers' representation. Stiglingh, an aspiring bourgeois with petit bourgeois ideas, was branded as a socialist who wanted to be the candidate of 'the Knights of Labour and the Coolies', and the Wesselton miners were discredited as 'a revolutionary element'. De Beers deserved support because of Rhodes, who had ushered in the new class alliance. The victory of the 'other Kimberley', and their kind, would inflict calamity, not only on the diamond industry, but also on the colony as a whole. Rhodes, the steadfast enemy of all these sinister forces, was the 'natural ally' of true 'Afrikanerdom'.[267]

The other major controversial issue, namely, the occupation of the north by Rhodes, touched, as we have seen, on much more sensitive nerves in the collective body of Cape Afrikaners. It evoked strong sentiments relating to the core of the Afrikaners' historical experience, to the myths of their collective creation, to their destiny and to their relations to their 'blood' brothers in the republics. Correspondingly, the challenge of the purists was viewed in much more serious vein, the Bond leadership and press being more defensive and apologetic about their collaboration with Rhodes against the Adendorff trek. This was manifested in Hofmeyr's speech at the Paarl meeting in mid-October 1891. He did not oppose the principle of settling new lands in the old way. On the contrary, he declared that 'he would have preferred by far that the country be thrown open and populated in the old Dutch Afrikander manner by the *Voortrekker*, the true pioneer of South Africa'.[268] The *ZA* also paraded its preference for a different way of occupying the north.[269] Hofmeyr claimed that he acted as he did in order to avert 'a fearful carnival of blood in the Northern territory' which could engulf both the imperial government and the Transvaal, with grave consequences for the latter. For this noble service for 'Afrikanerdom', he was prepared to estrange friends and relations and to suffer indignities.[270] The *ZA* was more modest in rationalising its support for the chartered company, simply resorting to the imperative of the politics of the possible: 'whoever cannot get what he wants must grab what he can'.[271] S.J. du Toit, in his elaborate open letter to the trekkers, simply exonerated both the chartered company and the Cape from any blame; it was all the fault of the British who had declared the north a British sphere of influence.[272] J.H. Smith, the MP for Graaff Reinet, echoing this legalistic argument, added Britain's superior power as a justification for the Bond's position.[273]

Other, more positive arguments were also used to rationalise and vindicate the opposition to the settlement of the north 'in the old Dutch Afrikaner manner'. In doing that, previous themes were picked up and elaborated upon. Much of this argument hinged on the personality of Rhodes and on the unlimited trust the Bond leadership had in him. *OL*, which was as close to the Bond's 'official mind' as possible, argued that since the north would have been occupied, in any case, Rhodes was preferable, not only to either Germany or Portugal, but also to the Transvaal. The reasons for this preference were that Rhodes 'had so much sympathy for the Afrikaners and acted in collaboration with them', and that he would govern his northern domain in accordance with 'Cape principles'.[274]

The foremost principle that they had in mind was 'native' policy. At best Rhodes would implement in the north the 'native' policy of the republics and Natal, at worst that of the Cape.[275] By 1892, Bondsmen could speak about that with much greater authority than before. Whereas previously they could refer only to Rhodes's promises, by 1892 Rhodes was delivering some goods. In getting his government, with its liberal wing, and Parliament to raise the franchise to the detriment of black political advance, Rhodes made a most significant contribution to the entrenchment of white domination. In the debate on the Franchise and Ballot Bill Rhodes made extra political mileage by confiding that 'personally he would have liked to copy the franchise of Natal in so far as the natives were concerned'.[276] According to Hofmeyr, this Bill removed the fear, among Afrikaners, that 'some Englishmen were not clear upon the line of demarcation between barbarism and civilisation as existed in India, in Natal and other countries, where the distinction was drawn between the coloured barbarian and the civilised European'.[277] *OC*, praising Rhodes for getting the Bill through, pointed out that only Rhodes could have done it.[278] For this achievement Rhodes was hosted to a lunch by the Bond MPs, whom he told, for further lubrication, that 'his education had instilled in him a sympathy towards the land owner'.[279] In contributing to the shaping of an ideal Afrikaner order in the Cape, Rhodes secured a solid launching pad for his northern expansion.

Thus, Rhodes was perceived and presented, because of his proven position on 'native' policy, as the ideal agent for the establishment of an appropriate, indeed ideal, regional order. As in the Cape, so in the north, Rhodes, the political 'Midas' who had so much influence in England, was the only one who could carve new settlement spaces in the region in which proper distinction between 'coloured barbarism' and 'white civilisation' could be upheld.[280] When the British Liberal government in 1892 was reported to have been opposed to the 'native' policy in Mashonaland, omnipotent Rhodes was relied upon to keep them at bay.[281]

Rhodes's credibility was further enhanced by his manifesting a preference for Afrikaners as settlers in his northern realm: 'Rhodes recognises the value of the colonists for the purpose of colonisation and wants to settle the interior with a settler race.'[282] The *ZA* used more evocative language: 'Rhodes shares the view that there is value in settling Native countries by a people who has forged ahead since the days of Van Riebeeck.'[283] The north was presented, as before, as an ideal settlement space, an additional reason for this view being that it was believed that Rhodes intended to grant it a Cape-like self-government and ultimately to unite it with the Cape. The north was presented as a colonial rather than an imperial project. No wonder that *OL* proclaimed enthusiastically: 'It is a victory for the Cape that the expansion to the North is undertaken and controlled in such a way by RHODES [sic].'[284] Rhodes was a political alchemist transforming what seemed an imperial project into one with a clear Afrikaner character.[285] T.P. Theron confirmed that on the issue of imperialism versus *Afrikanderism* Rhodes was in full harmony with Hofmeyr and S.J. du Toit.[286] Rhodes in the north was the agent of the ideal colony that was beginning to emerge in the Cape under his blessed influence – the victory of Afrikaner ideas under the British flag.[287] There was no incongruence in the claim that Rhodes was, in a sense, following in the footsteps of the *Voortrekkers*: 'He does not strive to get rid of British rule, but, like the *Voortrekkers*, his enterprise is daring and it is also possible to expect the development of a country for the European race.'[288] The *Voortrekkers'* experience had been updated, and Rhodes's northern project was ideologically legitimised through full Afrikanerisation. The Bond press and the party actively encouraged Cape Afrikaners to settle in this Afrikaner Utopia.[289]

As before, the north was presented not only as a political Utopia, but also as a fabulous economic Eldorado. The Bond press continued to marvel at the economic wealth of the north, the glittering of the gold, the green colour of the pasture and the magic sound of flowing streams continuing to provide a congenial backdrop.[290] The importance of the north to the economic prosperity of the Cape was underlined by a further increase in the import duties imposed by the Transvaal on Cape produce. Indeed, the preference for Rhodes, over the Transvaal, as the developer of the north was justified by the continuing economic hostility of the latter.[291] The north was also perceived as a means to solve the worsening socio-economic decline among the Afrikaner farming community. Indeed, in the early 1890s, the Bond became increasingly aware of the problem of the 'poor whites' (predominantly Afrikaners).[292] In April 1893, *OL* wrote that 'the upliftment of our needy whites and the salvation of their children is for us, as Afrikaners, a question of survival'.[293] C.W.H. Kohler, a prominent Bondsman from Paarl, proposed that the few hundred farmers who were getting ready to trek to Mashonaland take along with them a number of '*bijwoners* [squatters] of the better classes', who would assist in farm work and supervise black labour. Their main role would be to serve the company as volunteers in the event of 'native' wars and they would be able to settle newly available land.[294]

Rhodes himself joined the Afrikaner discourse again, making contributions designed to maximise support for his project. In September 1891, with the Banyailand trek controversy still raging, Rhodes told an audience in Cradock in the Eastern Province: 'His aim was to settle the country with Colonial men ... He wished to bind this country with the Cape Colony in the closest of bonds. He has worked for its acquisition in the interests of the Cape Colony, and to provide an outlet for them and their children (applause) ... He wished ... to lead in the future to the extension of the Cape boundaries to the Zambesi. (applause)'[295] A year later he whetted the appetite of his Little Karoo audience: 'Mashonaland is a good land with unlimited resources, and it will be the inheritance of the next generation in this colony ... (loud applause).'[296]

Some Afrikaners, at least, seem to have been intoxicated by Rhodes's aggressive expansionism. The *ZA* enthused about the prospects of Afrikaner farmers settling even across the Zambesi and joining hands with fellow Afrikaner farmers who had settled in the highlands of southern Angola.[297] Referring to Rhodes's Cape to Cairo telegraph line plans, the *ZA* predicted a Cape to Cairo railway line and envisaged tickets to Cairo being sold in the Cape.[298] Cape expansion into the interior, in collaboration with Rhodes, not only awakened Afrikaner material desires; it also stirred their imagination. No wonder that Rhodes's dual position, as premier and head of the chartered company, a major target for the challengers, was perceived as beneficial: 'The dual position is not a disadvantage; it is one of the strong arguments in favour of Rhodes.'[299] The Colossus had dragged the parochial Afrikaners to new heights, where a vast Promised Land lay at their feet. They could not resist the temptation; they were crossing into the dangerous zone of the politics of the desirable.

There was another important issue relating to its alliance with Rhodes which the Bond had to defend against the assault from within and without, namely the relations between Rhodes and the republics, particularly the

177

Transvaal. This was related to the northern project, which the Transvaal perceived as the ultimate act in the process of its encirclement by the forces of imperialism. By association, the Bond was accused of conniving with imperialism and newspapers in the Transvaal branded its leaders and its press as Rhodes's paid agents.[300] In persistently refusing to accept Rhodes's north as an imperialist endeavour, it , indirectly, addressed this embarrassing accusation. The Bond tried to resolve the contradiction between the two northern options and between the requisites of their alliance with Rhodes and those of close co-operation with its ethnic brothers in Transvaal, by convincing its members, and attempting to persuade Transvalers, that Rhodes, far from being the enemy of the independent republics, was, in fact, their natural ally. The *ZA* insisted that Kruger was wrong in viewing Rhodes as his personal adversary,[301] while S.J. du Toit was short and clear: 'Mr. Rhodes has got nothing against the existing Republics, he will not interfere with their independence, he wishes to promote friendly intercourse with them in the same manner as the Bond.'[302] The British refusal to hand over Swaziland to the Transvaal, on the basis of the 1890 Swaziland convention, was a source of grievance in Pretoria and embarrassment for the Bond. In the Transvaal, the Cape government and Rhodes were blamed for the Swaziland impasse. The Bond was, understandably, very keen to remove this obstacle in the way of improving relations with the republic.[303] With a view to another conference on Swaziland, the *ZA* suggested that if annexation to the Transvaal were to be effected, it would be, 'not to a small extent', attributable to the position taken by Rhodes and the Cape parliament.[304] The *ZA* took advantage of the statement of the spokesman of the 'National Union', the *Uitlanders'* protest movement in Johannesburg, that Rhodes had nothing to do with them. It also tried to sell its class analysis to the Transvalers:

> People like Rhodes, who possess clear views on South Africa, and support the rights of the settlers as the natural rulers of our region, also belong to the 'haves' who are the natural allies of Kruger and the Transvaal farmers.[305]

Rhodes himself contributed his share to the validity of this particular argument. Responding to allegations that he was hostile to the independence of the Transvaal, he said that 'nothing is more remote from my thinking and more contrary to my view'. *OL*, quoting him, made political capital, saying: 'These words by Rhodes, must, not only assuage our friends in the North, but also arouse them to work enthusiastically for the attainment of the unity Rhodes expects.'[306] Needless to say, Transvalers remained unconvinced.

Rhodes was thus perceived by his Cape Afrikaner followers as the promoter of South African unity. Not less importantly, they portrayed him, during his premiership more than before, as the amalgamator of the two white 'races' into a new white nation. This had been, as we have seen, the Bond's vision from its inception. This attribute of Rhodes was best articulated by his staunch supporter, D.C. de Waal, in an interview to the *Review of Reviews*:

> I am Dutch by birth and language, but I recognise that South Africa will be European; the English and the Dutch must unite, as did the Dutch and the Huguenot in the earlier years of the colony. The harmonious union of the two white races is the condition of progress and peace in South Africa. It is the glory of Rhodes that he, more clearly than any other Englishman, recognised this truth, and has at last secured its recognition as the axiom of South African policy.[307]

Indeed, Rhodes the premier, in his open alliance with the Bond, legitimised it in the eyes of many Englishmen. During this period many English-speakers joined the Bond and some represented it in Parliament, facts that were greatly prized by the Bond leadership.

Thus, during Rhodes's first premiership, he was at the centre of an ideological controversy within the Bond's ranks about central socio-economic and ethno-political issues. The conflicting parties contested the appropriateness of the emerging internal, South African and regional orders. Verbal exchanges were loaded and bitter, and emotions heightened. However, the extent of the controversy and the depth of the rift can be overstated. Beyond the verbal extravagance and emotional outbursts, there was sufficient ideological and political common ground to ensure that the threats of a split remained merely threats. It would be wrong to deduce from the pro-republic, anti-imperialist stance of the challengers that they represented ethnic chauvinism, extreme anti-imperialism and xenophobic anti-English feelings. This was clearly not the case. D.P. van den Heever, the firebrand and the most prominent Bond leader among the challengers, was neither anti-British nor anti-English. He remained as loyal to the bone as he had ever been. His reasons for claiming that the Bond did not fly the Bond's flag, would disappoint searchers for the origins of Afrikaner ethnic nationalism: 'The Bond was established to bring Afrikaners and English together ... can it be denied that the Bond acts on occasion unilaterally?'[308] The editor of the *GR*, the pro-trekkers, anti-imperialist crusader, and the apostle of *Afrikanderisme* who denounced Bond leaders for not being 'genuine Afrikaners', responded rather meekly to the accusation that he advised the Adendorff trekkers to shoot British soldiers: 'I am too loyal to the British Government to speak in such a manner.' In advocating the case of the trekkers he wrote: 'They do not wish to discard the British flag

179

or to be disloyal subjects.'[309] McCusker, the Afrikaner patriot, like Van den Heever, accused the Bond of sowing discord between English and Dutch-speakers.[310] With all the violent verbosity, the challengers never turned Bond congresses into arenas of vehement confrontation on the pan-Afrikaner Banyailand trek issue.

Likewise, Rhodes's staunch allies and admirers were not, in their perceptions and professions, traitors to the 'national' cause either. S.J. du Toit, in his open letter to the trekkers, addressed the issue of his ethno-ideological credentials:

> The alienation which separates us now cannot be attributed to a change on my side ... The 7,000 who protested to the English Queen, when injustice was done against our republican brothers, have not yet bent their knees before the Baal of British Imperialism. We have not become Jingoes. Rhodes does not have enough money to buy us out ... No, we are still the same men, with the same sympathy for justice and truth, driven by the same patriotism, nationalism and love of freedom. Africa for the Afrikaners! we call now as before.[311]

Du Toit also continued to propagate the idea that language was the fountain of national feeling.[312] Hofmeyr also continued to promote the Dutch language as the focus of Afrikaner collective identity and consciousness. Dr J.M. Hoffman, who travelled from Paarl to Philipstown to gain support for Rhodes against the Banyailand trekkers, said nothing on this controversial issue. His speech was, rather, geared to infuse organic national feeling among the Afrikaners: 'Keep your language ... also be proud of your nationality and of your language. "The language is the *Volk*."'[313] Referring to being denigrated as 'Judas Iscariot', Hofmeyr wrote that 'the real patriot works for his people even when he is condemned'.[314] For Rhodes's adherents there was no contradiction between support for him and devotion to their 'nationalist' cause: 'We are pleased that we have a prime minister who wishes to cooperate with our National party in our struggle for a United South Africa in a national sense.'[315]

In January 1893, the *taal* (language) celebrations were held in Burgersdorp in eastern Cape. During the celebrations, at which the foundation stone for the Dutch language monument was laid, the monument committee marched under the British flag. Of the three speakers one, D.P. van den Heever, was a leading challenger from the east, whereas three, Hofmeyr, S.J. du Toit and Kohler, were Rhodes's supporters from the west.[316] This episode highlighted the underlying unity which enabled the Bond to contain diversity.

They were all, challengers as well as Rhodes's loyalists, part of the same process of evolving Afrikaner political consciousness and assertion. All of them shared, to a greater or smaller degree, the experience of dramatic economic, social, cultural and political changes ushered in by the penetration of imperialism and capitalism. They were also subjected to the contradictions and ambiguities which marked this transition. They all developed a corresponding world outlook and strategies, characterised by eclecticism and ambivalence. The mixtures were obviously different. What was at the root of this ideological division between them? A conclusive answer is tempting but perhaps premature. There was definitely a noticeable regional variation, with the west being the bastion of Rhodes's loyalists. However, there were many Rhodes supporters in the Midlands and the east, the strongholds of the challengers. A socio-economic perspective may also be useful. In Rhodes's camp one finds many of the economically more progressive elements in Afrikaner society – farmers, businessmen and professionals – while the challengers seem to have drawn their support mainly from the relatively marginal sheep farmers. This socio-economic correlation overlapped to a certain extent the regional one, with the more progressive elements being concentrated mainly in Cape Town and the west whereas the sheep farmers were largely in the Midlands and the east. Yet Rhodes had support also in marginal sheep farmers' constituencies. A.S. le Roex, representing a sheep farming constituency, and a staunch Rhodes supporter, was not an exception. A class analysis explaining the anti-Rhodes opposition within the Bond in terms of a petit bourgeois response to the growing influence of big capital, also runs up against another embarrassing piece of evidence. S.J. du Toit, who had been the arch-articulator and propagator of the petit bourgeois position at the early stages of the evolution of the Bond, was now one of Rhodes's closest collaborators. His short disastrous experience of big speculative capitalism in the highlands left him with no money and many bitter memories. It seems that to be sustainable, any interpretation of diversity of the Afrikaner political consciousness must take account of the overall socialisation process of the Cape Afrikaners, with its multi-dimensional complexity. There were those who could adjust to the vast increase in the scope of their economic and political horizons, and to the requisites of power and responsibility in a political game whose stakes were much higher than ever before; there were others who for various reasons clung to the innocence and purity of their political adolescence.

Clearly, throughout Rhodes's first premiership, the balance between the two camps within the Bond leaned heavily on the side of Rhodes's supporters. While being at the centre of heated controversies, Rhodes enjoyed the trust and solid support of the Bond. In December 1892, *OL*, while enthusing about the reception Rhodes received in England, stated that 'in the Cape his influence has not diminished, and he stands higher in the eyes of the public here than ever before'.[317] Yet, it seems that the assault on the alliance made its supporters cautious. Thus, in presenting the toast to the government at a 1893 Bond congress dinner, even S.J. du Toit was somewhat reticent, claiming that 'we are not blind followers of Rhodes'. While summing up Rhodes's record in a positive manner, he concluded that 'the Bond will not support the government one day too much, but also that the Bond will not do it a day less'. The subsequent response of the participants reflected a less inhibited attitude: 'The toast was drunk with a thundering and prolonged applause and with cries Rhodes! Rhodes! and with the singing of "For he's a jolly good fellow".'[318]

RHODES'S SECOND MINISTRY

The demise of Rhodes's first ministry had nothing to do with his relations with the Bond. In fact, it occurred when his standing with the Bond establishment was at a peak. The ministry's fall, almost entirely of English origin, was caused by the infamous 'Logan affair'.[319] Towards the end of 1892 it became known that Sivewright, the Commissioner for Crown Lands and Public Works and a close associate and ally of Rhodes, had granted J.D. Logan, his friend, a contract to supply refreshments on the entire Cape railway network for 18 years, without inviting tenders and for a ridiculously low payment. Rhodes, who was then on his way to England with Sivewright, faced the music only upon returning to the Cape in March 1893. The music was played by the liberal 'trio' in his cabinet – Merriman, Innes and Sauer – who insisted on the removal from the cabinet of the perpetrator of this political immorality as a condition to their remaining in it. While Rhodes was very reluctant to give up the service of the three, who provided his ministry with talent it otherwise lacked, he found it especially difficult to dump Sivewright. Not only was he a faithful and capable ally of Rhodes in his various projects and schemes; he was also the 'Afrikaner from Aberdeen', a Bond member and a close associate and confidant of Hofmeyr. The *ZA* surmised, in early December 1892, that Sivewright would come out clean, adding that he was not only highly capable, but also a man who could 'march together with the prime minister and the Bond ... and offer Rhodes great assistance in other ways as well'.[320] The *BG* did not want to see the government fall because of the 'Logan affair'.[321] When the crisis broke after Rhodes's return, the *ZA* hoped that Sivewright would survive it. It thought that if he was out and Innes, 'the knight of the philanthropic principles' was in, it would be a 'severe blow' to Rhodes's government.[322]

As often happens in sound relationships, the crisis reaffirmed and reinforced the relations between Rhodes and the Bond. This was manifested in Rhodes's relationship with Hofmeyr which was particularly important in the evolution of the alliance. Rhodes used to consult Hofmeyr regularly in matters concerning the alliance and the government of the colony. However, as when the alliance was struck in 1890, Hofmeyr was not fully available in 1893. In July 1890 he was in Pretoria, negotiating the Swaziland convention. On 24 April 1893, the day of Sivewright's return from overseas, as the crisis was nearing a climax, he was mourning the death of his father. At first hesitating to disturb him in his mourning, Rhodes eventually wrote to him: 'My dear Hofmeyr, – I feel very much ashamed of myself to write to you amidst all your trouble, but I will say, that I have a Cabinet crisis upon me, and I need greatly your calm judgement.'[323] The crisis was, however, sufficiently consequential for Hofmeyr to oblige. The meeting between the two bore evidence to their political intimacy. Together, they worked out a strategy to resolve the crisis by forming a new government. Rhodes tendered his resignation on 2 May, the original idea being to get J.H. de Villiers, the venerable Chief Justice to head the new government. He would certainly have restored to it some of the respectability and decency the former government had lost. Their idea was, however, that the new government, like the old, would be essentially a Bond–Rhodes government with Rhodes within and Hofmeyr without exerting vital influence. When De Villiers refused to accept the list of possible ministers, in Hofmeyr's handwriting, but handed to him by Rhodes, he lost his chance. He took his position as future premier too seriously and too independently.[324] In the end Rhodes himself formed the new government, with Sprigg and two of his men taking the place of the departing ministers. For Merriman the Rhodes–Hofmeyr collaboration during the ministerial crisis was abhorrent: 'Now that the whole thing is over one feels a sense of relief at being free ... also from [the] Rhodes–Hofmeyr way of doing business – the lobbying, the intrigue and utterly cynical disregard of anything approaching moral principle in the conduct of public affairs.'[325]

Clearly, the Bond did not perceive this infringement of political morality as sufficient reason to forego the services of Rhodes or even those of Sivewright. The resolution of the crisis, and the formation of the second Rhodes ministry, was an occasion to reaffirm the Bond's attitude towards Rhodes. *OL* was greatly relieved: 'Had Mr Rhodes retired at this moment it would have been fatal for the welfare of the Colony and the Afrikaner party.' Indeed, their satisfaction had a clear party perspective: 'We have got every reason to expect that he would lead the government safely through the forthcoming session, and would further contribute to the forthcoming elections being of greater significance for the Bond than it is thought.'[326] On the same day *ZA* also expressed joy that Rhodes had taken upon himself to form a new government because 'without him no government will survive'.[327]

Political morality and the general election of 1893–1894

From a strictly political point of view, the ministerial crisis was satisfactorily resolved. However, the 'Logan affair' highlighted the issue of
political morality, which subsequently became a major bone of contention within the Bond and between the Bond and its external Afrikaner
critics. Rhodes, again, was at the centre of this stormy debate. With the
mineral revolution in the Cape, the scope and stakes in the political game
increased considerably. Moreover, the mineral revolution introduced to
the Cape a qualitative, as well as quantitative, transformation. The
diamond industry attracted a new breed of economic entrepreneurs who
adhered much more to market value than to the moral values of the
political market place. Seeing that government policy could determine
the fortunes of the diamond industry, these entrepreneurs were ready to
be as scrupulous, or unscrupulous, in their attitude to politics as they
were in their economic dealings. Rhodes was, essentially, an archetype
of this new breed of pushy unscrupulous capitalists. Merriman, lamenting
the corruption creeping into Parliament, referred to members of the
mercantile classes, chasing railways and other government contracts.[328]
T.P. Theron, the Bond's secretary, wrote bitterly: 'We live in a period
when the motto is: money is more important than principles.'[329]

The challengers to the alliance argued, as we have seen, from a highly
moralistic point of view. Their attacks on the prevailing concepts of socio-
economic and politico-ideological orders were morally loaded. Moreover,
in their moral critique they had already, during Rhodes's first ministry,
gone beyond concepts and orders, passing moral judgement on persons,
as much as on causes. Rhodes was the epitome of the immoral politician,
the 'Mammon', the 'Octopus', greedy and possessed of insatiable appetites.
His immorality was shown, not only in his establishment of an immoral
economic and social regime in the diamond fields, and in preventing the
trekkers from carving a legitimate space for themselves in the north. In
search of these immoral projects he also corrupted Cape politicians and
Cape politics. The *GR* grieved that the power of the money in the hands of
'Mammon Rhodes' was so great. People were afraid of the consequences
when speaking the truth, and whoever did not comply with 'Mammon' was
persecuted.[330] Not only the corruptor, but also the corrupted were taken
to task, Bond leaders being accused of receiving shares and diamonds as
presents.[331] It was argued that MPs did not speak, and editors did not
write, against either De Beers or the chartered company, because they
held shares in both.[332] The Transvaal newspapers attacking the *Patriot* and
the *ZA* wrote of paid agents in Rhodes's service.[333] R.P. Botha was asked
by the *GR* whether it was true that he received £3,000, the sum required
to qualify for the Legislative Council, from Rhodes. Although he refused

to respond to an allegation, made in a public meeting, that he had received material benefits from Rhodes, it was confirmed that he had received a small diamond from Rhodes.[334] In April 1893 it was reported that Rhodes offered Hauptfleisch, a Bondsman from the Midlands, a lucrative job in Kimberley in exchange for political services.[335] It was alleged that people were joining the Bond to gain profit and influence.[336]

Bond leaders were forced to respond to insinuations and straight-forward accusations. In August 1890, P.G. Wege had denied having received material benefits from Rhodes.[337] At a public meeting in Paarl Hofmeyr strongly denied that he had ever been offered bribes.[338] Responding to the *GR*, *OL* asked, rhetorically, whether an MP could not invest in shares in a public company. It further argued that only one or two Bond MPs possessed shares in De Beers and the chartered company, and claimed that those known as 'Rhodes's friends', owned none;[339] this was, of course, untrue. Referring to the Logan contract, Innes wrote that 'the attitude of Hofmeyr in regard to Sivewright, and also the position taken up by Rhodes, has caused great searching of heart among Bond members, who hold very strong views upon the whole Logan contract matter'.[340] If this was true, it is understandable why Bond leaders denied the above allegations.

In Kimberley, De Beers demonstrated how, by applying money and influence, political domination could be gained and consolidated. By the early 1890s all four local MPs were De Beers nominees, farmers and traders having none.[341] The Kimberley electoral experience served as a model for both Rhodes and the Bond. At a time when political stakes were much higher than ever before, the governing alliance needed more solid parliamentary support. The ministerial crisis highlighted the fragility of the coalition and the incompatibility of its components. The new coalition included supporters, on Sprigg's side, who were not known for their love for the Bond. Worse still, the Bond itself was not a solid political platform, lacking as it was in coherence and discipline. This was doubly true for the broader 'Afrikaner National Party'. The establish-ment, in 1889, of the supervision committee's to control election can-didates, was geared toward transforming the Bond into a more effective, disciplined party. Referring to the 1893 parliamentary session, Innes suggested that this goal was as urgent as ever: 'Since I have been in parliament Bond members have not been so divided as in the final session.'. They were divided mainly on regional lines but also on the basis of economic interests.[342] With a view to the general election due to be held in early 1894, it was clearly in the interest of both Rhodes and the Bond leadership not only to increase the parliamentary power of the Bond and of Rhodes, but also to promote more capable candidates with better debating ability[343] and more potential for cabinet positions.

As we have seen, there is evidence that in the 1888 elections there was some collaboration on electoral strategy between Hofmeyr and Rhodes. In 1893, with the alliance having been consolidated, the extent of collaboration increased considerably. The supervision committee actively intervened to secure parliamentary seats for capable, professional, mostly English-speaking, Bond members and supporters like Sivewright, the medical doctors A. Vanes, T.W. Smartt and T.N.G. te Water, and W.P. Schreiner, a barrister.[344] The Bond's electoral efforts were, however, geared not only to improving the quality of future MPs, but also to tightening discipline and enhancing loyalty to the Bond–Rhodes alliance. Indeed, as R.P. Botha told a Bond meeting in Kimberley, loyalty to Rhodes was a prerequisite for Bond candidacy in the forthcoming elections: 'At the Stellenbosch congress Stiglingh spoke too much against Rhodes on the Wesselton [mine] question, and we cannot allow the election of MPs who do not follow Rhodes in everything. We, as Bond, support Rhodes, and, therefore, all [Bond] MPs must support Rhodes.'[345] According to R. Solomon, who in a previous by-election had been promoted by De Beers, he was rejected in the 1894 elections 'because he would not be bound hand and foot to vote for every measure introduced into Parliament'.[346] T.P. Theron said that 'Bondsmen needed a leader and Rhodes was their elected leader'.[347] Botha's position made sense from a party point of view. The *GR* claimed that there was 'a clique of ring leaders, living in Cape Town, who want all the country to dance to their tune', usurping the selection of candidates for the forthcoming elections from the local branches.[348] The message of S.J. du Toit, a member of the Supervision Committee, to Barkly West Bondsmen certainly rendered this allegation credible:

> Bondsmen should not have a will or an opinion. The Bond is everything. If the Supervision Committee decides on a candidate you have to nominate him, because the Supervision Committee knows better than you what is better for the Bond.'[349]

In a meeting of the district executive of the Barkly East Bond branch, letters from T.P. Theron, S.J. du Toit and R.P. Botha strongly recommended the candidacy of Dr.T.W. Smartt, an Irishman, in the forthcoming elections.[350] The Bond leadership clearly attempted not only to improve the quality of its MPs, but also to transform the party into a tightly controlled and disciplined one.

The intervention of the Supervision Committee, in contravention of the traditional local autonomy, was not always uneventful. In a few cases, it aroused strong local opposition and bitter controversy. Dr Smartt's nomination for the Wodehouse seat, which involved the unseating of the incumbent, was secured only after some angry correspondence. In

Griqualand East, the local Bondsmen, who preferred a non-Bondsman to Sivewright, did not succumb to the pressures of the Supervision Committee. As a last resort, the latter freed Bondsmen from voting for the officially nominated candidate.[351] In Graaff Reinet, a conference which elected Dr T.N.G. te Water as candidate, caused division in the local Bond branch.[352]

It was, however, in Barkly West, Rhodes's own constituency, that the intervention of the 'clique' caused the bitterest controversy. It also exposed the extent of its commitment to Rhodes. The local branch chose P.J. Marais as Rhodes's partner, and H.D. Stiglingh as his substitute. Both were keen opponents of De Beers and Rhodes. This was not only an embarrassment but also an affront to Rhodes. Whereas Marais was persuaded to stand down, Stiglingh, who became automatically the official candidate, refused to submit. Even assurances to Rhodes that his arch-critic was a changed man who would prove a 'strong supporter',[353] did not pacify him. An elaborate strategy was worked out to remove Stiglingh and to ensure the candidacy of W.P. Schreiner, a bright barrister and a close confidant of Rhodes, who was not even a Bondsman. Schreiner claimed that he agreed to stand for Barkly West 'only at the request of Mr Hofmeyr'.[354] At the first stage a special meeting, held on 10 November 1893, elected S.J. du Toit, who intended to contest a Paarl seat, as a candidate for Barkly West. A month later Schreiner was elected as his substitute, and subsequently, S.J. du Toit conveniently withdrew his candidacy and Schreiner was approved as the Bond candidate. Stiglingh stubbornly refused to accept the results of this manipulation even in the face of threats of expulsion from the Bond. In this he was supported not only by Bondsmen in Barkly West, but also by leading members of the Kimberley branch.[355]

The troubles for the Bond were not over with the completion of the nomination procedures. In seven constituencies, Bondsmen fought the elections against official Bond candidates. In order to secure the election of their candidates the Bond leadership was involved in intra-Bond struggles during the election campaign. Rhodes was not simply an innocent beneficiary of the leadership's efforts to promote the election of their/his favourites. He, in fact, played a vital role, at least in some of the electoral contests. And as had already been shown in Kimberley in previous elections, he did so with singlemindedness and unscrupulousness. It seems that Rhodes was keen to see his devoted ally, S.J. du Toit, in Parliament and perhaps also in the government. It was alleged that the election campaign in Paarl alone cost him £500. In addition, it was claimed that De Beers obtained votes and providers of votes by applying pressure on local factories and wagon builders with whom it was doing business. Coaton, the owner of a tannery in Wellington, switched his support from J.S. Marais to S.J. du Toit, apparently after being promised a contract with De Beers.[356] When all this failed to secure Du Toit a seat, Rhodes apparently tried to persuade a candidate for the Swellendam constituency to withdraw in his favour.[357]

It was, however, in his own constituency that Rhodes unleashed his well-tried electoral machine and tactics. Hauptfleisch, the secretary of the Bond in Kimberley, who was also working for De Beers, actively promoted the candidacy of Schreiner, for which he was expelled from the branch.[358] According to a correspondent, Rhodes spent £10,000 on the election campaign for himself and his partner. According to this account S.J. du Toit travelled around the constituency for 14 days, accompanied by a lawyer from Kimberley, on a De Beers cart drawn by four horses. In addition 50 carriages hired in Kimberley for £5 each were used, probably on election day, and 350 men were employed to canvass for votes. Shortly before election day a Kimberley firm sent appropriate letters to shop owners. The expensive and elaborate election campaign also included 'smoking concerts' and half a bottle of brandy for each 'native' who voted for Rhodes and Schreiner.[359] Even if this account is somewhat exaggerated it is a telling one. The 'octopus' from Kimberley was sending his tentacles out into rural Cape. It was a novelty on the Cape political scene; a taste of a cocktail of aggressive capitalism and unscrupulous politics. Another novelty was that the Bond colluded with Rhodes openly and unashamedly.

All this was bound to invoke a response from the opponents of the Bond–Rhodes alliance who had already been disgusted by earlier fore-tastes of these activities. There were, as we have seen, local branches which refused to submit to the dictates of the centre and promoted candidates of their choice. In Barkly West the resistance was particularly strong. Despite the efforts of the Bond leadership and the huge resources employed by Rhodes, Stiglingh, the rebels' candidates received only 110 votes fewer than Schreiner, and 145 fewer than Rhodes. According to a correspondent, only eight Bondsmen in the constituency did not vote for Stiglingh.[360] The *Volksbode* asserted that there was a rebellion in the Bond.[361] So severe was the division within the Bond that D.C de Waal asked whether, in view of the lack of discipline in the various branches, it was not best to dismantle the party.[362]

As the case of Barkly West shows, local struggles also involved a fierce debate on political morality. Not only were the actions of the 'clique' condemned as 'illegal' and 'unconstitutional', but words like 'wilful', 'deceit', 'bunglers', 'infringement on the people's rights', were also used.[363] Unfortunately, much of what must have been a most instructive local discourse has not survived. This local discourse was manifested, however, in a much greater contribution to the broader debate through letters to the editor. It was, as before, the challengers' press which both reflected and fed, local and general debate on political morality. This time the *GR* was not alone in the moral battle field. It was, however, the first to wage the battle in a series of articles on the forthcoming election from late May 1893.[364] It was joined in late 1893 by the *Volksbode*. The *Volksbode*, representing a benevolent paternalistic, rather than liberal outlook, had been involved in a running ideological and moral battle against the Bond's attitudes to the 'natives'. It had combined this, however, with support for Rhodes and his government. In late June 1893, it still sang Rhodes's praise and defended him against his detractors:

> He has some great ideas with regard to the opening up of Africa to civilisation. He dedicates a large share of his ability to the fulfilment of these ideas and is prepared to make a personal sacrifice. We have never been able to understand why a citizen is not suitable for a public office because he is the head of a big commercial company.[365]

By the end of the year it had joined the *GR*'s chorus.

For the *GR* the 1894 election campaign was a vindication of the crusade it had undertaken against the Bond–Rhodes alliance. The critique of the newspaper was, as before, largely from a populist perspective, lamenting the fall of the small men and the rise of the big ones of the new era of high capitalism and high politics. Rather than dealing with complex and interlinked impersonal economic and political forces, it continued to indulge in personalisations. Rather than understanding the decline of old groups in terms of the advent of powerful new forces, it was presented as a function of human failings and a manifestation of the fall of the political man. The source of evil was, as before, the greed of Rhodes, the 'octopus'. Having monopolised the diamond industry, Rhodes was now engaged in the monopolisation of Parliament.[366] And the Bond leaders, who did not perceive the danger, had betrayed their calling: 'We thought that the Bond leaders will never abuse their influence, will act as patriots and refrain from selfishness.'[367] The betrayal of the Bond was manifested in slavishly following Rhodes.[368] If, previously, S.J. du Toit was the main scapegoat of the challengers, now the disease had spread and even Hofmeyr was affected. It was Hofmeyr who was responsible for presenting Rhodes to the Afrikaners as a 'political Messiah', as patriotic and as an honest man: 'But they bring no grounds for this assertion. No, Hofmeyr has the greatest trust in Rhodes and that is sufficient.' Hofmeyr abused his leadership and influence in spreading a false gospel: 'And since Hofmeyr swears in Rhodes as the best Afrikaner from London, most Bondsmen follow Rhodes to the slaughter.'[369] A correspondent, signing himself 'still a Bondsman' gave a popular perspective to the fall of Hofmeyr: 'But has Hofmeyr not tarnished himself together with S.J. du Toit in the Barkly West election ... S.J. du Toit appears in the open with his character, but *Onze Jan* stands behind the curtains and uses others in his despicable acts.'[370] Instead of consolidating a colonial regime, Bond leaders had been instrumental in establishing a 'De Beers – Chartered Company – Rhodes Government'.[371]

This regime representing capitalist monopolistic predators, dedicated to profit rather than to the welfare of *land en volk*, required a different political base from the good old Bond of the golden age. Indeed, the challengers perceived the 1894 election as a determined attempt to adjust the Bond to the requisites of Rhodes's tyranny. The attempt to 'modernise' the Bond's contingent in Parliament, by the infusion of more talent and degrees, was not seen as an essential adjustment to the vastly changed economic and political scale. Rather, it was presented as a nefarious thrust designed to marginalise the middle farmer, the backbone of the Bond, who provided it with its essential political values of honesty and patriotism. With reference to the imposition of candidates on local branches the *GR* grieved: 'The majority of land owners were trampled upon by Dick, Tom and Harry and their instigators, Rhodes's or De Beers clique, who are assisted in their efforts by S.J. du Toit and Hofmeyr.'[372] Their goal was to change the character of Parliament: 'May heaven prevent it ... The farmers will then cordially resign in order to have a Parliament composed of attorneys, advocates, clergymen, medical doctors, diamond merchants and company floaters.'[373] The Parliament was correspondingly becoming a 'hunting ground for ambitious, incapable, tyrannic men'.[374]

The fallen leaders brought about a decline of values: 'Is there a need for a Bond which sows and furthers political immorality among our people?'[375] Instead of true patriotism, loyalty to Rhodes was demanded, 'and whoever does not follow is not a good patriot because Rhodes is the patriot *par excellence*'.[376] And yet, under Rhodes's regime there occurred 'scandals which enrage every honest patriot'.[377] This decline was measured against the golden age of the Bond: 'Has the pure, honest Bond sunk so low?'[378] A correspondent gave the perspective of many bewildered common Bondsmen: 'The Bond used to be a respectable organisation and had good principles, but now it has become a speculation for the sake of ring leaders.'[379] Another correspondent gave a religious touch to the sense of decline: 'Even the Bond which at the beginning seemed a Christian organisation has lost its prestige and seems more as a curse than anything else.'[380] The Bloemfontein *Express* was quoted for a more articulate version of the fall which resulted from the association with Rhodes:

> The Bond is too much involved and identified with the 'man of the three stools'. The Afrikaners have been used too much as play balls by capitalists these days. The Bond has left its course; it is not any more the previous

conservative, patriotic Afrikaner farmers' party. The old ideals, dreams, aspirations of the Afrikaners have been buried under the big speculation of Rhodes and Company.[381]

The new Bond attracted new people. The influx of expatriates, especially Englishmen, to the Bond, who were highly prized by its leaders, was perceived differently from a challenger perspective: 'It is dangerous when strangers, who have got no respect for the Bible, and people who do not enjoy a good name in the community, join the Bond and become leaders through the use of smooth tongue and crafty brain.'[382]

The *Volksbode* added a touch of religious moral indignation to the critique of the political corruption which was manifested in the election campaign: 'It does not matter if society's sense of morality is trampled upon, or if the conscience of the Afrikaner population is killed. It does not matter if the religious faith of our devout fathers is destroyed. The end justifies the means, even at the expense of what is sacred and precious in the national life of the Afrikaner.'[383] It also declared that it would support any party, as long as it was guided by the ten commandments.[384] While infusing a religious moral blood to the veins of the challengers, the *Volksbode* discovered, all of a sudden, the plight of the poor in the diamond fields whom it had ignored before. It also came to the realisation that Mashonaland was, after all, a speculation rather than a promise of civilisation.[385]

With reference to the electoral assault of De Beers on Griqualand West, the *GR* appealed to Griqualanders: 'Conduct yourselves as men, as the free sons of the land.'[386] And when they rose to the challenge and faced the forces of political evil, they were hailed as 'courageous farmers, who follow in the footsteps of Uys, Maritz and Retief [famous *Voortrekker* leaders]'.[387] They deserved that honour because they fought for a new/old Bond and for a new/old order: 'The sons of the land must rule the land. Away with those who use our land as a milch cow.'[388] Faced with painful socio-economic convulsions and disturbing political corruption, the *Volksbode* articulated a more future-oriented, sophisticated vision – 'development combined with justice'.[389] South Africa, with much of the world, is still searching for this elusive, magic formula.

The moral and ideological critique which sharpened around the 1894 elections presented the Bond leadership with a much graver challenge. This was so, not only because the *GR* was joined by the *Volksbode*, but also because it had a much greater resonance among Bondsmen than during Rhodes's first ministry. Then, the issues related to the diamond fields with their unique conditions, and to the far north. Now, the moral and ideological battle was not only for sectoral interests and political control, but also for the soul of Cape 'Afrikanerdom', the backbone of the Bond.

At the political level, the Bond leadership dealt with the challenge through the Supervision Committee, manipulation and employment of superior resources. The result was that the Bond–Rhodes alliance managed to secure the election of their favourites. However, the reactions from the party's periphery were too strong to be ignored. The success of the leadership in preventing, at the 1894 Bond congress, a debate on the elections did not pacify the disgruntled; it only infuriated them further. Thus, a moral and ideological response was crucial if the Bond were to sustain its organisational integrity, and if the leadership were to maintain its influence on the grassroots. Since, the Bond–Rhodes alliance was, more than before, at the centre of the controversy, it had to be reaffirmed, rationalised and justified, to reassure the converted, to persuade the sceptics, and to neutralise the critics.

The response of the Bond leadership consisted of three main thrusts: one was aimed at undermining the credibility of the critics; the second at refuting their particular arguments; the third at reaffirming the benefit to the Afrikaners of the alliance with Rhodes. The Paarl press battery, under the command of S.J. du Toit, served as a basis for a long-range moral artillery directed at silencing the Transvaal ideological guns or at least at minimising their effectiveness. Du Toit had an opportunity to revenge his own private political and material defeat in Transvaal. Reports of corruption in the Pretoria government provided him with ample moral ammunition. The Transvaal was presented as the 'Land of the scandals': 'Where shall one begin and where shall one end the cleaning of the Augean stables'.[390] In August 1894 he wrote: 'If one follows the situation in the Transvaal in the last few years, one must prefer ... to live under an English government.'[391] The *Patriot* criticised the Transvaal government for denying political rights to the *Uitlanders*, who contributed most of its income, under the slogan 'no taxation without representation'.[392] The material damage suffered by the Cape as a result of the Transvaal's hostile customs and railway policies was also highlighted.[393] The main thrust of the republican press, namely that the Bond, through serving Rhodes, was serving the cause of imperialism in South Africa, was boldly countered: 'But then we find the opportunity to point out how Rhodes is, indeed, the powerful opponent of imperialism, and that it is the duty of everyone who cherishes the free development of our South African nationality, to rally around Rhodes, in order to make him invincible in this struggle.'[394] Rhodes himself, in repeating his assurance that he harboured no intention of violating republican independence, rendered assistance to his Afrikaner supporters in repealing the republican assault.[395] The *ZA* also launched a counter attack, accusing the *Volkstem* of sowing seeds of dissent between the Cape and the Transvaal.[396]

The main battlefield was, however, within the Cape. The western Cape Bond press did not bother about the continuing anti-Bond campaign of the *GR*. A local Midlands Bond mouthpiece, *OC*, had been established to deal with the local source of trouble. Wider coverage of its anti-Rhodes, anti-Bond crusade would only have given it wider circulation. *OC*'s response was not commensurate with *GR*'s onslaught. It must have been assumed that its bark was worse than its bite. Just the same, *OC* tried to undermine its local rival in the eyes of Afrikaners by highlighting its association with, and support for, known *boerenhaters* (Afrikaner farmer haters) holding views, mainly on the critical 'native' question, which were anathema to the middle Afrikaner farmer.[397]

The Bond press in western Cape left the *GR* alone, probably because it faced a more serious challenge at the centre of the Bond operation from the *Volksbode*. The challenge of the *Volksbode* was potentially more damaging, not only because it occurred at the centre, but also, more importantly, because of the influence of the church on Cape Afrikaners. By the admission of *OL*, which had by now swallowed the *ZA*, the *Volksbode* 'was controlled by a few influential predikants in our church'.[398]

Like *OC*, *OL* sought to establish guilt by association. The reason for the *Volksbode*'s volte-face, it was argued, was the exclusion of the liberal 'trio' from the second Rhodes government. The newspaper was portrayed as the mouthpiece of the opposition led by Merriman, Sauer and Innes.[399] This was a damning association for the average Bondsman, because the three were known for both their negrophile and anti-Bond, if not anti-Afrikaner, sentiments. The newspaper was accused of being 'ultra-oppositionist' and of resorting to 'dirty insinuations', instead of pursuing a legitimate political debate. With regard to the accusation that Rhodes was involved, during the elections campaign, in widespread political corruption, *OL* denied that he invested money in other constituencies to undermine candidates who opposed his policy. Finally, it was argued that it was in the interests of the church and the predikants, to refrain from involvement in politics.[400]

The Bond and the north – the Matabele War and the Ngami Trek, 1893–94

The main effort to thwart the challenge to the alliance was directed, however, towards restating the validity, soundness and usefulness of the Bond's collaboration with Rhodes. As before, the regional and domestic fronts were invoked. By the middle of 1893, the north, from a Cape Afrikaner perspective, seemed a dying horse. Despite Rhodes's invitation, the Bond's press propaganda and the Bond's encouragement and

193

recruitment, Mashonaland had not become the destination of particularly large-scale emigration from the Cape. In mid-May it was reported that many Afrikaners were trekking to German South West Africa and Portuguese Angola, rather than to the Cape's promised land.[401] Soon, however, the north received a boost, as the war between the chartered company and the Matabele, which had been looming, rekindled both interest and enthusiasm among frustrated propagators.[402] The war was perceived as an opportunity to throw Lobengula out of his country and to transfer the Matabeles' land and cattle to the victors. To stir enthusiasm, it was reported that 50 farmers' sons were ready, 'under certain conditions', to take part in the war.[403] For the editor of the ZA it was an occasion for recanting his 'promised land' piece, but also for lamenting the lack of enthusiasm among Cape Afrikaners to face both challenge and opportunity.[404]

It was also an opportunity to parade Rhodes again in his anti-imperialist garb. Responding to reports that Britain was preventing the chartered company from waging war against Lobengula's kingdom, Rhodes was called to assume the role of South Africa's Washington.[405] Rhodes's friends, headed by D.C. de Waal, intended to convene in Cape Town a 'big meeting that the Cape has not yet seen' to protest against imperial interference in the conflict in Matabeleland.[406] Congratulating Rhodes on the capture of Bulawayo, the ZA was suggested that his success would bring an end to Britain's ability to pester the Boers.[407] The victory stirred a new wave of enthusiasm. W.A Krige, contesting a Stellenbosch seat in the general elections, pronounced Rhodes 'the instrument in the hand of Providence to put an end to the cruel Matabele power'.[408] Hofmeyr, in Stellenbosch, was ecstatic: 'In Rhodesia, in which a brilliant victory was obtained, the whole North will open up with all these healthy highlands, gold veins, and thousands of industrious farmers [who] will soon settle there.'[409] For the ZA, the victory vindicated Bond support for Rhodes.[410] The advantages of the north were again paraded – an independent market in the face of Transvaal's commercial hostility, space for both farmers and miners and a utopian 'native' policy.[411]

While the conflict in the north was brewing, Rhodes was opening a new trekking frontier. On 27 July 1893, the Patriot recommended a trek to Lake Ngami organised by I. Bosman, a young adventurer who claimed that the settlement area was within the confines of the chartered company.[412] Bosman was very active in promoting the trek in the Cape and the Orange Free State. At a meeting in March 1894, he circulated a prospectus from the chartered company containing conditions for land acquisition.[413] In May 1894 a committee was set up to organise the trek on behalf of the company, its members including Dr Harris as secretary, and five leading Bondsmen from the western Cape, among whom were S.J.

du Toit and D.C. de Waal. Shortly afterwards, T.P. Theron was elected as the permanent chairman of the committee.[414] The premises of the *Patriot* and *OL* served as recruitment offices, and it was reported that many applications had been received. The committee sent a group of ten men, headed by Bosman, to dig wells along the route to the trek's destination.[415]

Despite this positive, indeed enthusiastic, beginning, the road to Ngamiland was strewn with obstacles. While Bosman was marvelling in Cape Town that Ngamiland was a Land of Canaan, a correspondent warned against both the area and Bosman. Bosman urged Afrikaners to trek in order to solve the problem of poverty which 'will exacerbate in the next generation'.[416] L.J. Coetzee, a lawyer from Phillipstown and a new anti-Rhodes crusader, responded by warning against settling in Rhodes's north. He warned, in particular, that poor whites settling under the chartered company's conditions would become its slaves.[417] The *GR* feared that 'women and children will die, perhaps from thirst and hunger',[418] while the *Volksbode* pointed an accusing finger at Rhodes:

> Does the prime minister of the Colony have no obligation towards the citizens of the land? Has it not been his duty long ago, when matters were so dark, to warn the people? Is it a small matter that so many of our best citizens are leaving the country? Is it a small matter to let hundreds of families trek to the desert when the memory of the previous trek [the disastrous Kalahari trek] is so fresh?

It was also critical of the Bond press and 'other accomplices'.[419]

On 7 June 1894, Merriman raised the question of the Ngami trek in Parliament. Pointing to the danger to the Cape of losing its best people, he urged the development of big tracts of uncultivated land in the Cape which could carry a large population. He was supported by A.S. le Roex, Rhodes's staunch supporter, and by I.J. van der Walt, his bitter opponent, who were keen on irrigation projects along the Orange River. Rhodes, while paying lip-service to these sentiments, claimed that the trek spirit could not be extinguished, and that all he was doing was to assist those who, in any case, would have left the colony.[420] In fact, Rhodes and the chartered company were directly and heavily involved in financing and organising the trek. Nevertheless, by September 1894, Rhodes conceded in Bulawayo that the trek would probably not succeed.[421] This view was echoed by the *Paarl*, which regretted the failure. Three months later the *Patriot* argued that it had not really failed, and that Rhodes and Harris were in London sorting out the difficulties arising from the objection of local tribesmen to the trek.[422] The *Patriot* was, in fact, flogging a dead horse. The trek was a story of controversy and human suffering which brought neither honour nor prestige to those who promoted it.[423]

In announcing the failure of the Ngami trek, some suggested that, after all, it might turn out for the best since Rhodes then offered the trekkers farms in Mashonaland and Matabeleland.[424] Indeed, as the Ngami trek was fading, attempts were being made to awaken interest in Mashonaland and Matabeleland. With the end of the parliamentary session, it was again the season of travel to the north. S.J. du Toit, who had done so much to focus the trek spirit on Rhodes's north, went to see the area for himself. His account of his journey ran in the *Patriot* for more than a year ending on 12 September 1895, and was subsequently published as a book.[425] Romantic headlines like 'King Solomon's mines are reopened' and 'Zimbabwe, the city of the Queen of Sheba', conveyed the enticing nature of Du Toit's account.[426] D.C. de Waal again went on his annual pilgrimage to Rhodes's territory, sending back enthusiastic reports and urging the Cape young to hasten and settle there.[427]

That year, however, there was another spy on the northern trail – J.L. Coetzee – who, like the original Israelite spies, saw different things from those seen by the modern Joshuas. On the way from Salisbury to Mozambique he saw not rolling hills, beautiful valleys, gushing streams and glittering gold, but rather 'the biggest locust swarms I have ever seen ... I think that they are like those our elderly have told us about, those who eat not only the leaves but also the bark'. He also saw the graves of a few settlers murdered by a 'native'. He concluded that most of the land was unhealthy for white settlement.[428]

Rhodes continued to take part in the Cape Afrikaner discourse. Returning triumphant, after crushing the Matabele, he told a special banquet in Cape Town that the victory was their sons'. Taking his audience along with him in a flight of the imagination, he suggested that in 25 years 'you might find a gentleman called your Prime Minister sitting in Cape Town and controlling the whole area, not only to the Zambesi but to Lake Tanganyika'. He also promised them that for many years only they would be able to trade with Matabeleland.[429] At the end of October 1894, at a dinner in honour of Jameson, Rhodes recycled his vision of Cape sub-imperialism to these parochial colonists:

> As I have told you once before, those old people at the Blockhouse might have said that was the limit; and when members of Parliament get up and say you must go no further ... and that you are taking away the best blood and energy of the country, the only reply to them is, that it is an absurdity. The people will go on, and you must follow them, and when you follow them, follow them with your laws and administration, and make everything the same, waiting – waiting ... for the ultimate amalgamation.[430]

Rhodes, in his verbal interventions, could still enthuse his select audiences and the loyal Afrikaner press. The latter continued to sing the praises of the promised land and to present it as the hope of Cape Afrikaners. However, for Cape Afrikaners, the north remained, until the Jameson Raid, a promise to be fulfilled, perhaps a comforting hope. Relatively few of them settled there; gold was in the realm of rumour; and the vast market remained a matter for the future. Essentially, the north was a flop. Yet, while the north did not fire the imagination of the Cape Afrikaner masses, the credulous Bond leadership and press continued to present Rhodes's exploits there as a vindication of their support for him.

Rhodes, the Bond and the Glen Grey Act

With a view to maintaining his alliance with the Bond Rhodes had, as before, another trump card to play – namely, 'native' policy. This question was not unrelated to the north. In its response to Rhodes's speech at the Jameson banquet, *OL* wrote: 'These were words to the heart of every true Afrikaner, when Mr Rhodes spoke on the question of native labour and the price paid for it, as the main question facing South Africa.' Pointing in his speech to the cheapness of labour in the north compared to the Cape, Rhodes must have intended to whet the appetite of labour-hungry Afrikaner farmers.[431] But the north was the province of hope and expectation. Rhodes had to prove his worth in the Cape, the realm of reality. He had shown some promise before, in word and action, in relation to the franchise question, and the 'native' problem generally. However, especially when his alliance with the Bond was facing increasing ideological and moral challenge, he could not afford to rest on his laurels. Of course, Rhodes's interests, as the head of De Beers, in matters concerning 'native' labour and political rights, were not dissimilar to those of Cape Afrikaner farmers. Still, the escalating challenge demanded swifter action.

There were 'natives' within the Cape and Rhodes was under pressure to prove that his promise in the north could shape the reality in the south. By 1894, according to Rhodes, they 'had now 700,000 people savages and barbarians – under our rule, and it made one feel overweighed almost with responsibility'.[432] From a Cape Afrikaner perspective, the new African territories in the east contained two sought-after commodities – land and labour. They also posed, under the Cape non-racial constitution, a serious long-term threat of black political power, and a short-term danger of an alliance between black voters and white, mainly English-speaking liberals. Rhodes, to please his Afrikaner supporters and to neutralise Afrikaner critics, had to address both Afrikaner expectations and apprehensions. He was constrained, however, by the Cape con-stitution, by the Cape liberals and, especially since the Liberals came to power in 1892, by the British government. In producing a policy to deal with the Cape's 'natives' he had to consider these contradictory pressures.

At the beginning of the 1894 parliamentary session, before tackling decisively the problem of the large 'native' population in the Transkei, he annexed Pondoland, the only remaining autonomous 'native' polity between the Cape and Natal. In the mid-1880s, in trying to get Cape Afrikaner support for the annexation of Bechuanaland, Rhodes had commended the concept of annexing land rather than 'natives'. Pondoland, however, was full of 'natives' and there was no way to dispose of them. Because, according to Rhodes, 'the question of having a barbarian power between two civilised powers had been proved by experience to be almost impossible',[433] Pondoland had to come with the Pondos. In fact, commending, during the debate, the Cape's record in the Transkei, he sounded almost like a Cape liberal:

> It was often believed by people at a distance that the Cape people were most unfair to the natives. Our progress in the Transkei was a bright record. The natives there had repeatedly rebelled, but we have left the natives in sole possession of the land. The Transkei was simply thick with people and stock. We asked nothing for it. All we did was to give them government at a loss to ourselves.[434]

This was as far as possible from the Afrikaner solution advocated by the *ZA* for Matabeleland.[435]

Little wonder that during the debate I.J. van der Walt doubted the benefit of annexation: 'It would be an annual burden on the Colony. There would be no advantage derived from it, and he was sorry it had been done.'[436] At a public meeting in Hanover he was more blunt about the annexation of Pondoland: 'There are there 400,000 natives but no land for the colonists.'[437] Clearly, Rhodes had to produce something better to satisfy broad Cape Afrikaner opinion. According to his contemporary, J.T. Molteno, Rhodes made the 'native question' the focus around which he hoped to consolidate his 'dispersing forces'.[438]

This Rhodes hoped to achieve in his boldest and most important piece of legislation – the famous, or infamous, Glen Grey Act, which he introduced towards the end of the session in late July 1894.[439] The Glen Grey Bill sought to implement in the Glen Grey district a comprehensive solution to the 'native problem', which would serve as a model. He pushed it through Parliament in a show of determination, and at time ruthlessly, not merely to please his Afrikaner allies. It was also in his own interest, as a large employer of 'native' labour, as the Cape premier and head of the chartered company, to offer a thorough, all-embracing solution to the most vital question facing the southern African white minority communities. However, there is little doubt that, in conceiving and presenting the Bill, the Bondsmen were uppermost in Rhodes's mind. First, he needed to improve his standing among them at a time when another major piece of legislation he was pushing through, the Scab Bill, threatened, as we shall see, to tear his power base to pieces. Second, being as committed as ever to the unification of South Africa, he wished to propose a 'native' policy which held an attraction for the Boer republics.

The Bill, according to the well-informed *OL*, was a result of deliberations between 'the heads of the government and Hofmeyr'.[440] It is astonishing, however, that on an issue the Bond considered of prime importance, there was no meaningful Bond participation in the debate. Perhaps it was because Hofmeyr, the only able parliamentary debater, was abroad. Thus, Rhodes was left to fight it out alone against an impressive battery from the liberal opposition. For Cape Afrikaners the Bill was a mixed bag. There were elements in it, and in Rhodes's presentation thereof, that pleased them. In his long speech introducing the Bill, Rhodes made a particular effort to court Bondsmen and to compensate them for what he did not provide in the Bill.[441] His reference to the 'natives' as lazy, as at best 'children' and at worst 'barbarians', were sweet music to Afrikaner ears. Of the two desired resources of the African areas – land and labour – the Bill deprived the Afrikaners of the former. In stabilising land ownership, and in preventing the purchase of land in the Glen Grey district by whites, he denied them an area they had coveted.[442] If the Bill was to be, as expected, a model for other African areas, it was a considerable loss. On the other hand, in limiting land ownership, introducing primogeniture and imposing a labour tax, the Bill looked most promising from a labour supply point of view. Rhodes intended to teach the 'natives' the 'dignity of labour'. It could be expected that the African areas would provide ample and cheap labour. The Bill was also satisfactory in allaying the fear that the Cape electorate would be swamped by newly enfranchised Africans. On this principle Rhodes was blunt: 'The natives were not in a position to deal with the politics of the country.' Local councils were to be set up to channel their political energy to local matters. Although, enfranchised Africans were not disenfranchised, the land plots provided by the Bill were not to be taken into account in assessing the £75 property qualification required of new voters. This prevented the voter lists being flooded by new African voters. Rhodes even tried, and failed, to please his western Cape supporters by providing for the sale of liquor in the district.[443]

OL viewed Rhodes's speech, in presenting the Bill, 'the most important speech in this session and perhaps the most important one he has ever delivered'. It was pleased that the Glen Grey district would become a labour reserve, but was unhappy with the exclusion of white settlers, possibly from the whole of the Transkei: 'These areas are among the best in the whole Cape and we cannot see why whites will be permanently prevented from occupying land there'.[444] Some three weeks later, with better perspective and insight, the newspaper passed its judgement:

> It is not a final solution to the native question but it is a step in the right direction. It all depends now on the implementation of the Act. In other words, will those in charge of the implementation of the act turn the native into a race of servants, or will they deviate out of sentimentalism or fear of Britain.[445]

In January 1895, I.J. van der Walt linked his criticism of Rhodes's 'native' policy in the Cape with his unflattering view of his policy in the north:

> Why does he behave differently in Charterland? There he offers us land because he wants Afrikaners to cultivate the land ... But in Tembuland and Pondoland, where there is land at our doorstep, we get nothing. So it is in the case of Glen Grey. To the natives who rebelled and have been conquered by us, he gives 4 morgen which cannot be purchased from them. Where does a white man in this country get such a privilege?[446]

Rhodes, however, received support from an unexpected quarter. The *Volksbode* was sympathetic to his speech in Parliament, praising his view that 'the natives were not a source of difficulty and threat, but rather offer an advantage to the state compared to the difficulties with the labour force in America. Properly governed, the natives could become a source of prosperity'. It was also sympathetic towards Rhodes's wish 'to keep the natives *apart*'.[447] On the whole Rhodes could count the Glen Grey Act, not merely as an offering to the Bond, but as a veritable political success.

The Scab controversy

There was, however, hardly opportunity for celebration. By the time the Glen Grey Act was enacted, Rhodes had already become involved in a bitter political controversy over his anti-Scab legislation, which was to haunt him to the end of his premiership. Rhodes, who appealed to the Cape Afrikaners' concern for immediate material interests and their parochial inclination, was now entangled in the web of Afrikaner parish pump politics. The affair was caused by a small insect which attacked the sheep flocks and damaged both wool and hide. This affected the prosperity and prospects of one of the most important sectors in the Cape economy. The extent of the financial damage caused by the *brandziekte* (scab) was debated, ranging from the official £500,000 to £150,000 a year.[448] The government appointed a Scab Commission whose report and recommendations served as the basis for a Scab Bill which set up a compulsory country-wide offensive against the disease, including inspection, dipping and quarantine.[449]

The agitation which the presentation of this Bill and its enactment caused was the most widespread, intensive and enduring Cape Afrikaner protest, indeed resistance, movement since the beginning of modern Afrikaner politics in the late 1870s. It much surpassed, in intensity and emotion, the response of Cape Afrikaners to the pan-Afrikaner crises in the late 1870s and early 1880s. As in other colonial situations involving economic transformation, Afrikaner politics in the Cape were primarily motivated not by broad political allegiances and lofty ideologies, but rather by state intervention in the economic life of farming communities. The anti-excise movement was much more confined and restrained, not only because it was the first such properly organised political response, but also because of the geography and nature of the wine farming community. The anti-Scab movement was more widespread and more determined, not only because sheep farming covered a much greater area of the Cape and involved many more farmers, but also because of the different nature and temperament of the sheep farmers. In addition, by the time it erupted, Cape Afrikaner farmers had accumulated political experience and gained confidence.

It is astonishing that Rhodes brought the controversy upon himself. Surely, the modest saving the curing of the disease might have brought about was not worth the political upheaval that threatened his premiership. Rhodes was well aware of the parochial nature of Cape Afrikaner politics. The Scanlen government fell in 1884, with Rhodes losing his short-lived ministership, at least partly because of the phylloxera 'bug'.[450] In courting the Bond and consolidating their support for him, he was very sensitive to their immediate economic needs, showing great diligence in satisfying them. Why should he have antagonised such a large economic sector which was one of the solid bases of his political ally? There is little doubt that had he anticipated a widespread violent response, he would not have pushed through this controversial legislation. It seems that Rhodes simply had not expected such a response. While demonstrating understanding and sensitivity towards his Cape Afrikaner allies, he failed to understand fully the complexity of the socio-political basis on which his premiership rested.

In initiating and pushing through the Scab Bill, Rhodes fell victim to the clash between economic modernity and pre-modern conservatism. In an age when science and technology offered a simple solution to the disease it was difficult for Rhodes, the modern man, to understand and justify the resistance to the government's willingness to invest a large sum of money in helping the sheep farmers. The conflict over the Scab Act also mirrored the conflict between progressive English and conservative

201

Afrikaner sheep farmers. The government was under pressure from the English Farmers Association to pass stringent legislation to eliminate the disease. In presenting his 1894 budget, Sprigg, the Treasurer General and a leader of the progressive English farmers from the east, conveyed a great sense of urgency: 'if this Parliament did nothing else than pass that Scab Act and they neglected everything else, this Parliament would have done more to advance the interests of the people of this country than any Parliament that has sat during the last forty years'.[451] In stating, in his 1895 budget speech, that the opponents of the Scab Act were 'stirred ... by the Demon of Ignorance and Prejudice',[452] Sprigg gave expression to the gap between the English progressive and the Afrikaner conservative farmers and to the impatience of the former when faced with the 'ignorant' intransigence of the latter. The chairman of the Scab Commission, Dr T.W. Smartt, himself a progressive farmer from the east, gave the commission a definite progressive bias and did not convey the degree of resistance on the part of many Afrikaner sheep farmers to a stringent compulsory Act.

Rhodes was urged on by the Bond itself. Shortly before the parliamentary session, the Bond congress, convening in Cape Town, passed the following resolution, which was proposed by S.J. du Toit:

> That so long as the Scab Act Commission did not hand in its report, the meeting should not express its decisive opinion upon that point. In the meantime the meeting is of the opinion that the existing Scab Act should be repealed and that a new and more efficient Act should take its place. Also that the peculiar conditions and difficulties of the North Western districts be considered and be met as far as possible.

Although there were dissenting voices against a compulsory Act, the resolution was adopted by 'acclamation'.[453] Rhodes subsequently tried to excuse himself, when confronting the opponents of the Act, by stating that he had acted on the expressed desire of the Bond congress.[454] Even an opponent of the Act excused Rhodes, saying that he would not have submitted the Bill if the congress had expressed its opposition to it.[455] Rhodes must have been unaware of the severity of the divisions within the Bond which was, beyond a broad ethnic front, a coalition of regional and/or economic interests. There was a major division between the wine and wheat farmers centred mainly in the western province, and the sheep farmers inhabiting mostly the outlying areas of the Midlands, the east, the south west and the north west. This divide was not simply about the type of agricultural activity pursued; it was, in fact, a multi-dimensional cleavage reflecting the complex economic, social, cultural and political history of the Cape.

In February 1895, the committee of the anti-Scab movement, attempting to expand the socio-economic basis of their opposition, went to Paarl, the capital of viticulture, with the express intention of forging an alliance between sheep and wine farmers. At an important meeting of the opponents of the Act, in December 1894, Nigrini from the north west stated: 'the sheep farmer had supported the wine farmer; now is the time for the wine farmer to learn the needs of the sheep farmer so that he could support him'.[456] Shortly before the Paarl meeting, S.J. du Toit also articulated the need for an alliance between the sheep, wheat and wine farmers. He argued that each of these sectors was too weak to protect its interests and that only an alliance between them would make them a political force to reckon with in Parliament.[457] And yet, the meeting in Paarl failed to achieve unanimity. The wine and wheat farmers present, while expressing sympathy with the sheep farmers, refused to support their campaign to transform the compulsory Act into a permissive one, and implored them to pursue their grievances through the Bond. In view of the performance of the 1894 Bond congress, it is hardly surprising that the visitors felt betrayed. In addition they felt insulted by the arrogance of some of the local speakers.[458] In a subsequent meeting in Tulbagh, the leader of the anti-Scab movement, D.P. van den Heever, said that although in the past the sheep farmers had supported the wine farmers in their campaign against the excise, in Paarl he 'got the impression that the wine farmers do not want to help the stock farmers'.[459]

At the root of this division were the diverse economic interests of the two groups, which placed a limit to the degree of support one group was prepared to give to the other. It went both ways. While the stock farmers did support the wine farmers in their struggle against the excise, they had also supported legislation restricting drinking among the 'coloureds'.[460] The wine farmers, while being prepared to support 'reasonable' modification of the Act,[461] found it difficult to go along with the anti-Scab movement because their economic cleavage was reinforced by overlapping contradictions between the two groups.

The first contradiction was that between progress and conservatism. The wine and wheat farmers were on the whole more progressive than the sheep farmers and were not inclined to support anti-progressive legislation. There were also other progressive elements in the Bond, like the representatives of the Afrikaner business community and others. This contradiction between conservatism and progress came to light in the debate on the Scab Act in the 1895 Bond congress. T.P. Theron urged the congress to pass 'not a retrogressive resolution, but a progressive one'. Revd Pienaar delivered a progressive sermon to the sheep farmers:

> He thought the law was one which made for the progress of the country (Hear, hear). The Scab Act was to protect them, it was to protect the energetic against the lazy farmer. A great many inherited from their fore-

fathers certain ideas, but the farming methods of their forefathers could be considerably improved on at present.[462]

The progressive–conservative divide was also manifested in a contest between the former's modern scientific knowledge and the latter's traditional, experience-based wisdom. It was not incongruent that I.W.J. van der Vyver, in opposing the Bill in Parliament, referred to the Bible, the Afrikaner farmer's source of wisdom:

> but in the Bible they would see how matters went when rulers made laws that were impracticable or unjust. The rulers were in each case punished, and the same call to Heaven which went up in those days was being raised to-day ... The Lord said he would not punish Sodom if there were five righteous men, but under the law the House was for punishing thousands of righteous men.

He warned that the government would suffer the fate of King Rehobaam, who instead of listening to the advice of the elders [experience] took that of the young [science].[463] The wine farmers, who knew nothing about sheep farming, gave advice based on universal scientific knowledge. Sheep farmers were enraged that a man like S.J du Toit, who 'had never seized a sheep by his hind legs', would decide for them.[464] For them, the only legitimate knowledge was that derived from experience. Some even disputed the fact that the disease was caused by an insect. Others countered the prognosis of the experts with their particular, contradictory experience. For the modern progressive wine and wheat farmers from the west, the Scab Act represented economic salvation, or at least improvement. For the conservative sheep farmer it spelled disaster and economic ruin. For the wine and wheat farmers it was a question of macro-economic prosperity, for the conservative sheep farmers it was a matter of individual economic survival. It was a gulf difficult to bridge.

There was also an overlapping cleavage between the agriculturalist from the western Cape and the stock farmers, which informed two sub-political cultures. The former had a long sedentary tradition, living in the fertile valleys of the western Cape and firmly linked, both to the modern economy and to the centre of the state, also by virtue of proximity. They had learnt to accommodate the state, to enjoy its benefits and to endure and tolerate its unwelcomed interventions. Most of the sheep farmers lived far away from Cape Town, many of them in marginal, inhospitable areas. Their full integration into the modern economy was of relatively recent origin, and their isolation and geographic distance from the centre of state power for many years engendered among them intense individualism, a love for freedom and dislike of state meddling. They represented the tradition of the *trek boers*, of whom there were still quite a number, at least in the north-western districts,[465] but even many of the more settled sheep farmers were bearers of this tradition. From this perspective their rejection of state interference with their private property[466] stemmed from this tradition, rather than from adherence to the modern bourgeois value system.

Indeed, a distinct pre-modern, anti-capitalist protest was manifested in the anti-Scab movement. Furthermore, since the big capitalists were expatriates, this anti-capitalism was reinforced by xenophobia. Thus, A.S. le Roex asked Parliament whether it was right that men should come from other countries to legislate for the Afrikaner farmer.[467] I.J. van der Walt asked a series of rhetorical questions on behalf of the less privileged farmers: 'Was it the duty of the parliamentary representative to protect the interests of his wealthy constituents only? Should he not protect the interests of his poor constituents? Was the poor farmer to be oppressed still further?'[468] There was also a town versus country, and farmer versus merchant element to the poor–rich dichotomy: 'The people of Cape Town were not to suffer by this Bill, only the poor Boer. The merchant was to get all the benefit, the Boer was to bear the expense.' A particular dislike for the modern professionals was also shown: 'If the Bill went through, it would go through by the votes of merchants, lawyers and doctors, not by the votes of the farmers'.[469] Nigrini from Frasenburg articulated a capitalist conspiracy worthy of Hobson. According to him the insistence on implementing the Act stemmed from the operation of a coalition of interests:

> The company which produces the dip tanks; the merchants who distribute the dip tanks; the loafers who have become inspectors and receive good salaries; there are wealthy farmers who want to impoverish the poor farmers so that the latter will work for them as labourers; if the farmers will get bankrupt, foreign companies will be able to buy our farms and then we will become servants and *bijwoners*. Rhodes's company will be the biggest beneficiary and then his flag will fly on all the area from Table mountain to Ngami Lake.[470]

For Nigrini, as for Hobson, Rhodes was at the centre of a grand conspiracy. The analysis of M.J. Coetzee was similar: 'The small farmer will be forced to sell his sheep and go out to work. And to whom will the sheep be sold: to Jim for a few shillings. The capitalist will also buy our land. And what will become of our children? They will be forced to work for Jim and look after our sheep.'[471]

This anti-capitalist peasant salience of the anti-Scab Act movement reinforced traditional suspicion of the state. Indeed, it was the responsible colonial state that was the instrument of the coalition of inimical interests. As Theunissen told his audience in Caledon, the source of trouble was colonial rather than imperial: 'The existing Act is unheard of under the British flag.'[472] The local state and local socio-political forces were at the root of the conservative sheep farmers' predicament. This may explain why, at a later stage, they appealed to the governor, representing the Crown, to dissolve the freely elected parliament which had overwhelmingly voted for the Scab Act.

The sheep farmers faced an antagonistic coalition of forces which included, of course, the progressive English-speaking farmers and townsmen. Worse still, important segments of Afrikaner society ranged against them. This was, as we have seen, the case of the wheat and wine farmers in western Cape whose socialising experience had given them a different perception of their interests and of the state. On the eve of the meeting in Paarl, S.J. du Toit urged the anti-Scab leaders to learn a lesson from the political culture of the wine farmers. He argued that the excise duty had been much more oppressive for the wine farmer than the Scab Act was for the sheep farmer. The duty had caused the wine farmer sheer economic hardship and loss of freedom in his private domain. In the sheep farmers' case, the state was at least prepared to invest considerable sums in curing the disease. 'And yet', wrote du Toit, 'we bore patiently this insufferable burden; we gave the act a trial period and showed that it was impracticable and got it repealed ... Will our friends the stock farmers not be able to take a small lesson from this?'[473] It was possible for such a patient, accommodating and pragmatic political response, even in the face of severe loss of both profit and dignity, to develop in the settled, comfortable conditions under the shadow of Table Mountain and in the beautiful valleys of western Cape. The rugged, hard and isolated conditions in the marginal sheep producing areas did not offer a congenial habitat for a similar political culture and response.

The anti-Scab movement faced hostility not only from the wheat and wine farmers among the Afrikaners. The sheep farmers themselves were divided. Wine farmers used this division to justify their own position towards the Act.[474] There were Afrikaner sheep farmers, like Becker who, at a public meeting in the Little Karoo, defended the Act from a progressive perspective.[475] They faced a problem even in the Bond whose main preoccupation was the protection and promotion of Afrikaner farmers' interests. Despite the fact that most Bond branches and Bond parliamentary constituencies were in sheep producing areas, the Bond passed the resolution calling for an 'effective' Scab Act in its 1894 congress, and most Bond MPs supported the Bill in Parliament. This outcome resulted from the fact that the sheep-producing areas were not necessarily represented in congress and Parliament by conservative sheep farmers. Some representatives were progressive sheep farmers, but others were not sheep farmers at all. In normal times sheep farmers tended their lambs rather than feathering their political nests. Thus, prominent Bond supporters of the Bill in Parliament represented sheep farming constituencies. The chairman of the Scab Commission, Dr T.W. Smartt, was a Bond candidate in an eastern constituency, while P.J. du Toit, a member of the Commission and a prominent Bond leader, represented a sheep producing constituency as did T.P. Theron, R.P. Botha, Dr Te Water, N.F. de Waal and A.S du Plessis, who represented Midlands and eastern constituencies.

Leaders and supporters of the anti-Scab movement, from their narrow perspective, could not accept that there was a legitimate alternative position and strategy. They tended to attribute their failure to mobilise the Bond to the betrayal of the party and its leaders. Kruger from Venterstad asked: 'Is this the Bond which had been formed for the sake of the farmers?'[476] Another correspondent suggested that the Bond had fallen into the hands of 'ring leaders'.[477] Yet another was astonished that the Bond leaders had voted for the 'tyrannic act which will cause the downfall of the *trek boer*'.[478] The *GR* pointed out that most of the speakers on the Scab Act in the 1895 Bond congress were clergymen, foreigners, lawyers and shopkeepers.[479] The author made a clear, morally loaded distinction between the Bond MPs and the agitators: 'Away with those who use our legislature as a stepping stone to acquire influence, fame and wealth! All the blessing and success to the people's agitation which is for the benefit of *land en volk*.'[480] The anti-capitalist Nigrini had a more sinister interpretation: 'Who will guarantee that our leaders who support the Act do not receive bribes?'[481]

In trying to ward off the encroaching state the representatives of the sheep farmers also resorted to the principle of individual freedom, demanding their rights as free people in their private spheres. D.J. van Zijl, the MP for Clanwilliam, argued: 'Since childhood they had been free burghers, and now they are to have masters over them in their own business.' D.J. van Wijk argued that the Act 'will encroach on the liberties of a free people'.[482] Representing their grievances to the government Viljoen said that 'the farmers want freedom' and that they objected to the inspectors 'who will practically be masters of the farm'.[483]

These arguments failed to impress either Parliament or government. Pressure had to be exerted if the anti-Scab protestors were to be taken seriously. In pursuing this strategic option they drew on the *Voortrekkers*, tradition of disengagement from an oppressive state. J.A.D. de Vages stated in Parliament the golden rule of trekking: 'Compulsory law of any kind invariably result in treks, and one might say that this Bill has been introduced with the intention of swelling the treks.'[484] I.W.J. van der Vyver adopted a more evocative and threatening posture: 'Blood would flow, as in the case of Retief and others, if the law was enacted, and before 1896 farmers and their families would trek to uncivilised regions.'[485]

D.J. van Zijl was more specific, informing parliament of the intention to approach the German Consul with view to settling across the border in South West Africa.[486] He also threatened that there would be a revolution 'in certain areas' if the Act were enforced.[487] Van der Vyver warned that there would be 'a rising of the people'.[488] Probably inspired by his parliamentary leaders, a correspondent wrote with great pathos: 'Revolution, death, murder, but there will be no mercy.'[489] As the time of enforcement came near, there was passive resistance in certain areas.[490]

In case the threats should have no effect, the anti-Scab movement also pursued a more conventional constitutional thrust. The constitutional struggle started with an attempt to persuade Parliament to make the Act permissive rather than compulsory. This was accompanied by a stream of spontaneous petitions to Parliament from different sheep farming constituencies.[491]

This campaign was not totally without effect. Initially, Rhodes refused to bow, and only his threat to resign convinced the caucus to rescind its decision to refer the Bill to a select committee.[492] However, the vigorous stand of the opponents prompted the leadership of the Bond to press for the softening of the Bill. Rhodes succumbed to their pressure to such an extent that members of the opposition, who had strongly supported the Bill, voted against a new diluted version of it.[493] Innes noted Rhodes's unwillingness to push the original bill through against the sheep farmers' opposition and described the process of its modification: 'Caucuses are being held daily. Rhodes does not like the angry feelings of his Dutch supporters, and though he is standing firm upon the question of making the Bill permissive, ... he is quite prepared to water it down to a very considerable degree.'[494]

To the anti-Scab group this watered-down version was still objectionable, and they continued to campaign for a permissive Act. To provide the campaign with public backing a meeting was convened in De Aar in early October 1894 which rejected the Act and elected a *Volkscomite*, chaired by the indefatigable D.P. van den Heever.[495] A meeting in Victoria West, in December, representing 34 areas, called on Hofmeyr to negotiate with them the withdrawal of the Act. It also condemned the bias of the Dutch press against them. Another resolution adopted by the meeting, opposing the extension of the railway line northwards, was distinctly anti-Rhodes.[496] Many meetings of opponents of the Act were subsequently held across the country.[497]

The Bond congress, convened in Port Elizabeth in March 1895, was an obvious arena for the sheep farmers to pursue their campaign. On the eve of the congress S.J. du Toit feared that the anti-Scab agitation would split the Bond.[498] The Bond did not split, but the debate on the Scab Act, which occupied much of the time of the congress, was fierce and bitter.

The opponents of the Act managed to push through a resolution calling for a permissive Act, with a majority of two, only because two supporters of the compulsory Act had to leave the conference. The anti-Scab movement suffered a small setback when the congress adopted a resolution strongly disapproving of the agitation outside the framework of the Bond.[499]

With the beginning of the parliamentary session in May 1895, Cape Town and the Parliament became the battle front between supporters and opponents of the Act. The opponents organised a deputation of some 200 sheep farmers who took the trouble and time to press their case. They carried with them petitions signed by more than 10,000 farmers, and met MPs and the government. Addressing them twice, in public and over lunch in his home, Rhodes used all his charm and power of persuasion to pacify them and to convince them to give the Act a 'fair trial', refusing to make the Act permissive.[500] D.P. van den Heever expressed the hope that Rhodes 'will not drive them to despair'.[501] In Parliament two amendments to the Bill were proposed – one to make the original Act permissive and the other to draw a dividing line between a compulsory and a permissive zone. Rhodes threatened to dissolve Parliament if either was adopted, but finally accepted a compromise which left the Act compulsory but conceded careful implementation in sensitive areas and called for new legislation in the following session should it be deemed necessary. Rhodes himself undertook to visit, during November and December, the problematic areas in the north west and south west, and judge the practicability of the Act. This compromise was adopted in Parliament by a large majority, including the opponents of the Act.[502]

This compromise did not bring an end to the agitation. The leader of the anti-Scab Act movement, Van den Heever, did advise his followers to suspend their struggle until Rhodes's visit. Towards the end of 1895 he was shifting his attention to the Bond, advising his adherents to elect suitable delegates to the following party congress. He clearly set out to follow up his success in March 1895 by capturing the Bond and making it more representative of its grass-roots basis: 'It is now time to rally your forces to make the Bond again what it should be. The Bond must be purified of the ring leaders who want to shorten its life.'[503] He was aiming at the base of Rhodes's political power. Van den Heever, it should be recalled, was not only an avowed opponent of Rhodes on the Scab issue. However, his temporary moderation notwithstanding, resistance to the prospective implementation of the amended Act continued. The anti-Scab Act movement was essentially a spontaneous, grass-roots movement, guided by open letters in the press rather than by effective leadership and organisation. The strategy of the die-hards shifted from petition signing to preparations for passive resistance through non-cooperation.[504] With regard to Rhodes's prospective visit to the problematic Scab areas, *OL* suggested that he had undertaken a difficult mission 'even for a capable man like him'.[505] But poor health prevented Rhodes from undertaking the promised tour. The student of this fascinating movement may have lost a climax, or at least a wealth of additional source material. By the end of the year, the Jameson raid had taken place and a veritable ethno-political crisis pushed the politics of grievances to the background. Judging by his handling of the Scab crisis, we would probably have been deprived of a climax in any case. His response to the grass roots pressure was characterised by concession rather than determination. The colossus was bowing to the dictates of the parish pump.

The political marriage between Rhodes and the Bond was thus stormy. The hopes that Rhodes would lead them to a terrestrial political garden of Eden came to naught. Worse still, their alliance with Rhodes sharpened and exacerbated the contradictions within the social base of the Bond. The alliance was a perpetual source of controversy and division in the Bond, its leadership constantly attacked over their wisdom, loyalty to the cause and personal integrity. The divisions within the Bond were nearing their climax towards the end of Rhodes's premiership, with the anti-leadership challenge resting on a broad, popular and militant socio-political base. Hofmeyr, the Bond's uncrowned leader, and a pillar of the alliance, retired from Parliament in early April 1895. His resignation was undoubtedly related to the internal upheavals in the Bond and the personal attacks against him. His biographer attributed his resignation to the bitter controversies surrounding the 1894 elections. On 10 February 1894 Hofmeyr wrote: 'I am dead tired of the whole business. And I would thank the Lord, if I could with decency retire from the Bond and Parliament. I love peace, and yet I am always in the wars.'[506]

There is little doubt, however, that the anti-Scab Act agitation also contributed to his final decision. It came on the heels of the 1895 Bond congress, much of which was dedicated to acrimonious exchanges between supporters and opponents of the Scab Act. It was a considerable loss for Rhodes and the alliance, at a time when Parliament had become increasingly an arena in which they were challenged. Within the Bond itself the alliance was treading on shakier ground than before. The anti-Scab movement was able to mobilise, in the 1895 congress, half of the delegates to support its cause. Although the resolution condemning the extra-Bond activities of the agitators won a comfortable majority, Van den Heever was urging his followers to elect suitable candidates for the 1896 congress. The controversies involving Rhodes and the alliance were not about minor issues. They related to vital interests and to crucial questions of economic, social and political morality.

The motives of the Bond in supporting Rhodes

And yet right to the end of his premiership Rhodes enjoyed the over-whelming support and trust of the Bond leadership, its caucus and its press. At a banquet during the 1895 congress, T.P. Theron said that the Bond did not regret the 'fair chance' it had given Rhodes.[507] In mid-May, *OL* wrote that 'Mr Rhodes has, for five years conducted his office to the great satisfaction of the majority of the population.'[508] In October, a brilliant young Afrikaner, Jan Smuts, who had recently completed a law degree at Cambridge, was sent by Hofmeyr to Kimberley to defend Rhodes against attacks by the Cronwright-Schreiners. Smuts's speech, which was at least inspired by Hofmeyr, was the best articulation and defence of Rhodes and of the alliance between Rhodes and the Bond.[509] Young Smuts, who was not only bright, but also very perceptive and insightful, identified with the Bond's alliance with Rhodes and wished to launch his political and professional career through association with Rhodes.[510] His mission to Kimberley was a golden opportunity for him. He would not have undertaken it unless he believed that Rhodes's star was still shining. The trust of Bond supporters in Rhodes was demon-strated in a leader article less than a month before the Jameson raid: 'What Mr Rhodes expects from the future is generally known. His plans cannot be secret and if one is for or against his plans, one knows what our Prime Minister wants.'[511]

How can one account for the unwavering support the Bond lent Rhodes, and for the trust, bordering on credulity, the Bond leadership had in him? This trust was not easy to sustain. The alliance was constantly challenged from Afrikaner elements, both internal and external. Further-more, even from the Bond leadership's perspective, its balance sheet was mixed. There were definitely lights, but there was no want of shadows. Although Rhodes made supreme efforts to prevent the contradictions inherent in his multifarious pursuits from surfacing, he was not always successful. Thus, the chartered company's relations with Gungunyane, the Gaza chief, which included the supplying of weapons to the latter, were certainly not in line with the Bond's idea of dealing with a 'kaffir' chief. The *ZA* pointed out, disapprovingly, that the company appeared to have behaved in the spirit of the 'infamous' missionary, Mackenzie. While suggesting that the weapons deal was a local initiative on the part of company officials, the *ZA* indicated that it expected Rhodes would clarify the matter. The editor was disappointed when Rhodes did not condemn the officials' misconduct.[512] Likewise, the *ZA* was unhappy with the hostility of the Company towards the Portuguese in Mozambique.[513] There was also a recurrent grievance relating to Rhodes's inability or unwillingness to reinstate Bamberger, a magistrate who had been dismissed for his harshness towards 'natives'.[514] Rhodes could not make good his promise to reinstate Bamberger because of strong opposition from the liberal 'trio' – Merriman, Sauer and Innes – in his government.[515] There was, indeed, dissatisfaction with the presence of at least two of these avowed negrophiles in his first cabinet. While Rhodes, the Cape politician, in courting the Afrikaners promoted their economic interests in many ways, Rhodes, the employer of 'native' labour, was a determined campaigner for restricting their drinking of liquor. This was, according to the *Patriot*, a greater threat to the wine industry than the devastating phylloxera which had decimated the vines.[516] Rhodes did 'improve' the franchise, but only at the cost of conceding the ballot, to which the Bond was strongly opposed. While elements in the Glen Grey Act much pleased Bondsmen, others, and the terms of annexation of Pondoland, were not in accordance with their ideas of dealing with 'native' chiefs and land. While the north was presented to the Cape Afrikaners as a promised land, the inheritance of their children, it remained, until the end of Rhodes's premiership, an essentially unfulfilled promise. The Ngami Lake project turned very sour. Their alliance with Rhodes cost them dearly in very strained relations with their ethnic republican brothers. It divided their own ethnic house. The price of upholding the alliance was, indeed, high.

In accounting for the preparedness, indeed eagerness, of the Bond leadership to pay the price, we must re-emphasise an important element in their political culture. In their political temperament they were, as we have seen, essentially moderate, accommodating pragmatists, practising politics as the art of the possible. They were clearly aware of the limits of their political power, their goal being to occupy the available political space, rather than conquering new exciting ones. M.M. Venter, Rhodes's close friend and ally, gave, expression to this important salience in December 1892: 'Our experience has taught us that friends who stubbornly adhere to principles do not achieve much.'[517] The *ZA* reconfirmed this essential motivating inclination of the Bond leadership: 'One has to row with the oars one has.'[518] For them the good rather then the best was the goal of the political game.

They accepted that the balance sheet had to be mixed, and they judged Rhodes by the balance of this mixture which appeared to them good enough. On essential issues – support for their economic interests, 'native' policy, Cape sub-imperialism, the fusion between English-speakers and Afrikaners, colonialism versus imperialism – Rhodes's record was perceived as good. Indeed, from a Cape Afrikaner pragmatic perspective, Rhodes embodied the ideal imperialist – providing external protection but not meddling in their internal affairs – and the ideal English-speaking colonist who identified with them and shared their policies and their prejudices whilst being eager to collaborate with them. The verdict of *OC* on the Franchise and Ballot Act of 1892 was: 'the Act, however, was a compromise, and one must take what one can get'.[519] This pragmatic evaluation was also echoed in the *Patriot*'s verdict on the 'all important' Glen Grey Act: 'if it does not lead to a general solution of the Native difficulties, it is a tremendous step in the right direction'.[520] This was also the gist of Kohler's more general assessment of Rhodes's record at the 1895 Bond congress: 'No cabinet had done for us what Rhodes's cabinet has done'.[521] The assessment was experiential and comparative – present performance against past record. In a panegyric on Rhodes, in early 1894, the emphasis was on Rhodes's unusual ability to implement his ideas.[522] From their pragmatic perspective, they admired Rhodes as the ultimate artist of the possible, rather than as a dreaming visionary.

However, the journey of Bondsmen with Rhodes to the boundary of the possible was not without hazard. The boundary of the possible was also the border with the territory of the desirable, and between reality and imagination. Rhodes made the desirable seem possible. Even in the heart of an avid pragmatist there hides a spark of romanticism, inclined towards flights of imagination, and bent on mythicising the past and contemplating a glorious future. Rhodes fired the biblical imagination of the Old Testament-loving Afrikaners. To some, like D.P. van den Heever, he was an oppressive Pharaoh.[523] For many others he was Moses,[524] leading the modern Israelites from the Egyptian bondage to the promised land of Canaan. On the frontier between political reality and imagination, even an accomplished artist of the possible can be transformed into a romantic hero, and admiration for him into hero-worship. Cape Afrikaner Bondsmen began to see in Rhodes a Midas who could turn complex reality into political gold. It is in this spirit that *OL* wrote about Rhodes's visit in England in late 1892: 'Rhodes can be rightly called the hero of the day. All England, yes, the entire civilised world, is amazed in the face of what he has already achieved, and in the face of the great plans which he has conceived.'[525] In early January 1894 it was even more positive: 'There is not such a prominent personality, not only in South Africa, but also in the British Empire, and we are tempted to say the entire civilised world, like Rhodes the prime minister of the Cape.'[526] In late 1891, the *ZA* was relieved that a riding accident had ended only in injury: 'Even important people have got substitutes. But to lose Rhodes would be an eclipse for South Africa.'[527] At the time of the ministerial crisis in 1893 *OL* suggested that it would be 'fatal for the welfare of the Colony' to lose Rhodes.[528] The editor of *OC* added a personal touch, informed by Biblical imagery, English romanticism and frontier Darwinism, to the hero worship:

He is a young man of Davidian rosiness and freshness of countenance. He has about him the air of the woodlands, heaths and hedges of the southern counties of Old England; but much exercise in the affairs of life, as they are found in a mining camp, has made him a very Methuselah in shrewd, business-like qualities, so that it is currently reported to be necessary to sit up all night in order to take this old burgher in.[529]

For the editor of *OL*, he was a historic hero modelled on Carlyle's 'The Man Who Can'.[530] Referring to Rhodes's position on the 'cardinal question of South Africa' (the 'native question), the *ZA* implied that Rhodes was performing the will of Providence.[531]

There was, however, more to the Cape Afrikaners' attitude towards Rhodes than pure hero-worship and trust. As Olive Schreiner observed, there was love as well.[532] This emotion was also expressed by Jan Smuts himself shortly after, when writing on the Jameson raid.[533] The key to this deep attachment of many Cape Afrikaners to Rhodes was his unusual charisma. In January 1894 the editor of the *Volksbode* referred, with some trepidation, to Rhodes's exceptional talent for influencing people and using them for his own purpose: 'Such convergence of spirit and money in one man threatens not only the independent existence but also the independence of the thought and of the character.'[534] Smuts wrote, in retrospect, in a similar vein: 'He had that amplitude of mind which throws a glamour round itself and draws men and undermines their independence in spite of themselves.'[535] The nature of Rhodes's charisma is crucial to understanding the attachment of so many Cape Afrikaners to him. It was not the charisma projected from the distance of speaking platforms in town squares and relying on magnetic oratory and pathos. Rhodes was, in fact, a bad public speaker, discussing with his audience rather than addressing them. His charisma was not one that rested on the talent and power to force a detached leader on faceless masses. It was one born of a unique combination of projection of power and humility and the ability to identify with his followers and to invade and inhabit their innermost personal domains. He, in turn, allowed them access to his own personal domain. It was a charisma that could flourish in the particular frontier ambience of the Cape and southern Africa.

Cape Afrikaners were particularly vulnerable to such a combination in a person like Rhodes. They were well disposed towards his particular charisma because of their unhappy encounter with the English-speaking settlers in the Cape. Suffering from a deep sense of inferiority *vis-à-vis* the representatives of a superior economic, political and cultural power, they craved recognition and dreamt of amalgamation of the two white 'races' into a great South African nation. What they got in return was a combination of arrogance and contempt which greatly hurt and grieved them. They could never surrender themselves to an English-speaking leader like Sprigg, who could speak of the 'Demon of Ignorance and Prejudice' motivating decent and respectable Afrikaner farmers. Rhodes was different. Not only was he a much greater figure than the other English-speaking politicians who despised the Afrikaners; he also appeared to identify with them, to respect and even to like them. He was their vindication. It was an irresistible combination.

Rhodes had cultivated and courted not only the Afrikaner farmers' material interests, but also their egos and their souls. Rhodes was candid about courting the Afrikaners by doing more than support their material interests:

> Well, I have great sympathy with them; they have needs and experiences which we are all, I sincerely think, apt to overlook. I help them as far as I can, instead of opposing them. Is not that the better way? It pleases them and it pleases me. As for other minor measures, which I have supported, if men like to put blue ribbons on their cattle when they send them to market, why shouldn't they?[536]

He liked to visit Afrikaner farmers in their farms, and also opened his own home and heart to them. His mansion was also a manifestation of his battle for the Afrikaners' hearts and minds. Merriman asked Herbert Baker, Rhodes's architect, why he had not built 'a fine Tudor House'. Rhodes, however, not only instructed Baker to build his new home following the original Cape Dutch design, but also restored its original Dutch name, *Groote Schuur*, and furnished it with specimens of fine Cape Dutch furniture. Rhodes also restored on his estate an old Dutch summer house, and showed respect for three Dutch family graveyards which he found neglected on his estate, one of which belonged to the Hofmeyr family. He was largely responsible for the conservation of the old farm houses of Boschendal and Rhone which belonged to Rhodes Fruit Farms, and collaborated with Mrs Koopmans de Wet in preserving the 'antiquities' of the Cape.[537] Baker was convinced that Rhodes was 'impelled by a deeper feeling of sympathy for the history of the early settlers and of respect for their achievements in civilisation'. Others laughed at Rhodes's actions in this regard, suggesting that he was motivated by a desire to curry favour with Cape Afrikaner politicians and court the Afrikaner vote.[538] Smuts confirmed that Cape Afrikaners were influenced by Rhodes's demonstrated love for Dutch furniture.[539]

Coming to his home, where he used to entertain many of them, Cape Afrikaners were impressed and captivated not only by the Englishman who manifested love for their artistic heritage, but also by his openness, warmth and hospitality.[540] His attitude towards them contained no trace of the arrogance they had experienced from lesser Englishmen. Rhodes had a way with the Afrikaners which totally disarmed them. He gave them the impression that he not only liked them and enjoyed their company, but also needed them. L.J. Coetzee, who had been invited with a friend to Groote Schuur, recalled how successful was Rhodes in capturing the heart of Afrikaners:

> when he showed us all his deers, horses, etc., my unforgettable friend told me: 'Man, how can you be against Rhodes? This is the first Englishman I have seen who is exactly like an Afrikaner.' The reason for this remark was undoubtedly that Mr Rhodes was so homely, and perhaps also because, in his presence, he gave one of his stable men a kick on his buttocks. Mr Rhodes was indeed as homely as the homeliest *boer*, and his attention was given only to his Dutch guests.[541]

Perhaps the best example of Rhodes's way with the Afrikaners was his address to the deputation of the anti-Scab Act movement during the luncheon he gave them in Groote Schuur. He started off saying that he sympathised with 'those who lived on the land' because he himself had been brought up on the land. He then explained the reason for his generous hospitality: 'he had travelled much through Africa, and when he came to a farm they treated him well and gave him of everything they had, and he felt that if he did not receive them well, he would be ashamed to call at a farm again'. He then reiterated his support for their cause and interests, and told them in his direct manner that he 'did not see farmers often, so he would speak plainly to them – they must do all they could to keep the old population on the land' (loud applause). Then he made them feel wanted: 'They must not think that a compliment. They wanted a conservative element on the land to check the new population and to keep the natives in their places, and for this reason they would find him with the farming population.' He then paraded his love for their heritage: 'When they looked around Groote Schuur they would see that he liked old things (applause). It was in his nature, and he could not alter it.' He ended up by promising them 'not to drive them to despair' (Loud and continuous cheers).[542] At the end of his speech, even the tough and rugged sheep farmers, who had left their farms at considerable cost to voice their bitter opposition to his government, responded with 'for he is a jolly good fellow'.[543]

It is an intriguing, but moot, question whether the feelings Rhodes expressed towards the Afrikaners were authentic or contrived. Contemporaries who were close to him were convinced that he was genuine.[544] At best his attitude towards them was ambivalent, but a conclusive answer is not possible. What is interesting for our investigation is the way his manifestations were perceived by their objects. Many Cape Afrikaners believed that he was genuine. Referring to Rhodes's statement that he occupied the north for the Cape, *OL* wrote: 'One sees that he spoke from

216

the depth of his heart. There is no reason to doubt what he has said.'[545] The *ZA* asserted that Rhodes collaborated with the Bond out of deep conviction, and that he earned their support because he knew their nature.[546] *OC* stated that Rhodes loved the *platteland*, the habitat of the Afrikaners, whereas W.A. Krige said, at a public meeting, that the Afrikaners were close to Rhodes's heart.[547] An Afrikaner historian captured Cape Afrikaners' perception of Rhodes as a person: 'He was not an arrogant and inaccessible British who stood on formalities, but frank and humble in his dealings, just the man to win the trust of Afrikaners.'[548] Afrikaner Bondsmen were particularly gratified that Rhodes did not treat them as a political mistress. Referring to his speech in parliament, *OC* was pleased that, rather than being ashamed of the Bond's support for him, Rhodes was proud of it.[549]

In this way Rhodes acquired not only the trust of many Cape Afrikaners, mainly Bond leaders, but also their friendship. In consolidating his position among Bondsmen, Rhodes took special care to cultivate Hofmeyr's friendship and confidence. As he candidly told Parliament in the debate on the Franchise Bill in 1892, he consulted Hofmeyr even on minor issues:

> He would take the House into his secrets. He did consult the hon. member for Stellenbosch. He consulted him in the first place, because he represented a large section of the people of this country; in the second place, because he found his sound judgement was of enormous assistance to him. On a purely trivial question they had a couple of hours' discussion.[550]

Hofmeyr was, indeed, the most important among an inner circle of Rhodes's friends in the Bond. Fuller gave an insight of the rapport between the two: 'It was most interesting to meet Rhodes and Hofmeyr in friendly consultations at Groote Schuur, each perfectly understanding the other and what the other wanted.'[551] Other close friends were D.C. de Waal and M.M. Venter who accompanied him on his trips to the north. In mid-January 1892, the evening before Rhodes left for England, De Waal gave a dinner in his honour which was attended also by the MPs J.A. Combrinck, D. de Villiers Graaff, M.M. Venter, Hofmeyr, Sivewright and Tielman, Hofmeyr's brother. De Waal's biographer described this gathering as a 'real brotherly company'.[552] There must have been many such occasions, and many more leading Bondsmen whom Rhodes befriended. Moreover, by supporting their material interests, identifying with their ideals and prejudices, and through his unique charisma, Rhodes's influence went much further than those who knew him personally. Merriman, a keen and insightful contemporary observer wrote: 'There was a very genuine regard among the majority of Dutch-speaking Colonists for C.J. Rhodes. His personal generosity and his undisguised expression of admiration for Boer ways took their fancy.'[553] The best account of the special attitude of many Cape Afrikaners towards Rhodes was given by Jan Smuts, writing in the wake of the Jameson raid:

> It is generally known in England that Mr Rhodes formed his Ministry on the promise of the Dutch Afrikanders that they would support him; and that they stuck with unswerving fidelity to their promise. But it will never be known there to what extent Mr Rhodes had in six or seven years become the national idol of the Dutch Afrikanders. I who had an opportunity to watch the growth of this profound devotion could find nothing comparable to it in the sphere of political relationships except the beautiful, truly religious attachment of liberals of the old school to Mr Gladstone. The Dutch are perhaps a suspicious people, but when they do come to put their trust in a man ... then the trust becomes almost absolute and religious: such was their faith in Mr Rhodes.[554]

It was in this context that Smuts dismissed bribery and corruption as accounting for Cape Afrikaners' support for Rhodes. Flint, who also dismisses such an interpretation, warns against another mistake, namely, 'to picture Rhodes as bamboozling the Afrikaner farmers' party with his magnetic charm'. The relations between them, he argues, stemmed from a give-and-take calculation, Afrikaners rendering support and Rhodes furthering their interests, mainly material.[555] This is a narrow view which can account for their previous support for Upington and Sprigg. It is insufficient to account for their attachment and devotion to Rhodes. Cape Afrikaners had not only stomachs and pockets, but also souls and dreams. Rhodes appealed, successfully, to the totality of their personality, and his reward was handsome. It is true that the alliance with the Bond was not smooth and uneventful. However, until the Jameson raid, the recurring crises confirmed among Rhodes's Cape Afrikaner supporters their love and admiration for him, rather than precipitated a break.

Rhodes, the Bond and the Jameson raid

This was the state of the alliance on the eve of the Jameson raid. It is not the intention here to deal with the raid itself. Numerous studies, Rhodes's biographies, studies of the Anglo-Boer war and specialist studies cover most aspects of this intriguing and bizarre episode.[556] The imperial connection, the Rhodesian connection, the relations between Rhodes and the Johannesburg reform movement, the economic angle and even Rhodes's psychological disposition have been considered. Yet, the Cape Afrikaner angle is conspicuously absent from the accounts and analyses of the raid. This is rather surprising, because the Cape was the centrepiece of Rhodes's southern African project, and the alliance with the Bond was its political foundation. From this narrower vantage point, the

218

focus of our interest is not so much the chain of events in late 1895 which led to Jameson's invasion of Transvaal. The direct responsibility of Rhodes for Jameson's march into the Transvaal is thus of little relevance. From the perspective of this study, there is the irrefutable evidence that from late 1894, for more than a year, Rhodes was deeply involved in a conspiracy, whose network stretched from Johannesburg and Cape Town to London, and which involved heavy expenditure, transfer of arms and ammunition into Johannesburg, acquiring a stretch of territory along the western border of the Transvaal, and placing there of a military force commanded by his trusted lieutenant, Jameson. He was definitely planning and making preparations to overthrow the Kruger regime and to reassert imperial authority in Transvaal.

On the eve of the raid, Rhodes explained why he was taking this considerable risk:

> I don't want to annex the Transvaal, but I want to see it a friendly member of a Community of South African States. I want equal rights for the English language, a Customs Union, a common Railway policy, a common Native policy, a central South African Court of Appeal, [and] British coast protection. I have tried to do a deal with old man Kruger and I have failed. I never shall bring him into line ... What I want to do is to lay the foundations of a united South Africa.[557]

Most of these goals were perfectly in line with the South African policy of the Bond. And yet, while many people in Johannesburg and in London knew of the plan and of Rhodes's deep involvement in it, Rhodes never divulged it to his closest Afrikaner friends, not even to Hofmeyr. Hofmeyr would not have sent Jan Smuts to Kimberley to defend Rhodes against the accusations of the Cronwright-Schreiners, some of which related to his involvement with the reform movement in Johannesburg, had he suspected that he was, indeed, involved. His allies did not suspect his plans. On the eve of the raid, *OL*, which was very close to Hofmeyr, displayed understanding of the suspicions of the Transvaal towards Rhodes, but its solution was to show them that they were wrong.[558] As is often the case in human relations, a loving partner is the last to know.

On one occasion, on the eve of the raid, Rhodes did reveal to a Cape Afrikaner his true sentiments, though not his plans, towards the Transvaal. When, during an interview, F.S. Malan, the new editor of *OL*, argued that the republics were prepared to make concessions on the questions of customs and railway tariffs, Rhodes moved impatiently about the room and finally said:

> No, they do not want to do it at all! It seems that they will never do it! As long as the present *Volksraad* plays boss in Transvaal we shall get no improvement in the situation. The country will never progress if they will adopt such a conservative policy.

Rhodes became so agitated that it seemed as if he 'was jumping on Transvaal's throat'. His face got red and he continued in his famous falsetto voice: 'Something has to be done. The situation is intolerable. Certain steps will have to be taken to improve the situation.' The surprised look with which Malan received this outburst must have alerted Rhodes and he ended up more cautiously, saying that 'we must not be too rash'. It was only after the raid that Malan understood, in retrospect, the significance of this bizarre encounter.[559]

Rhodes kept his Cape Afrikaner friends uninformed, because he knew full well that his plan was anathema to them. Upon his entry to Cape politics, he had witnessed the response of Cape Afrikaners to the 'first War of Liberation' of the Transvalers. He had also observed their sympathetic attitude towards the Transvaal during the Bechuanaland crisis of the mid-1880s. That he fully internalised the Cape Afrikaners' solidarity towards their republican ethnic brothers is amply proved by the care he took, while courting them, to parade his sympathy and positive disposition towards the republics. He was fully aware that his views earned him handsome dividends among Cape Afrikaners. He knew that 'colonialism', as distinct from and in opposition to 'imperialism', was an essential pillar of his alliance with the Bond. He must have been aware that he was particularly praised as a bulwark against an imperialism of the kind that could have undertaken a brutal intervention of the Jameson raid variety. During his premiership he continued to demonstrate his pro-Transvaal proclivities. He even took care to calm down leading Afrikaner Bondsmen, enraged by the increase in Transvaal's tariffs on Cape produce.[560] He also condemned the demonstration of Uitlanders during the High Commissioner's visit to Pretoria in 1894.

If that was not enough, his Cape Afrikaner allies stated clearly the parameters of their alliance. Despite their economic grievances against the Transvaal, Bondsmen cherished the independence of the republics. This was not merely out of ethnic solidarity, but also because the independent republics were perceived as a bulwark against imperial intervention and guarantors of an appropriate South African 'native' policy. In October 1892, ZA made it clear that anything like the Jameson raid was an abhorrence: 'The Bond will never harm the republics, even for the advancement of South African unity.'[561] On 7 July 1891 it stated that Rhodes would forfeit Hofmeyr's friendship if he were to harbour indecent intentions towards the republics.[562] In May 1892 it made it clear that a condition for the collaboration of Cape Afrikaners with Rhodes was that he would not harm the republics.[563] In late 1893, while still believing that there were no two people in the region who could collaborate better than Kruger and Rhodes, it added the following:

But it is certain that if such conflict [between Kruger and Rhodes] will occur, the whole state of affairs in South Africa will change, and Colonial Afrikanerdom will view Rhodes in exactly the opposite way they now view him.[564]

At a banquet in his honour in June 1895, in the presence of Rhodes, Hofmeyr said that if the republics were harmed he would do again what he had done during the 1880–81 Transvaal crisis.[565]

The parameters of the alliance were, thus, clearly defined and there is little doubt that Rhodes was fully aware of them. On 4 November 1895 Sir Hercules Robinson, who had again been appointed Governor and High Commissioner, wrote the following to Chamberlain, the Colonial Secretary, on the possible response of Cape Afrikaner to military intervention against the Transvaal:

> The Cape Dutch sympathised with their Transvaal kinsmen in the war of 1881, but the ungrateful and hostile attitude of President Kruger since, and the conciliatory policy of H.M.G, have greatly changed that feeling. Nevertheless, if a race war broke out, the ill-deeds of Kruger might be forgotten in a burst of national sentiment.[566]

Robinson was a close confidant of Rhodes and it is highly probably that the latter was not only aware of this assessment but also shared it.

How can we account, then, from a Cape Afrikaner perspective, for Rhodes's involvement in the raid? What could have motivated him to contemplate the destruction of the political base he had cultivated so diligently and so patiently? It should be recalled that during the Scab crisis, as he was preparing for his act of aggression, he laboured hard to keep his Cape sheep in his political *kraal*. The answer lies in the perceived irresolubility of the contradiction between the requisites of maintaining his Cape political base and his broader imperialist designs. The Cape political base was important not for its own sake but rather as a launching pad for sub-imperialist expansion and ultimately as the foundation stone for a self-governing united South Africa within the British imperial orbit. When Rhodes conceived his grand strategy, during the 1880s, it made perfect sense. The Cape, with its large, more settled white population, with its developed and prosperous economy, with its more stable and solid political institutions and with an Afrikaner population socialised into the British Empire, was an obvious choice. When gold was discovered in the Transvaal, Rhodes hoped to cajole Kruger into a customs and railways union which would preserve the Cape as the political focus of South Africa while turning the wealth of the Transvaal into a South African asset. This would have paved the way for his united South Africa. Kruger, however, did not play ball, intending to transform his wealth into political power. Rhodes then turned to the north also in an attempt to discover wealth which would checkmate the Transvaal. By the end of 1894, however, it became evident that neither Mashonaland nor Matabeleland would become a match for the Rand.

It was not a coincidence that after failing, in late 1894, in his attempt to win over Kruger for the last time, Rhodes began to conspire against his regime. By then, there was a twin danger – either a strong Kruger republic with broader republican aspirations and designs, or an *uitlander* republic which, Rhodes suspected, would not be less inimical to his designs. In either case the balance of power in South Africa would tilt heavily towards the Transvaal. Rhodes sought to resolve the contradiction between his old political base and the changing economic realities by conquering the new economic citadel. It was then, in late 1894, that Rhodes crossed, from a Cape Afrikaner perspective, the Rubicon into the territory of political immorality. It was then that the big betrayal of his trusting Afrikaner followers had its origin. On the eve of the raid, during the drifts crisis, Rhodes betrayed his Bond allies yet again. Without their knowledge he committed the Cape government to assisting a prospective British military intervention against the Transvaal,[567] and such action was, of course, anathema to them.

This was the background to the raid. Molteno suggests: 'Success he thought would attend the Raid, and *ex post facto* Hofmeyr with the Bond would come into line.'[568] This suggestion could be reinforced by an argument that Rhodes may have believed that Transvaal's hostile trade policies towards the Cape would ensure the Bond's support for his anti-Transvaal conspiracy in the event of a successful execution. Such a belief could have been further bolstered by the drifts crisis on the eve of the raid when Kruger closed two drifts on the Vaal river which were used to transport goods from the Cape to the Transvaal and Johannesburg in particular. In doing this Kruger prevented Cape merchants from evading the high railway tariffs imposed on Cape goods from the Vaal river to the Rand.[569] However, those who suffered from the closure of the drifts were mostly English-speaking merchants from Cape port towns.[570] Generally speaking, commercial relations between the Cape and the Transvaal flourished in 1895. The opening of the Delagoa railway line and the Transvaal's hostile customs and tariffs policies notwithstanding, the Cape enjoyed the lion's share of the Transvaal market. While Rhodes's north was a promise, the Transvaal proved to be an actual commercial Eldorado.[571] During the drifts crisis, *OL* expressed understanding and sympathy towards the Transvaal.[572] In relation to this crisis, even the *Patriot*, Kruger's bitter enemy, while critical of the Transvaal, opposed imperial intervention.[573] This position made definite sense. Involvement in aggression against the Transvaal could certainly burn the commercial bridge to the most lucrative market. Pragmatic Bond leaders, representing farming interests desiring a profitable market, were not likely to risk a gamble such as that which Rhodes was contemplating.

Even if Rhodes believed that there was a chance that the Bond might swallow a successful military action against the Transvaal, it was certainly not a major determinant of the raid. The simple truth was that the Cape, and with it the Bond, had lost their usefulness as a base for the pursuance of Rhodes's South African imperial project. The battle front shifted to the Transvaal and, for the only strategy Rhodes could conceive, the Cape could not serve as an operational launching pad or even as a support base. For his new aggressive strategy he mobilised his own financial resources and his Rhodesian forces. He also counted on the disgruntled *uitlanders* in Johannesburg seeking reform and appearing to have come close to exploding. Ultimately, he relied on the backing of the imperial government and its local agents. In 1894 the High Commissioner, Loch, had tried to promote the plan of using an *uitlander* rebellion for the forceful reoccupation of the Transvaal. This strategy was, however, flatly rejected by Lord Ripon, the Liberal Colonial Secretary. Indeed, perhaps the critical determinant of the raid was the new Conservative government, which came to power in 1895, with Joseph Chamberlain as Colonial Secretary. Chamberlain was prepared to entertain an aggressive design against the Transvaal in upholding British supremacy in South Africa.[574] This new coalition of forces and strategy was, from an Afrikaner Bond perspective, in direct opposition to everything on which their alliance with Rhodes was premised. It involved using Rhodesia not as a bridge between the Cape and the republics, but rather as the base for aggression against one of them. It also involved, not the promotion of cordial relations between Afrikaners and English-speakers, but rather the employment of the latter in a violent action against the former. Ultimately, Rhodes planned to act not as a buffer to aggressive British imperialism but rather as a conduit for it.

Once Rhodes had conceived such a plan and contemplated such a coalition, he crossed the Rubicon, leaving the land of Cape 'Afrikanerdom' behind him. With the political decline of the Cape, the alliance with the Bond, while still worth preserving, was, in the last resort, expendable. The Cape without the Transvaal was not worth much. The high stakes were in the Transvaal, and Rhodes, the gambler, shifted all his chips from the Cape to the Transvaal. And, as is often the case when gambling for high stakes, he lost everything.

Shortly before the raid, J.H. Smith, the Bond MP for Graaff Reinet, said that although he did not know what Rhodes's goals were there was nothing to worry about since 'a watchful eye is scrutinising his deeds'. The *Volksbode*, pointing out that the future of South Africa had never before been in the hand of one man as it was, at that time, in the hands of

Rhodes, sounded a warning: 'Is there no danger that they will follow Rhodes blindly until it will be too late, and as a clergyman has told a great Rhodes supporter, "the Afrikaner people has been sold for ever"?'[575] When the 'great Rhodes supporter' opened his eyes on 1 January 1896, it was, indeed, too late.

It is possible that Rhodes's lukewarm response to the imminent threat from Jameson's unauthorised departure for his ill-fated raid was at least partly linked to his relations with the Bond. Indeed, Rhodes acted in a way that suggests that, although he was not responsible for the departure of Jameson, he welcomed it, or at least was resigned to it. This response can perhaps be partly attributed to the gambler in him who hoped that it might succeed. However, this fatalistic disposition could have also resulted from the frustration of the colossus who had been entangled in the web of parochial Afrikaner politics. At the time when he was primarily preoccupied with his grand Transvaal design, he was deeply involved in the Scab agitation and was expected to visit, at the end of 1895, the remote districts of the Cape to deal with an insect which affected the sheep. Perhaps the ill health which prevented him from undertaking this promised tour was, at least partly, diplomatic. The tension between his colossal designs and the parish pump inclinations of his local collaborators might have engendered in Rhodes a disposition which made him eager to cut the Gordian knot once and for all.

NOTES

1. See, for example, A. Wilmot, *The History of Our Own Times in South Africa* (London, 1899), pp. 11–12.
2. Rhodes Papers, Mss. Afr. C26, No. 7, Hofmeyr to Rhodes, 3 Oct. 1888.
3. *Notulen*, 1889, pp. 34–5.
4. *OL*, 10 March 1892.
5. Wright, *Innes, Selected Correspondence*, Innes to S.C. Cronwright, 2 Sept 1893.
6. Fuller, *Rhodes*, p. 145.
7. *Hansard*, 21 July 1890, pp. 162–3.
8. Ibid., 21 July 1890, pp. 164–5.
9. Ibid., 21 July 1890, pp. 165–6.
10. Ibid., 28 July 1890, pp. 197 and 202–3.
11. Ibid., 30 July 1890, pp. 221–4.
12. *CA*, 5 Sept. 1890.
13. Hofmeyr Papers, 16C, J. Hofmeyr to Harris, 5 Nov. 1890.
14. J.H.H. de Waal, *Die Lewe van David Christiaan de Waal* (Cape Town, 1928), p. 137; *ZA*, 14 Oct. 1890.
15. *Burghersdorp Gazette* (*BG*), 4 Sept. 1890; *GR*, 15 Sept. 1890.
16. *BG*, 17 July 1890.
17. *GR*, 7 and 10 July 1890.
18. *Volksbode*, 24 July 1890.

19. *ZA*, 15 July 1890.
20. Ibid., 22 July 1890.
21. *Patriot*, 7 Aug. 1890.
22. *BG*, 24 July 1890.
23. *GR*, 1 Sept. 1890.
24. *BG*, 23 Oct. 1890.
25. *GR*, 24 Nov. 1890.
26. *Volksbode*, 18 Sept. 1890.
27. *ZA*, 25 Sept. 1890.
28. Ibid., 4 Dec. 1890.
29. Ibid., 28 Oct. 1890.
30. Ibid., 2 Dec. 1890.
31. Ibid., 11 Dec. 1890.
32. Ibid., 21 Oct. 1890.
33. Ibid., 8 Nov. 1890.
34. Ibid., 29 Nov. 1890.
35. Ibid., 25 Oct. 1890.
36. Ibid., 18 and 28 Oct. 1890.
37. Ibid., 28 Oct. 1890.
38. Ibid., 13 Sept. 1890 and 21 Oct. 1890.
39. Ibid., 28 Oct. 1890.
40. Ibid., 20 Dec. 1890.
41. Ibid., 31 July 1890.
42. Ibid., 1 Jan. 1891.
43. Ibid., 31 July 1890.
44. Ibid., 2 Dec. 1890.
45. *Patriot*, 13 Nov. 1890.
46. Scholtz, 'Ds. S.J. Du Toit', p. 194.
47. J.D. du Toit, *Ds. S.J. du Toit*, p. 335.
48. Scholtz, 'S.J. Du Toit', p. 194.
49. Davenport, *Afrikaner Bond*, pp. 105–6.
50. *GR*, 21 April 1890. Du Toit subsequently denied having said that.
51. *ZA*, 6 Sept. 1890.
52. *CA*, 14 April 1891
53. *CA*, 16 April 1891.
54. Rhodes Papers, Mss. Afr. 2A, The Cape 1890–3, S.J. du Toit to Rhodes, 3 April 1891.
55. Ibid.
56. Rhodes Papers, Mss. Afr., 2A, The Cape, S.J. du Toit to Rhodes, 14 April 1891.
57. *ZA*, 7 Aug. 1890.
58. Ibid., 11 Oct. 1890.
59. *BG*, 23 Oct. 1890.
60. *ZA*, 13 Nov. 1890.
61. Davenport, *Afrikaner Bond*, p. 134; *ZA*, 7 April 1891.
62. Ibid., 6 Nov. 1890; see also 11 Nov. 1890.
63. Ibid., 4 April 1891.
64. *CA*, 2 April 1891.
65. Worger, 'The making of a monopoly', pp. 257–76.
66. *Diamond Fields Advertiser* (*DFA*), 6 March 1891.
67. *DFA*, 14 March 1890.

68. Ibid., 14, 17, 18 and 27 March 1891.
69. The Adendorff letter was, in fact, not brought to the attention of the congress; see S.J. du Toit's open letter, *CA*, 7 May 1891.
70. For the menu, see *ZA*, 4 April 1891.
71. *CA*, 1 April 1891.
72. Ibid., 2 April 1891.
73. Rhodes Papers, Mss. Afr. 2A, The Cape 1890–3, S.J. du Toit to Rhodes, 3 April 1891.
74. *ZA*, 9 April 1891.
75. Vindex, *Cecil Rhodes*, pp. 264–77.
76. *GR*, 13 April 1891.
77. Ibid., 6 April 1891.
78. Ibid., 9 April 1891.
79. Ibid., 13 and 30 April 1891.
80. *Patriot*, 2 April 1891.
81. *ZA*, 7 April 1891.
82. *Patriot*, 9 April 1891.
83. Rhodes Papers, Mss. Afr. 2A, The Cape, 1890–93, S.J. du Toit to Rhodes, 3 April 1891.
84. *Paarl*, 15 April 1891; *ZA*, 14 April 1891.
85. Rhodes Papers, Mss. Afr., 2A, The Cape 1890–93, S.J. du Toit to Rhodes, 14 April 1891.
86. Vindex, *Cecil Rhodes*, pp. 261–4.
87. Hofmeyr Papers, 'De Afrikaander Bond en de Dreigende Botsing in het Noorden'; *ZA*, 21 April 1891.
88. *Paarl*, 25 April 1891.
89. Vindex, *Cecil Rhodes*, pp. 278–91.
90. *Paarl*, 25 April 1891.
91. Ibid., 6 May 1891; *CA*, 7 May 1891.
92. *Paarl*, 9, 16, 23 and 27 May 1891; *ZA*, 7, 9, 12, 14, 18 and 21 May 1891.
93. Ibid., 9, 12 and 23 May 1891, 4 and 20 June 1891, 1 and 19 Sept. 1891 and 13 Oct. 1891.
94. Ibid., 30 May 1891.
95. Ibid., 30 June 1891.
96. *Volkstem*, 23 April 1891; See also 27 April 1891 and 21 July 1891.
97. *Express*, 21 April 1891.
98. Ibid., 5 May 1891; see also 26 May 1891 and 2 June 1891.
99. Ibid., 12 May 1891.
100. *GR*, 30 April 1891 and 14 May 1891.
101. Ibid., 11 and 22 June 1891 and 16 July 1891.
102. Ibid., 11 and 22 June 1891, 9, 16, 27 and 30 July 1891 and 10 Aug. 1891.
103. Ibid., 4 May 1891.
104. Ibid., 25 June 1891, 10 Aug. 1891 and 28 Sept. 1891.
105. Ibid., 22 June 1891.
106. Ibid., 10 Aug. 1891, signed 'Eleven-year Bondsman'.
107. *ZA*, 30 April 1891.
108. *Patriot*, 21 May 1891.
109. Ibid., 18 June 1891.
110. *GR*, 14 May 1891; the resolution must have been in support of the Cape Town branch circular.
111. Ibid., 14 May 1891.

112. Ibid., 10 Sept. 1891.
113. Ibid., 16 July 1891.
114. Ibid., 16 July 1891.
115. Ibid., 3, 14 and 28 Sept. 1891, 8, 15 and 26 Oct. 1891 and 9 Nov. 1891.
116. Ibid., 9 July 1891, 17 and 24 Aug. 1891, 3, 14 and 28 Sept. 1891, 5, 8, 15 and 22 Oct. 1891 and 9 Nov. 1891.
117. Ibid., 22 Oct. 1891.
118. J.E. McCusker, the editor of *GR* was a Catholic.
119. *GR*, 14 Sept. 1891.
120. Ibid., 29 Oct. 1891.
121. Rhodes Papers, Mss. Afr., 2A, The Cape 1890–93, S.J. du Toit to Rhodes, 8 Aug. 1891.
122. *GR*, 22 June 1891.
123. Ibid., 3 Aug. 1891; the circular letter was issued on 14 July 1891.
124. Ibid., 10 Aug. 1891.
125. Ibid., 27 July 1891.
126. Ibid., 30 July 1891.
127. Ibid., 8 Oct. 1891.
128. Ibid., 29 Oct. 1891.
129. Ibid., 15 and 26 Oct 1891.
130. Ibid., 29 Oct. 1891.
131. *GR*, 29 Oct. 1891.
132. *ZA*, 2 May 1891; *Patriot*, 16 April 1891.
133. *Hansard*, 4 June 1891, pp. 32–3.
134. Ibid., 30 June 1891, p. 149.
135. *ZA*, 30 June 1891.
136. *Hansard*, 4 June 1891, p. 35.
137. *ZA*, 2 July 1891.
138. *Hansard*, 19 June 1891, p. 107.
139. *ZA*, 17 Oct. 1891; see also 22 and 29 Sept. 1891 and 10 Oct. 1891.
140. Ibid., 1 Sept. 1891.
141. Ibid., 17 and 22 Oct. 1891.
142. See for example, *Paarl*, 19 and 30 July 1891.
143. Ibid., 22 Oct. 1891; see also *ZA*, 10 and 13 Oct. 1891.
144. See, for example, ibid., 1 Oct. 1891.
145. Ibid., 20 Aug. 1891.
146. Hofmeyr, *Hofmeyr*, p. 416; Davenport, *Afrikaner Bond*, p. 135.
147. Rhodes Papers, Mss. Afr. 2A, The Cape 1890–93, S.J. du Toit to Rhodes, 8 Aug. 1891.
148. *ZA*, 8 Sept. 1891.
149. Ibid., 12 and 15 Sept. 1891.
150. *CA*, 12 Oct. 1891.
151. *Paarl*, 1 Oct. 1891; *ZA*, 22 and 29 Sept. 1891.
152. *GR*, 12 Oct. 1891.
153. *GR*, 15 Oct. 1891.
154. *CA*, 13 Oct. 1891; Hofmeyr, *Hofmeyr*, pp. 418–9.
155. *CA*., 24 Oct. and 4 Nov. 1891.
156. *ZA*, 5 Nov. 1891.
157. Hofmeyr Papers, 1/A, South African Bond party policy, Official report of an interview of the Burgersdorp Committee with the High Commissioner, 16 Nov. 1891.

158. Davenport, *Afrikaner Bond*, p. 137.
159. *ZA*, 24 Jan. 1891.
160. Ibid., 19 May 1892.
161. Ibid., 29 Feb. 1892.
162. Ibid., 2 May 1892.
163. Ibid., 29 Feb. 1891.
164. Ibid., 3 March 1892.
165. Ibid., 14 April 1892.
166. See, for example, *Patriot*, 19 and 26 May 1892 and 2 June 1892.
167. *ZA*, 1 and 15 March 1892.
168. *Patriot*, 24 March 1892; *CA*, 26 Jan. 1892 and 29 Feb. 1892.
169. *GR*, 29 Feb. 1892.
170. *ZA*, 15 March 1892.
171. *CA*, 26 Jan. 1892.
172. *Notulen*, 1892, pp. 56–7.
173. Ibid., pp. 58–65.
174. *GR*, 24 Oct. 1892.
175. Ibid., 7 Nov. 1892; see also 8, 12 and 31 Dec. 1892.
176. *OL*, 30 June 1892.
177. *Paarl*, 1 and 3 Nov. 1892.
178. Ibid., 24 Oct. 1892.
179. Ibid., 7 Nov. 1892.
180. *OL*, 10 Nov. 1891; *GR*, 21 Nov. 1892.
181. Ibid., 24 Nov. 1892.
182. Ibid., 29 and 31 Dec. 1892; *OL*, 17 Dec. 1892.
183. Ibid., 23 and 26 Jan. 1893.
184. *CA*, 27 April 1892; *ZA*, 30 April 1892.
185. *Patriot*, 9 March 1893.
186. *GR*, 27 March 1893.
187. Ibid., 30 March 1893.
188. *ZA*, 3 Oct. 1892, 3, 22 and 24 Nov. 1892; *OL*, 29 Oct. 1892 and 24 Nov. 1892.
189. *GR*, 29 Feb. 1892, 17 March 1892 and 10 Oct. 1892; *OL*, 30 June 1892 and 23 July 1892; *ZA*, 15 March 1893.
190. *GR*, 22 Feb. 1892.
191. Ibid., 7 April 1892.
192. Ibid., 29 June 1892.
193. Ibid., 29 Feb. 1892, 11 March 1892 and 9 Jan. 1893.
194. Ibid., 29 Feb. 1892.
195. Ibid., 3 March 1892.
196. Ibid., 3 Oct. 1892.
197. *ZA*, 17 May 1892 and 2 June 1892.
198. *Notulen*, 1892, pp. 45–6.
199. Rhodes Papers, Mss. Afr. 2A, The Cape 1890–93, S.J. du Toit to Rhodes, 3 April 1891.
200. Davenport, *Afrikaner Bond*, p. 142.
201. Ibid., pp. 142–3.
202. F.A. van Jaarsveld, 'Dr. J.W.G. van Oordt (1826–1904) – Erflater van 'n wereldgeskiedenis aan Suid Afrika', *Tydskrif vir Gewetenskappe*, Vol. 23, No. 1 (March 1983).
203. A. Dreyer, Hollandse Joernalistiek in Suid-Afrika Gedurende die 19de Eeu, *OL*, 8 April 1930, p. 14.

204. *GR*, 11 Jan. 1892 and 31 Dec. 1892.
205. Davenport, *Afrikaner Bond*, pp. 142–3.
206. He was reported to have offered £10,000 for the mine; see *GR*, 7 Nov. 1892 and 26 Jan. 1893.
207. *DFA*, 13 March 1891.
208. Davenport, *Afrikaner Bond*, pp. 50–1.
209. *GR*, 19 March 1893.
210. *OL*, 10 March 1892.
211. *Notulen*, 1892, p. 60; see also *GR*, 24 Oct 1892.
212. *Paarl*, Nov. 1892.
213. *GR*, 8 Dec. 1892.
214. *OL*, 26 Nov. 1892.
215. Ibid., 10 March 1892.
216. *Paarl*, 3 Nov. 1892.
217. *Notulen*, 1892, p. 60.
218. *Paarl*, 3 Nov. 1892.
219. *GR*, 19 March 1891.
220. Ibid., 10 Aug. 1891.
221. *OL*, 30 June 1892.
222. *GR*, 24 Oct. 1892.
223. Ibid., 27. Dec. 1892.
224. Ibid., 7 Jan. 1892.
225. Ibid., 16 Nov. 1891.
226. Davenport, *Afrikaner Bond*, pp. 32–3.
227. Scholtz, 'S.J. du Toit', p. 199.
228. Rhodes Papers, Mss. Afr. 2A, The Cape 1890–3, G.J. Malherbe to P.H. Faure, 9 Aug. 1891; Scholtz, 'S.J. du Toit' p. 199.
229. *GR*, 25 Jan. 1892 and 31 Dec. 1891.
230. Ibid., 22 June 1891.
231. Ibid., 22 June 1891.
232. Ibid., 22 June 1891.
233. Ibid., 16 Nov. 1891.
234. Ibid., 14 Sept. 1891.
235. Ibid., 17 March 1892.
236. Ibid., 16 May 1892.
237. Ibid., 8 Dec. 1892.
238. Ibid., 11 March 1891 and 11 June 1891.
239. Ibid., 11 March 1892.
240. Ibid., 16 July 1891.
241. Ibid., 22 Feb. 1892.
242. Ibid., 22 June 1891.
243. Ibid., 31 Dec. 1892.
244. Ibid., 10 Aug. 1891.
245. Ibid., 3 March 1893.
246. Ibid., 29 Feb. 1892.
247. Ibid., 25 Sept. 1892.
248. Ibid., 17 March 1892 and 14 April 1892.
249. Ibid., 25 June 1891, 16 and 23 Nov. 1891, 10 Aug.1891, 22 and 28 Feb. 1892 and 17 March 1892.
250. Ibid., 25 Feb. 1892.
251. Ibid., 4 May 1891, 10 and 31 Aug. 1891, 22 and 29 Feb. 1892, 14 Nov. 1892,

31 Dec. 1892 and 24 April 1892.
252. Ibid., 23 Nov. 1891, 21 and 24 March 1892 and 16 May 1892.
253. Ibid., 15 Oct. 1891, 22 Feb. 1892 and 16 May 1892.
254. Ibid., 31 Aug. 1891.
255. Ibid., 27 March 1893.
256. *OL*, 7 April 1892.
257. *GR*, 25 Feb. 1892, 19 Oct. 1891, 16 Nov. 1891, 28 Feb. 1892 and 17 Aug. 1891; see also 17 March 1892, 24 Oct. 1892 and 12 Dec. 1892.
258. Ibid., 16 May 1892.
259. Ibid., 11 March 1892.
260. Ibid., 15 Oct. 1891.
261. Ibid., 27 Aug. 1891.
262. Ibid., 17 Aug. 1891; see also 14 Nov. 1892.
263. Ibid., 15 Oct. 1891.
264. Ibid., 22 June 1891, and 27 March 1893; *Volkstem*, 6, 23 and 27 April 1891 and 21 July 1891; *Express*, 14 and 21 April 1891, 5, 12 and 26 May 1891, 2 June 1891, 22 Sept. 1891, 19 Jan. 1892, 12 and 26 April 1892 and 17 March 1893.
265. *ZA*, 12 March 1892; *Patriot*, 16 Aug. 1892.
266. *ZA*, 12 March 1892 and 24 Nov. 1892; *OL*, 10 March 1892.
267. *ZA*, 13 and 1 Oct. 1891, 12 March 1892, 12 July 1892, 10 and 17 Jan. 1893; *OL*, 10 March 1892 and 24 Nov. 1892; *Patriot*, 16 March 1893; *GR*, 4 Aug. 1892.
268. *CA*, 13 Oct. 1891.
269. *ZA*, 17 Sept. 1891 and 15 Nov. 1892.
270. *CA*, 13 Oct. 1891.
271. *ZA*, 15 Nov. 1892.
272. *Paarl*, 6 May 1891.
273. *GR*, 22 Oct. 1891.
274. *OL*, 2 Aug. 1892 and 29 Dec. 1892.
275. Ibid., 2 Aug. 1892; *Patriot*, 27 Aug. 1891; *ZA*, 24 Nov. 1891.
276. *Hansard*, 11 July 1892, p. 151.
277. Ibid., 18 July 1892, p. 203.
278. *OC*, 8 Sept. 1892; see also, *OL*, 30 Aug. 1892.
279. *ZA*, 23 Aug. 1892.
280. *OC*, 8 Sept. 1892; see also, *ZA*, 31 Dec. 1891.
281. Ibid., 12 May 1892.
282. *OC*, 5 Dec. 1892.
283. *ZA*, 6 Aug. 1892.
284. *OL*, 7 July 1892.
285. *ZA*, 5 Jan. 1892.
286. *Patriot*, 5 Nov. 1891.
287. *ZA*, 22 Dec. 1891.
288. Ibid., 10 Sept. 1892.
289. Ibid., 12 April 1892, 26 March 1892, 21 May 1892 and 26 July 1892; *Patriot*, 26 May 1892, 2 and 9 June 1892, 23 March 1893, 11 and 18 May 1893.
290. *ZA*, 12 and 16 April 1892, 16 and 23 June 1892, 26 July 1892, 10 and 22 Sept. 1892, 24 Jan. 1893 and 25 Feb. 1893; *OL*, 16 April 1892; *Paarl*, 16 June 1892, 1 and 8 Sept. 1893 and 22 Oct. 1892.
291. *OL*, 2 Aug. 1892.
292. *Paarl*, 27 Dec. 1892; *OL*, 7, 16 and 26 Jan. 1893 and 18 April 1893.
293. Ibid., 18 April 1893.
294. *ZA*, 22 Dec. 1892.

295. *Paarl*, 24 Sept. 1891.
296. *OL*, 13 Sept. 1892.
297. *ZA*, 12 and 28 Jan 1892.
298. Ibid., 22 Nov. 1892.
299. *OC*, 24 Oct. 1892; see also *ZA*, 23 June 1891.
300. Ibid., 15 Oct. 1892; *Patriot*, 30 April 1891.
301. *ZA*, 21 June 1892.
302. *Paarl*, 12 Sept. 1891.
303. *ZA*, 6 Oct. 1892.
304. Ibid., 13 April 1893.
305. Ibid., 6 Oct. 1892; see also 15 Oct. 1892.
306. *OL*, 2 Aug. 1892.
307. *Review of Reviews*, Feb. 1892, p. 193.
308. *GR*, 3 March 1892.
309. Ibid., 8 and 26 Oct. 1891.
310. Ibid., 15 Dec. 1892.
311. *Paarl*, 6 May 1891.
312. *Patriot*, 3 Dec. 1891.
313. *Paarl*, 23 May 1891.
314. Hofmeyr Papers, Hofmeyr to H.P. van Heerden, 24 June 1891.
315. *Paarl*, 27 Dec. 1892.
316. *OL*, 24 and 17 1893.
317. Ibid., 10 Dec. 1892.
318. Ibid., 11 March 1893.
319. Rotberg, *The Founder*, pp. 372–4; C.E. Viney, 'A new look at the Logan crisis – with special reference to the role played by C.J. Rhodes and J.X. Merriman', BA Honours thesis, University of Cape Town (1975).
320. *ZA*, 6 Dec. 1892.
321. Ibid., 8 Dec. 1892.
322. Ibid., 22 April 1893, 2 May 1893 and 28 March 1893.
323. Hofmeyr Papers, 15/G, Rhodes to Hofmeyr, undated [April 1893].
324. Hofmeyr, *Hofmeyr*, p. 445; E.A. Walker, *Lord de Villiers and his Times* (London, 1925), pp. 229–31.
325. Lewsen, *Selections*, Vol. ii, Merriman to Curry, 9 May 1893, p. 151.
326. *OL*, 4 May 1893.
327. *ZA*, 4 and 6 May 1893.
328. P. Lewsen, *John X. Merriman: Paradoxical South African Statesman* (Johannesburg, 1982), p. 117; Lewsen, *Selections*, Vol. i, Merriman to Curry, 24 March 1886.
329. Te Water Papers, Theron to Te Water, 6 Nov. 1890.
330. *GR*, 10 Nov. 1892.
331. Ibid., 4 May 1891 and 31 Aug. 1891.
332. Ibid., 14 Nov. 1892.
333. *Patriot*, 30 April 1891.
334. *ZA*, 31 Aug. 1891, 8 Sept. 1891 and 10 Oct. 1891.
335. *GR*, 24 April 1893.
336. Ibid., 16 Feb. 1893.
337. *ZA*, 2 Aug. 1890.
338. *Paarl*, 15 Sept. 1891.
339. *OL*, 29 Oct. 1892 and 5 Nov. 1892.
340. Wright, *Innes*, Innes to S.C. Cronwright, 2 Sept. 1893, p. 117.

341. *GR*, 17 and 31 Dec. 1892.
342. Wright, *Innes*, Innes to S.C. Cronwright, 2 Sept. 1893, p. 117.
343. Davenport, *Afrikaner Bond*, p. 149.
344. Ibid., pp. 150–1.
345. *GR*, 19 Oct. 1893.
346. *CA*, 17 Jan. 1894; *CT*, 16 and 17 Jan. 1894.
347. *GR*, 12 June 1893.
348. Ibid., 1 June 1893.
349. Ibid., 15 Jan. 1894.
350. Ibid., 1 June 1893.
351. Davenport, *Afrikaner Bond*, p. 150; Hofmeyr, *Hofmeyr*, pp. 453–4.
352. *GR*, 10 Aug. 1893.
353. Rhodes Papers, Mss. Afr. 2/A The Cape, 1890–3, de Kock to Rhodes, 24 Aug. 1893.
354. *CA*, 7 Feb. 1894.
355. Hofmeyr Papers, 3/Barkly West elections 1893–4, 'An open letter to all Bondsmen in the Barkly West constituency', by J.H. Hofmeyr, 18 Jan. 1894, published by *Paarl*; J.J. Michau to Hofmeyr, 22 Jan. 1894; Davenport, *Afrikaner Bond*, pp. 150–1.
356. *Volksbode*, 7 and 11 Jan. 1894, 24 and 28 Feb. 1894.
357. Ibid., 10 Feb. 1894.
358. *GR*, 23 Nov. 1893 and 21 Dec. 1893.
359. Ibid., 24 May 1894.
360. Ibid., 22 Feb. 1894 and 5 March 1894.
361. *Volksbode*, 21 March 1894.
362. *GR*, 12 Feb. 1894.
363. Hofmeyr Papers, 3/Barkley West election, 1893–4, letter to the editor, *Paarl*, by W.C.A. Scholtz; *GR*, 11 Jan. 1894, Jan Vorster to the editor.
364. Ibid., 29 May 1893, 1, 5, 8, 12 and 15 June 1893.
365. *Volksbode*, 29 June 1893.
366. *GR*, 10 June 1893.
367. Ibid., 15 June 1893.
368. Ibid., 19 Oct. 1893.
369. Ibid., 23 Nov. 1893.
370. Ibid., 9 April 1894.
371. Ibid., 23 Nov. 1893.
372. Ibid., 12 April 1894.
373. Ibid., 5 June 1893.
374. Ibid., 8 and 5 June 1893.
375. Ibid., 11 Jan. 1894.
376. Ibid., 19 Oct. 1893.
377. Ibid., 5 June 1893.
378. Ibid., 11 Jan. 1894.
379. Ibid., 14 May 1894.
380. Ibid., 7 May 1894.
381. Ibid., 1 March 1894.
382. Ibid., 9 April 1894.
383. *Volksbode*, 18 Jan. 1894; see also 7, 10 and 17 Feb. 1894.
384. Ibid., 14 Feb. 1894.
385. Ibid., 25 Jan. 1894, 17 Feb. 1894 and 7 March 1894.
386. *GR*, 21 Jan. 1894.

387. Ibid., 12 April 1894.
388. Ibid., 5 Nov. 1894.
389. *Volksbode*, 18 Jan. 1894.
390. *Patriot*, 7 June 1894 and 22 Feb. 1894; see also 15 June 1893, 3 May 1894, 13 Dec. 1894 and 22 Aug. 1895; *Paarl*, 24 April 1894.
391. *Patriot*, 28 Aug. 1894.
392. Ibid., 23 Nov. 1893 and 18 April 1894.
393. Ibid., 12 Dec. 1894; see also *Paarl*, 27 Sept. 1894; *ZA*, 22 Aug. 1893.
394. *Patriot*, 26 Oct. 1893; see also *ZA*, 23 and 28 Sept. 1893 and 7 Nov. 1893.
395. Ibid., 9 Jan. 1894.
396. Ibid., 14 July 1894.
397. *OC*, 2 Nov. 1893 and 11 Dec. 1893.
398. *OL*, 13 Feb. 1894.
399. Ibid., 23 Jan. 1894 and 13 Feb. 1894.
400. Ibid., 13 and 15 Feb. 1894 and 17 March 1894.
401. *ZA*, 16 May 1893; see also 24 June 1893 and 18 July 1893.
402. For the events leading up to the war, see Rotberg, *The Founder*, pp. 432–45.
403. *ZA*, 29 and 31 Aug. 1893.
404. Ibid., 16 Sept. 1893, 14 and 26 Oct. 1893.
405. Ibid., 5 Sept. 1893.
406. De Waal, *De Waal*, p. 188.
407. *ZA*, 2 Nov. 1893.
408. *CT*, 15 Jan. 1894.
409. *ZA*, 28 Nov. 1893.
410. Ibid., 7 Nov. 1893.
411. Ibid., 28 Nov. 1893, 5, 16 and 28 Dec. 1893 and 4 Jan. 1894.
412. *Patriot*, 27 July 1893. The area is in present-day Botswana.
413. Ibid., 29 March 1894.
414. *Paarl*, 12 May 1894; *Patriot*, 24 May 1894.
415. Ibid., 3, 10 and 24 May 1895.
416. *CT*, 24 and 25 April 1894; *ZA*, 12 May 1894.
417. *Patriot*, 10 May 1894.
418. *GR*, 31 May 1894.
419. *Volksbode*, 9 and 16 June 1894 and 29 Sept 1894.
420. *Hansard*, 7 June 1894, pp. 77–9.
421. *Volksbode*, 19 Sept. 1894.
422. *Paarl*, 13 Sept 1894, *Patriot*, 13 Dec. 1894; *Volksbode*, 7 July 1894.
423. See for example, *Patriot*, 23 Sept. 1894; *OL*, 5 Feb. 1895; *CT*, 14 Sept. 1894 and 11 Jan. 1895; *Volksbode*, 29 Sept. 1894.
424. *Paarl*, 13 Sept. 1894; *Patriot*, 20 Sept. 1894.
425. S.J. du Toit, *Sambesia, Salomo's Goudmijn Bezocht in 1894* (Paarl, 1895).
426. *Patriot*, 11 July 1895 and 5 Sept. 1895.
427. *OL*, 2 and 27 Oct. 1894; *Patriot*, 4 Oct. 1894.
428. *OL*, 22 and 27 Nov. 1894; see also 9 Oct. 1894 and 31 Jan. 1895.
429. Vindex, *Cecil Rhodes*, a speech at the Good Hope Hall, 6 Jan. 1894, pp. 335–60.
430. Ibid., pp. 405–6.
431. *OL*, 30 Oct. 1894; Vindex, *Cecil Rhodes*, pp. 409–10.
432. *Hansard*, 21 May 1894, p. 10.
433. Ibid., p. 7.
434. Ibid., p. 10.

435. *ZA*, 29 Aug. 1893.
436. *Hansard*, 21 May 1894, p. 12.
437. *OL*, 19 Jan. 1895.
438. Molteno, *The Dominion of Afrikanerdom*, p. 47.
439. For a detailed account of the Glen Grey Act, see Rotberg, *The Founder*, pp. 467–77.
440. *OL*, 17 July 1894.
441. *Hansard*, 26 July 1894, pp. 362–9.
442. Davenport, *Afrikaner Bond*, p. 153.
443. Rotberg, *The Founder*, p. 474.
444. *OL*, 31 July 1894.
445. Ibid., 21 Aug. 1894.
446. Ibid., 19 Jan. 1895.
447. *Volksbode*, 1 Aug. 1894; italics added.
448. *Hansard*, 22 June 1894, p. 157.
449. *Paarl*, 21 Aug. 1894.
450. Rotberg, *The Founder*, p. 163.
451. *Hansard*, 14 June 1894, p. 108.
452. Ibid., 11 June 1895, p. 221.
453. *CA*, 6 March 1894; *Paarl*, 15 March 1894.
454. *CA*, 23 May 1895.
455. *CT*, 21 Dec. 1894.
456. *OL*, 22 Dec. 1894.
457. *Patriot*, 17 Jan. 1895.
458. *Paarl*, 7 Feb. 1895.
459. Ibid., 12 Feb. 1895.
460. *Patriot*, 17 Jan. 1895; *Paarl*, 7 Feb. 1895.
461. *Patriot*, 27 Dec. 1894.
462. *CT*, 18 March 1895.
463. *Hansard*, 5 July 1895, pp. 397–8, 22 June 1894, p. 158; see also 5 July 1895, p. 398, 16 July 1895, p. 475.
464. *CT*, 21 Dec. 1894.
465. *Hansard*, 26 June 1895, p. 350.
466. Ibid., 16 July 1895, p. 475.
467. Ibid., 26 June 1894, p. 166.
468. Ibid., 25 June 1894, p. 161.
469. Ibid., 25 June 1894, p. 161.
470. *GR*, 22 July 1895.
471. *Albert Gazette*, 26 Oct. 1894.
472. *OL*, 9 Feb. 1895.
473. *Paarl*, 5 Feb. 1895.
474. *OL*, 9 Feb. 1895.
475. *CT*, 11 April 1895.
476. *GR*, 6 May 1895.
477. Ibid., 16 May 1895.
478. *OL*, 13 Dec. 1894.
479. *GR*, 28 March 1895.
480. Ibid., 5 Nov. 1894.
481. Ibid., 22 July 1895.
482. *Hansard*, 2 July 1894, p. 199.
483. *CT*, 23 May 1895.

484. *Hansard*, 25 June 1894, p. 161.
485. Ibid., 5 July 1895, p. 397.
486. Ibid., 26 June 1895, p. 350.
487. Ibid., 23 July 1895, p. 516.
488. Ibid., 22 June 1894, p. 158.
489. *Albert Gazette*, 26 Oct. 1894.
490. *OL*, see, for example, 7, 19 and 26 Sept. 1895.
491. *Hansard*, 11 June 1894, p. 89; 14 June 1894, pp. 106 and 108; 25 June 1894, pp. 158–9; 26 June 1894, p. 166; 2 July 1894, p. 196; 6 July 1894, p. 246.
492. *OL*, 19 Jan. 1895.
493. *Albert Times*, 3 Nov. 1894; *CT*, 4 June 1895.
494. Wright, *Innes*, Innes to Hockly, 2 July 1894, p. 142–3.
495. *OL*, 10 Oct. 1894.
496. *CT*, 21 Dec. 1895; *OL*, 19 Jan. 1895.
497. See, for example, *CT*, 8 July 1895; *OL*, 9 Feb. 1895.
498. Te Water Papers, S.J. du Toit to Te Water, 28 Feb. 1895.
499. *CT*, 19 March 1895; *OL*, 19 and 21 March 1895.
500. *CT*, 23 and 25 May 1895 and 4 June 1895.
501. Ibid., 4 June 1895, a letter from Van den Heever to Rhodes, 2 June 1895.
502. *Hansard*, 1895, pp. 346–51, 396–407, 422–7, 468–76; *OL*, 18 and 20 July 1895.
503. *Paarl*, 28 Sept. 1895, open letter by D.P van den Heever, 12 Sept. 1895.
504. *OL*, 23 and 25 July 1895, 13 Aug. 1895, 3, 7, 19 and 26 Sept. 1895.
505. Ibid., 13 Aug. 1895.
506. Hofmeyr, *Hofmeyr*, pp. 473–4.
507. *Patriot*, 4 April 1895.
508. *OL*, 16 May 1895.
509. Hancock and Van der Poel, *Jan Smuts Papers*, Vol. i, pp. 80–99; *South African Telegraph*, 7 and 11 Nov. 1895.
510. H.C. Armstrong, *Grey Steel: Jan Smuts – a Study of Arrogance* (London, 1937), pp. 44–7.
511. *OC*, 5 Dec. 1895.
512. *ZA*, 19 and 26 March 1891, 7 April 1891 and 2 June 1891.
513. Ibid., 17 March 1891, 23 April 1891 and 28 May 1891.
514. See, for example, *ZA*, 2 Feb. 1892 and 23 June 1892.
515. Ibid., 23 June 1892.
516. *Patriot*, 10 Jan. 1895.
517. *OL*, 3 Dec. 1892.
518. *ZA*, 13 April 1893.
519. *OC*, 18 July 1892.
520. *Patriot*, 21 March 1895.
521. *Patriot*, 21 March 1895.
522. *OL*, 9 Jan. 1894.
523. *Volksbode*, 23 Nov. 1895.
524. *ZA*, 2 Dec. 1890; Hancock and van der Poel, *Jan Smuts Papers*, Vol. i, p. 173.
525. *OL*, 10 Dec. 1892.
526. Ibid., 9 Jan. 1894.
527. *ZA*, 24 Dec. 1891.
528. *OL*, 4 May 1893.
529. *OC*, 25 July 1892.
530. *OL*, 9 Jan. 1894.
531. *ZA*, 18 Nov. 1892.

532. R. Rive (ed.), *Olive Schreiner: Letters, 1871–99* (Cape Town, 1987), pp. 286–7, O. Schreiner to Smuts, 1 July 1896.
533. Hancock and van der Poel, *Jan Smuts Papers*, Vol. i, p. 125.
534. *Volksbode*, 7 Jan. 1894.
535. Hancock and van der Poel, *Jan Smuts Papers*, Vol. i, p. 124, a leading article in the *South African Telegraph*, 18 July 1896.
536. Fuller, *Rhodes*, p. 168.
537. H. Baker, *Cecil Rhodes by his Architect* (London, 1934), pp. 20–1, 41–2; C. de Dosdari, *Cape Dutch Houses and Farms* (Cape Town and Amsterdam, 1953), pp. 53, 78–9.
538. Baker, *Cecil Rhodes*, p. 25; P. Jourdan, *Cecil Rhodes: his Private Life by his Private Secretary* (London, 1910), p. 188; Roberts, *Cecil Rhodes: Flawed Colossus* (London, 1987), pp. 198–9.
539. Hancock and Van der Poel, *Jan Smuts Papers*, p. 113.
540. Baker, *Cecil Rhodes*, p. 26; Joelson, *Kohler*, p. 52.
541. *OL*, 21 July 1896.
542. *CT*, 25 May 1895.
543. *GR*, 1 June 1895.
544. Fuller, *Rhodes*, p. 146; G. le Sueur, *Cecil Rhodes: the Man and his Work* (London, 1913), p. 272; Jourdan, *Cecil Rhodes*, pp. 194–5; G.A.L. Green, *An Editor Looks Back: South Africa and Other Memoirs* (Cape Town and Johannesburg, 1947), p. 40.
545. *OL*, 7 July 1892.
546. *ZA*, 1 Nov. 1892, 19 Sept. 1893.
547. *OC*, 25 July 1894; *OL*, 16 Jan 1894.
548. A.J.H. van der Walt, J.A. Wiid and A.L. Geyser, *Geschiedenis van Suid Afrika*, Cape Town, 1951), Vol.1, p. 460.
549. *OC*, 8 Sept. 1892.
550. Hofmeyr, *Hofmeyr*, p. 496.
551. Fuller, *Rhodes*, p. 143.
552. De Waal, *De Waal*, p. 151.
553. Lewsen, *Selections*, Vol. ii, notes on South Africa by Merriman, 22 Jan. 1896.
554. Hancock and van der Poel, *Jan Smuts Papers*, Vol. i, p. 173.
555. J. Flint, *Cecil Rhodes* (Boston and Toronto, 1974), pp. 160–2.
556. See, for example, Rotberg, *The Founder*, pp. 515–50; J.S. Marais, *The Fall of Kruger's Republic* (Oxford, 1961), pp. 1–89; J. van der Poel, *The Jameson Raid* (Cape Town, 1951); E. Pakenham, *The Jameson Raid* (London, 1961); E. Langford, *Jameson's Raid: The Prelude to the Boer War* (n.d); A.N. Porter, *The Origins of the South African Raid: Joseph Chamberlain and the Diplomacy of Imperialism, 1895–99* (Manchester, 1980), pp. 49–94.
557. Rotberg, *The Founder*, p. 531.
558. *OL*, 23 Nov. 1895.
559. B. Cloete, *Die Lewe van Senator F.S. Malan* (Johannesburg, 1946) pp. 113–5; see also, F.S. Malan Papers , 'Rhodes and "A Youngster"', pp. 2–3.
560. Michell, *Cecil Rhodes*, Vol. i, pp. 221 and 236.
561. *ZA*, 15 Oct. 1892.
562. Ibid., 7 July 1891.
563. Ibid., 19 May 1892; see also 29 Nov. 1892.
564. *ZA*, 19 Oct. 1893.
565. *CT*, 20 June 1895.
566. Garvin, *Joseph Chamberlain*, p. 61.

567. *Hansard*, 6 April 1897, pp. 17–19. Rotberg, *The Founder*, p. 484.
568. Molteno, *The Dominion of Afrikanerdom*, pp. 80–1.
569. Van der Poel, *Railway and Customs*, pp. 85–6; R. Mendelsohn, 'The Cape and the Drifts Crisis of 1895' (BA Honours thesis, University of Cape Town, 1971), p. 15.
570. Mendelsohn, 'The Drifts Crisis', pp. 15–20.
571. Ibid., pp. 25–31; *Patriot*, 31 Jan. 1895 and 29 Aug. 1895.
572. *OL*, 9 and 14 Nov. 1895.
573. *Patriot*, 7 Nov. 1895.
574. Robinson, Gallagher and Alice Denny, *Africa and the Victorian*, pp. 419–29.
575. *Volksbode*, 23 Nov. 1895.

4

The divorce, 1896–98

At the beginning of 1896 the political marriage between Rhodes and the Afrikaner Bond came to an abrupt and violent end. On the last day of 1895 the news about Jameson's incursion into the Transvaal reached the Cape Town public. When W.P. Schreiner told P.H. Faure, a cabinet minister and one of Rhodes's staunchest Afrikaner supporters, of the raid, he dismissed it with disbelief: 'It is all absurd. Rhodes would not be doing anything of this sort without having spoken to us about it.'[1] Soon, however, even the most credulous had to come to grips with the rude reality. The shock of the news was shared by both Rhodes and his Cape Afrikaner allies. Rhodes, while deeply involved in the conspiracy, and although he could have been more determined in calming Jameson down, seems, on the eve of the raid, to have been resigned to the fact that the Johannesburg revolution had fizzled out. Certainly, an unco-ordinated march into the Transvaal seemed a recipe for disaster. Garrett, the editor of the *Cape Times*, gave in the 1896 New Year's Day entry of his diary a vivid expression of gloom and despondence:

> Jameson spoiled all – given us all away – damned Rhodes and himself and the future of South Africa ... Rhodes may say and do what he likes, but on Jameson's luck in the next 4 and 20 hours hangs his career, and perhaps his career in this Colony is past hanging already. All his years of work ... thrown away. All our carefully conquered Afrikander sympathy flung into Paul Kruger's arms.[2]

Similar thoughts passing through Rhodes's head must have been responsible for his state of mind after learning about Jameson's departure, as described by his close friend W.P. Schreiner:

> The moment I saw him I saw a man I had never seen before. His appearance was utterly dejected and different. Before I could say a word he said, 'Yes, yes, it is true. Old Jameson had upset my apple-cart.' ... He was really broken down absolutely in feeling.[3]

Such was also the impression of Colonel David Harris: 'I was shocked to

238

see the change that had taken place in his appearance in so short a time. He seemed to be in a terribly depressed and agitated condition.'[4]

Initially, the Jameson raid crisis in the Cape had a definite element of a great personal drama. The Bond–Rhodes alliance was cemented by a remarkable political understanding, friendship and trust between Rhodes and Hofmeyr. From a Cape Afrikaner perspective the central role played by Hofmeyr was due to the fact that Parliament was in recess and the Afrikaner Bond lacked an effective central organisation and leadership to deal with the crisis. Hofmeyr, who had resigned his parliamentary seat in 1895 and seemed disillusioned with Cape Afrikaner politics, was sucked into the political vacuum, and again played a vital role. For him, much more than for Rhodes, the Jameson raid had a strong touch of personal tragedy. Rhodes, had, for more than a year, lived with his betrayal of Hofmeyr's trust. If he was 'broken down' it was more for fear of the future of his imperial project than because of the loss of past friends. It was not coincidental that in one of his meetings with Rhodes soon after the news of the raid had reached Cape Town, Hofmeyr used the marriage metaphor:

> I could explain better if you had ever been a married man. You were never married. I have not yet forgotten the relation of perfect trust and intimacy which a man has with his wife. We have often disagreed, you and I, but I would no more have thought of distrusting you than a man and his wife think of distrusting each other in any joint undertaking. So it was till now; and now you have let me go on being apparently intimate while you knew that this was preparing, and said nothing.[5]

For Hofmeyr, at the personal level, the choice was clear: 'If Rhodes is behind it, then he is no more a friend of mine.'[6]

However, for Hofmeyr, as for other like-minded Cape Afrikaners, it was more than a personal tragedy and loss. It was also a crashing failure of a grand political strategy. They were attracted to Rhodes because he seemed to offer them a semblance of harmony in an increasingly complex and confused colonial world. He was, as we have seen, their Moses leading them from the wilderness to the happy middle ground which suited their interests and their political outlook and temperament. All this came to an abrupt end the moment the news about Jameson's expedition broke out. It all looked a fraud as soon as Rhodes's involvement came to light or was suspected. The grief and anger of Hofmeyr and other of Rhodes's Afrikaner supporters must be understood against this background of a great promise broken, of a wonderful dream turned into a nightmare.

Nevertheless, as the initial attempts to resolve the crisis show, the raid did not cause an immediate irreversible break. Hofmeyr and Rhodes met for the first time after the raid was launched on 31 December 1895. According to Hofmeyr, Rhodes said to him:

> I have been thinking over this matter, as I have been so intimately connected with Jameson, people will not relieve me of responsibility for his march into the Transvaal. I have therefore tendered my resignation to the Governor, but he will not accept it.

This, however, did not satisfy Hofmeyr:

> Rhodes, mere resignation will not clear you, but I tell you what might. Issue a proclamation or manifesto as fast as it can be printed, repudiating Jameson's move, instantly dismissing or suspending him as Administrator, and providing the criminal law (if there be such a law bearing on the subject) will be enforced to the utmost against him.

To this Rhodes responded: 'Well, you see, Jameson has been such an old friend, of course, I cannot do that.' Hofmeyr turned away saying: 'I quite understand, that is quite enough – you need say no more.'[7] Hofmeyr may have been offended that Rhodes's friendship with Jameson outweighed his own friendship and the demands of justice.

However, what was uppermost in Rhodes's mind at that time was neither justice nor friendship, whether Jameson's or Hofmeyr's. At that stage, as Garrett wrote, Rhodes 'cherished a wild hope that Jameson might somehow win and tumble Paul Kruger down'.[8] Indeed, as Rotberg convincingly shows, Rhodes tried, in the few days after the raid started, to give it a chance of success.[9] Caught between the prospect of mending his fences with his Cape Afrikaner collaborators and the slim chance of success in using the raid for its original imperial purpose, he gave preference to the latter. He may also have assumed that his complicity would come to light anyway, and that, consequently, his chances of appeasing the Bond were minimal.

Hofmeyr, in playing his peace-making role, was again placed between empire and republic. Between the crisis of the early 1880s and the Jameson raid he dedicated himself to cultivating an option which would resolve the contradiction between the imperial urge for control and the republican desire for independence. The raid had destroyed this option, at least temporarily, and Hofmeyr again mediated between the two antagonistic forces in order to restore peace and save the colonial Afrikaners from being torn between their conflicting loyalties. Over and above the need to secure credibility in both camps, the raid proved to Hofmeyr what he had repeatedly declared: 'blood is thicker than water'. Indeed, his instinctive solidarity and identification with his republican co-ethnics overrode all the negative residues that had accumulated since the early 1880s. This spirit of pan-Afrikaner solidarity was in Hofmeyr's initial cable to Kruger: 'I hope your burghers will acquit themselves like heroes against Jameson's filibusters.'[10] He was also quick to congratulate Kruger on his victory over the raiders on 2 February 1896.[11] At the same time Hofmeyr engaged the imperial actors locally and in London. He convinced the high commissioner, Sir Hercules Robinson, to issue a proclamation, which he had drafted, repudiating the raid, calling on Jameson to withdraw and instructing British subjects to refrain from assisting him. Hofmeyr also facilitated the meeting between Robinson and Kruger in Pretoria, and communicated with Chamberlain asking him to take action against the chartered company.[12] As in the Transvaal crisis of the early 1880s Hofmeyr manifested remarkable even-handedness. He urged Kruger to prevent 'the firing of a single shot' in Johannesburg, and to be magnanimous in making 'as many concessions as possible', presumably to the *uitlanders*. He also beseeched him to show leniency towards the captured raiders, and was publicly highly critical of the famous Kaiser Wilhelm telegram congratulating Kruger for beating the raiders 'without appealing to the help of friendly Powers'.[13]

With the surrender of Jameson on 2 January and the publication of the proclamation of the High Commissioner, Rhodes's imperial project lay in ruins. He had to come to terms with the local reality and local forces in order to salvage its remnants. The Afrikaner Bond was a decisive determinant in this salvage operation. According to Hofmeyr's biographer, his friendship with Rhodes came to an end at their meeting on 31 December 1895.[14] But Hofmeyr proved during the crisis that he was still the unchallenged, though uncrowned, leader of the Bond, and some understanding with him was essential. Rhodes worked his way to Hofmeyr mainly through D.C de Waal and Revd Adriaan Hofmeyr, close, trusted friends who also happened to be Hofmeyr's brother-in-law and cousin respectively. Rhodes assured De Waal that Jameson had acted against his will and restated his sympathy towards the Afrikaners. When De Waal suggested that it might be desirable for him to disown and condemn Jameson, Rhodes responded that he could not betray a helpless friend who had given his life for Matabeleland. De Waal, while condemning the raid, urged his Afrikaner friends not to condemn Rhodes before he was given an opportunity to defend himself.[15]

It was, however, Revd Hofmeyr whom he used to get a second interview with Hofmeyr. On 7 January Hofmeyr received a letter from his cousin begging him to meet Rhodes:

> He is terribly depressed. He longs very much to see you, but thinks that you will refuse to see him ... Much good can arise out of it. Take pity, Cousin Jan. Really, my heart bleeds for my poor friend. He does not defend himself, he admits he was wrong ... Dear Cousin, let us display a Christian spirit of forgiveness.

On 8 and 9 January the two met at Groote Schuur and at the house of T.J. Louw, one of Rhodes's closest Afrikaner friends. According to Hofmeyr's biographer the following was the outline of his message to his former friend:

> What he advised, was that Mr Rhodes should either resign his seat or absent himself from Parliament, and stay away in Rhodesia for some time, that he should further issue a manifesto in the interests of reconciliation and peace, and this manifesto he offered to write out for him. After two or three years, he might return to politics with the prospect of regaining Africander support.

The biographer suggested that Rhodes's approach should indicate that he also 'felt the parting keenly'. Rhodes's prime motivation lay, however, in what the biographer wrote at the end of this account: 'All through Mr Rhodes showed himself excessively anxious about the safety of his Charter.'[16] Rhodes was engaged in a rearguard battle for his imperial dream. He was not keen to accept Hofmeyr's advice for a lengthy political abstention. He only promised to consider it.

On 10 January, a day after his last meeting with Hofmeyr, Rhodes sent De Waal on another errand to his brother-in-law. He told Hofmeyr that Rhodes intended to go to Bulawayo, but could not do so if Hofmeyr was going to attack the charter. De Waal delivered to Rhodes a reassuring message: 'Hofmeyr says he adheres to what he told you yesterday. The chief man he has his eye on is not yourself. He will not gratuitously agitate against you.' Rhodes proceeded to Kimberley where he declared that his career was only beginning. He also despatched a provocative message to an American newspaper, and *The Times*, in which he had some influence, published what Hofmeyr's biographer called 'mischievous fictions'. Worried about what he considered to be attacks on the chartered company by Hofmeyr, on 8 February, Rhodes cabled a message to him through D.C. de Waal: 'Tell Hon. J.H. Hofmeyr, I hear he continues to attack my Charter. He informed me he would leave it alone.' In his response Hofmeyr referred to Rhodes's provocative behaviour and stated that he 'reserves perfect liberty of action, but has hitherto not made further attacks on the Charter, though freely giving legitimate information ... bearing on Jameson's raid, when asked'. This was the last communication between the two former friends.[17]

THE IMPACT OF THE RAID ON CAPE AFRIKANER POLITICS

By then, the raid crisis had been resolved. However, the impact of the raid on Cape politics, and on Afrikaner politics in particular, persisted. Long after Rhodes and Hofmeyr had parted, Rhodes continued to haunt

Cape politics. No less than before, he continued to feed the political discourse and processes among Cape Afrikaners. The disengagement from Rhodes lasted until its culmination in the crucial 1898 general election. The divorce took longer to reach finality than might have been expected, because of the deep impression left by the marriage on the aggrieved Afrikaner partners. It was also a painful divorce, involving personal and collective soul searching, rethinking of basic premises and restatement of identity, policies and ideology. The raid contributed greatly to the politicisation of Cape Afrikaners. On the eve of the raid it was the Scab Act which precipitated the most extensive and aggressive movement ever unleashed by Cape Afrikaners. In the aftermath of the raid this movement subsided, giving way to one concerned with broad political, ideological issues relating to the essence of their collective colonial existence. It was, essentially, another attempt to sort out old contradictions which seemed to have been resolved by the alliance with Rhodes. This involved a much greater popular political awareness and participation by Cape Afrikaners and Bondsmen. It entailed an increasing political tempo which manifested itself in editorials, letters to the editor, Bond branch meetings, congress debates and contributions to parliamentary debates. By the time the disengagement from Rhodes and his heritage was completed, the political map of the Cape had markedly changed, the Bond finding itself in the company of new, strange political bedfellows. However, as we shall see, on essential issues relating to Cape Afrikaners' self-identity and to the major thrust of their political ideology and strategy it perhaps took the form of an evolutionary adjustment rather than a revolutionary change.

The continuity in the Bond's political strategy was already evident at the height of the raid crisis. With the resignation of Rhodes having been accepted on 7 January 1896, the Bond was faced with a ministerial crisis. As the largest and most compact parliamentary group representing specific interests, the Bond could not remain aloof. The opposition, which included prominent negrophiles and free traders, was not a particularly attractive alternative. When Hofmeyr and Supreme Court Judge J. H. de Villiers apparently declined to accept the premiership, Sprigg made himself available. As the Bond did not have a functioning central decision-making body to handle the ministerial crisis, it was left to Hofmeyr to sanction the Bond support for the new government. Sprigg had no difficulty getting two Bondsmen, P.H. Faure and J. Sivewright, who had not even sought party approval, to join his cabinet. Dr T.G.N. Te Water, a novice in Parliament was hesitant and wished to secure the party's blessing. The telegraphic exchange between the two reveals Hofmeyr's general political mood and his particular approach towards the government. Initially he refused to commit himself or advise Te Water

243

whether to join the cabinet or not, being particularly worried that Sprigg might be unacceptable to the republics. When Te Water insisted on getting a straight answer to the question 'whether you will support, as the head of our party, the government as Sprigg intends to constitute it?', Hofmeyr reluctantly replied: 'I would support Sprigg's or anybody else's ministry as long as I could.'[18] It was the traditional external support policy involving individual participation of Bond members in the government and conditional support of the party. There was no break with past political strategies, the Bond, in fact, having greater representation in government than ever before.

Likewise the raid, while causing separation from Rhodes, did not predetermine the inevitability of divorce. In being linked to the raid, Rhodes had infringed a sacred Afrikaner ethnic taboo and had to pay a political price. However, as we have seen, Hofmeyr himself offered him the prospect of regaining Bond support at the end of a cooling-off period of a few years. Indeed, in understanding the political divorce between the Bond and Rhodes we must also consider the dynamic of the relations between them after the raid.

It is indicative of the inefficacy of the Bond that the response to the raid received no central institutional guidance. The Bond did not convene a special conference to deal with the crisis; it did not even advance the date of its planned annual congress. Neither did they press for a special session of Parliament to discuss the raid in which the ex-prime minister was obviously involved and to vote confidence in the new government. With the exception of Hofmeyr's initial 'fire extinguishing' intervention, the Bond leadership proved surprisingly inactive and inept. In mitigation one can argue that the brevity of the crisis and the humiliating defeat of the invaders took the edge off it. For whatever reason, the initiative was left, until the Bond congress which convened in March 1896, to the Bond press and to local branches.

Among the Bond newspapers *OL*, which had given the lead in worshipping Rhodes, now led the attack on him. The new young editor, F.S. Malan, who had taken over shortly before the raid, played a very important role in the anti-Rhodes campaign. He belonged to a new breed of well-educated young Cape Afrikaners who were imbued with a strong sense of ethno-cultural identity. While not always representing Hofmeyr's views, he seems to have had his backing. On 4 January, with Rhodes still prime minister, he called on Faure, Schreiner and 'other well-meaning ministers' to resign. He also called for the annexation of Rhodesia to the Cape. He was, however, careful not to implicate Rhodes, only stating that 'unless the situation is clarified we cannot support Rhodes any more'.[19] By mid-January, in response to Rhodes's declaration that his career had only begun, *OL* did not see fit to refer to the raid: 'The Afrikaners who have for many years supported and loved him have been pushed to the side and he does not think it is worth while to clarify his conduct.' It stated that the suspicion against Rhodes was such that no Afrikaner should support him.[20]In response to Rhodes's provocative telegram to the *New York World*, *OL* articulated a deep sense of betrayal by 'the great imperialist':

> What kind of a man is he if, in order to fulfil his ideals, he must betray the Afrikaners? He is an Englishman and has no feelings for the Afrikaners. This he has now shown and therefore we say that we cannot trust him, and if it is true that his political career only begins, then we hope that it will not happen in South Africa.'[21]

A similar attitude was expressed a few days later: 'We know how he has misled the Afrikaners and struck the face of his bosom friends.'[22] With a view to the forthcoming Bond congress, the newspaper took stock of the relations between the Bond and Rhodes. All the benefits accrued to Cape Afrikaners through their association with Rhodes could not, it was argued, justify further trust in him. By then the leader writer was sufficiently convinced of Rhodes's complicity: 'Because of the information we possess we have withdrawn our political support from Rhodes and we hope that the Bond congress will do the same.[23]

OC, the Bond organ from the Midlands, referred, on 6 January, to reports that weapons had been distributed in Johannesburg on the premises of Rhodes's Consolidated Goldfields:

> It places Rhodes in a dark colour and we expect from him a full and frank statement. We hope and wish that he will be able to remove all the suspicion. If not, he would forfeit the support of those whose hearts beat warmly for South Africa.

By 9 March, with Rhodes's complicity in the raid becoming increasingly clear, *OC*'s conclusion was unequivocal: 'Rhodes, the Afrikaner, has become an impossibility – thus now begins the career of Rhodes the Jingo.'[24] *Het Oosten* on 23 January was still lenient, stating its unwillingness to judge Rhodes before giving him a chance to defend himself.[25] The editor was probably inspired by the Paarl Bond press edited by S.J. du Toit.

At the beginning of the crisis S.J. du Toit acted in full concert with Hofmeyr.[26] On 9 January, the *Patriot* stated a position which served as a basis for Du Toit's approach for more than a year:

> We said that we would support Rhodes as long as he served the land and the people. Has Rhodes deceived us? This we do not say. We must not judge prematurely. We have demanded a response from him and we await it. The facts speak against him. But the danger is over – let now give him

the time to respond. If it will appear that he was involved in treason we will not be able to work with him.[27]

The *Paarl* stated that while pressing for an investigation of Rhodes's involvement 'we keep quiet' until then. And the *Patriot*, in mid-February, promised that 'if Rhodes or anybody else is found guilty, then he will be branded for all times as enemy of our nation'.[28] Responding to criticism of his apparent leniency towards Rhodes, Du Toit stated that while the suspicion against Rhodes was such that the Bond could not co-operate with him any more, he could not pass judgement on him. He referred to St Paul in his policy of not judging a man prematurely, and stated that he was against lynching '(like the half barbaric Yankees)'.[29] By then, Hofmeyr was sufficiently convinced of Rhodes's complicity to state categorically:

> Through these reasons (and also through others which I cannot now reveal) I am forced to the sad conviction that it is impossible for me to work any longer with the man whom I had perceived for so long as my most trusted friend.[30]

There was one newspaper, *GR*, for which the raid was a victory, an occasion to tell all lost Afrikaner lambs, 'I have told you'.[31]

Afrikaner Bond branches, without guidance from the provincial leadership, took the initiative and organised meetings to discuss the raid and pass resolutions. They were inspired by the Bond press, and by the example of Hofmeyr and other branches. On the whole, however, this response was not only unco-ordinated but also sporadic and unimpressive. The lead was given by meetings held on 2 January in Paarl and Graaff Reinet. In Paarl a meeting, which was hastily organised and attracted some 200 people, passed a resolution condemning the raid and requesting Rhodes to make a speedy and clear statement regarding the act of his subordinate. It was also decided to elect 'a Vigilant Committee' to follow events and act according to the circumstances 'in the interest of peace and order'. It was indicative of the Bond's organisational and operational weakness that even in such a major crisis a local branch had to take such initiative. Similarly, the meeting in Graaff Reinet resolved to send copies of its resolution to all the branches of the Bond to support them in their effort to preserve 'peace and friendship between the Transvaal and other states in South Africa'. However, this meeting, while condemning the raid, failed even to mention Rhodes.[32] The response from the other towns was rather slow and limited. During January fewer than ten meetings were held, and a few more were reported by mid-March. Some condemned the raid while others added a demand for clarification from Rhodes. Some were more extreme, calling for the abolition of the charter and for the resignation of Rhodes from Parliament. The latter

demand came from Bond branches in Barkly-West, Rhodes's constituency. It was an opportunity to take revenge for the 1894 election.[33]

In mid-March 1896 the annual Bond congress convened in Burgersdorp. *OL*, stating that the raid was the most important subject to be dealt
with at the forthcoming congress, asked:

> What kind of a resolution will the Bond adopt? Will it be a miserable ...
> resolution? Or will the Bond be manly and not only condemn the most
> serious act in our generation but also speak the truth about the politician
> who so badly disappointed our people? Will they condemn Jameson and
> leave Rhodes alone until this brave man defends himself, who knows
> where and when?'[34]

Malan, the editor, could not condemn the resolution as he was the one to
propose it. The rather long resolution described the raid as treacherous
and congratulated Kruger and his burghers for their victory; it thanked
Hofmeyr 'for the firm stand made by him'; it urged Sprigg to convene
Parliament for a special session and institute an inquiry into the raid. As
far as Rhodes was concerned it recommended that 'radical changes be
made in the administration of Rhodesia to prevent inroads such as that
by Dr Jameson in the future'; it expressed regret that the raid had taken
place with Rhodes 'not only the Managing Director of the Chartered
Company and the Chairman of De Beers Company, but also the Premier
of the Cape Colony, and as such trusted and supported by the Africander
people'; it criticised Rhodes for not providing 'a clear explanation of his
conduct' in connection with the raid; he was asked to provide a 'public
refutation' of a list of accusations implicating him in the raid. The last
paragraph of the resolution underlined its essentially moderate nature:

> unless Mr Rhodes succeeds in clearing himself of these accusations, and of
> all participation in, foreknowledge and countenance of the conspiracy,
> and of all subsequent shielding of its chief originators and instruments, it
> would be impossible for the National Africander party to co-operate with
> him in political matters'.[35]

It was moderate because by then the direct and indirect circumstantial
evidence, while perhaps not sufficient for criminal prosecution, certainly
justified an unconditional political disengagement. S.J. du Toit would not
have seconded the resolution unless he had believed it was moderate.[36]

The conditionality of the resolution provided sufficient space for
Rhodes's remaining supporters to reveal themselves within the Bond.
OL took on the task of exposing and condemning them. They were pre-
dominantly Bond MPs, who had been exposed to Rhodes's charm more
than ordinary members or local leaders. On 23 March, after the congress,
OL reported that two Bond MPs from the east, F.F. Wienand and
L. Abrahamson were treading in the footsteps of P.S. Bellingan, from

Uitenhage, who had been exposed earlier. At a public meeting in Bedford they tried to silence a discussion on the raid. They also, apparently, glorified Rhodes and voiced the opinion that he would soon be prime minister again. Wienand said:

> We must not be harsh on Rhodes before we have heard him. He did err, but is it justified to condemn him and call 'away with him'? ... Rhodes is not the only one who makes mistakes and thus it is not right to hasten and condemn him. Rhodes has done a lot for the country and he is not a capitalist who spends his money abroad.

OL was deeply hurt: 'Can one think of anything more humiliating for the Afrikaners. The congress proved that it was not to be intoxicated by Rhodes. The small lights from Parliament think differently!' He ended on a threatening note: 'The time has come to purge the Bond', F.F. Wienand being reminded that 'the voters and the Bondsmen possess a good memory'.[37] Two days later Sivewright was reported to have said that he was still Rhodes's friend and that he had not discarded him in his difficult time. *OL* hastened to remind the readers that there was a difference between personal and political friendship.[38] Dr T.W. Smartt, the new English recruit, while mildly critical of Rhodes, stated that it was 'not fair and generous of Rhodes's former supporters to attack him so bitterly', and opposed the call 'away with Rhodes'.[39] D.C. de Waal, addressing his constituents in Piketberg and Porteville, was too apologetic for *OL*'s taste. He hailed Rhodes's contribution to the well-being of the Cape, stated his belief that Rhodes had not been aware of the conspiracy, and urged his audience to leave him alone until he had defended himself. Worse still, a vote of confidence in De Waal was passed by the meetings. The newspaper was exasperated:

> If he must choose between the people who supported him and the friend who betrayed him is it impossible to expect that he will stand on the side of the people? De Waal is perhaps not the best authority on patriotism.'[40]

A correspondent from Paarl complained that *Paarl* did not publish letters critical of Rhodes, while willingly publishing ones supporting him. Criticising S.J. du Toit and De Waal he ended up: 'Away with *Paarl*! This is the watchword of many with me.'[41] News of these embarrassing calls reached London where *The Times* wrote that MPs addressing their voters praised Rhodes, that most of the people in the western province supported him, that the DRC was behind him, and that the disengagement from the Bond gave him large Afrikaner support and independence. *OL* called on MPs and clergymen to clarify their position.[42] All this was happening while information about Rhodes's complicity was accumulating.[43]

In a leader article on the eve of the opening of the 1896 parliamentary session, *OL* betrayed anxiety regarding the conduct of Bond MPs:

> Never was the demand of the Afrikaners to take their political salvation into their own hands so strong ... Will those who see South Africa as their home assert this right or will imperialism triumph? ... The critical moment has arrived.[44]

In view of the proceedings unfolding in Parliament this anxiety was hardly misplaced. Soon after the opening of the session Merriman gave notice of a motion calling on the British government to consider

> the revocation or alteration in the terms of the Charter granted to the said company, to make such provisions for the government of the territories comprised therein as may to her seem advisable.[45]

Even *OL*, the anti-Rhodes crusader, admitted that any alternative to the chartered company could only be worse for the Afrikaners.[46] As soon as Merriman finished presenting his motion, W.P. Schreiner proposed a motion calling for a British and Cape inquiry into the raid, and for measures to prevent a recurrence of such aggression. In his speech Schreiner called on Parliament to 'follow the golden mean in all matters' and urged his colleagues that: 'they must not hotly allow their feeling to run away with their reason and compel them at once to give a verdict, for which they required the fullest information'.[47] A week later *OL* described this moderate man as the 'leader of the Afrikaner party'.[48] In fact, the Schreiner amendment was decided upon in a meeting chaired by Hofmeyr.[49]

The subsequent debate revealed a sharp division in the Bond with regard to Rhodes. One group of MPs, led by I.J. van der Walt, an anti-Rhodes die-hard of repute, was bitter and uncompromising towards Rhodes and the chartered company. He called for the abolition of the charter and for the handing over of at least part of its territory to the Transvaal, saying: 'Poor Dr Jameson got all the blame, whilst the greatest criminal in this case was being shielded by many ... There was one man whom the Government ought to have tried and to have kept here, but he escaped.'[50] A few other Bondsmen, using less extreme language, nevertheless identified with Merriman's vicious attack on Rhodes and supported the revocation of the charter.[51] Bondsmen however, were openly sympathetic to Rhodes and critical of the extremists. P.J. Weeber said that he thought that Van der Walt was a Transvaal rather than a Cape colonist. T.J. Louw paraded his friendship with Rhodes, and after relating all that Rhodes had done for the farmers he lamented: 'Mr Rhodes had fallen, and the fact grieved all his Afrikaner friends most deeply.[52] P.H. Faure, a cabinet minister, in a similar vein, 'said farewell to his late Premier with heartfelt sorrow. He was not going to kick his friend now that he was down.'[53] D.C. de Waal lauded Rhodes for his support for the interests of the Afrikaners and declared that he did not regret having followed him, while his colleague from Piketberg, D.J. Marais did not believe that Rhodes was involved in the raid because 'he was too clever a man to plan such a stupid plot'. J.H. Smith from Graaff Reinet was less sure, not being able either to condemn or defend Rhodes.[54] Merriman's motion was heavily defeated, the vote being 60–11 with only seven Bondsmen having supported it.[55]

This was a bitter pill for the zealous young editor of *OL* to swallow. On 21 May he preached to the Bond MPs that they should give preference to patriotism over personal friendship. He was becoming a self-appointed witch hunter, advising voters not to send to parliament those who preferred personal friendship (with Rhodes).[56] Two days later he stated that if it had not been for the few 'righteous' MPs, it would have been appropriate to inscribe on the doors of Parliament the word 'Ichabod', adding: 'It is with a feeling of shame and scandal, as much as rage, that I have written the above about some of my fellow Afrikaners.'[57] This criticism of prominent Bondsmen precipitated a flood of letters to the editor. Indeed, one of the outstanding results of the raid was a considerable increase in the general participation in Afrikaner public discourse on issues related to 'high politics' rather than to material interests. Some encouraged the editor in his crusade, while other attacked the pro-Rhodes MPs. L.J. Coetzee, who had been anti-Rhodes before the raid, was disappointed that after Merriman's 'brilliant speech' most Bondsmen praised Rhodes for what he had done for South Africa and Matabeleland, instead of going even further than Merriman. He went on:

> It is difficult to describe how sad it was for us to read these speeches. All true Afrikaners felt immediately that our leaders were captured by the greatest enemy of South Africa ... There are Afrikaners who begin to despair with regard to the prospect of achieving our ideal.

Fortunately there were also those, 'who will leave no stone unturned to purge the Afrikaners who bow to the Great Baal'. He urged the editor of *OL* to expose them: 'This is no time to spare men like brothers De Waal, Marais, Louw, Abrahamson and others who manifest such a Jingoistic spirit with regard to Rhodes and the Charter.'[58]

For the Afrikaner zealots the worst of the session was still to come. On 4 July 1896, a few days after it again pronounced Schreiner the leader of the Afrikaner party, *OL* reported that he intended to move for leave of absence from Parliament on behalf of Rhodes. The editor was upset that the leader he had crowned was proposing to take such a step before the report of the Cape parliamentary enquiry was published. He stated that it was not too late to postpone the motion and ended up gloomily: 'The future of the Afrikaners is, indeed, not bright.'[59] This was an opportunity to eliminate Rhodes from Parliament by refusing to grant him leave of absence. A correspondent who was more openly critical of Schreiner also directed a veiled threat to Bond MPs: 'Each Afrikaner will, in connection with Schreiner's motion, print his own mark on his forehead, by which he will be recognised.'[60]

Rhodes was at that time in Rhodesia where the combined Ndebele–Shona rebellion was raging. On 11 April 1896 his friend D.C. de Waal urged him to attend the forthcoming parliamentary session: 'Face them in spite of whatever you might have to say ... You know the nature of human being: the man with courage is theirs.'[61] Rhodes ignored this advice and instead asked Schreiner at the end of June, to secure him leave of absence.[62] At the 1897 party congress the Bond secretary confirmed that the motion approving the leave of absence, as presented by Schreiner, 'was formulated at a meeting of many Afrikaners with Hofmeyr at the head'.[63] In presenting the motion on 14 July, Schreiner justified the leave of absence on the grounds that Rhodes was 'combatting barbarism in the North'. He explained to the House that he wished to separate this issue from the report of the commission of inquiry into the raid,[64] which was, in fact, published only three days later. By then, Schreiner, as a member of the commission, was aware of the full extent of Rhodes's complicity. I.W.J. van der Vyver, opening the debate, 'hoped that the motion would be thrown out by a large majority', claiming that 'the entire world would be surprised at their action and it would degrade them'. A few Bondsmen identified with him and some suggested postponement of the debate on the motion until after the publication of the commission of inquiry's report. A motion to that effect was submitted by J.S. Marais from Paarl. I.J. van der Walt introduced the witch hunt to the parliamentary floor, threatening that those voting for the motion would be 'earmarked'. T.P. Theron, expressing regret at differing from many of his friends, and exhibiting indifference to what a newspaper had to say (*OL*, his party's principal organ) stated: 'His sense of right made it impossible for him to condemn a man unheard.' J.S. Marais's amendment was defeated, 49–19, with the 'Afrikaner party' divided evenly. Schreiner's motion was passed by a large majority, 52–12, with most Afrikaner members voting for it.[65]

Three days later, before there was an opportunity to come to terms with the above vote, the report of the commission of inquiry was submitted to Parliament. The majority report was unequivocal about Rhodes's role:

> As regards ... Rhodes your committee can come to no other conclusion than that he was thoroughly acquainted with the preparations that led to the inroad. That in his capacity as controller of the three great joint-stock companies ... he directed and controlled the combination which rendered such a proceeding as the Jameson raid possible.[66]

While Schreiner, the only speaker on the motion, was, on the whole, unemotional, his only explicit moral judgement was most unwelcome to the anti-Rhodes purists among the Bondsmen: 'But he [Mr Schreiner] would never be led into the suggestion that Mr Rhodes's motives were at any time low, or grovelling, or sordid ... The aim of Mr Rhodes was a high one. He ... wished it had been a right one.'[67] *OL* regretted that Schreiner could not believe that Rhodes's ideals were 'low and vile'.[68] The editor was also disappointed with the debate, or rather the lack thereof: 'This debate made an unfavourable impression on most orthodox [*rechtzinnige*] Afrikaners. It is clear that the warm national spirit which prevailed in 1880 and 1881 does not reside in the heart of some who were present in Parliament.' He asked some penetrating questions on the state of Cape 'Afrikanerdom':

> Is it possible that the heart of the Afrikaners beats weakly now? Has the *volk* declined in the last 15 years in cherishing its nationality? Did the spirit of the debate reflect what goes on in the heart of the *volk*? If not, what is the reason that the Afrikaners were so divided in Parliament?'[69]

During the parliamentary session another embarrassing development for the Bond took place. One of those on the receiving end of *OL*'s witch hunt approached D.C. de Waal with a proposition to found an alternative newspaper 'where justice can be made to those who think differently to Burg Street [i.e. *OL*]'. De Waal approached D.F. du Toit & Co. asking them to publish a Dutch daily. According to a correspondent who quoted a reliable source, the meeting which decided on the establishment of the newspaper was held in the office of D.J. Logan, an English-speaking MP and Rhodes supporter, in the presence of known Afrikaner supporters of Rhodes – MPs T.J. Louw, D.C. de Waal, P.G. Wege and M.M. Venter, and also S.J. du Toit. According to De Waal's biographer, nine English-speaking MPs purchased shares and a Rhodes associate provided additional capital.[70] In the beginning *OL* welcomed the *Dagblad*, but by the end of July 1896 it began to suspect its pro-Rhodes inclinations,[71] and at the end of August it claimed that both the *Patriot* and *Dagblad* were Rhodes organs.[72]

Afrikaner press and caucus were evidently seriously divided on the main subject of the day – Rhodes. In his criticism of the debate on the report of the commission of inquiry, the editor of *OL* expressed his belief that the *volk* still felt as it did in 1881.[73] There was a great divide between the *volk* and its leaders, and the young enthusiastic editor obviously pinned his hopes on the *volk*. Malan did not rely on hope alone. He had transformed *OL* from a moderate elite-orientated organ into an activist, militant, mobilising one, out to indoctrinate and incite the grass roots into political activism and initiative. As we have seen, it had already begun to create a groundswell among local leaders and rank and file against moderate Rhodes-inclined leaders and waverers. This acquired momentum in the wake of the parliamentary session. On 1 August, summing up the session, Malan revealed his strategy, juxtaposing leadership and *volk*:

> Now is the time for the *volk* to speak out. The representatives of the *volk* must promote its interests in the institutions of the land. Have they done it in the spirit of the *volk*? Have they really been the representatives of the people? Are the voters happy with the conduct of their representatives? If the *volk* will not speak out clearly now, others will undertake to do it. What will be the result thereof? Nobody will know what is the position of the *volk* and the enemy of the Afrikaners will make political capital from their silence.

He was more specific in pointing to the appropriate strategy of putting pressure on local MPs returning home at the end of the session.[74]

In late 1896 *OL* responded to Merriman's claim that the Bond had disintegrated in the last parliamentary session. The editor attributed the decline to the effect of Rhodes on the Bond leadership, some of whom were still hoping that he would be reinstated. For the decline of the Bond he had a populist cure: 'Deep in the heart of Afrikanerdom the same nationalist feeling simmers ... Give the Afrikaners a leader who will understand them and whom they could trust, *Onze Jan* for example, and you will see that they will be stronger than ever'.[75] He should have known better. Conservative, pragmatic Hofmeyr was not cut from such a leadership role. It was left to young Malan to urge the *volk* on through his newspaper. The target of this populist campaign was Rhodes.

The grass roots' response to the clarion call of *OL* was remarkable. Popular political participation and initiative within the Bond was not one of the party's outstanding features. Branch meetings and the meetings of MPs with their voters were normally uneventful, revolving mostly around issues of local concern. Votes of confidence in the MPs for supporting local interest were a foregone conclusion. As we have seen, the Scab Act precipitated a widespread grass roots response in the affected areas. The cause of this impressive large-scale political mobilisation was, however, economic and sectoral rather than broad and political. It was, all the same, an impressive manifestation of popular assertion and protest against the unresponsiveness of the Bond leadership and MPs to the grass roots. As such it prepared the ground for future popular intervention. The Jameson raid and the betrayal of Rhodes provided a powerful stimulus to the process of politicisation of the Bond grass roots. The issues at stake were, however, primarily neither micro-economic nor sectoral. They related to broad ethnic political, ideological and moral issues. It was the first time in the history of the Bond that its grass roots had been so agitated over such issues, and it had a considerable potential for political mobilisation. The Bond leadership, however, caught between their ambivalence towards Rhodes and their conservative, élitist political culture, failed to grasp the opportunity. F.S Malan, young, highly capable, an eager and aspiring young politician, who had already in his Cambridge days developed a strong sense of ethnic identity and mission,[76] stepped in to fill the leadership vacuum. It is hardly surprising that many old-fashioned politicians resented both the ideological message and the crusading style of this eager parvenu.

The grass roots, however, responded to Malan, and there developed, especially after the 1896 parliamentary session, very interesting relations between this anti-Rhodes crusader and his grass roots knights. Malan not only continued to provide general ideological and political guidance, but also encouraged and directed popular initiatives. He expressed satisfaction with local responses and tried to curb excesses.[77] Thus, in reply to press intervention from Pretoria, he assured his troops that 'three cheers' for the Queen is acceptable in Bond meetings.[78] He applauded others' initiatives, like that of P.J. du Toit that resolutions against the reinstatement of Rhodes in Rhodesia should be passed in the branches and sent to the high commissioner.[79] He also identified specific targets for popular attacks. Thus *OL* reported that De Waal and Wege, two close friends of Rhodes, had attended a dinner at Groote Schuur at the invitation of Rhodes's sister.[80] On one occasion, at least, Malan took a more direct, active part in the campaign, his target being D.C. de Waal. He took the trouble to travel to Piketberg to stir up opposition to De Waal among his constituents. De Waal wrote that by the time he reached Porteville Malan had everything prepared: 'I was the first to speak. I spoke in favour of Rhodes more vigorously than if Malan would not have been present. I wanted to show Malan what I thought of him.'[81] Little wonder that Malan hailed this meeting in particular: 'In this meeting there was unanimity – nobody defended Rhodes and it was as clear as day light that the two MPs did not represent their voters' views.'[82]

This was, however, an exception, and in most cases it was left to local initiative to fulfil the mission. At first, local response took the form of Bond and public meetings. There were the traditional meetings of local MPs reporting back to constituents at the end of which a vote of confidence was unanimously passed. These meetings focused almost exclusively on the raid, on the betrayal of Rhodes and on the way the local representatives had spoken and voted on these issues.[83] There were also meetings of local Bond members and executives, mainly to voice their opinion and to pass resolutions on issues stemming from the raid and its aftermath. The resolutions adopted by these meetings were invariably anti-Rhodes and anti-charter and critical of Rhodes's sympathisers and supporters.[84] At a meeting in Rietfontein, Dirk Viljoen was rather undiplomatic about his former prime minister: 'Rhodes is a murderer and deserved to be hanged.'[85] A large meeting in Venterstad stated categorically that 'whoever supports Rhodes did not deserve to be a member of either the Bond or the national party'.[86]

Another medium for the expression of local opinion and discontent was letters to the editor, the earlier stream turning into a flood. These letters related to issues dealt with by the Bond meetings and were invariably critical of, and hostile to, anything that smacked of Rhodes. They also took to task MPs who had taken pro-Rhodes positions in the last session.[87] The top leadership was not spared. One correspondent expressed disappointment with Schreiner for asking for leave of absence for 'treacherous Rhodes'.[88] N.A.J. van Rensburg, a local leader from the east, expressed regret and rage over the 'coolness' exhibited by Hofmeyr.[89] Some of the attacks on individual leaders smacked, indeed, of witch hunting. Thus, a correspondent from Calvinia warned P.G. Wege, the local MP: 'The day of reckoning will still come.'[90] Another paid compliment to *OL*: 'Luckily *Ons Land* does not yet smack of Rhodes because this smell is objectionable to a genuine Afrikaner and to those who desire the welfare of South Africa.'[91] A few of the above meetings also passed votes of thanks to the editor of *OL*. A meeting in Barkly East praised Malan for reflecting the feelings of genuine Afrikaners and for conveying them courageously to the public. Meetings also hailed the similar role played by the *GR*.[92]

What was the impact of this press and popular anti-Rhodes campaign on the Bond and Rhodes's sympathisers therein? Since the Bond lacked effective central organisation, leadership and discipline, the results could be expected to be uneven. Indeed, it is remarkable that the raid, which not only was a crisis of great magnitude in itself but also gave rise to an ongoing crisis, did not induce the party leadership to improve and tighten its organisation and its capability for mobilisation. Perhaps it was the fault of Hofmeyr, who performed magnificently during the raid crisis but faded into the background soon after. He left a leadership vacuum while still being perceived by Bondsmen as their leader. It must also be borne in mind that the effects of scarcity of resources, vastness of space and poor communication were exacerbated by the lack of a tradition of party political organisation in the Cape. The bold initiative of the young editor of *OL* could not compensate for the lack of effective central organisation and leadership. Consequently, the effects of the popular campaign were varied, and were determined by local and personal differences. On the whole it seems that in the west the response of the constituents to the performance of their MPs was more moderate and approving. While

Malan managed to orchestrate opposition to De Waal in Porteville, where the latter and D.J. Marais were censured for their support for Rhodes's leave of absence, they secured unanimous votes of confidence in four subsequent meetings in their constituency.[93] T.J. Louw, one of Rhodes's closest Afrikaner friends, also secured a unanimous vote of confidence.[94] In the Stellenbosch constituency, P. de Waal and G. Krige were well received by their voters. In Somerset West, while condemning the raid, Krige was not unkind to Rhodes, whereas De Waal praised Rhodes for opening up the north. Worse still, a resolution congratulating Rhodes on restoring peace in Rhodesia and wishing him many years 'so that he will be able to manage the affairs' was unanimously adopted. The vote of confidence in the two MPs was also unanimous.[95] Western Province, it should be recalled, had always been a bastion of support for Rhodes.

In other parts of the Cape the response was more varied. A Bond meeting in Colesberg adopted unanimously a vote of no confidence in M.M. Venter, a staunch Rhodes supporter.[96] In Britstown a Bond meeting was highly critical of the behaviour of the local MPs on the Rhodes issue. A vote of no confidence in T.P. Theron and P.J. du Toit, two of the most senior Bond leaders, was carried by a large majority.[97] A meeting in Calvinia strongly condemned P.G. Wege's conduct on the issue of Rhodes's leave of absence.[98] On some occasions, however, some of the above-mentioned leaders fared better. In another meeting, Wege, while criticised for his vote on the leave of absence, received, together with two other MPs, a vote of confidence. One meeting passed a vote of thanks to, as distinct from confidence in, T.P. Theron and M.M. Venter, while another voted confidence in the latter after he clarified his conduct on the leave of absence.[99]

By the end of 1896 the supporters of Rhodes and those who were lenient towards him, while feeling some pressure, were definitely not ostracised or isolated in the Bond. Not only were some of the MPs among them well received by their constituents, but at least some of the more prominent among them were active in the broad front of Cape Afrikaner ethnic assertion. Thus we find, side by side at the table of honour at a meeting of the 'Language Association', Revd Adriaan Hofmeyr, one of Rhodes's most ardent collaborators, and F.S. Malan, the anti-Rhodes crusader.[100] A committee elected by the Cape Town Bond branch to deal with the question of the cemetery consisted of F.S. Malan and four prominent Rhodes supporters.[101] But perhaps the most significant manifestation of this strange cohabitation of obviously ideological and political extremes under the Bond's roof was the visit of S.J. du Toit to Somerset East, the heartland of the purists in the east. On 10 October, a meeting of the district executive was informed that S.J. du Toit was coming at the beginning of November as a member of the committee responsible for the erection of the Slagtersnek Monument. Many of the participants thought that it was 'very good to invite Du Toit to the village and hold Bond meetings because people wanted to listen to him'. The following was the speech of welcome offered to the visitor by the reception committee: 'Our most respected friend ... we offer you a most hearty welcome in our midst ... and we assure you that we, as well as the Bondsmen here highly prize your coming.' Du Toit was received with loud applause from the 250 people present, and was described as one to whom 'we owe our awakening'. Du Toit told his audience that he was walking on two legs: the one was the service of god and the other the love of the *vaderland*.[102] Two aspects of this episode are indicative of the lingering ambiguities and contradictions inherent in the ethnic assertion of the Cape Afrikaners. First, S.J. du Toit, who by then was clearly behind Rhodes, was also actively involved in the promotion of Afrikaner 'nationalist' historical myths. Second, local Bond leaders and the rank and file, in warmly receiving him, seem to have been oblivious of the contradiction between this and his support for Rhodes.

Looking at 1896 from the perspective of its last few months, it seems clear that the Jameson raid and the consequent collapse of the Bond–Rhodes alliance had not launched the Bond on a clear new course. The storm had a devastating effect on the party, which plunged from peak to abyss. In the face of the storm the Bond looked like a captainless and rudderless ship. Merriman's assessment that the Bond was disintegrating does not seem to have been too wide off the mark. Rhodes's continual influence among many Bond leaders was a cancer in the body of the Bond. *OL* and the grass roots produced some anti-bodies, but at the end of 1896 the disease was still raging. The future of the Bond hung in the balance and it was not yet clear which way it was going. However, the popular thrust to drive Rhodes and his heritage from the Bond was not without effect. For the first time in the history of the Bond its leaders were taken to task and scrutinised on issues relating to the essence of 'Afrikanerdom'. Even if many of them still held the confidence of their electors, they were forced to disguise their inner convictions and feelings and to adopt an apologetic position. As early as April 1896, before the parliamentary session and at the end of a tour of his constituency, D.C. de Waal wrote to a friend that he feared that the harmony between him and his voters which had lasted 12 years was coming to an end.[103]

RHODES'S TRIUMPHANT RETURN AND BOND RESPONSE

At the end of 1896, the movement to purify the Bond of Rhodes received a shot in the arm from Rhodes himself, who made a dramatic reappearance on the Cape political arena. On 7 November 1896 it was reported that

Rhodes would pass through the Cape on his way to London and that victory demonstrations by the jingoes in the big cities could be expected. One newspaper wrote that it would be unsafe for Hofmeyr to be in Cape Town.[104] Rhodes, after defeating the Matabele and having held his legendary encounter with the leaders of the Matabele in the Matopos hills, was in the eyes of many in the Cape, certainly the English-speaking jingoes, a returning hero. Many English-speaking imperialists strongly resented the anti-Rhodes offensive on the part of elements in the Bond and founded, in early 1896, what was to become the South African League, an ultra-imperialist, anti-Bond organisation.[105] Rhodes was to many of the English speakers, who were politically disorganised when compared with the Bond, a potential leader or at least a hero. The tone was set in Rhodes's first stop at Port Elizabeth in late December 1896. *OC* described the reception given to Rhodes as the biggest the city had ever known: 'No effort was spared to welcome the hero from the North.' According to Fuller: 'The horses were removed from his carriage, and it was dragged to the spot where a vast crowd of all nationalities awaited him.'[106]

Rhodes, who had kept quiet for almost a year, broke his silence in Port Elizabeth. His message showed that Hofmeyr's advice to keep clear of Cape politics for a few years had not been heeded. He delivered, according to his own admission, an impromptu speech. It was, however, his usual one with the important messages hidden under piles of anec-dotes, stories, and intimate discussion with his audience. Although he was speaking in a predominantly English-speaking city, he also addressed the Afrikaner gallery, parading his loyal burghers in Rhodesia and emphasising his desire to promote 'racial' understanding and unity. The main political thrust of the speech was certainly out of tune with the new music in the Bond. He reminded his audience that he had declared, at the beginning of the year, that his political career was only beginning. His victorious exploits in Rhodesia certainly did not change his mind:

> I am going home to meet a committee of my own countrymen. As soon as they release me from their assiduous attentions, I mean to return to this country; and when I say this country, I mean South Africa. I shall go to the north and do my best to develop that part, in co-operation with the Cape colony and any other state which may desire to co-operate. I shall keep my seat in the Cape House, because it is part of my programme to show to the people of South Africa that I don't undertake a career of isolation.[107]

Rhodes ended his triumphant trip in Cape Town, where his reception was equally enthusiastic.[108] Fuller invited some 30 of Rhodes's old parliamentary colleagues to dinner at his residence. At this intimate gathering Rhodes came close to giving what many of his ex-Afrikaner allies had expected of him for the last year, namely a show of regret and remorse:

> I do not so much regret, joining in an attempt to force President Kruger into a juster and more reasonable policy, when he had resolutely refused all redress of grievances; but what has been a burden to me is that I was Prime Minister at the time, and that I had given a promise that I would not do anything incompatible with the joint position I held as Director of the Chartered Company and Premier of the Cape Colony. On every ground I was bound to resign, if I took such a course as assisting in a revolution against an officially friendly State; and I did it. I can only say that I will do my best to make atonement for my error by untiring devotion to the best interests of South Africa.

Perhaps Rhodes needed the confidence of a victory to confess a bad mistake. Fuller recalled, when writing Rhodes's biography: 'Ah, how I wished, at the time, I could reproduce that scene in public! It was just the statement all his friends wished he would make publicly.' Apparently this was also the wish of Schreiner, the 'leader of the Afrikaner party', who hoped that it would pave the way for the resumption of leadership by Rhodes. Fuller asked Rhodes to make the same 'avowal' at the public meeting he was to address later. Rhodes promised to do so. According to Fuller the promised words were uttered

> but before he had got through the second sentence, it was met with such a hurricane of protesting applause that the remainder of his words, although heard on the platform, were lost to the audience. In the hot blood of the welcome to their hero the crowd did not want to hear any confessions of error.[109]

Was the course of South African history changed as a result of this applause by hero-worshippers? One doubts it.

The adulation of Rhodes by the English-speaking jingoes was an affront to many Afrikaners. *OC* from Graaff Reinet fulminated over the reception in neighbouring Port Elizabeth:

> This reception can so clearly be seen as a blow in the face of the Dutch Afrikaners ... Not only that the hero of the North has brought evil and disunity to South Africa ... not only were our good relations with the Republics endangered; not only blood poured ... now comes Port Elizabeth.[110]

Worse, however, was what occurred between Port Elizabeth and Cape Town. On Rhodes's trip to Cape Town, crowds, including many Afrikaners, greeted him in Cradock, Beaufort West, Worcester, Wellington and Paarl. In Worcester the Afrikaner mayor and other prominent Afrikaners presented him with a welcoming address.[111] The worst was the

259

reception in Paarl, where an address signed by some 400 residents was submitted to Rhodes. The address congratulated Rhodes on securing peace in Rhodesia and expressed the hope that the country would be opened for mining and other industries. Rhodes's contribution to safe-guarding the trade route to the interior was hailed and the hope was expressed that Rhodes would return to complete the job. According to the *Patriot* those who cheered Rhodes in Paarl were not 'Rhodes agents and the Crethi and Plethi'. Among them were some of 'the most independent and influential of our inhabitants, not Jingoes but true Afrikaners'. Someone from the crowd called: 'Rhodes, your best friends are in Paarl.' Rhodes, apparently moved by this support, said that while in Rhodesia he thought he had lost 'those with whom he sympathised [the Afrikaners] and who would have seen him in a different light if they knew the facts'.[112] T.J. Louw and P.G. Wege were at the harbour in Cape Town to welcome Rhodes, and Jan Faure was on the Cape Town reception committee.[113]

In early January 1897 Rhodes left for England to appear before the parliamentary select committee. In terms of mending fences with the Bond his short triumphant journey through the Cape was disastrous. It delighted those in the Bond who wished to purify it and to carve a new course for the party free from Rhodes and his admirers. It sparked off a much more bitter and powerful backlash than had been caused by the raid itself. This perhaps did not bother Rhodes particularly. He must have come to terms with his inability to restore the alliance with the Bond in a way that would serve his imperialist project. He was moving towards an alternative power base – the English-speaking, pro-imperialist elec-torate. He probably believed, or hoped, that he could split the Bond and secure the support of at least some of his erstwhile Afrikaner adherents who could also mobilise a portion of the Afrikaner electorate. This political shift was underlined by his contribution, before leaving for England, of £11,000 to secure registration of voters for the forthcoming elections.[114]

The Bond organ in Graaff Reinet immediately identified the positive potential in the outburst of adulation for Rhodes: 'The Jingo with his usual ignorance has again woken up the almost sleeping Afrikaner and the *Cape Times* and its consorts will soon witness the inevitable reaction.'[115] Indeed, the 'Rhodes worshipping' sparked off the '*contra stem*' (counter voice) which belittled not only the Afrikaners' welcome to Rhodes but also the anti-Rhodes protest that followed the raid. After the *contra stem* had gained momentum Hofmeyr told Reuters that the movement stemmed from the heart of the people and did not require his involvement.[116] It is true that the *contra stem* was largely a grass roots response rather than an organised and centrally guided and directed movement. The Bond's central leadership had still to prove their organisational and leadership ability. Indeed, the response of Cape Afrikaners was so uneven that J.L. Coetzee claimed that Rhodes's admirers were fortunately limited to the 'Highlanders', namely Afrikaners from the west and that the 'Lowlanders', namely those from the Midlands and the east, were proved right in not trusting the former's patriotism.[117]

About ten days elapsed before the first *contra* meetings took place. The Bond press again played a vital role in alerting Cape Afrikaners to their political duty. On 7 January 1897, *OL* was not satisfied with lamenting that 'the name of Paarl was tarnished and continues daily to be dragged in the mud' and that 'the suppressors of our rights as a *volk* were glad that they have succeeded to defile the Mecca of Afrikanerdom'. He also argued that it was not sufficient to protest in letters to *OL*, and urged Cape Afrikaners to hold protest meetings and send resolutions to the high commissioner. He argued that Afrikaners had to cleanse themselves in the eyes of their republican brothers. Indeed, the response from the Transvaal urged on the Cape Bond zealots. Kruger himself was enraged by the warm welcome offered to Rhodes and called on Cape Afrikaners to protest against it.[118] On the same day, the editor of *GR* also encouraged Bond branches to arrange to adopt resolutions condemning Rhodes and expressing sympathy with the Transvaal.[119] The Bond press was also pushed into action by the English press which tried to make capital out of the fact that there had been no counter demonstrations. *OC* predicted that the joy of the detractors would soon be proved premature.[120] Letters to the editor, from the Cape and the republics, expressing rage and dismay, also helped to create a conducive atmosphere for large-scale popular response.[121] An appeal was made for guidance by Hofmeyr, 'the great leader'.[122] The editor of *OL* also implored Hofmeyr to join Parliament at least for a short time: 'Is he, who in his ability and personality had transformed the party into a force in Parliament, not sad to see how the Afrikaner party wanders like a flock of sheep without a ram while the lion stands ready to devour those falling into his hands.'[123] 'The great leader', however, was still in his political closet and Bondsmen had to fend for themselves.

Soon the *contra stem* set off, and on 12 January 1897, *OL* jubilantly reported an anti-Rhodes meeting in Paarl: 'Paarl has cleansed itself courageously and in a praiseworthy manner from the stain which some Jingoes and Rhodes admirers have inflicted on her'. The meeting in Piketberg, on 9 January, showed the teething problems of an unco-ordinated popular campaign. While a resolution was passed, distancing the participants from the adulation of Rhodes and condemning the jingoes, the chairman of the meeting expressed the view that 'it was natural to congratulate Rhodes for restoring the peace to Rhodesia and for doing so much in the North.'[124] The meeting in Stellenbosch, on 12 March, was also not exactly what the *OL* had in mind. The two local MPs certainly lacked in zeal and determination. G.J. Krige was very gentle and moderate in his criticism, using the Transvaal market as his prime argument for supporting the resolution condemning Rhodes's reception. His colleague, P. de Waal, was even more lukewarm, stating that he was opposed to both pro- and anti-Rhodes demonstrations. So unsatisfactory was the tone of the meeting that Jan Smuts felt obliged to intervene and to stress that their relations with the Transvaal were about a 'sense of nationality' and brotherly love rather than about a market for Cape produce. Another external intervention, by Merriman, was needed to give the meeting the required stamp of an anti-Rhodes crusade.[125] Soon, however, meetings condemning Rhodes's reception were being held throughout the Cape.[126] By 19 January some 35 meetings had been held; by 30 January there had been 78; and by 6 February more than 100.[127] The editor of *OL* enthused: 'This is one of the most important events of our time. One fact is clear, Afrikaners . . . spoke in one voice'.[128] While Malan may have been carried away with regard to unanimity, the *contra stem* was certainly gathering considerable momentum.

The anti-Rhodes campaign, as manifested in the press and in the many public meetings, turned equally against his Afrikaner supporters and admirers. Greed as well as foreign influences were offered as explanations for the corruption and betrayal of leaders. These were labelled 'unprincipled favour-hunters, money worshippers and dastardly knee-benders to the money Baal and betrayers of Afrikanderism'. Country folk described them as 'the Crethi and Plethi from the towns'.[129] S.J. du Toit and his newspapers were singled out for what was perceived as their support for Rhodes.[130] Even in connection with his suggestion that the spelling of Afrikaans be changed, readers were reminded that he preached adulation of Rhodes.[131] Indeed, the witch hunt raged more fiercely than before. Individual leaders who showed any pro-Rhodes leanings, or who had any contact with him, were earmarked for the political day of reckoning.[132] At a meeting in Vryburg, Wessels gave this witch hunt a general perspective: 'There are Afrikaners, sons of old Afrikaner families, who bow to the Mogul. We must purge our ranks from the Afrikaner Jingoes.'[133]

As the anti-Rhodes campaign gained strength, Rhodes was becoming a political obsession, the dominant focus and concern in Afrikaner politics. Of the prospective by-election in Wodehouse, *OL* stated: 'Now there is one dominant issue – Rhodes.' It called on the voters to forget about personal and other issues and to unite behind a 'candidate who can represent the voters' feelings on the great national questions'.[134] The Bond was in the process of shedding its parochial nature. Correspondents were astonished that D.P. van den Heever, the anti-Scab Act crusader, called on voters not to vote for a Bond candidate who favoured the Act: 'The issue is related to the Dutch-speaking *volk*, with our nationality ... Let him continue with his agitation and leave us alone.'[135] Not all Cape Afrikaners were prepared to make a clear choice between *volk* and flock politics. At an anti-Scab Act conference in Victoria West, A.S. Le Roex refused to give an explanation for a night visit to Groote Schuur. The conference participants opted for a compromise – he was condemned for his support for Rhodes, but was praised for his performance in the anti-Scab Act campaign. The bottom-line sentiment of the meeting was shown in a vote of confidence in Le Roex.[136]

The gathering momentum of the anti-Rhodes campaign had an impact on Rhodes's supporters. A straightforward pro-Rhodes position was both politically hazardous and difficult to sustain. Some showed more poltical courage than others. T.J. Louw told some 500 listeners that while he could not support Rhodes in everything, he believed that Rhodes still harboured the same feelings towards the Afrikaners, and that he would come back to work with them.[137] Those who, like Louw and Jan Faure, were not afraid to be associated with Rhodes publicly were in a minority. A.S. Le Roex simply argued that his visit to Groote Schuur was a private matter, while some argued 'not guilty'. J.P. du Plessis, who declared that he had met Rhodes in Cape Town on behalf of a friend, and that he would not support Rhodes and his policy in the future, was absolved by a meeting.[138] Others used more elaborate verbal acrobatics to enable them to keep their political options open.

This was also the case with S.J. du Toit and his Paarl press. The *Patriot* and the *Dagblad* did not adopt an overtly pro-Rhodes stance and argued from a Bond point of view. Since the Bond's latest official position was stated in the March 1896 party congress, Du Toit argued and manoeuvred from that premise, repeatedly affirming his allegiance to the congress' resolution withholding support for Rhodes as long as he had not defended and cleared himself.[139] While the position of *OL* was that the Cape parliamentary commission of inquiry had found Rhodes guilty, thus removing the conditionality from the Burgersdorp resolution, Du Toit preferred to wait for the outcome of the British inquiry. Since the Bond had no decision-making mechanism between congresses, Du Toit's position was not altogether devoid of formal constitutional soundness. He also continued to insist that his newspapers were Bond organs.[140] With regard to Rhodes's triumphant return and the *contra stem*, Du Toit argued from a traditional moderate Bond perspective. To render his position legitimate he distanced himself from the receptions given to Rhodes for three reasons – first, because Rhodes was under suspicion, secondly, because they would be used by the Transvaal 'clique', and thirdly, because they would precipitate a counter movement which would exacerbate 'racial' hatred.[141]

Once Rhodes had completed his triumphant return, Du Toit sought to remain aloof, advocating a moderate response which would avert both 'racial' animosity between Afrikaners and Englishmen and a rift within the Bond.[142] A more partisan pro-Rhodes position, comparing Rhodes favourably with the Transvaal and Kruger, was contained in a letter to the editor signed by 'moderate'.[143] Du Toit's pro-Rhodes proclivities were manifested indirectly through his continuation of his blatant anti-Transvaal campaign,[144] which was in stark contrast to the sympathetic attitude of *OL* towards Kruger's republic after the raid. He also continued to present Rhodesia, and Rhodes's northern project in general, in bright colours and as most beneficial to the Cape.[145] In this vein he not only defended, but also praised M.M. Venter and T.J. Louw, who gave favourable evidence on Rhodesia and the chartered company to the London inquiry.[146] When news of the inquiry in London was received Du Toit delighted in the involvement of Chamberlain and the High Commissioners, Sir Henry Lock and Sir Hercules Robinson, in the preparations for the raid, presenting this as a vindication of his position of 'wait and judge'.[147] This contrasted sharply with *OL*'s conclusion that Rhodes was the arch-conspirator.[148]

The manoeuvring space of Rhodes's sympathisers within the Bond was further shrinking as the party's annual congress progressed during the second week of March 1897. The congress convened as the *contra stem* was beginning to subside. It was an opportunity to test the different forces that had been vying for power, influence or simply a living space within the party in the previous year. In particular, it was an opportunity for the local popular forces to display themselves at the party's highest decision-making body. The Malmesbury congress, much more than the one in Burgersdorp a year earlier, was preoccupied with high political issues stemming from the raid crisis and revolving, directly or indirectly, around Rhodes's person and politics. It was in this broad political front that the popular forces, from the geographical and political periphery, generated a challenge to the leadership and to the accepted mode of operation of the Bond. These forces possessed the zeal, the radicalism and the witch-hunt tendency which had characterised their pre-congress activities. The popular challengers came mainly from the remote areas of the Karoo and the Midlands. Compared to their militancy, even F.S. Malan who had urged them on appeared moderate.

It was Theunissen from Richmond who submitted a resolution based on the findings of the Cape commission of inquiry and Rhodes's evidence in London. The resolution, which dispensed with the conditionality of the one adopted at the Burgersdorp congress, simply asked Bondsmen to refrain from supporting Rhodes. In presenting the resolution, the proposer said that 'the Afrikaner who still supports Rhodes is the murderer of his own flesh and blood'. Dr J.M. Hoffman gave the debate on the resolution an Afrikaner historical perspective. Even S.J. du Toit agreed to the resolution although he also said that the last word had not yet been said. The resolution was accepted unanimously.[149] The link between the Bond and Rhodes's person was formally severed. The congress also adopted a resolution declaring that the two Bond MPs who gave evidence to the British parliamentary inquiry did not represent the party.[150]

The first controversial issue raised by the peripheral political forces was related to the claim of *Dagblad* to be recognised as a Bond organ. N.A.J. van Rensburg, who was in the forefront of the challengers' camp, put forward the following resolution: 'This meeting strongly denies the right of *Dagblad* to call itself a Bond organ and rejects the policy of the newspaper.' In arguing that the newspaper 'undermines our nationality' Van Rensburg referred to its refusal to express an opinion on Rhodes who had been found guilty by the Cape commission of inquiry. S.J. du Toit tried in vain to convince the congress that *Dagblad* strictly followed the principles of the Bond. The resolution which was finally adopted denied the newspaper the status of a Bond organ.[151] Van Rensburg also led the second assault in proposing another resolution: 'The congress institutes an inquiry whether the *Bondsmoderatuur* has done its duty on the issue of Rhodes's betrayal, and expresses no confidence in the executive commission.' In presenting his resolution Van Rensburg strongly attacked the office bearers of the Bond for their support of the motion to grant leave of absence to Rhodes when they already knew that the Cape commission of inquiry was to find him guilty: 'When our leaders vote for the traitor in our country the hope vanishes.' Coetzee, who seconded the resolution, tried to soften the blow: 'We lash our leaders out of love.'

The accused, T.P. Theron and J.P. du Plessis, the party's secretary and vice chairman respectively, made a desperate effort to justify their conduct. The former argued that the decision to support the leave of absence was also approved by Hofmeyr, while the latter implied that had he known what he knew now, he would have acted differently. Du Plessis betrayed the bewilderment of the leadership in the face of this assault: 'It was a pity that men like Dr Hoffman and other men did not tell the members of Parliament what they had to do when Rhodes asked for leave of absence.' At the end F.S. Malan stepped in, proposing a softened version of the resolution which was accepted by a large majority: 'This meeting regrets that the members of the executive did not act in the spirit of the last resolutions passed by the Bond.'[152] Two other motions which were rejected reflected the dissatisfaction of the party's periphery with the conduct of Bond MPs. One sought to minimise the participation of MPs in the party congresses, and the second wished to expel those who did not vote in parliament in accordance with congress resolutions. The disenchantment with the performance of Bond MPs was also manifested in the motion asking Hofmeyr to return to parliament which was carried unanimously.[153] There was definitely a leadership crisis in the Bond. Although the leadership survived the popular challenge, the message was clear – in the future they would have to take the sentiments of the party's rank and file more seriously. The Malmesbury congress also manifested a tendency towards greater political and ideological conformity and discipline in response to the confusion caused by the raid and the collapse of the alliance with Rhodes.

Yet, despite the anti-Rhodes-inspired popular challenge, the Bond had not yet reached the point of no return for Rhodes's sympathisers. Thus we find S.J. du Toit, not only present at the congress, but actively participating in the deliberations and in party committees. Most importantly, he remained a member of the vital Supervision Committee. Shortly after the congress, he signed, together with Hofmeyr and N.F. de Waal, a circular to Bondsmen in the Beaufort West constituency, confirming the candidate of the local branch for the forthcoming by-election.[154] It is also noteworthy that the resolution withholding recognition of *Dagblad* was opposed by 25 delegates against 35 who favoured it.[155] Even J.P. du Plessis, despite bending before the storm, felt sufficiently confident to tell the congress, when criticised for bidding farewell to Rhodes, that 'whenever Mr Rhodes came back he would like to shake hands with him again', and that 'in his belief Mr Rhodes was at present as perfect an Afrikaner as ever'. He also intimated that 'he had been told that there were several districts, even in the Western Province, where Mr Rhodes would get in at the head of the poll'[156] It should also be borne in mind that there were still three Bondsmen in the government and it was definitely not anti-Rhodes. When they visited the congress they were welcomed by the chairman as Bond members. One of them, P.H. Faure, a notable Rhodes supporter, told delegates that he hoped that all their resolutions would be in a 'patriotic spirit'.[157]

As the deliberations of the Malmesbury congress showed, the raid had another significant impact on Afrikaner politics. This was revealed by the following resolution which was adopted 'enthusiastically':

> The meeting regards it as an obligation for the Afrikaner party to express thanks to the predikants of the Dutch Reformed Church for standing faithfully by our party and especially to the predikants who sent an address to the Governor on the Rhodes issue.[158]

At the height of the Bond–Rhodes alliance the tension between party and church considerably exacerbated. In addition to the sharp disagreement on 'native' policy, the *Volksbode*, representing influential church circles, strongly condemned the corrupting influence of Rhodes on Afrikaner politics. After the raid the *Volksbode* took a strong anti-Rhodes line, corresponding to the purist popular thrust of *OL*, and joined the latter in condemning the lingering support for Rhodes in the Bond.[159] The last leader article, before it closed down, warned its readers against Rhodes's influence: 'To sympathise with Rhodes now is a hundred times more dangerous to the peace of South Africa than ever before.'[160] A common enemy makes good friends. *OL*, referring to this resolution, presented the *rapprochement* between the clergy and the Bond as one of the benefits of the raid.[161]

In arguing for moderation during the congress, S.J. du Toit pointed out that the number of Bond members had decreased by almost a third. By implication he urged congress not to follow the extremism of the purists. He was trying to carve a moderate space for himself and his kind in the party. Some thought that the Scab Act was responsible for the decline of the party. A voice from the floor suggested that the cause was different: 'Drastic measures like those now proposed will soon increase the members roll.' J. Luttig thought that the Bond declined because its policy was one of 'milk and water'.[162] Soon after the congress the parliamentary session was to begin and Bond leaders would have the opportunity to prove whether their policy was one of milk or of water.

THE 1897 PARLIAMENTARY SESSION AND RHODES'S RETURN TO ACTIVE POLITICS

Shortly after the opening of Parliament P.J. du Toit, the Bond chairman, submitted the 'Peace Motion'. Behind it was the increasing tension between Britain and the Transvaal in the wake of the raid, Chamberlain's apparent belligerency as manifested in the British inquiry,[163] and the revelations that the Cape government, during the drifts crisis in late 1895, had undertaken to support a prospective military action against the Transvaal.[164] The motion read as follows:

> That this House, being of opinion that the occurrence of hostility between the European communities of South Africa would for many years to come prove disastrous to the best interests of the country, and earnestly desiring to secure peace, and establish mutual confidence in and between the various South African states and colonies, wishes to express the conviction that these objects can be attained by the faithful and reciprocal observance of all obligations under treaties, conventions, or agreements; that means could be devised to obtain an amicable settlement of any differences which

267

may arise in the interpretation of such obligations, and that by the adoption of a policy of moderation, mutual conciliation, and fairness in the discussion of and dealing with all differences, the tranquillity of South Africa would be further assured.

In presenting the motion Du Toit was a model of moderation, his language being devoid of any traces of the purism and extremism of the recent congress. Innes moved an amendment which specified that adherence to the London convention and redress of the Transvaal *uitlanders'* grievances, as well as British moderation, were crucial to the securing of peace in South Africa.[165] In the ensuing long debate, participating Bondsmen emulated Du Toit's moderation, but all of them rejected Innes' amendment as interference in the domestic affairs of the Transvaal and adopted an apologetic posture towards the latter.[166] All the Afrikaners voted for Du Toit's motion which was adopted in a slightly amended version.[167]

In this debate there appeared the beginning of a process of disengagement of English-speaking Bondsmen from the party. L. Abrahamson spoke in favour of the Innes amendment and in particular for the redress of the *uitlanders'* grievances, but decided eventually to vote with the Bondsmen. Dr T.W. Smartt adopted a similar stance and went further, voting against the Bond. Sivewright was still sitting on two stools. He was the one who proposed the modification to Du Toit's motion that allowed him and the government to vote with the Bond.[168] One of the main contributions of Rhodes to the Bond, the transformation of the Bond into a bi-'racial' party, was withering away.

On 30 April 1897, Merriman moved a vote of no confidence in the government. He justified his motion in terms of the requisites of peace in South Africa, in view of the growing tension between Britain and the Transvaal. He took the initiative because 'others better fitted than himself had not been able to undertake the duty – others who were thoroughly in accord and entirely with him in that matter'.[169] The 'others' were certainly Bondsmen who had preferred to leave the task to him. The Sprigg government still contained three Bondsmen and enjoyed the lukewarm support of the Bond. Sprigg, as well, was lukewarm in his subservience to his main backers, vacillating between his sympathy with Rhodes and the need to maintain parliamentary support. In the first half of 1897, and more especially during the parliamentary session, the political haze of the the post-raid period, which shielded the Sprigg government, was clearing away and the lines of a new, potentially more rigid, party-political map began to emerge.

This development was closely linked to the political manoeuvres of Rhodes. During 1896, the period of his self-imposed exile in Rhodesia, at least some of his former political allies, Schreiner and Hofmeyr included, believed, or at least hoped, that Rhodes would repent and espouse again the causes he had championed before. His vigorous, triumphant and unrepentant return at the end of 1896 shattered these hopes. Merriman interpreted the pro-Rhodes demonstrations as a proof 'that Rhodes has burnt his boats'.[170] P.A. Molteno saw more in these demonstrations: 'their object being to divide the Colony into two camps'. Molteno was glad to learn that 'at last W.P. Schreiner and Hofmeyr are disillusioned with Rhodes and see him now in his true colours'.[171] Cape politics was, indeed, changing. The process of political amalgamation of English and Afrikaners, to which Rhodes had contributed so much, had been arrested, indeed, reversed. Now Rhodes was precipitating the re-racialisation of Cape politics – English against Afrikaners.

His return to the Cape around 20 April 1897, after giving his evidence in London, hastened this process. Rhodes made a point of travelling back to the Cape in the company of Schreiner who, while testifying against him, showed approval of his motives. Rhodes must have thought that this provided a basis for political *rapprochement* with him. Schreiner was not to be lured. On the contrary, this trip occasioned the final break between the two. Back in Cape Town, Schreiner wrote to a friend in London that if the British government was pursuing a policy of peace in South Africa, 'Rhodes should be regarded as the greatest enemy in Africa of the Imperial policy'.[172] Schreiner was moving closer to an alliance with the Bond.

After his return to Cape town, Rhodes attended the parliamentary session, which opened in early April. He may have told Garrett subsequently: 'humanly speaking, *qua* ambition at the Cape, one has had everything. There is no more to offer, only work and worry ... Really there are many other things to think of besides the Cape Town parish pump.'[173] The truth was, however, that the Cape, with its parish-pumpers, remained a vital component in his grand imperial design. Upon landing in Cape Town Rhodes addressed the cheering crowds at the docks:

> You recognise the higher motive which I had (cheers) and I still hope that constitutionally we shall arrive at that point we all desire (loud and prolonged cheering). And what is that point? It is not a question of race; it is this – that we desire equal rights for every white man south of the Zambesi (continued cheering) irrespective of race, and then gradually the union of Africa (renewed cheers).[174]

As a discussion in which he participated shortly after revealed, his strategy was to federate the Cape, Natal and Rhodesia as a preliminary to the ultimate union of South Africa under British paramountcy.[175] For this grand design the control of Cape politics was crucial. The Bond, with its post-raid pro-Transvaal inclination was clearly not a vehicle for implementing such strategy. There was also a personal element to the deteriorating relations between Rhodes and the Bondsmen. Fuller noted the 'bitterness with which he spoke of his old friends and allies'. Rhodes refused offers by mutual friends to arrange for him to meet Hofmeyr even socially. In interviews with Garrett Rhodes spoke of his former friends in a way which did not make for 'pleasant reading'.[176]

Thus, when Rhodes returned to the Cape, while not actively participating in the parliamentary debates, he was most interested in the outcome of the contest between the two emerging political blocs. On the eve of the no-confidence vote, Rhodes revealed his Cape political strategy in a discussion with James Rose Innes. He told the latter that Sprigg, if defeated, would advise the governor to ask him to form a new government: 'You will have 32 who voted for your Peace Amendment [all of whom were English-speaking], I could get you six Dutchmen and you will have four from the present government.'[177] Rhodes was aiming at a winning English-speaking bloc, supported by a few 'Rhodes Dutchmen'. This was the gist of a communication by Milner, the new governor, to Chamberlain, ten days later:

> The present Ministry, a weak one, ... has hitherto leant ... upon the Bond, though with mutual distrust ... *Now* there is something like an open rupture, and at the next election the Ministry will stand boldly upon the 'no more Bond dictation' platform. On that platform they will have all the English on their side, and some Dutchmen corrupted by Rhodes. But they cannot afford to show their hand yet.[178]

The Bond press responded immediately to the glove thrown down by Rhodes upon his return. *OL*, noting that Rhodes had used the opportunity to hurt and ridicule the Bond and the 'Afrikaner party', responded with rage, vigour and defiance:

> The courage, manliness, the independence and self-respect of our forefathers still characterises their offsprings. The contempt, ridicule and threats of Rhodes cannot harm us, because they will encounter the independent and strong national character of the Afrikaners.[179]

GR described the struggle between Rhodes and the Bond as one for political life or death, strongly criticising Bondsmen who greeted Rhodes upon his arrival in Parliament.[180] *OC* thanked Rhodes for parading his true colours:

> There were still among us, as unbelievable as it may appear, *many* [italics added] who wavered in their feelings towards the great traitor of the Afrikaners' trust, who still believed in the possibility of a compromise ...

country, let us be unanimous! We do not say this out of compassion for Mr Rhodes, but out of love for our country and people. Let us understand each other where formerly misunderstanding was rife, and let us co-operate as formerly in union and love and a blessing will result from such action.[192]

It is doubtful that Du Toit's conversion was altogether genuine. On the day after he published the first article in his series, he had 'a good chat' with D.C. de Waal about the Ngami trekkers who were still stranded with no scope for settlement. The gist of the discussion was to resolve the issue in a way which would improve Rhodes's image among Cape Afrikaners.[193]

The publication of the series did indicate, however, that it was becoming increasingly difficult for Afrikaners seeking legitimacy and support to parade their support for Rhodes openly. Indeed, the parliamentary session, the traditional tours of MPs in their constituencies, the forthcoming Upper House elections, the increasing tension between Britain and the Transvaal and the anti-Bond, anti-Afrikaner campaign in the Cape English press, further charged the political atmosphere. Sprigg, saying in England that some half of Cape Afrikaners supported Rhodes, provided another major provocation.[194] Milner, a keen participant and a very perceptive observant of Cape politics, was of the opinion that Sprigg had committed a grave error. He believed that:

> a number of the Dutch, quite a considerable proportion in the House, but not, I think, many in the country, are at heart quite ready to forgive Rhodes. But it was a great mistake for Sprigg to call such pointed attention to it, for he had excited the Bond to fury. They are agitating all over the country. The doubtful are being called upon with a pistol at their heads, for a profession of faith and under this pressure they are being compelled in many instances, much against their will I have no doubt, to renounce Rhodes and all his works with an emphasis which will make it very difficult for them to support Sprigg next session.[195]

As before, it was not merely the raid itself, but also, to a large extent, the insensitive provocation of Rhodes and his friends in its aftermath that shaped the Afrikaners' attitude towards him.

THE 1897 UPPER HOUSE ELECTION – THE CLOSING OF THE RANKS

Indeed, Rhodes became, in the wake of the 1897 parliamentary session, a political obsession for Cape Afrikaners: 'What further happens in the Cape Colony is closely related to the overshadowing Rhodes question.'[196] Rhodes who had cultivated the Afrikaner parish pump now caused them to abandon it. *OL* argued that of the two main issues on the Afrikaner agenda, the Scab on the one hand, and imperialism and Rhodes on the other, the latter was far more vital to the fate of *land en volk*.[197] Although Rhodes himself was still to be persuaded to become the leader of the anti-Bond party, Bondsmen increasingly saw him as such. The chairman of a Bond meeting in Wellington spoke of a Rhodes party and an anti-Rhodes one.[198] *OC* asserted that Rhodes was seen by the adherents of the opposing party 'or Rhodes party', as their head.[199] The electoral struggle in Paarl was described as one between the 'Rhodes party' and the 'anti-Rhodes party'.[200] Innes said that the forthcoming election was a struggle between Rhodes's party and Kruger's party.[201]

This struggle was increasingly perceived by Bondsmen in apocalyptic terms. This was how *OC* saw it when concluding the year:

> The year 1897 was a year of organisation for all the elements hostile to the Bond and in the coming year the Afrikaner will have to fight with all his powers for the national existence. 'Rhodes above and the Afrikaners under', this is the election battle cry of all those who hate the Bond.[202]

At a Bond meeting in Phillipstown it was claimed that Rhodes was trying 'to kill our nationality', while in Wellington Bondsmen were warned that 'if Rhodes wins our power will be broken for ever'.[203] An open letter to the voters of the South West Circle asserted that Rhodes wanted to turn the Afrikaners into 'hewers of wood and drawers of water'.[204] *OL*, articulating this approach, gave it a historical perspective:

> From the beginning of 1896 Rhodes's name has been linked to a social and political movement which had existed before Rhodes set his feet on South Africa's soil ... For many years this party systematically suppressed the Afrikaner people and ignored it.[205]

With such a prevailing mood, S.J. du Toit needed to do much more than publish his 'earthquake' if he sincerely wished to be readmitted to the 'Synagogue' of mainstream 'Afrikanerdom'. With the *volk* undergoing a survival crisis, suspicions of collaboration with the enemy were not easily washed away. Such conditions served as fertile ground for witch hunting, with people being branded traitors on the basis of flimsy evidence. Such conditions invariably generate an urge for purification. This tendency, which had already manifested itself since the raid, acquired a new urgency as the perceived *volk* crisis grew worse. *GR*, referring to those who had welcomed Rhodes upon his arrival in Parliament, including leading and respectable Bondsmen like Te Water and Theron, exclaimed: 'The time has come to throw the traitors out of the Synagogue.'[206] The term 'genuine Afrikaner', which had been used in the past by the marginal opponents of the Bond leadership, now became the weapon of the party mainstream. The supporters of the government in the no-confidence vote were denigrated as 'mish mash, the rag tag and bob tail of Rhodes',[207] while the opponents of Rhodes in the Paarl Bond branch were hailed as 'the purifiers'.[208]

S.J. du Toit could not have expected rehabilitation, not only because of his past position, but also because he continued to propagate his old position and views – attacking the Transvaal, promoting Rhodesia, criticising the Bond mainstream, supporting the Sprigg government, adopting an apologetic position towards Rhodes, and ultimately supporting pro-Rhodes candidates for the Upper House election.[209] It was, consequently, hardly surprising that he continued to be a target for bitter criticism and attacks as the arch-traitor in the Afrikaner cause. One correspondent wrote: 'Who is the man who not only sows discord in the Bond ... but also works day after day to bring about division and bitterness among the Afrikaners? Who is the man who employs the most loathsome means to achieve his despicable plans?' Another claimed that he had turned into 'a red Jingo', adding in despair: 'Is it possible that an Afrikaner will relinquish his nation for a handful of figs?'[210]

Du Toit was not alone in feeling the anti-Rhodes backlash from the Bond rank and file. The Bond press, in articles and in letters to the editor, continued the witch hunt, sniffing out suspected Rhodes sympathisers and targeting them. The known supporters of Rhodes were presented to the public for condemnation, and Afrikaners were asked not to support or vote for them.[211] However, as invariably happens in witch hunting, innocents also fell victim. Thus, a correspondent disputed the selection of Dirk Rabie as a Bond candidate on the basis of his past record.[212] Rabie was subsequently elected as an official Bond candidate. Another correspondent warned against voting for J.J. Michau in Kimberley because of his business contacts with De Beers.[213] He was subsequently defeated as an official Bond candidate. Even old M.L. Neethling, who stood as the candidate of the Bond leadership against a Rhodes candidate, was, according to a correspondent, suspected by many Afrikaners as a supporter of 'Rhodes politics'.[214] For witch hunters a man in the middle was a dangerous man not to be supported as a candidate in the election.[215] As is also the case with witch hunting, some people used the fire to fry other fish. Thus, a correspondent suggested that it was dangerous to support Steyn, because he was 'one of those who would have preferred to Anglicize his name', and also because he did not have influence, only money. De Villiers also had the same drawbacks – he was English-inclined and was wealthy and lived in a village rather than on a farm.[216] Poor old anti-Rhodes die-hard D.P. van den Heever was also taken to task for not mentioning Rhodes in his speech. He was, moreover, castigated for dividing the ranks by persisting in pursuing his controversial anti-Scab Act campaign.[217]

Thus, when targeted MPs visited their constituents after the 1897 parliamentary session, the latter were well prepared for the occasion. In a letter to Rhodes, T.J. Louw described the mood of his Afrikaner voters: 'the farming population is dead off, the very mention of your name is enough to put them against you.' In the case of Louw and his partner, the Bond and *OL* 'marshalled at the Malmesbury Town meeting men from the whole district and they came in large numbers and swamped the town people and actually passed a vote of censure upon Ryan and myself.'[218] They faced an overwhelming no-confidence vote in three other meetings, and only in Darling did a vote of thanks to the two of them receive a large majority.[219] In his letter to Rhodes Louw revealed his dilemma in the face of this crusade against him:

> I am inwardly sorry that I did not hit more straight from the shoulder, in fact show them my exact colours, instead of trying to pacify and sit on the rail for after all that will not help me a bit in the future . . . I must say it was my intention to do so, but many of my supporters persuaded me to be mild.[220]

Other Rhodes sympathisers faced a similar response from their voters and a similar dilemma, the outcome varying according to person and place. Of D.C. de Waal, Louw wrote: 'De Waal leaves tomorrow for Piketberg. I hope he may succeed in squaring his people.' He managed to do so with the exception of Porteville.[221] P.G. Wege had left for his constituency, according to Louw, 'in rather a troubled mind'. In Calvinia where he managed to scrape through by promising not to support the Sprigg government and disguising his sympathy towards Rhodes, a vote of no confidence in him was defeated by 61 to 54 votes.[222] M.M. Venter fared worse in the more radical Colesberg constituency. Despite his declaration that he would not support Rhodes in the future, a vote of no confidence in him was passed with a large majority.[223] Strangely, however, he was elected to represent his district in the 1898 Bond congress.[224] J.H. Schoeman saw fit to retract favourable comments towards Rhodes that he had made at an election meeting for the Upper House.[225]

However, despite increasing popular pressures on Rhodes sympathisers, the Bond and its supporters continued to exhibit a variety of views. P.H. Faure, addressing a large meeting in Paarl, displayed his only thinly disguised Rhodes colours and was well received by his audience.[226] Even in a meeting of Faure's opponents in Paarl, Dr J.M. Hoffman, a staunch Bondsman, declared that they were not against the former.[227] Dr te Water, who had voted against the motion of no confidence in the government and continued to serve in the government, was well received by his constituents and even *OL* was lenient towards him, stating that no one could decide for him when he should leave the government.[228] And a Bond candidate in a by-election in Worcester said, when asked how he would deal with Rhodes:

> I will conduct myself according to the issues and not the person. It is difficult to respond to this question decisively. I will not support Rhodes blindly. I will check the issue carefully and will be very cautious in my support for Rhodes.[229]

That association with both the Bond and Rhodes was not yet absolutely impossible is borne out by the fact that some 12 MPs, including repenting ones, responded to Rhodes's invitation to attend celebrations in Bulawayo.[230]

While those who were known to be Rhodes sympathisers had not yet been politically eliminated, they were, on the whole, under increasing pressure and were obliged, as we have seen, to withdraw to the political closet. There was a big difference between what D.C. de Waal, for example, could tell his constituents, without forfeiting their support, and what he revealed in a letter to Rhodes. In this letter he clearly appears as a faithful member of Rhodes's political entourage. Referring to the prospects of their camp in the forthcoming Upper House elections he wrote: 'If *we* succeed, about which I am sure *we* will, the wind will be out of *their* sail and *they* will collapse before the other comes off ... J.H. [Hofmeyr] can't stand a defeat.' To be on the safe side he asked Rhodes to destroy the letter lest it fell 'to the hands of the opposition'.[231] The Bond had not yet purified its ranks of the Rhodes contamination.

The Bond had to improve its organisation if it wished to stand a fair chance in the critical test of the approaching elections to both Houses of Parliament. The need to tighten up control and discipline was underlined by the crisis of nomination for the Upper House election in the Western Circle. While the Paarl branch which was controlled by S.J. du Toit nominated, as provided for in the Bond constitution, Jan Faure, an avowed Rhodes supporter, the Bond leadership in Cape Town favoured the old member, M.L. Neethling. Consequently, the Supervision Committee was hostile towards the Paarl branch.[232] This crisis was also accompanied by a schism in the Bond Paarl district branch, with the anti-Rhodes elements challenging S.J. du Toit's leadership.

The Bond annual congress, convened in Worcester in mid-February 1898, made the first attempt to secure control of the party branches by the centre. The congress adopted two major changes to the constitution – one gave the Provincial *bestuur* (executive) the authority to dissolve branch or district executives 'when it is their conviction that such *bestuurs* have fallen under influence which is prejudicial or inimical to the organisation', while the second gave the Supervision Committee the power to reject, in the interests of the party, any candidate elected by local branches. S.J. du Toit strongly objected to these changes because he knew that he would be their first victim. Indeed, the troubles in the Paarl branch must have motivated these far-reaching changes. Only 16 delegates opposed these consequential changes.[233] The Bond congress also turned against its founder. In the election for the chairmanship of the Bond S.J. du Toit received only one vote and for the vice chairmanship a mere four votes. Worse still, he lost badly in the election for the Supervision Committee, the most powerful agency of the party.[234] *OL* underlined this purification thrust following the congress:

> The interests of the *volk* demand, more than ever before, people who are prepared to work imbued by self-sacrifice. And if there are among us a few members who want, directly or indirectly, to act against our interests, we hope that the spirit of patriotism in the Bond will be so strong that these members may have to leave the Bond.[235]

The Bond finally took decisive action to eliminate whatever space was left within the party for Rhodes's sympathisers. The congress, in passing by a large majority a resolution thanking Merriman for his 'courageous conduct' in the last parliamentary session further signalled its shift towards a new anti-Rhodes alliance.[236]

S.J. du Toit responded after the congress in an article entitled 'The Bond Dictatorship established': 'What will now be the result: That the Bond dictatorship has been established for good.' He argued that local executives as well as MPs would have to submit to the dictate of the dictator in Camp Street (Hofmeyr). He concluded: 'Will, can Bondsmen any longer remain in an organisation which has in this manner become untrue to its own principles?'[237] The reply which Du Toit was to give shortly afterwards was negative.

Before Du Toit gave this response, Rhodes made, on the eve of the election to the Upper House, a dramatic and decisive re-entry to the Cape political stage. Garrett's biographer credited him with grooming Rhodes for the leadership of the Progressive Party.[238] At a mass meeting at the Good Hope Hall in Cape Town, on 12 March, Rhodes offered his services and his leadership to the party. He again underscored the importance of the Cape in his overall imperial scheme. His post-raid regional plan, which he had first outlined a year earlier, was presented more fully. Within five years he envisaged the union of the Cape, Natal and Rhodesia, to be subsequently sublimated in a South African union which would also include an *uitlander*-controlled Transvaal and the Orange Free State. The forthcoming elections to the two Houses were decisive to the implementation of this strategy. A Bond government in the Cape with its anti-Rhodesia bias and its post-raid sympathy towards

Kruger's Transvaal would hardly be a suitable agent for that. On the contrary, in pursuing its policies it would not only frustrate Rhodes's plans, but also deprive the Cape of a bright future. Consequently, a Progressive party victory was most important: 'And so I say it is the duty of the Progressive party to fight them perhaps even more than to support the broad principles that we have enunciated.' Rhodes launched a vicious attack on the 'little gang in Camp Street' who were 'terrorising the country'. He labelled the Bond as 'the non-Progressive ... *Ons Land* party'. which did not represent the Afrikaners. He appealed to the Afrikaners, especially the progressive ones, above the head of the Bond. He portrayed the policies of the Bond in a very unflattering manner, from a progressive perspective: 'My own idea is that they are not the politics of the Dutch people, but that they are the politics of a very small coterie. Let us think what the politics are – non-education, drunken coloured labour, anti-Fleet vote, anti-the-North, favourable to the present policy in the Transvaal.'[239] The speech was not simply programmatic. It was bitter and resentful, reflecting Rhodes's emotions in the face of the vicious attacks against him after the raid. As Smuts said from another vantage point, 'good lovers make good haters'. Rhodes was prepared to lend himself as leader of the Progressive party and to invest both energy and resources in order to win a political battle and achieve a small revenge.

Dagblad's response to Rhodes's speech was both apologetic and laudatory:

> His policy is practically the same as when he was premier of the Cape Colony and was supported by the Africander party ... His act of two years ago is generally condemned, but all are not so unchristianlike, unwise and impolitical to refuse on that account to see any good in whatever Mr Rhodes says or does.[240]

Some ten days later both Rhodes and Du Toit had cause for celebration. Earlier, Du Toit was jubilant that his candidate for the Upper House, Jan Faure, not only was elected but also won a majority in the predominantly Afrikaner Paarl Division. On 25 March the overall results showed an impressive Progressive victory of 14 against 9. Du Toit predicted that if the Bond did not study the cause of its defeat, the defeat in the election for the Lower House would be even greater. He himself offered the cause – the dictatorship instituted by the last congress. He claimed that the Bond leadership wanted to get rid of '12–14 of the most capable Bond Members of Parliament'.[241] In early April he was confident that the future belonged to the Progressives, advising the Bond to discard its retrogressive line and to adopt a moderate progressive one.[242] A few days later he launched a frontal attack on Hofmeyr, 'the Bond dictator'.[243]

On 11 April *Dagblad* reported an interview published by the *Cape Times* with Paul Myburgh, an old and influential Afrikaner from Stellenbosch, described as a 'South African Gladstone'. Old Myburgh rejected the view that most Afrikaners shared strong feelings against Rhodes. Most Afrikaners, as good Christians, while condemning the raid, had forgiven him. He maintained that Rhodes 'has done for the Colony more good than any other Englishman.'[244]

The more bitter attacks on the Bond and on Hofmeyr personally and the more overt sympathy and support for Rhodes signalled a change in Du Toit's political course. The considerable erosion in his leadership position, and the tightening up of party discipline, all but eliminated his political space within the Bond. At the same time Rhodes's assertion of the leadership of the Progressive party and its victory in the Upper House election seemed to open for him a promising new space. Du Toit must have been encouraged not only by the overall victory of the Progressives, but also by the success of some Afrikaner candidates sympathetic to Rhodes in predominantly Afrikaner areas. His own candidate for the Western Circle received more votes in Paarl than M.L. Neethling, while in Stellenbosch he received only marginally fewer. In the South Western Circle, two of the three successful candidates, M.J. de Villiers and A.G. de Smidt, were condemned by *OL* as a South African League candidate and a jingo respectively.[245] The new bandwagon was moving towards victory while his own political wagon sank in the mud of the Bond's post-raid politics. Yet, for Du Toit, the father of the Bond and Afrikaner ethno-cultural revival, joining the Progressive party – which included the anti-Afrikaner jingo South African League – was unthinkable at that stage. It would not have gone down well even among many moderate, progressive Afrikaners whom he viewed as his socio-political hinterland. He opted for a half-way political house between the extremes of the Bond and the South African League. This was manifested in the programme of the 'Colonial Union' which was founded in Paarl on 23 April 1898. It sought to occupy the political niche that the Bond had discarded, namely a moderate bi-ethnic party: 'an organisation by means of which the two great European races in our country may reach each other's hand and co-operate.'[246]

Rhodes had also received Afrikaner support from an unexpected quarter – McCusker, the editor of *GR*, the virulent anti-Rhodes crusader during the latter's premiership. McCusker persisted in his anti-Rhodes inclination after the raid, his attitude towards the Bond being adjusted accordingly. In August 1897 he proposed to present the candidates for the election with a simple question: 'What is your slogan, Africa for the Afrikaners or Africa for Rhodes?' In late September he wrote of a candidate who was known as a Rhodes supporter: 'Away with Bellingan!

long live *Afrikanderisme*.'[247] McCusker must have seen the light on the road to Bulawayo, which he visited at the invitation of Rhodes on the occasion of the celebrations for the completion of the railway line thereto. After his return he began to sing the praises of Rhodesia which he had previously described as a desolate, unhealthy and hopeless country.[248] He also supported G.H. Maasdorp, the local candidate of the Progressives, suggesting that the election's battle cry should be 'forward with South Africa and away with race hatred' rather than 'Rhodes or anti-Rhodes', arguing that precedence should be given to issues over people. He explained his transformation by saying, 'who does not change his mind ... See how the Bond has often changed its mind.'[249] While for the sake of maintaining some credibility with his readers he kept a safe distance from Rhodes, occasionally even adopting a critical position towards him,[250] his transformation was unmistakable. He not only propagated the cause of Rhodesia, but also continued to support anti-Bond candidates and even enthused about S.J. du Toit and his Colonial Union. He concluded a leader on the latter by pronouncing a new battle cry – 'long live progress'.[251]

Bondsmen who had viewed Rhodes as the leader of the opposing Party in 1897,[252] welcomed his determined re-entry to the Cape political scene on the eve of the Upper House election. In viciously attacking the Bond and showing his true colours, he not only provoked them to greater endeavour but also made it easier for them to present him as the Bond's anti-Christ. This was the line adopted by *OC* following Rhodes's Cape Town speech:

> Rhodes will find out that his attacks on the Bond are counter productive. He helped wavering Bondsmen to wake up from their dream. The more we recognise Rhodes as an open enemy of the Bond our work will be easier. As long as he had kept quiet it was difficult to convince our weak-minded brothers where the line of political division was.[253]

OL also used Rhodes's speech in Cape Town in drawing the political battle lines more clearly. Rhodes, it argued, had discarded the country in favour of the city, his 'progressiveness' spelling doom to the farmers and to the Cape as a whole: 'And this is called progress! Yes, this is progress in the direction of social and moral destruction.' A correspondent saw in Rhodes's speech the seed of war within five years.[254] Professor Lion Cachet, speaking in Burgersdorp, added a touch of blood and pan-Afrikanerism to the growing division between Rhodes and the Bond:

> We face a general election and it is certain that Rhodes will be re-elected to the Lower House, and will probably become prime minister ... And now they say, let's extend our hand to Rhodes. This, however, we cannot do. Between us and Rhodes there is a blood stain, the blood of Afrikaners in

Doornkop! ... De Beers has got a lot of money, but not enough to cover the stain. They say extend a hand to Rhodes. But between us and Rhodes lie corpses.'[255]

And yet even after Rhodes's Cape Town speech the lines of political battle were not finally drawn. Less than a week later, Dr Te Water received his voters' trust despite remaining in the government and saying that if Rhodes did something good for the Afrikaners he would be able to support him.[256] In mid-April 1898, T.P. Theron, the new Bond chairman, was reported to have said that 'Rhodes was the best friend the farmers have ever had in Parliament, and not withstanding the fault he had done, he was the man who will save the situation'.[257] It took Theron some two weeks from when his speech was quoted in the press to publish his own version of the speech – from which the words quoted above were conveniently omitted.[258] It is difficult to establish the truth although Theron's belated response renders his denial somewhat suspicious. The argument that the reporter of the *Midland News* did not understand Theron's Dutch[259] is not very convincing. At a meeting in Philipstown, I.J. van der Walt, one of Rhodes's bitterest opponents, conceded that the latter could use his influence to rally the support of most Afrikaners.[260] Indeed, the Bond, in the wake of the defeat in the election for the Upper House, looked somewhat demoralised and disoriented.

THE FINAL BREAK: THE REDISTRIBUTION BILL

Soon, however, Rhodes and his allies provided the Bond with the ultimate provocation which stimulated it to even greater efforts and helped them in drawing the political battle lines more sharply and harnessing more wandering sheep into their political kraal. This provocation occurred shortly after the opening of the 1898 session, when Sprigg submitted the second reading of the Redistribution Bill designed to adjust parliamentary representation to demographic changes.[261] As *OL* had pointed out a few weeks earlier, the enactment of the Bill would considerably strengthen urban representation to the detriment of the country districts. It viewed the Bill as the 'trump card' of 'Rhodes's Clique', and as one of the 'constitutional means' he had promised to use for the attainment of his goals.[262] Indeed, one of the domestic issues brought up by Rhodes in his speech on 12 March 1898 was redistribution. He stated the need to 'give the representation of this country on the basis of the number of the people who live in it ... It is the key of the whole of our politics.'[263] Indeed it was. Election on this basis would guarantee a convincing victory for the Progressives and Rhodes would get a new political base to pursue his imperial project.

A leader article in *OL*, on 14 May, elaborated on the implications of the Bill, viewing it as the ultimate defeat of the Afrikaner countryside by the English towns:

> This time Rhodes employs, as he told the committee of inquiry in London, constitutional means – redistribution of parliamentary seats. This will enable the submission of the country party to the will of the town. This will enable them to implement their designs – in Southern Africa and in the economic sphere ... It is time to consolidate the forces to thwart this attempt. If the friends of the welfare of South Africa will not unite everything will be lost for good ... The Parliament will convene within a week. The eyes of all the country will watch the representatives ... The trump-card of Rhodes's clique will be played. What will the ministers do? What will the representatives do in Parliament? What will the rural population do to protect its rights? It is a general, not a local question. Woe to those who will sacrifice the general interests for a personal or regional interest.[264]

I.J. van der Walt claimed that the passage of the Bill would be 'a great step towards the total revolution about which Rhodes has spoken lately'.[265] An immediate result of the government's intention to submit the Bill was the resignation of Te Water from it.[266] He was a faithful Bond member, and with all his reservations about the government he represented in it the interests of the 'Afrikaner party'. Support for the Bill would be in total contradiction of the Bond's interests and its very survival as a dominant political force in parliament. Even before Parliament convened the Bond began to hold meetings protesting against the Bill.[267] Dr Te Water was a confidant of Hofmeyr and with his resignation the last tenuous link between the effective Bond leader and the government was severed.[268]

When the Bill passed the second reading, Schreiner submitted a vote of no confidence, which also underlined his emergence as the parliamentary leader of the 'Afrikaner party'. The vote of no confidence went through with a small majority of five.[269] Rhodes and his allies brought upon themselves an early general election to the Lower House, unnecessarily and under conditions of great excitement among Cape Afrikaners which could only play into the hands of the Bond. Sprigg, most probably in collusion with Rhodes, submitted a Redistribution Bill which was much more favourable to the town vote than the majority report of a parliamentary commission. Dr Te Water implied in the debate on the Bill that he would have supported a Bill based on the majority report. He could not vote for the Bill which the premier had submitted to Parliament without consulting his ministers. He was unable to vote for a simple reason that: 'he felt convinced that if the Bill passed the influence of the country party would be destroyed ... The object of the Bill was solely to support the diamond-mining industry and the interests of the cities, and to neglect the farmers' interests.' Du Plessis, another Bond member, also said that he would have supported a Bill based on the majority report, 'although that went further than he personally wished'.[270] In the no-confidence debate Theron stated: 'Had the Premier abided by the majority report [on redistribution], he [Mr Theron] would have stood by the Premier even had he been covered with obloquy by his people.' He also said that 'it was not the Bond that had separated from the Government, but *vice versa.*'[271]

Through its political greed the government lost not only the Bill but also the confidence of the House. For the Bond the no-confidence vote was of critical importance and they apparently used all available influence and pressure to defeat the government. Dr T.W. Smartt may have exaggerated somewhat, but his account of the efforts of Hofmeyr, in particular, in securing a majority for the no-confidence vote sounds credible.[272] The government lost the confidence of Parliament mainly because even supporters of the government and of Rhodes, like D.C. de Waal, M.M. Venter, A.S. le Roex, G.S. Wolfaardt and P.G. Wege, representing rural constituencies, could not support the government on the issue of redistribution. Only five Afrikaners voted with the government. The votes underscored the hardening of party political lines.[273] Milner reported that the Bond members voting with the government were those who 'had already quarrelled irretrievably' with the party. The 'doubtfuls', with the exception of one, thought Milner, voted with the Bond.[274]

Parliament was dissolved and the Cape Colony was plunged into the most bitter and divisive general election in its history. The intensity of the election campaign reflected the culmination of a shift in the nature of Cape politics from parish pump politics to high politics for high stakes. This was the perception of both competing political blocs. Sprigg, in a speech to his electors, on 9 July 1898, outlined the programme of his outgoing government:

> I will tell you then, that the cardinal features of the policy of this govern-
> ment are two, and the first is to maintain British Supremacy in South
> Africa (cheers) – and, secondly, to push through a Bill providing for
> the better representation of the people in the Parliament of this Colony
> [redistribution] (cheers).'[275]

In other words, it was a policy of imperial supremacy in South Africa and English-speaking supremacy in the Cape. In advocating large-scale white immigration he further underlined his latter goal.[276]

These goals were in stark contradiction to the Bond's perception of the desired Cape and South African order. The redistribution of seats was viewed by the Bond, as we have seen, as a loss of the political influence of the party and of the economic privileges of the Afrikaner farming community it represented. The imperial supremacy of the Progressives seemed equally sinister, with a clear pro-*uitlanders*, anti-Transvaal bias, and with a touch of warmongering. Not surprisingly, the election was presented by the Bond as a political Armageddon, and the prospect of a Progressive victory was painted in apocalyptic colours. At the outset of the election campaign, a Bond MP wrote:

> It is known that the Sprigg–Rhodes–De Beers combination aims not less than to dispossess us once and for all from our privileges – our voice in Parliament – so that they will be able to implement their intentions against us and against the republics. What their aim is is very clear to us, but our heart shrinks when we think of the frightening consequences threatening our country.[277]

A correspondent predicted that the election would be the 'hottest' ever held in 'our beloved country', because the capitalist clique wanted to try 'to suppress the Afrikaner nation once and for all'.[278] The threat, ultimately, focused on Rhodes. In early May, following the resignation of Dr Te Water from the government Milner had observed: 'the extreme Dutch party are increasingly inclined to take up the attitude that every man who is not on their side in the Rhodes controversy, is to be treated as enemy.'[279] Dr J.M. Hoffman, the Bond candidate for Paarl, told his audience that the question in the election was whether Rhodes would become prime minister or be permanently excluded from South African politics. He argued that peace and unity would evade them as long as Rhodes was among them.[280] Hofmeyr called on Cape Afrikaners not to be afraid of naming, 'the idol of the Jingo – Rhodes', claiming that the Progressive Party did not conceal the fact that they were struggling 'only for Rhodes'. And Chamberlain, he told his audience, saw the results of the election to the Upper House as proof that Rhodes would be the next prime minister.[281] This was echoed by a correspondent:

> The worshippers of Rhodes will make great efforts to suppress us in order to restore Rhodes. Large sums of money will be spent to place us, a people which had been born free, under the tyrannic yoke of Rhodes. If Sprigg (Rhodes) wins we will be finished for ever.

He referred not only to matters of high politics: 'They will dictate to us – there will be a Redistribution Act, the protective tariffs will be removed, Excise tax will be imposed.'[282]

Such a fateful election completed the process of forming political blocs. The approaching election consummated a process that had begun in the wake of the raid. This was captured by Olive Schreiner in May

1898: 'I should like to write an article ... showing how completely the raid altered the political face of matters at the Cape and *broke all parties* which *must* be formed again entirely anew'.[283] In previous elections, which followed traditional parochial lines, local issues and personal allegiances were prime determinants. Such elements were a luxury at a time when the stakes were so high and when everything depended on who would form the next government. The two blocs – the Progressives and the bloc around the Bond – closed ranks for the ultimate political battle. The closing of the ranks brought together political groups and politicians who in normal times would have been unlikely allies. Sprigg and his supporters, who shared with the Bond many aspects of internal policy, which in the 1880s formed the basis for a stable political alliance, found themselves bitter enemies. On the other hand the Bond allied with itself anti-Bond liberal negrophiles like Merriman, Sauer and their supporters. It was not an easy transformation. In May 1896 Olive Schreiner wrote to Merriman: 'Neither you nor Sauer can ever ultimately work with the Bond!'[284] Merriman, writing in March 1898, was rather unhappy with his prospective allies: 'The worst is that the Bond persists in running the most objectionable candidates [for the Upper House]: people with anti-Scab views in the east and pro-liquor in the west.'[285] A month earlier he wrote that his connection with the Bond was 'only in the imagination'.[286] Indeed, for Merriman, who felt strong antipathy towards the Bond, the prospective new alliance was difficult to swallow.

With the approach of the election Merriman and his friends joined the camp of the 'Afrikaner party'. Since Rhodes was running for Merriman's constituency and he had no chance of recapturing it himself, the Bond offered him the safe Bond constituency of Wodehouse. On 28 July he and his liberal friends appeared in the list of Bond and Bond-supported candidates.[287] It is interesting to note that the Bond and the liberals differed sharply on what had been before the raid the most vital issue to the survival of the Afrikaners, namely 'native' policy. With an overwhelming new danger, personified by the former saviour, looming large, the former critical issue had to be shelved for the sake of a new alliance. The Bond was also supported by Olive Schreiner, who had parted ways with Rhodes because of his support for the Bond's 'native' policy. Even more surprising was the courting of the black vote by the Bond. Hofmeyr paraded his pro-'native' record, while Tengo Jabavu, the editor of *Imvo*, responded positively and supported the Bond candidates.[288] Politics, indeed, makes strange bedfellows. With Hofmeyr still acting his role of background leader, the 'Afrikaner party' needed a real leader – Hofmeyr picked for the job W.F. Schreiner, an English-speaker who was not even a Bond member.[289] As the Bond won support from English-speaking liberals, it lost the support of English-speakers like Sivewright, Dr T.W.

Smartt, Dr A. Vanes, L. Abrahamson and many others, who had joined it in the heyday of its alliance with Rhodes, and who in many respects had more in common with it than its new allies.

The Progressive Party, too, was a strange political creation. 'Progressive', was, in fact, a misnomer. Some of the prominent Progressives (liberals) had joined forces with the Bond. James Rose Innes, perhaps the natural leader of the progressive forces in Cape politics, refused to join either bloc because too many who belonged to them were anything but progressive.[290] In fact, as the Bond was essentially an Afrikaner party, defending Afrikaner interests and privileges, with marginal English-speaking liberals for icing, so the Progressive party was essentially an English-speaking party with some open Afrikaner support, determined to end Bond political supremacy and to pursue a clearer imperial policy. In fact the new lines of political division were defined by Rhodes and what he personified and symbolised for friends and foes.

As befitted a political Armageddon, the competing blocs exploited all the power resources they could muster. Rhodes made a major contribution to the electoral campaign. He had brought from England an experienced campaign manager, and also secured the support of the English press, buying up the antagonistic *Diamond Field Advertiser* of Kimberley. The Dutch newspapers edited by S.J. du Toit also lent their support to the Progressive cause. Rhodes was personally deeply involved in the running of the campaign. Most importantly, he contributed large sums of money to finance an unprecedented lavish electoral campaign.[291] He was, of course, particularly concerned with his own election campaign in his old constituency of Barkly West, which had a large Afrikaner farming population. In November 1897, his agent informed him that he was ready for the election and that he enjoyed the support of 1,865 out of the 2,850 voters.[292]

While the Progressives enjoyed the organisational and financial resources provided by Rhodes, the Bond, which was lacking in such resources, employed political-moral ones, also derived from Rhodes. It was the threat of Rhodes that contributed so greatly to the zeal, determination and moral fervour of their election campaign. Indeed, the raid, and Rhodes's re-entry to Cape politics gave it new emotional intensity. It was this new dimension of Cape politics that drove many Englishmen and Afrikaners to rally behind their ethnic banner. This served the electoral campaign of the Progressives as well.[293] For the Bond, suffering from organisational and financial weakness, the moral case was a critical resource. This was articulated by a correspondent:

> Our enemies will go to the election with all possible forces, with unusual financial resources and with wicked violence on their side, whereas the

> Afrikaner party is without means. But we have a just cause. We have an open way to the grace throne of the faithful covenant of God ... Every patriot must be mobilised.[294]

God was invoked by another correspondent who gave his moral fervour an anti-capitalist and biblical touch:

> The question is whether the just God, who controls the destiny of every man, will allow that in this part of South Africa the money will continue to rule. Of course not. Afrikaners who do not want to sell their national sentiment for any sum of money, mobilise to the struggle and with God's help you will win, as the people of Israel was freed from tyrants in the ancient times.[295]

In the search for moral zeal and power, an appeal was also made to ethnic history. A correspondent from Paarl resorted to sub-ethnic mobilisation, appealing to 'my brother Huguenots and compatriots', while another was more specific in exploiting the Huguenot tradition: 'My compatriots – remember that our fathers the Huguenots arrived in South Africa with the Bible in their hand. Let us show that we also struggle for our people and for our homeland.'[296]

This combination of perception of threat and a conviction of possessing the high moral ground was a considerable mobilisation asset. It gave its leadership a strong lever to bring recalcitrant and wavering MPs back to the fold. For example, Hofmeyr promised P.G. Wege that he would endorse him if he would give a written promise to support the Bond in Parliament on redistribution and on issues related to Rhodes.[297] Wege, who refused to make this promise, must have felt the pressure once he started canvassing in his constituency. Obviously his support for Schreiner's vote of no confidence did not absolve him. Towards the end of July he tried to court his voters by telling them that he had told Rhodes, who had offered him a political bribe for his vote for the government: 'How do you think that I will sell my homeland for money?'[298] This manifestation of patriotism did not save him. He was not selected as a Bond candidate and contested the election against it. M.M. Venter, who also tried to repent by supporting the no-confidence vote was not spared by his constituents either, ending up as a Progressive candidate.[299] A.S. le Roex suffered the same fate despite the fact that he had been hailed by his constituents for his stand on the Scab Act.[300] Parochial issues could not save those who, as supporters of Rhodes, were perceived as traitors. When a correspondent tried to defend T.J. Louw on his record of service to his constituents in building roads and bridges, lowering of the price of guano etc., the editor argued that, in voting for redistribution, Louw supported a move which would bring to power the enemies of the farmers.[301] Among Rhodes's supporters, only D.C. de Waal received the support of the Bond, after promising that in the future he would oppose the government and the Redistribution Bill.[302]

The ethno-moral weapon of the Bond, which Rhodes helped to sharpen, enabled it to purify its ranks, to eliminate local and sectoral issues from the elections, to impose more discipline on its branches, and to prevent Bond members from competing against each other. In only two constituencies was the Bond unable to impose discipline. In Paarl, where the original branch was still in the hands of S.J. du Toit and his supporters, there were two sets of unofficial Bond candidates. In his Barkly West constituency, Rhodes enjoyed the support of some Bond branches who nominated him as party candidate. The Supervision Committee intervened and used its new powers to cancel the nomination.[303]

The Bond bloc won the election by a margin of only one seat. This in itself was a significant political victory. However, a close examination of the election results shows that despite the country bias of the distribution of seats which favoured the Bond, its electoral performance was not as impressive as the victory itself suggests. According to Milner's calculations the Progressives received 44,403 votes against 37,901 for the 'Afrikaner party'. Furthermore, three seats fell to the Afrikaner party by majorities of 2, 10 and 20 votes respectively. Milner calculated that a shift of 20 votes in these constituencies would have turned a victory into a defeat.[304] The goddess Fortune was definitely smiling on the Bond. However, as Milner himself admitted, the Progressives were also served by the coincidental presence of many English-speaking volunteers in Vryburg, which tipped the balance in their favour and gave them two unexpected, and perhaps undeserved seats. The Bond succeeded in eliminating from Parliament most of Rhodes's Afrikaner supporters whom they had targeted. Only two Afrikaners supporting Rhodes and the government were elected – Olivier in Oudtshoorn and Haarhoff in Vryburg. However, the results in the contested Afrikaner constituencies show that Rhodes and the Progressives received a not insignificant share of the Afrikaner vote. In Stellenbosch, Sivewright headed the poll, eliminating one of the Bond candidates. In Paarl, the hub of Cape 'Afrikanerdom', the Bond won the two seats, but only with a narrow margin. In other predominantly Afrikaner constituencies like Malmesbury, Caledon, Riversdale, Worcester and Richmond (where S.J. du Toit tried his luck), while the margin was larger, Progressives must have secured hundreds of Afrikaner votes.[305] In Barkly West Rhodes was elected with a comfortable majority and secured the election of his unknown partner as well, against stiff Bond opposition. As we have seen, he had been supported in his campaign by some Bond branches. However, since many miners resided in the constituency it is difficult to assess the degree of grass-roots Afrikaner support he received.

Politically, the election was clearly a victory for the Bond. Rhodes and Sprigg were both frustrated and tempted by the narrowest possible margin. They tried to postpone the resignation of the government in the hope that petitions, which might force re-election in some constituencies or defection from the Bond side, would still save the day. Rhodes apparently believed that his old trusted friend and ally D.C. de Waal would cross the floor. 'I should think De Waal will be right', he wrote to Milner, at the same time informing him of his tactices: 'I feel sure the right course is that Sir G. Sprigg should hold on as long as there is a chance of a majority and with the various chances now before him I think he has a fair chance of success.'[306] *OL* reported that £3,000 were offered to an MP to join the Progressives.[307] There were also rumours that D.C. de Waal was considering crossing the floor. He however, promised, a delegation from his constituency that he would abide by his electoral promises.[308] Furthermore, Milner refused to collaborate with the Progressives' shady strategy and forced Sprigg to summon the new Parliament on 7 October 1898 and to submit to its verdict.[309] On 11 October Schreiner, the leader of the 'Afrikaner party', moved a vote of no confidence in the government which was won by 39 to 37 votes. Six days later he presented the policy of his new government.[310] The Cape political game was virtually over for Rhodes. His relations with the Afrikaner Bond had gone full circle – from persistent courting, to an eventful but, on the whole, happy marriage, and a relatively long divorce ending up on a very bitter note.

THE IMPACT OF THE DIVORCE ON THE POLITICAL OUTLOOK OF THE BOND

As we have seen, Rhodes, before and especially during his premiership, had made a deep impact on the evolving political outlook of his Afrikaner allies. It remains to investigate more systematically the impact the Jameson raid and the subsequent deteriorating relations between the former allies had on the Cape Afrikaners' self-perception and political outlook. This impact was not as clear cut as might have been expected. Rhodes's deep impression on the Bond and Cape Afrikaners more generally notwithstanding, their self-perception and their outlook were primarily the products of the complex process of socialisation under British rule. The raid and the disengagement from Rhodes, traumatic though they may have been, did not erase the deep imprint of this experience. Neither did they revolutionise the conditions under which they lived.

What did change dramatically after the raid were those aspects of their outlook that were more purely associated with Rhodes personally. With

290

regard to the domestic Cape order, the attitude to the role of capitalism changed markedly. As we have seen, the alliance with Rhodes was rationalised and articulated as one that rested on the common interests of national mining capital and Afrikaner landowners. This alliance was to protect the farmers from the English-speaking merchants and to ensure that the 'natives' performed their appropriate role as providers of free land and cheap labour. After the raid, which was perceived as a capitalist plot engineered by Rhodes, the Bond organs and many Bondsmen changed their tune. In a way, the marginal voices which had been heard faintly before the raid and which had been articulated by the *GR*, became prevalent in its wake. There was the small man, the populist anti-capitalist thrust, using the Biblical metaphors of Baal or Mammon. The contribution of newspaper correspondents to the anti-capitalist thrust indicated that editorial exhortations touched sensitive chords among rank-and-file Afrikaners.

Rhodes, the former benevolent capitalist who was the ally of the Afrikaner farmer, was transformed into the epitome of the malevolent, selfish, profit-seeking capitalist. The weapon in the struggle of the small man against capitalism was, almost inevitably, morality: 'What we are struggling against is the despicable influence of Mammon and the oppressive policy in South Africa since the beginning of 1896, which is associated now with the name of Rhodes.'[311] Rhodes had abandoned the country in favour of the town and represented the tyranny of capitalism whose progress augured the destruction of the farmer.[312] M.L. Neethling, the Upper House candidate, argued that the election of his rival, Jan Faure, who was supported by Rhodes, would adversely affect the triple alliance of the wine, wheat and stock farmers.[313] Implied was the notion that the Afrikaner farmer could rely only on his own power against his former capitalist allies. In the western Cape capitalism also brought actual dispossession of farmers when, after the raid, Rhodes and other capitalists began to buy out distressed Afrikaner farmers, leaving former owners to work on the farms.[314]

Capitalism was not only a threat to the economic interests of the farmers. It brought in its wake the demoralisation of society. The editor of *OL* argued that the yoke of a political tyrant was much preferable to the tyranny of Mammon, because the former could not infringe on morality. The tyranny of Mammon brought about the demoralisation of man: 'It arouses in him the lowest urges and transforms the crown of creation into a selfish coward and valueless creature.'[315] Rhodes was associated since the raid with a movement which threatened to corrupt 'our institutions' and destroy 'our public morality'.[316] Writing of the forthcoming election, Dr Hoffman was particularly concerned with the prospect of capitalist control of the legislature, which would bring about its emasculation, and transform it into 'a place in which people would come to fill their sacks'.[317] The opposition was not to capitalism as such. In fact, socio-economic inequality was presented as necessary for both material and human progress. Capitalism, however, also had its dark side, and in a poor country like South Africa there was a danger that 'squaring', introduced in the wake of the mineral revolution, would usher in the tyranny of Mammon.[318] This anti-capitalist thrust was definitely of a populist, rather than socialist, vintage.

Capitalism was a threat to the Afrikaners not only as class and society but also as a *volk*. Thus, the Afrikaners who greeted Rhodes on his return from Rhodesia were depicted not only as 'a few unprincipled favour hunters and money worshippers', but also as 'dastardly knee benders in front of the money Baal and betrayers of *Afrikanderisme*'.[319] Afrikaners were called upon to demonstrate that 'patriotism' was stronger than Mammon.[320] The election was portrayed as a contest between 'the true friends of the welfare of the land' and 'the self seekers and capitalists'.[321] It was a struggle 'against the internal capitalist politics which threatens to destroy the social freedoms of the population'.[322] A correspondent urged readers to elect representatives who would further the welfare of '*land en volk*' and repulse the 'Mammon worshippers' so that 'our posterity will not be under the iron yoke of capitalism'.[323] H.D. Stiglingh, campaigning against Rhodes in Barkly West, told his audience that the struggle was one between capitalism and nationality.[324]

Another victim of the Jameson raid was Rhodesia. Rhodes had, as we have seen, diverted the economic imagination and the political energy of Cape Afrikaners from the Transvaal to his new promised land north of the Limpopo. Rhodesia had become not only the economic salvation of the Cape farmers, but also the vehicle for the fulfilment of hidden desires and dreams. The Bond press and leaders had presented the north, even when its promises were slow to materialise, in glowing terms. The raid put an end to the Bond's sub-imperialism, and Rhodesia began to be presented in a totally different light. The aversion of F.S. Malan to Rhodesia was so great that he preferred to name it Zambesia, even when the former name gained wide circulation. In a leader article published shortly after the raid he demolished all the arguments which had been previously employed in support of Rhodes's project in the north. He showed, in particular, that there was no economic profit for the Cape in Rhodesia and called on his readers to discard previous illusions.[325] Potential settlers were warned and the country was painted in the darkest possible colours.[326]

The transformation of Rhodesia from a promised land to an economic mirage did not put an end to the interest of Cape Bondsmen in their northern hinterland. The yearning for the north stemmed not from fancy dreams but from a persistent economic reality which made it essential for the Cape economy to expand beyond its borders. As we have seen, Cape sub-imperialism was only one option, the other economic expansive option being the gold fields of the Transvaal. The Transvaal's commercial obstructionism and the fascination with Rhodes combined to lure the Bond to the former. With the disappearance of the fascination, economic choices became more rational, reality supplanting hopes as the foremost determinant of policy. It should be mentioned in passing that Cape Afrikaner supporters of Rhodes continued to exhibit strong enthusiasm for Rhodesia and to present it as the economic salvation of the Cape.[327] For those who rejected Rhodes morally and politically, this option was, in any case, objectionable. The political glasses certainly coloured the economic landscape. Statistic and economic realities played into the hands of Rhodes's opponents in the Bond. Rhodesia's economic usefulness depended on the discovery of gold. In the post-raid period, as it became increasingly clear that rich gold deposits were unlikely to be discovered, the tremendous wealth of the Transvaal gold reserves was being established. Thus, with the raid freeing Bondsmen from the magic of Rhodes, the reorientation of their economic and commercial thrust towards the Transvaal was natural.

The substitution of sub-imperialism for pan-Afrikaner solidarity made perfect economic sense. Shortly after the raid, *OL*, after parading the sympathy and support of Cape Afrikaners for the Transvaal as a manifestation of Afrikaner unity, mentioned that the Transvaal's commercial policies alienated Cape Afrikaners. It argued that for a small loss of customs revenue the Transvaal could secure much greater benefit, namely, the support of their Cape brothers.[328] At a meeting convened in Stellenbosch to condemn the demonstrations of welcome for Rhodes, the proposer of the resolution stated that the Transvaal was a good market and that they could not substitute it for an uncertain one in Rhodesia.[329] A speaker at a similar meeting in Worcester, also a wine farming district, was more candid and blunt:

> What will be the consequence of the welcoming of Rhodes in Worcester, Paarl, Wellington etc.? No other than the imposition of tax on our wine by the Transvaal. The worshippers of Rhodes tell us that he has opened the North for us, but in what way has he opened it for us? Who will settle there and how shall we trade with this country? Who wants to give up the Transvaal market for a market in the North which has not yet been opened?[330]

In Malmesbury, a resolution expressed the hope that mutual consideration in the spheres of 'commerce and industry' would remove misunderstandings between the Cape and the Transvaal.[331]

As had already been clear before the raid, despite Transvaal's disadvantageous commercial policies towards the Cape, its large expanding market proved most beneficial to the latter. In January 1897 statistics of the sales of Cape fruits showed that the Transvaal had consumed the same quantities as the Cape as a whole.[332] In an editorial entitled 'Rhodesia versus Transvaal', *OL* refuted the claim of a Rhodes sympathiser that the Rhodesian market was more beneficial: 'The Rhodesian market exists in the imagination whereas the Transvaal market is already opened for us.'[333] In July 1898 it claimed that many Cape products were not taxed in the Transvaal.[334]

Economic considerations certainly contributed to the change in the regional orientation of the Bond. However, the change of attitude towards the Transvaal in the wake of the raid was more than a simple pursuit of commercial benefits. At the meeting in Stellenbosch Jan Smuts claimed that the market argument was not sufficient: 'What is at stake is a sense of nationhood and brotherly love (applause).'[335] Indeed, the attitude of the Bond towards the Transvaal after the raid brings us closer to a crucial question related to the impact of the raid on the Cape Afrikaner collective consciousness and identity. Here again one must contend with the 'nationalist' conventional wisdom which views the Jameson raid as another turning point in the march of pan-Afrikaner nationalism. Such a view can be sustained only with a very heavy dose of the wisdom of hindsight. 'Nationalist' historiography looks at the Jameson raid from across the Anglo-Boer war, the great watershed in South African and Afrikaner history, which transformed South Africa into a single geo-political unit. Things looked somewhat different in the period before this watershed when South Africa still consisted of four distinct states. A late-nineteenth-century Cape perspective is needed for a late-nineteenth-century episode.

There is little doubt that the raid stimulated the evolution of Cape Afrikaners' self-consciousness and strengthened their ethnic identity. As in the case of their relations with Rhodes, it was not merely the raid that influenced the evolution of Cape Afrikaner ethnic consciousness and political outlook. The subsequent provocations and challenges by Rhodes and his Afrikaner and English supporters in the Cape, and by the British government, which posed a threat to their position and their achievements as Cape Afrikaners, also made a crucial contribution to this evolution. The feeling of betrayal and abandonment by their trusted English-speaking ally certainly pushed them towards their more exclusive ethnic *laager*. The impact of Rhodes's betrayal on the Cape Afrikaner self-consciousness was captured by Jan Smuts:

> He whom we had followed and who was to lead us to victory, had not only deserted us but also had, in the deepest sense of the word, betrayed us. We

have again begun to write our history in blood ... Indeed, Afrikanderdom has sunk deeply in the mud.

Rhodes's violent intervention against their Transvaal brothers had swung the Cape Afrikaners' collective pendulum from reason to blood. The result, through the agency of Providence, was that

> the Raid which aimed at paralysing Afrikanerdom mainly in the republics served as an electric shock sent to the national heart. This has brought about an awakening of the Afrikaners in consciousness and seriousness we have not witnessed since the glorious liberation in 1880.[336]

Shattered by the impact of the crisis and excited by the gushing of the collective blood, Smuts produced a text which could be easily construed as the maturing of a veritable pan-Afrikaner nationalism.[337]

Smuts, however, was anything but representative of the prevalent intellectual and ideological mood of Cape Afrikaners. He belonged to a relatively small group of young, highly educated Cape Afrikaners who had probably been influenced, while pursuing their studies in Europe, by a strong sense of ethnic identity and by the prevailing nationalism on that continent.[338] Yet even Jan Smuts himself had not returned from Cambridge an organic nationalist. As we have seen, before the raid he fully identified with the Bond outlook and its Rhodes-centric orientation. Deeply disappointed by the betrayal of Rhodes, whose bandwagon he had wished to join, he must have swung to the more ethno-centric outlook of his friend Malan, the editor of *OL*. He certainly did not represent the bulk of the Bond leadership and rank and file. Even Malan's own subsequent contribution to the Cape Afrikaners' ethnic discourse qualified the tone and impression of Smuts's fiery exhortation. It is doubtful that Smuts himself had undergone the conversion which the above quotation suggests. In order to capture the full scope of the post-raid Cape Afrikaner ideological and political discourse, we must take into consideration other texts, as well as the impact of the context.

Professor de Vos, a theologian from Stellenbosch, made a major contribution to the ethno-cultural 'nationalist' discourse in a series of articles entitled 'National Questions', published by *OL* in late October and early November 1896. De Vos's main thrust was a cultural *volkish* one. He took advantage of the shock of the raid and Rhodes's betrayal to awaken Cape Afrikaners to the dangers of cultural erosion and assimilation by the aggressive English culture. He called on Cape Afrikaners to adhere to, and defend, their linguistic, religious and cultural heritage which formed the basis for their *volk* community: 'All Afrikaners say: we choose not to become English, we shall not allow that you will wash out our *volk* as long as we can prevent it.'[339] The raid gave a strong stimulus to the struggle for the preservation of the cultural identity of Cape

Afrikaners, who also had common material interests as members of a predominantly farming community. The triple alliance between wine, wheat and stock farmers was the material *alter ego* of the cultural community. It was in this broad sense that terms like *volk, land en volk, nationaliteits gevoel* (sense of nationality), and *vaderlandliefde* (patriotism) were so often employed in the ideological and political discourse of Cape Afrikaners after the raid. In a speech in May 1898, T.P. Theron, by now the Bond chairman, referred to *'Nationaliteits gevoel en Patriotisme'* (as) 'two words which have been recently on everybody's lips'.[340] The strengthening of the sense of solidarity among many Cape Afrikaners was manifested in the definition Theron gave to *Nationaliteits gevoel*:

> A sense of nationality means *volkliefde* [love of the *volk*]. A sense of nationality exists when it is just as warm in one's innermost being as in one's mouth. Then it brings him to sacrifice himself for his *volk* ... He can forgive and forget the weaknesses of his *volk*, he can help carry their burdens and protect them against opponents.

This was not yet a reality, but rather an ideal to strive for. Theron's message was to transform the verbal manifestations into a deep motivating feeling.[341]

This perception of the *volk* was not restricted to Rhodes's opponents in the Bond. S.J. du Toit continued to propagate the adoption of Afrikaans as the focus for the *volk*'s cultural identity, while Revd Adriaan Hofmeyr, Rhodes's trusted collaborator, continued to promote the cause of Dutch as a bulwark against cultural assimilation. From this perspective, the differences between pro-Rhodes and anti-Rhodes Bondsmen were ones of nuance rather than essence. They were all engaged in a continuous effort to contain the contradictory pressures stemming from their various, at least potentially conflicting, identities and to construct a satisfying syncretic, unifying one. As before, Cape Afrikaners were still, concurrently, Cape Afrikaners, white Cape colonists, South African Afrikaners and British subjects. As we have seen, they evolved a complex identity which harmonised the conflicting pressures on their loyalty. Rhodes had played an important role in facilitating this harmonisation, but it was not of his making. Consequently, even his betrayal did not free Cape Afrikaners from the need to struggle with this salience of their existence, and imaginatively to adjust the balance of their identities to the post-raid conditions.

It is from this perspective that we must view the warming of relations between Cape Afrikaners and their Transvaal brothers. It should be stated at the outset that although the raid brought the Afrikaners in the Cape and the republics closer together, this process was by no means universal. S.J. du Toit and his press, as well as other Rhodes sympathisers, continued to be highly critical of the republican regime in the Transvaal.[342] F.S. Malan, on the other hand, used *OL* to promote the idea of pan-Afrikaner unity. In a leader article entitled, 'Afrikaner rapprochement' he blamed Rhodes for being 'a sort of dividing wall between the Colonial Afrikaners and the brothers in the republics'. He wrote in the spirit of *la patrie en danger*:

> Never has Afrikanerdom needed more colonial and republican unity. A psychological moment has now come, now our *volk* throughout South Africa has awakened, now a new flame rages in our hearts – let us now lay the foundation stone of a truly united South Africa on the ground of a pure and comprehensive sense of nationality. In our past blood has always been thicker than water. The blood of the *Voortrekker* is the same as that of those left behind.[343]

This, indeed, sounds like a veritable organic *bloot und bodem* nationalism. There is ample evidence that the Cape Bondsmen exhibited much more sympathy and understanding towards their brothers in the Transvaal than before. This was shown not only in their initial response to the raid. It persisted throughout the period under consideration and was reflected in the Bond press, in Bond meetings and congresses and in the contributions of Bond MPs in parliamentary debates.[344]

It would be, however, an exaggeration to conclude from these manifestations of sympathy and from a few fiery articles that the Cape Afrikaner ethnic consciousness and political outlook were qualitatively transformed after the raid. Solidarity and sympathy for their republican brothers had been an integral part of their Cape Afrikaner self-perception before the raid. As we have seen, they demonstrated their pan-Afrikaner solidarity even at the height of their alliance with Rhodes when their relations with the Transvaal were at a low ebb. As in the Transvaal crisis of 1880–18, Cape Afrikaners discovered again that 'blood was thicker than water'. This was an expected, almost instinctive, response. The difference was that whereas the former crisis was concluded with magnanimous British concessions, which brought it, from a Cape Afrikaner perspective, to a happy conclusion, the raid crisis never really subsided. The conduct of the *uitlanders*, the British government, Rhodes and the Cape jingoes transformed the raid crisis into a continuing, low-intensity crisis always threatening to erupt. Cape Afrikaners lived under the spectre of an imminent 'race' war which they dreaded.[345] Even Milner believed that the excessive manifestations of sympathy by Cape Afrikaner leaders towards the Transvaal were primarily motivated by a desire to avert such war:

> They loathe very naturally and rightly, the idea of war, and they think that if they can only impress upon the British Government that in case of war with the Transvaal it would have a great number of its own subjects ... against it, that is a way to prevent such calamity.[346]

He may have had in mind an interview in which Hofmeyr told a London newspaper that were Transvaal's independence to be threatened Cape Afrikaners would support them.[347]

As before, the distinction between the ethnic core and the ethnic diaspora still informed Cape Afrikaners' consciousness and political behaviour. Their solidarity with their ethnic diaspora was an integral part of their Cape 'Afrikanerdom', rather than a manifestation of its transformation into full-blown pan-Afrikaner nationalism. This trans-Cape ethnic solidarity was counterbalanced, in the shaping of Cape Afrikaners' comprehensive consciousness and identity, by two competing identities. First, the Bond, representing mainstream Cape 'Afrikanerdom', did not discard, in the wake of the raid, its goal of amalgamating the Afrikaners and the English-speakers into one white colonial voluntary political community or nation. There is no doubt that the betrayal of Rhodes was a severe blow to the cherished goal of 'racial' amalgamation. The 'nationalist' editor of *OL* lamented this particular consequence of the raid:

> We have thought that the path followed by the Rhodes–Bond alliance will be a long and enduring one and that along this path our ideal of the unification of the two white races will be achieved. Rhodes is one of the few English-speaking politicians we have trusted.

The betrayal of Rhodes, however, as painful and disappointing as it was, did not divert the Bond from the march along this path:

> The policy we have adopted so far has no doubt been the best for us and for South Africa's interest as a whole. We have in our land two white races – and the pragmatic politician must acknowledge the fact that we can hate one another or live together in friendship. Is there anyone who doubts that we must choose friendship? We must eradicate from our midst racial hatred, contempt, agitation and suspicion. We must not withdraw from our ideal because of the recent events.

The editor was aware that such a policy sowed the seeds of suspicion in the Transvaal against Cape Afrikaners. This 'dark side' of the policy of 'racial' reconciliation did not, however, deter the Bond from pursuing it. It was only hoped that 'our leaders' conduct during the crisis will convince our friends across the Vaal that our intentions are fair'. The hope was expressed that the Transvaal would 'seek a policy of appeasement to the problems of Johannesburg' because 'racial' hatred would cause the fall of the Afrikaners.[348]

The inspiration of Hofmeyr, the editor's patron who had reasserted his leadership of the Bond, is noticeable in every line of this policy-setting editorial. Clearly, the Bond continued to view solidarity for their ethnic diaspora and 'racial' amalgamation at their core as being as compatible as they had been before the raid. In the same series of articles in which he put forward strongly the case for cultural nationalism, Professor de Vos also advocated the amalgamation of 'the two brave races, the English and the Afrikaner'. In fact, he argued that, since the British only respected 'manliness' and despised weaklings, the manly assertion of Afrikaner culture was a condition for a proper alliance with them. His message was clear – Cape Afrikaners were interested in the amalgamation of English and Afrikaners into one big white nation.[349] Responding to a letter by an 'English Afrikaner' who had advocated collaboration between the two races, *OL* wrote: 'The spirit of the letter is refreshing like cold water to a thirsty soul in the desert.' However, like De Vos, it insisted that the amalgamation must be on the basis of equality, rather than a result of the swallowing of the thin cows by the fat ones.[350] When W.T. Stead wrote that Rhodes saw the struggle between English and Afrikaans in Darwinian terms, *OL* argued that the struggle for the survival of the fittest should be waged between both against the 'natives'.[351] Speaking at a meeting in Paarl against the pro-Rhodes demonstrations, Dr J.M. Hoffman, a 'nationalist' ideologue, claimed that no one wanted the amalgamation of the two 'races' more than he.[352] At the 1898 Bond congress, D.P. van den Heever, in proposing a resolution praising Merriman, 'a true Afrikaner and an upright Englishmen', reiterated the Bond's known position: 'The Bond knows no nationality.'[353] A.J. Herholdt, a member of the Upper House, wrote in an open letter that on the 'big issues' he had always followed Hofmeyr whose aim was to encourage good relations between the 'races'.[354] In the debate on the no-confidence vote, H.C. van Heerden from Cradock said: 'It was deplorable that race feeling was raised in that House. They were all living in one country, their interests were the same, and they ought to work together for the good of the country.' Du Plessis said that 'if any man, or any member of the House had used the word "rooinek" [red neck, i.e. Englishman], he would condemn it, even were it his own friend.'[355]

It is true that, despite the unchanged desire to promote co-operation, even political amalgamation, the Bond became increasingly an ethnic Afrikaner party after the raid. Most, if not all, English-speakers who had joined the Bond especially during the height of the alliance with Rhodes, had left it before the 1898 elections to join the Progressives. This, however, neither reflected a desire of the Bond leadership, nor resulted from any direct action by the party. The heightened ethnic sentiments within the Bond may have indirectly contributed towards it. The defection of English-speaking Bondsmen seems to have been more directly caused by the increasing jingoism and anti-Afrikanerism among the English-speakers in the Cape and by the return of Rhodes to active politics. As Innes wrote: 'Apart from the years of the actual war, I remember no period when racial feelings ran higher than ... during

1896–99.'[356] For this increasing 'racial' tension, the English-speakers were more responsible than the Afrikaners. Cape Afrikaners, and the Bond in particular, were subjected to a campaign of abuse and accusations by English-speaking politicians. The response of Cape Afrikaners to this barrage was primarily defensive. *OL* insisted that it was the South African League, rather than the Afrikaners, who were instigating 'racial hatred'. It even recommended that weapon demonstrations and anti-Scab meetings should not be held, in order not to arouse suspicion that Afrikaners were encouraging inter-'racial' tension.[357] In remaining faithful to their accommodating position towards the English-speakers, in the face of continuous provocations, the Bond exhibited remarkable consistency and moderation. In the elections of 1898 many more Afrikaners voted for the 'English' party than the other way round. The Bond proved their adherence to their policy of inter-'racial' collaboration when despite their electoral success in the election of August 1898, they installed W.P. Schreiner, a non-Afrikaner, non-Bondsman, at the head of a government which included only two Afrikaner Bondsmen.

The second identity which constrained the evolution of pan-Afrikaner nationalism was the imperial one. One of the thrusts of the jingoes' attack on the Bond was that it was disloyal and that it was converted to republicanism. James Rose Innes's brother, living in the east, wrote of a discussion with a well-to-do Afrikaner farmer who had told him that most of the Afrikaner farmers in the district would have welcomed the transformation of the Cape into a republic.[358] This could be considered, by any standard, as disloyalty to the Crown. It is, however, difficult to accept one piece of evidence as representative of broad Afrikaner opinion. James, more experienced in Cape politics, qualified his brother's story:

> Now, I have no doubt that a great many Dutch Africanders have a sort of academic preference for a Republic in the dim and distant future ... on their part it is at best a pious opinion; and once show them the difficulty and danger of setting up house for themselves and they fully recognise it.[359]

At a meeting in Paarl in March 1898, after parading the record of his loyalty and services to the British empire, Hofmeyr addressed the allegation that he harboured republican inclinations:

> When I joined the Bond it was, amongst others, to scrap a clause regarding an independent South Africa which had been sneaked in by someone who is now a Progressive [S.J. du Toit]. I wanted to remain under the British flag and even Majuba and Doornkop did not change my mind.[360]

Indeed, the evidence of loyalty to Crown and Empire is so voluminous, so universal and so convincing, that only political blindness, prejudice and fanaticism could account for the accusations of disloyalty levelled against Cape Afrikaners in general and Bondsmen in particular. In 1897, on the occasion of the celebration of the Diamond Jubilee of the Queen's rule, the Bond submitted an address to her:

> Recognising the material progress experienced by the Cape Colony as a part of the British Empire under Your Majesty's wise rule, and the world-wide ennobling influence by Your Majesty ... the members of the Bond beg to assure Your Majesty of their feelings of loyalty to Your Majesty's throne and of their attachment to Your Majesty's person.[361]

At an executive meeting of the Cape Town Bond branch, in January 1898, Hofmeyr responded to a British MP who had said that he wished to destroy the Bond for its opposition to British rule, by comparing the Jubilee celebrations in Ireland and the Cape. He also asked the secretary to read a resolution adopted by the branch in 1885: 'The branch expects that none of its members will contribute to the severance of the existing link between the Cape and the British Empire, on the contrary, he will strive to maintain the link.' This resolution was readopted unanimously.[362] In a speech in Britstown, T.P. Theron, after enthusing about the freedom enjoyed by Afrikaners as British citizens, suggested to his audience: 'Ask the Germans, the Russians, and anybody else, where would they have enjoyed more freedom, in their own land or under a British government?' He then added: 'Imbued with this feeling, do I say too much if I say, "I thank the Lord that I am a British subject"?'[363] Such a statement to a large audience, in one of the foremost centres of 'genuine Afrikanerdom', at a time when ethnic feelings ran so high, cannot be construed as mere lip-service. *OC* claimed that 'there was probably more disloyalty in England than here'.[364] It also stated categorically and unequivocally: 'We have never supported republican ideas.'[365] *OL* responded disapprovingly to Milner's claim that were there to be confrontation between the Transvaal and England, the majority of Cape Afrikaners would support the former warmly and without a vestige of neutrality: 'It is possible that there are a few who are prepared to act in such a manner, but it is certainly untrue with respect to the great majority of Dutch Afrikaners in the Cape.'[366]

These are only some of the expressions of loyalty by Afrikaner Bonds-men, at different levels of organisation and leadership, after the raid.[367] Non-Bondsmen, observing from without, confirmed the veracity of these manifestations. J.H. de Villiers, the much respected Judge of the High Court of Justice, assured the London *Daily News* that he knew not one Afrikaner who would approve the separation of the Cape from Britain.[368] James Rose Innes said that no one who knew the Afrikaners would claim that they were disloyal.[369] Of Hofmeyr, the London *Pall Mall Gazette* wrote: 'Hofmeyr has always been a loyal subject of the Queen and, in his own way, an imperialist.'[370] Milner, soon after his arrival to take up his new position in Cape Town, reported: 'All I can say is that, so far as I am able to judge, these racial differences have not affected the loyalty of any portion of the community to H.M. the Queen. People of all races ... have vied with one another in demonstrations of affection for her person and devotion to her throne.'[371] A year later, on the eve of the election to the Lower House which was marred with heightened 'racial' feelings, he was still basically of the same view. Despite manifestations of sympathy towards Transvaal he did not believe that Cape Afrikaners were disloyal.[372] A final proof of the Bond's sound loyalty lay in the fact that they had selected as their parliamentary leader, and after the successful election as prime minister, Schreiner – and he was loyal to the bone.

Innes believed that the loyalty of the Afrikaner was 'of the head and not of the heart'.[373] The evidence suggests that he might have been wrong. Dr te Water, speaking in Somerset East, said that he had 'never seen such a great enthusiasm as in the Jubilee celebrations that have been recently held here.'[374] In Paarl the Jubilee celebrations, which attracted 5,000 participants, included a three-mile long procession and all Paarl celebrated. The Mayor of Paarl remarked jubilantly: 'No one will be able to call Paarl disloyal.'[375] In Montagu some 2,000 people from the town and the surrounding countryside participated in the procession, while in neighbouring Robertson their number was 4,000.[376]

The Queen also inspired poetic talents among Cape Afrikaners. J.M. Brink, a known poet, wrote a short poem for the occasion of the Jubilee:

> We respect her as a Queen
> As mother and as wife
> As subjects of her Empire
> We are loyal and faithful
>
> And those who suspect us of unfaithfulness
> And see us as disloyal
> The heart of our people do not know
> And utter only blasphemy
>
> We live under England's flag
> Almost a hundred years
> But disloyalty has never here
> This flag in danger placed
>
> We live under her rule
> In liberty, in freedom
> And we wish her well in her Jubilee
> From the bottom of our heart.[377]

A year later, election fever did not silence the muses:

302

No, we are not unhappy
And still less disloyal
England can rest assured
Her flag has nothing to fear ...

Under which flag or ruler
Will you Afrikaner be
Jingoes! you have nothing to fear
Our answer will always be
If the question be posed
Because despite blasphemy and lies
Which you spread every day
You will make us no rebels
Nor make us renounce our trust
In Britain and her flag.[378]

This enthusiastic poetry saw the light, it should be emphasised, in the vanguard of Afrikaner ethnic 'nationalism'. Evidently devotion to the Queen and loyalty to her Empire, were as fresh, fervent and sincere after the raid as they had been before it. They were informed by the heart as well as by the head.

It is worthy of note that the response of the Afrikaner Bondsmen to the accusations of disloyalty was apologetic rather than defiant. There was one noticeable change in the way Bondsmen related to the loyalty issue after the raid. The constant challenge from the local jingoes, and from a metropolitan policy feeding the tension between Britain and the Transvaal,[379] forced them to address the apparent contradiction between loyalty to the Crown and the call of the blood. It was in line with the political culture of the Cape Afrikaners that in dealing with this apparent contradiction, they sought not to heighten and sharpen it but rather to submerge and resolve it by offering a syncretic, ambivalent and inclusive outlook, which facilitated the cohabitation of British imperialism and Afrikaner ethnicity. They do not seem to have felt the contradiction. Theron, for example, while enthusing about the empire, also propagated, to the same audience, the virtues of an emotional, organic ethnic 'sense of nationality'.[380] Likewise, Professor de Vos, who advocated the cause of ethnic 'nationalism' with a strong cultural bias, also stated: 'I acknowledge God's hand in this, that the Queen of England reigns here, and I will fulfil my duties as a loyal and faithful subject.'[381] M.L. Neethling, appealing to his electors, wrote the following: 'This I enunciate as a loyal subject and at the same time as an Afrikaner patriot of the right sort.'[382]

However, the challenge from the jingoes forced Bondsmen to deal more directly with the apparent contradiction. The well-informed Hofmeyr took a comparative view – arguing that, as in the case of Scotland and Ireland, 'local patriotism' was not incompatible with loyalty.[383] *OC* took a leaf from British politics: 'If opposition to the British government's policy is disloyalty then the opposition in England and half the English people are disloyal.'[384] While M.L. Neethling presented himself as the most loyal subject Britain had ever had, he saw no discrepancy between his loyalty and his wish to live 'in friendship and love with his brothers and sisters in the republics'.[385] For others it was, in fact, a duty as loyal subjects to fight against the evil, which for the jingoes was a manifestation of disloyalty.[386] It was in this sense that J.S. Marais argued, at a meeting at Paarl, that he was more loyal than Rhodes.[387] A correspondent from Mossel Bay wrote: 'We are loyal to our Queen and thank God that has given us such [a] God-fearing, virtuous and pious ruler. God bless her and extend her realm. But as British subjects we must safeguard our rights and protect our privileges.'[388]

The loyalty of the Afrikaner Bondsmen to the Queen and the Empire was as sincere and as deep as it had been before the raid. They disowned Rhodes but not what he had stood for during their alliance with him. The raid, from Rhodes's perspective, represented his inability to contain the contradiction which was inherent in his alliance with the Bond. Consequently, in the wake of the raid he had to carve a new road and devise new strategies. This path led him to direct confrontation with the Bond. The Afrikaner Bond made tactical adjustments, but remained faithful to the political outlook which was informed by their collective experience. The Bond remained, essentially, a manifestation of Cape Afrikaner ethnic identity and mobilisation, rather than of ethnic nationalism. Because of the complexity of their situation, and as a result of the nature of their socialisation under British rule, their ethnic identity and consciousness were not bent on exclusivity. On the contrary, their identity was of a hybrid variety. They carved out a space, in which Cape Afrikaner ethnicity, white Cape colonialism, pan-Afrikaner solidarity and British imperialism lived side by side, not without tension, but on the whole quite happily. English colonists, imbued with cultural arrogance and prejudice, exacerbated by frustration stemming from Afrikaner political dominance, as well as metropolitan officials, intolerant of ambiguities, could neither comprehend the harmonious confusion of Cape Afrikaners nor come to terms with it. Accusations of disloyalty stemmed from this misapprehension or ignorance. This was not merely an unharmful intellectual ineptitude. It played a role in pushing Britain along the catastrophic road leading to the Anglo-Boer war.

NOTES

1. *Index of the Reports from the Select Committee on British South Africa, with Digest of Evidence, ordered by the House of Commons, to be printed 13 July 1897* (London, 1897), p. 172.

2. G. Shaw (ed.), *The Garrett Papers* (Cape Town, 1984), pp. 42 and 45.
3. *Index of the Reports ... on British South Africa*, pp. 173–4.
4. Rotberg, *The Founder*, p. 544.
5. E. Garrett and E.T. Edwards, *The Story of an African Crisis* (London, 1897), p. 160.
6. Hofmeyr, *Hofmeyr*, p. 498.
7. *Hofmeyr Papers*, 8/A/2.
8. Garrett and Edwards, *African Crisis*, p. 159.
9. Rotberg, *The Founder*, pp. 544–5.
10. Hofmeyr, *Hofmeyr*, p. 490.
11. Hofmeyr Papers, 8/A/1, Hofmeyr to Kruger, 2 Jan. 1896.
12. Hofmeyr *Hofmeyr*, pp. 491–3; N.J. Hofmeyr, *De Afrikaner Boer and de Jameson Inval*, (Cape Town and Amsterdam, 1896), pp. 390–2.
13. Hofmeyr, *Hofmeyr*, pp. 492–6.
14. Hofmeyr, *Hofmeyr*, p. 499.
15. De Waal, *De Waal*, pp. 220–1.
16. Ibid., pp. 499–500.
17. Hofmeyr, *Hofmeyr*, pp. 500–1.
18. Vanstone, 'Sprigg', pp. 347–351.
19. *OL*, 4 Jan. 1896.
20. Ibid., 14 Jan. 1896.
21. Ibid., 6 Feb. 1896.
22. Ibid., 11 Feb. 1896
23. Ibid., 7 March 1896.
24. *OC*, 9 March 1896; see also 5 March 1896
25. *Het Oosten*, 23 Jan. 1896.
26. Hofmeyr Papers, 8/A/1, S.J. du Toit to Hofmeyr, 1 and 13 Jan. 1896.
27. *Patriot*, 9 Jan. 1896.
28. Ibid., 21 Jan. 1896 and 13 Feb. 1896.
29. Ibid., 5 March 1896.
30. *Paarl*, 3 March 1896.
31. *GR*, 6 Jan. 1896.
32. *Paarl*, 4 Jan. 1896.
33. *OL*, 18, 21, 23 and 30 Jan. 1896, and 4, 15, 18 and 22 Feb. 1896, 3, 7, 10 and 12 March 1896; *OC*, 6 Feb. 1896.
34. *OL*, 7 March 1896.
35. Public Record Office (PRO), CO, 48, 528.
36. *OL*, 17 March 1896.
37. Ibid., 26 and 31 March 1896.
38. Ibid., 28 March 1896.
39. Ibid., 9 and 23 April 1896.
40. Ibid., 18 April 1896.
41. Ibid., 25 April 1896.
42. Ibid., 23 April 1896.
43. Ibid., 30 April 1896 and 2 May 1896.
44. Ibid., 2 May 1896.
45. *Hansard*, 4 May 1896, p. 9.
46. *OL*, 7 May 1896.
47. *Hansard*, 12 May 1896, pp. 88–9.
48. *OL* 19 May 1896.
49. E.A. Walker, *W.P. Schreiner: a South African* (London, 1937), pp. 79–80.

50. *Hansard*, 13 May 1896, pp. 106–7.
51. Ibid., p. 107; 15 May 1896, pp. 125–6; 18 May 1896, p. 138.
52. Ibid., 18 May 1896, p. 136.
53. Ibid., 20 May 1896, p. 145.
54. Ibid., 21 May 1896, pp. 158–9.
55. Ibid., 28 May 1896, p. 145–6.
56. *OL*, 21 May 1896.
57. Ibid., 23 May 1896.
58. Ibid., 4 June 1896; see also 4 June 1896 (four other letters), 11, 13, and 18 June 1896.
59. Ibid., 4 July 1896.
60. Ibid., 9 July 1896.
61. De Waal, *De Waal*, pp. 229–30.
62. Walker, *Schreiner*, p. 80.
63. *OL*, 13 March 1897.
64. *Hansard*, 14 July 1896, pp. 568–9.
65. Ibid., pp. 568–75.
66. Ibid., 17 July 1896, p. 602.
67. Ibid., pp. 661–8.
68. *OL*, 25 July 1896.
69. Ibid., 28 July 1896.
70. De Waal, *De Waal*, p. 231; *OL*, 1 Sept. 1896.
71. Ibid., 28 July 1896; see also 18 and 27 Aug. 1896.
72. Ibid., 27 Aug. 1896; see also *OC*, 20 Aug. 1896.
73. *OL*, 28 July 1896.
74. Ibid., 1 Aug. 1896.
75. Ibid., 29 Aug. 1896.
76. Cloete, *F.S. Malan*, pp. 55–6.
77. *OL*, 25 Aug. 1896.
78. Ibid., 1 Oct. 1896.
79. Ibid., 24 Sept. 1896.
80. Ibid., 17 Nov. 1896.
81. De Waal,*De Waal,*, pp. 232–3; *OL*, 19 Sept. 1896.
82. *OL*, 19 Sept. 1896.
83. Ibid., 30 July 1896, 15, 20, 22 and 27 Aug. 1896, 10, 12 and 19 Sept. 1896, 3, 6, 10 and 22 Oct. 1896.
84. Ibid., 30 July, 29 Aug. 1896, 1, 10, 24 and 29 Sept. 1896, 1 and 15 Oct. 1896; *GR*, 15 and 19 Oct. 1896.
85. *OL*, 24 Oct. 1896.
86. Ibid., 20 Aug. 1896.
87. Ibid., 28 and 30 July 1896, 4, 11, 13 and 20 Aug 1896, 1 and 22 Sept. 1896, 3, 6 and 10 Oct. 1896.
88. Ibid., 8 Aug. 1896.
89. Ibid., 3 Oct. 1896.
90. Ibid., 22 Oct. 1896.
91. Ibid., 12 Sept. 1896.
92. Ibid., 20 Aug. 1896; see also 1, 12 and 29 Sept. 1896.
93. De Waal, *De Waal*, pp. 232–3.
94. *OL*, 15 Aug. 1896.
95. Ibid., 27 Aug. 1896.
96. Ibid., 15 Aug. 1896.

 97. Ibid., 14 Nov. 1896.
 98. Ibid., 10 Oct. 1896.
 99. Ibid., 1, 22 and 24 Oct. 1896.
100. Ibid., 8 Sept. 1896.
101. Ibid., 10 Dec. 1896.
102. Ibid., 17 Nov. 1896; *Het Oosten*, 15 Oct. 1896, 12 and 17 Nov. 1896. The monument commemorates the clash in 1815 between some Afrikaners and the British authorities which resulted in the execution of the Afrikaner culprits, see T.R.H. Davenport, *South Africa: a Modern History* (Bergulei, 1987), p. 3.
103. De Waal, *De Waal*, p. 229.
104. *OL*, 7 Nov. 1896.
105. M.F. Bitensky, 'The South African League: British Imperialist Organization in South-Africa, 1896–1899' (MA thesis, Witwatersrand University, 1950).
106. *OC*, 28 Dec. 1896; Fuller, *Rhodes*, p. 207.
107. Vindex, *Rhodes*, pp. 495–506.
108. Rotberg, *The Founder*, pp. 578–9.
109. Fuller, *Rhodes*, pp. 208–10; Walker, *Schreiner*, p. 85.
110. *OC*, 28 Dec. 1896.
111. *GR*, 7 Jan. 1897; *OL* 12, 14 and 21 Jan. 1897.
112. *Patriot*, 7 Jan. 1896; *OL*, 31 Dec. 1896; *Dagblad*, 1 Jan. 1897.
113. *OL*, 31 Dec. 1896.
114. Michell, *Rhodes*, p. 314.
115. *OC*, 7 Jan. 1897.
116. *OL*, 23 Jan. 1897.
117. Ibid., 12 Jan. 1897.
118. Ibid., 7 Jan. 1897.
119. *GR*, 7 Jan. 1897.
120. *OC*, 11 Jan. 1897.
121. *OL*, 7, 12 and 14 Jan. 1897.
122. Ibid., 12 Jan. 1897.
123. Ibid., 18 Feb. 1897.
124. Ibid., 12 Jan. 1897.
125. Ibid., 14 Jan. 1897.
126. Ibid., 14, 16 and 21 Jan. 1897.
127. Ibid., 19 and 30 Jan. 1897 and 6 Feb. 1897.
128. Ibid., 6 Feb. 1897.
129. Ibid., 7, 12 and 19 Jan. 1897.
130. Ibid., 14, 21, 23 and 28 Jan. 1897.
131. Ibid., 2 Feb. 1897.
132. Ibid., 14, 19, 21 and 23 Jan. 1897.
133. Ibid., 26 Jan. 1897.
134. Ibid., 28 Jan. 1897 and 2 Feb. 1897.
135. Ibid., 13 Feb. 1897 and 6 March 1897.
136. Ibid., 23 Jan. 1897.
137. Ibid., 21 Jan. 1897.
138. Ibid., 13 March 1897.
139. *Patriot*, 17 Dec 1896, 14 Jan. 1897; *Dagblad*, 6 Jan. 1897.
140. Ibid., 13 March 1897.
141. *Patriot*, 14 Jan. 1897.
142. *Dagblad*, 6 and 12 Jan. 1897.
143. Ibid., 11 Jan. 1897.

144. Ibid., 25 Feb. 1897, 6 and 9 March 1897.
145. Ibid., 18 Feb. 1897.
146. Ibid., 8 and 11 March 1897.
147. Ibid., 18 and 22 Feb. 1897.
148. *OL*, 9 March 1897.
149. Ibid., 16 March 1897.
150. Ibid., 18 March 1897.
151. Ibid., 13 March 1897.
152. Ibid., 13 March 1897; *CT*, 13 March 1897. The terms *Moderatuur* and executive committee refer to the office bearers of the Bond.
153. *CT*, 13 March 1897.
154. *OL*, 30 March. 1897.
155. Ibid., 13 March 1897.
156. *CT*, 13 March 1897.
157. *OL*, 16 March 1897.
158. Ibid., 13 March 1897; the address, signed by many predikants, protested against reports in England that the DRC was solidly behind Rhodes.
159. *Volksbode*, 8 and 18 Jan. 1896, 5 Feb. 1896 and 1 April 1896.
160. *Volksbode*, 29 April 1896.
161. *OL*, 16 March 1897.
162. Ibid., 13 March 1897; *CT*, 13 March 1897.
163. See, for example, *OC*, 12 April 1897.
164. *Hansard*, 6 April 1897, pp. 17–19.
165. Ibid., 14 April 1897, p. 79.
166. Ibid., pp. 84–142.
167. Ibid., pp. 142–3.
168. Ibid., pp. 108–9, 112–16, 135–6, 138 and 142–3.
169. Ibid., 30 April 1897, pp. 172–3.
170. Lewsen, *Selections*, Vol. ii, p. 251, Merriman to Curry, 24 Jan. 1897.
171. V. Solomon, *Selections from the Correspondence of Percy Alport Molteno, 1892–1914*, (Cape Town, 1981), pp. 46–7, Molteno to Merriman, 12 Feb. 1897.
172. Walker, *Schreiner*, p. 94.
173. Rotberg, *The Founder*, p. 600.
174. G. Shaw, *Some Beginnings: the Cape Times, 1876–1910* (Oxford, 1975), p. 94. Shaw wrongly dates Rhodes's return as March.
175. Walker, *Schreiner*, p. 102.
176. Fuller, *Rhodes*, pp. 214–15.
177. Wright, *Innes*, p. 209, J.R. Innes to J.D.P Innes, 2 May 1897.
178. Rotberg, *The Founder*, p. 603.
179. *OL*, 22 April 1897.
180. *GR*, 26 April 1897.
181. *OC*, 26 April 1897.
182. *Hansard*, 30 April 1897, pp. 182–5.
183. Ibid., p. 183.
184. *OL*, 1 May 1897.
185. *Hansard*, 30 April 1897, p. 193.
186. *OL*, 26 June 1897.
187. Flint, *Rhodes*, p. 210.
188. *Dagblad*, 5 Aug. 1897.
189. Ibid., 14 Aug. 1897.
190. Ibid., 25 and 28 Aug. 1897.

191. Ibid., 31 Aug. 1897.
192. Ibid., 7 Sept. 1897.
193. *Rhodes Papers*, Mss Afr., 2A, The Cape 1896–1902, D.C. de Waal to Rhodes, 6 Aug. 1897.
194. *OC*, 2 and 26 Aug. 1897; *OL*, 31 July 1897.
195. C. Headlam (ed.)*The Milner Papers*, (London, 1931), p. 90, Milner to Chamberlain, 29 Aug. 1897.
196. *OC*, 30 Dec. 1897.
197. *OL*, 24 July 1897.
198. Ibid., 21 Aug. 1897.
199. *OC*, 25 Oct. 1897.
200. *OL*, 30 Sept. 1897
201. Ibid., 11 Dec. 1897.
202. *OC*, 30 Dec. 1897.
203. *OL*, 13 May 1897 and 11 Dec. 1897.
204. Ibid., 22 Jan. 1898.
205. Ibid., 17 Aug. 1897.
206. *GR*, 26 April 1897.
207. Ibid., 3 May 1897.
208. *OL*, 30 Sept. 1897.
209. See, for example, *Dagblad*, 22 Sept. 1897, 8, 9, 20 and 29 Oct. 1897, 8, 16, and 27 Nov. 1897, 13 Dec 1897, 7 and 24 Jan. 1898.
210. *OL*, 28 Sept. 1897.
211. Ibid., 17, 19, 21 and 24 Aug. 1897, 23 Sept. 1897 and 16 Nov. 1897.
212. Ibid., 14 Aug. 1897.
213. Ibid., 16 Sept. 1897.
214. Ibid., 18 Nov. 1897.
215. Ibid., 9 Dec. 1897.
216. Ibid., 16 Feb. 1897.
217. Ibid., 31 Aug. 1897 and 8 Dec. 1897.
218. *Rhodes Papers*, Mss. Afr., 2A, the Cape 1896–1902, T. Louw to Rhodes, 11 Sept 1897; *OL*, 26 Aug. 1897.
219. Ibid., 28 Aug. 1897.
220. See also ibid., 31 Aug. 1897.
221. Ibid., 16 Sept. 1897; see also 18, 21 and 25 Sept. 1897.
222. Ibid., 18 Sept. 1897.
223. Ibid., 15 July 1897.
224. Ibid., 17 Feb. 1897.
225. Ibid., 20 Oct. 1897 and 30 Sept. 1897.
226. Ibid., 14 Aug. 1897.
227. Ibid., 26 Aug. 1897.
228. Ibid., 18 and 28 Sept.1897.
229. Ibid., 15 Feb. 1898.
230. Ibid., 2 and 6 Nov. 1897.
231. *Rhodes Papers*, Mss. Afr., 2A, the Cape 1896–1902, D.C. de Waal to Rhodes, 6 Aug. 1897 (Italics added).
232. Davenport, *Afrikaner Bond*, pp. 173–4.
233. *Patriot*, 3 March 1898; *Dagblad*, 26 Feb. 1898; Davenport, *Afrikaner Bond*, pp. 174–5.
234. *OL*, 19 Feb. 1898.
235. Ibid., 24 Feb. 1898.

236. Ibid., 22 Feb. 1898.
237. *Dagblad*, 26 Feb. 1897.
238. E.T. Cook, *Edmund Garrett: a Memoir* (London, 1909) p. 138.
239. Vindex, *Rhodes*, pp. 520–47.
240. *Dagblad*, 15 March 1898.
241. Ibid., 25 March 1898.
242. Ibid., 7 April 1898.
243. Ibid.
244. Ibid., 11 April 1898.
245. *OL*, 12, 22, 24 and 26 March 1898.
246. *Dagblad*, 26 April 1898.
247. *GR*, 23 Aug. 1897 and 30 Sept. 1897.
248. Ibid.,15 and 18 Nov. 1897 and 16 Dec. 1897.
249. Ibid., 6 Dec. 1897.
250. Ibid., 23 Dec. 1897 and 17 March 1898.
251. Ibid., 28 April 1898; see also *OC*, 6 and 9 Dec. 1897.
252. *OC*, 25 Oct. 1897.
253. Ibid., 17 March 1898.
254. *OL*, 15 March 1898.
255. Ibid., 5 May 1898.
256. *OC*, 17 March 1898.
257. Ibid., 18 April 1898.
258. Ibid., 2 May 1898.
259. *GR*, 21 April 1898.
260. *OL*, 12 May 1898.
261. *Hansard*, 1 June 1898, pp. 31–40.
262. *OL*, 12 May 1898.
263. Vindex, *Rhodes*, pp. 525–6.
264. *OL*, 14 May 1898.
265. Ibid., 26 May 1898.
266. Ibid., 17 May 1898.
267. See, for example, ibid., 17, 21, 24 and 26 May 1898.
268. *PRO*, CO 48/537, Milner to Chamberlain, 18 May 1898.
269. *Hansard*, 22 June 1898, p. 235.
270. *Hansard*, 1 June 1898, pp. 41–2.
271. Ibid., 22 June 1898, pp. 225–6.
272. Ibid., p. 212.
273. Ibid., p. 235.
274. *PRO*, CO 48/538, Milner to Chamberlain, 29 June 1898.
275. Vanstone, 'Sprigg', p. 371.
276. Ibid., p. 374.
277. *OL*, 25 June 1898.
278. Ibid., 2 July 1898.
279. *PRO*, CO 48/537, Milner to Chamberlain, 18 May 1898.
280. *OL*, 30 July 1898.
281. Ibid., 30 June 1898.
282. Ibid., 2 July 1898.
283. Rive, *Olive Schreiner*, p. 329, O. Screiner to W.P. Schreiner, 26 May 1898.
284. Ibid., p. 278.
285. Solomon, *Molteno*, p. 65, Merriman to Molteno, 20 March 1898.
286. Lewsen, *Selections*, Vol. ii, p. 297, Merriman to J. Merriman, 23 Feb. 1898.

287. *OL*, 28 July 1898.
288. Davenport, *Afrikaner Bond*, pp. 184–6.
289. *OL*, 30 June 1898.
290. Tindall, *Innes*, p. 169; Wright, *Innes*, p. 234, Innes to R. Solomon, 7 Feb. 1898.
291. Rotberg, *The Founder*, pp. 607–8.
292. *Rhodes Papers*, Mss. Afr., 2A, the Cape 1896–1902, Brown to Rhodes, 17 Nov. 1897.
293. Rive, *Olive Schreiner*, p. 335, O. Schreiner to F. Schreiner, 13 Aug. 1898.
294. *OL*, 25 June 1898.
295. Ibid., 9 July 1898.
296. Ibid., 19 and 23 July 1898.
297. Ibid., 5 July 1898.
298. Ibid., 30 July 1898.
299. Ibid., 28 and 30 July 1898.
300. Ibid., 11 Aug. 1898.
301. Ibid., 28 July 1898.
302. Ibid., 14 and 21 July 1898.
303. Ibid., 7, 9, 12 and 30 July 1898 and 4 Aug. 1898.
304. *PRO*, CO 48/538, Milner to Chamberlain, 20 Sept. 1898.
305. *OL*, 18 Aug. 1898.
306. Headlam, *Milner Papers*, p. 270, Rhodes to Milner, Aug. 1898.
307. *OL*, 29 Sept. 1898.
308. Ibid., 6 Oct. 1898.
309. Vanstone, 'Sprigg', p. 376.
310. *Hansard*, 11 Oct. 1898, pp. 10–19.
311. *OL*, 5 March 1898.
312. Ibid., 15 March 1898.
313. Ibid., 13 Jan. 1898.
314. Ibid., 6 Jan. 1898, 15 Feb. 1898; Le Sueur, *Cecil Rhodes*, p. 68.
315. *OL*, 6 Jan. 1898.
316. Ibid., 17 Aug. 1898.
317. Ibid., 29 March 1898.
318. Ibid., 20 Jan. 1898.
319. Ibid., 19 Jan. 1897.
320. Ibid., 15 July 1897.
321. Ibid., 4 June 1898.
322. Ibid., 26 July 1898.
323. Ibid., 16 July 1898.
324. Ibid.
325. Ibid., 25 Feb. 1896; see also 21 Aug. 1897, 25 Nov. 1897 and 4 Dec. 1897.
326. Ibid., 4 and 9 Sept. 1897 and 29 March 1898.
327. See, for example, *Dagblad*, 13 Jan. 1897, 8 and 11 March 1897, 8 and 11 Oct 1897 and 13 Dec. 1897
328. *OL*, 16 Jan. 1896.
329. Ibid., 14 Jan. 1897.
330. Ibid., 19 Jan. 1897.
331. Ibid., 21 Jan. 1897.
332. Ibid., 25 Jan. 1897.
333. Ibid., 25 Nov. 1897.
334. Ibid., 12 Jul. 1898.
335. Ibid., 14 Jan. 1897.

336. Ibid., 12 March 1896; Hancock and van der Poel, *Selection from Jan Smuts Papers*, Vol. i, pp. 103–6.
337. See, for example, the interpretation of this article in J.A. Coetzee, *Die Politieke Groepering in die Wording van die Afrikanernatie* (Johannesburg, 1941), pp. 185–6.
338. *OL*, 5 Nov. 1896 and 14 Sept. 1897.
339. Ibid., 31 Oct. 1896, 3, 7, 10 and 12 Nov. 1896.
340. *OC*, 2 May 1898.
341. Ibid.
342. *Dagblad*. See, for example, 20, 24 and 25 Feb. 1897, 4 and 18 May 1897, 28 Jan. 1898, 17 Feb. 1898 and 6 and 8 June 1898.
343. *OL*, 12 March 1896.
344. See, for example, ibid., 11 and 16 Jan. 1896, 22 Aug. 1896, 15 and 19 Dec. 1896, 19 Jan. 1897, 1 May 1897, 26 Aug. 1897, 2 Oct. 1897 and 10 April 1897; *Hansard*, 1897, pp. 105–106, 109 and 130.
345. Headlam, *Milner Papers*, p. 64, Milner to Chamberlain, 25 May 1897; *OL*, 17 Aug. 1897.
346. Headlam, *Milner Papers*, p. 245, Milner to Mrs Gaskell, 22 June 1898.
347. *OL*, 7 Dec. 1897.
348. Ibid., 18 Jan. 1896.
349. Ibid., 5 Nov. 1896.
350. Ibid., 7 Nov. 1896.
351. Ibid., 9 April 1896.
352. Ibid., 12 Jan. 1897.
353. Ibid., 22 Feb. 1898
354. Ibid., 28 April 1898.
355. *Hansard*, 15 June 1898, p. 163; 21 June 1898, p. 216.
356. Tindall, *Innes*, p. 166.
357. *OL*, 9 and 20 April 1896.
358. Wright, *Innes*, p. 199, R.W. Rose Innes to J. Rose Innes, 13 March 1897.
359. Ibid., pp. 200–1, J.R. Innes to R.W. Innes, 22 March 1897.
360. *OL*, 29 March 1898.
361. Ibid., 3 June 1897.
362. Ibid., 8 and 13 Jan. 1898.
363. *OC*, 2 May 1898.
364. Ibid., 12 April 1897.
365. Ibid., 15 April 1898.
366. Ibid., 5 March 1898.
367. See also, for example, *OL*, 31 Oct. 1896, 2 Feb. 1897, 13 March 1897, 9 Sept. 1897, 8 Jan. 1898, 23 and 30 July 1898; *OC*, 6 June 1896 and 12 April 1897.
368. *CT*, 9 July 1897.
369. *OC*, 25 July 1896.
370. *Barkly and Diggers News*, 28 May 1898.
371. Headlam, *Milner Papers*, p. 49, Milner to Chamberlain, 23 June 1897.
372. Ibid., pp. 244–5, Milner to Mrs Gaskell, 22 June 1898.
373 Wright, *Innes*, pp. 200–1, J. Rose Innes to R.W. Rose Innes, 22 March 1897.
374. *OC*, 30 Sept. 1897.
375. *OL*, 3 July 1897.
376. Ibid., 6 July 1897.
377. Ibid., 22 June 1897.
378. Ibid., 13 Aug. 1898.

379. Robinson and Gallagher, *Africa and the Victorian*, pp. 430–57; A.N. Porter, *The Origins of the South African War*: Joseph Chamberlain and the Diplomacy of Imperialism, 1895–1899 (Manchester, 1980), pp. 95–175; *OL*, see, for example, 7 Aug. 1897, 7 Sept. 1897, 7 Dec. 1897 and 5 March 1898.
380. *OC*, 2 May 1898.
381. *OL*, 31 Oct. 1896.
382. Ibid., 17 Feb. 1898.
383. Ibid., 29 March 1898.
384. *OC*, 15 April 1897.
385. *OL*, 1 Feb. 1898.
386. *OC*, 8 Jan. 1897; *Het Oosten*, 3 Sept. 1896.
387. *OL*, 30 July 1898.
388. Ibid., 22 Jan. 1898.

Conclusion

The evolution of the relations between Rhodes and the Afrikaner Bond, the foremost manifestation of Cape Afrikaner political awakening and assertion, is a fascinating story. It is also an episode of great significance in the history of the Cape and South Africa as a whole. It formed an important part in the march of South Africa to the Anglo-Boer war which so dramatically changed the course of its history. In representing aggressive British imperialism, bent not only on expansion into the vast regions beyond South Africa, but also on consolidating British supremacy in South Africa itself, Rhodes himself made an important contribution towards this cataclysmic war. Rhodes developed, while in South Africa, a strong sense of imperial mission. But he was only a wealthy man who made his money in the diamond fields of Kimberley. Since he had little trust in the the imperialist zeal of successive British governments, he developed the strategy of local sub-imperialism which received the blessing and support of the reluctant imperialists in London. But he had no local political base to pursue his imperialist project, only money. His choice of the Cape as his local political base was perfectly congruent with his vision, the Cape being the most developed, established and solid British imperial outpost in South Africa. The choice of the Afrikaner Bond as his political launching pad was less congruent. At first sight, Cape Afrikaners, who had shown sympathy to their republican ethnic brothers during the crisis in 1880–81, were not natural allies of Rhodes's imperialist design. The Bond, however, was the only relatively organised party with influence over a large contingent in the Parliament of the self-governing Cape. In courting the Bond throughout much of the 1880s Rhodes laboured to establish his credibility and to groom Bondsmen for the role he had allocated to them.

The Bond, in lending itself as a base for Rhodes's political career, contributed to the chain of events which culminated in a South African war which the Bond had dreaded more than anything else. In this study I have tried to account for the Bond's support for, and trust in, perhaps the most aggressive British imperialist of the day. It is clear to me that had Bond leaders suspected that Rhodes was the aggressive imperialist that he was, they would have neither supported nor trusted him. The inevitable conclusion is that the Bond fell into a political trap set by Rhodes. Rhodes, in courting the Bond, and also during their political marriage, not only lured but also deceived them. As we have seen, from late 1894, at the height of the Rhodes–Bond alliance, when the former enjoyed the loyalty, the trust, the admiration and the love of the Bond leadership, he was involved in a betrayal which culminated in the Jameson raid at the end of 1895.

Rhodes lured his Cape Afrikaner allies by supporting their immediate economic interests and by offering them a long-term economic promised land in Rhodesia. In supporting them on the 'native' question he addressed one of the most pressing economic problems afflicting Afrikaner farmers, namely the labour problem. In supporting them on the issue of 'native' political rights he addressed a more general and more acute concern among Cape Afrikaners – the threat of English-'native' political alliance and the fear of ultimate black domination. Rhodes also tempted some prominent Bondsmen with personal material benefits. Rhodes manifested a desire to collaborate with the Bond and to facilitate the emergence of a non-ethnic white colonial nation. He also enticed Bondsmen by clever employment of his charismatic personality. In identifying with them and invading their emotional domain, he earned both their devotion and their love.

Rhodes found Afrikaner Bondsmen very responsive to his courtship through these means. Representing a vulnerable farming community which found it difficult to keep its head above the turbulent water in an increasingly competitive free market, the Bond craved protection by the state. They also longed for a symbiosis with the English-speaking settlers in order to improve their chances of prosperity and survival in the black continent. In their encounter with the English-speaking community which represented a more advanced economic, political and cultural front, Cape Afrikaners suffered from an acute sense of inferiority and craved recognition as equals. This was denied to them by other English-speaking politicians but lavished on them by Rhodes.

Tempting and alluring as all this was, it is not sufficient to account for the Bond's devoted support for Rhodes. Over and above it there was the great deception practised by Rhodes with regard to the true nature of his vision and goals. He disguised his aggressive imperialism under a cloak of 'colonialism', presenting his project in the north as Cape rather than British expansionism. In the second half of the 1880s Cape expansion into its hinterland was becoming increasingly acceptable to Bondsmen, and this was partly in response to insistent propaganda by Rhodes. They accepted this expansion as essential for their position in South Africa.

Thus, Rhodes, in word and deed, conjured up an environment which was very attractive to Bondsmen. He captured them and fired their imagination because the blueprint he drew up was modelled on the interests, inclinations and desires of the backbone of Cape Afrikaner society. It held the promise of consolidating in South Africa an order which corresponded to, and stemmed from, their collective experience. It was a colonial Cape-centric order with which they could identify because their collective ethnic identity and consciousness developed under the aegis of British imperialism. As the balance of their colonial experience improved towards the end of the nineteenth century, they evolved a political outlook which harmonised their interests and aspirations with the colonial and imperial reality. In delineating and articulating this cohabitation space, or common ground, Rhodes engendered among Cape Afrikaner Bondsmen the illusion of convergence of both interests and outlook. This illusion served as a basis for the alliance.

There was, however, one apparent contradiction which had to be resolved before full convergence could be perceived and an alliance could be struck. It was the contradiction between the essence of Rhodes's project, namely the expansion to the north and the solidarity of Cape Afrikaners towards their republican ethnic brothers which formed part of their ethnic consciousness. It related to the broader contradiction with regard to the vision of South Africa – imperialism versus republicanism. These two conflicting visions of South Africa, the origins of which were external to the Cape, posed a constant threat to the stability of the common ground upon which Rhodes sought to build the alliance with the Bond. This hurdle was also the last to be removed before the alliance was struck. Rhodes made his contribution to the apparent resolution of the contradiction by presenting his northern expansion as a colonial rather than an imperial venture, by promoting the unity of South Africa in a way which did not seem inimical to the independence and well-being of the republics and by exhibiting a favourable disposition towards them. For Rhodes, the adoption of Cape sub-imperialism did not pose any problem. After Majuba and the Warren expedition this was essentially the policy of the British government. Furthermore, Rhodes believed, or hoped, that the Transvaal could be enticed into a South African federation under the imperial umbrella.

While the Bond accepted Rhodes's utterances at their face value, they had also to contend with the attitude of the Transvalers towards Rhodes and his designs. These not only viewed Rhodes as a British imperialist and an enemy of their republic, but also saw the Bondsmen themselves as collaborators with their imperial foe. The Bond was apologetic rather than defiant in the face of what it considered to be false accusations. They did not waver in their solidarity towards, and commitment to, the Transvaal, and opposed any move regarded as injurious to it. However,

316

Transvaal's hostile trade policies towards the Cape after the discovery of gold, weakened considerably the pull of the call of ethnic blood among Bondsmen and converted them to Rhodes's Cape sub-imperial expansionism.

Thus, the neutralisation of the two external foci of attraction – imperialism and republicanism – paved the way for the Bond–Rhodes alliance. The neutralisation of these foci created an external balance which allowed the full exploitation of the perceived internal common ground. In conclusion, only the combination of the positive cultivation of the common ground, and the weakening of the pull of the two external gravitation forces can fully account for the consummation of the *rapprochement* between the Bond and Rhodes into the full-blown alliance that installed the latter as premier of the Cape Colony in July 1890, and allowed him to launch his imperial project.

The Bond–Rhodes alliance during Rhodes's premiership, which lasted until the end of 1895, did not go unchallenged. Some members of the Bond disputed the existence of the domestic commond ground which was at the root of the alliance. They attacked the alliance, pointing to the contradiction between the interests and goals of its respective partners. With regard to the external foci of gravitation they perceived Rhodes as the epitome of aggressive British imperialism and manifested sympathy towards their republican ethnic brothers. These were, however, voices from the margins of the Bond. The leadership of the Bond as a whole stood firmly behind Rhodes, viewing his performance in his capacity as premier, the head of De Beers and the head of the Chartered Company as a vindication of the alliance and their support for him. Indeed, their sympathy towards Rhodes developed during this period into veritable hero-worship. This was manifested in the Bond press, at party congresses and in the performance of its MPs. To the Bond leadership, the balance between the pull of the empire and of that of republican 'Afrikanerdom' had not changed; the hostile trade policies of the Transvaal continued to weaken the pull of this external focus of attraction. Furthermore, they viewed Rhodes as a good colonialist, as good as he had ever been, as a veritable bulwark against aggressive imperialism, and as sympathetic towards republican independence. To the Bond leadership the alliance was at least as firm at the end of 1895 as it had been since 1890. They shared none of the blame for the abrupt, violent end of the alliance following the Jameson raid.

The blame landed squarely on Rhodes's head. In conceiving the Jameson raid he was contemplating the end of his alliance with the Bond. Towards the end of 1894 he was no longer able to contain the contradiction between the requisites of maintaining the alliance with the Bond and the call of the imperial sirens. For him the internal common ground, premised on the ideology of 'colonialism', was primarily a platform for the pursuit of imperialist goals. When the balance between 'colonialism' and republicanism appeared to him to be shifting irretrievably towards the latter, Rhodes lost much of his interest in cultivating the colonial common ground. For more than a year before the raid, while he conspired against the Transvaal unnoticed by his Cape Afrikaner allies, Rhodes was torn between the increasing pull of the call of Empire and the need to uphold the alliance. All this time he was openly wearing his 'colonial' garb. Jameson, in marching into the Transvaal, violently opened Rhodes's colonial closet and exposed him for the jingo that he was. Once the news of Jameson's departure reached Cape Town, the fate of the alliance and Rhodes's premiership was sealed. The balance between the external foci of gravitation was violently disturbed and the common ground which supported the alliance was exposed as a great illusion.

The break between Rhodes and the Bond leadership was not as swift as might have been expected. Quite a few Bond leaders remained loyal to Rhodes; many others were ambivalent towards him; and there were a few who followed him all the way, serving the cause of British imperialism as loyalists during the Anglo-Boer War. The Bond itself was rather slow to disengage from him fully. In all probability Rhodes could have regained the support of the Bond had he repented and reverted to the creed of 'colonialism'. Hofmeyr, as we have seen, offered him just this option. Had he taken this course, then the Jameson raid might have gone down in history as a political accident, an aberration. It was, however, neither an accident nor an aberration. Rather, it reflected Rhodes's deepest motives and commitment. Since the prospect of sub-imperialism after the raid was even worse than it had been before it, there was little point in repairing his colonial parish pump. Once revealed as an aggressive imperialist, Rhodes had no inclination to go back into the colonial closet. The only hope for imperial supremacy in South Africa was, for him, through direct imperial intervention, and Rhodes allied with the Cape domestic forces which were prepared not only to entertain but also to propagate and support such a course. As Rhodes's new strategy unfolded, and as he became associated with his new domestic allies, the chasm between him and his former allies grew wider and deeper. The definitive break between many Bond leaders and Rhodes was precipitated not merely by the raid, but also by Rhodes's professions and behaviour in its wake. The gradual process of disengagement between Rhodes and the Bond culminated in the 1898 general election, when the two camps, Rhodes leading the one and the Bond at the centre of the other, were engaged in a battle for political life and death.

The nature of the divorce between the Bond and Rhodes sheds light on their courtship and marriage. From a Bond perspective the alliance with Rhodes was cemented by three mutually reinforcing elements – the perception that Rhodes supported the material interests of Cape Afrikaner farmers; the perception that he shared with them an ideological and political outlook; and attachment to Rhodes's person. For the smaller number of Bondsmen who continued to follow Rhodes after the raid, these three elements were still valid, and consequently they saw no reason to withhold their support for, and loyalty to, him. For most Bond leaders two of the above elements lay in ruins. With regard to the personal element, Hofmeyr said what many Bondsmen would have echoed. 'If Rhodes was involved he is no more a friend of mine.' They viewed the raid as a serious breach of friendship and trust. His transgression against the Transvaal was also perceived as a serious infringement on Cape Afrikaners' economic interests. With the failure of Rhodesia to live up to its economic promise and with the concurrent flourishing of the gold fields in the Transvaal, continuing support for Rhodes could seriously undermine the Cape economy – which benefited handsomely from the Transvaal markets despite its hostile trade policies. The Bond did not turn its back on the essence of the ideological and political creed which formed part of the common ground. Rather, adjustments were made, as necessary, to those elements in it which were associated with Rhodes personally, namely, the perception of Rhodes and his associates as representatives of 'good' national capitalism, and of Rhodesia as the ultimate manifestation of the appropriate Afrikaner order. The main thrust of the ideological and political rationale of the alliance, however, continued to be upheld, with only minor changes in degree and nuance. The Bond remained, as before, a white non-ethnic home rule party engaged in ethnic mobilisation in the internal political area. Their political outlook and behaviour continued to be informed, as before, by a combination of colonial Cape-centricism, by loyalty to the empire and the Crown, by solidarity with their ethnic brothers in the republican diaspora, and by the pursuit of immediate and longer-term economic interests. The durability of this outlook is hardly surprising; it must be remembered that, in striking the alliance, Rhodes did not drag Cape Afrikaners to his ideological and political domain, but rather invaded and settled in theirs. This outlook was shaped in a long and thorough process of integration into the British colonial and imperial world, and as Hofmeyr said, 'even Majuba and Doornkop has not changed my mind'.[1] Rhodes was thrown out of the Cape Afrikaner Synagogue because the 'devout' adherent of their creed proved to be an imposter – indeed a heretic.

NOTES

1. *OL*, 29 March 1898.

Bibliography

PRIMARY SOURCES

Borcherds, P.B., *Autobiographical Memoir, being a plain narrative of occurrences from early life to advanced age, chiefly intended for his children and descendants, countrymen and friends*, Cape Town, 1861.

Bower, Graham, Private papers, The South African Library, (Cape Town).

Bryce, J., *Impression of South Africa* (London, 1897).

British Parliamentary Papers, Africa, 38, sessions 1884–5. Cape Colony, House of Assembly, Hansard.

British South Africa Company Papers, Rhodes House, Oxford.

Cape of Good Hope Almanac for 1845, The (Cape Town).

Cape of Good Hope Almanac and Annual Register, 1855, The (Cape Town).

Cape Town Directory for 1865, The (Cape Town).

Churchill, R.S., *Mines and Animals in South Africa* (London, 1892).

Conference of Loyalists held at Paarl, August 29 and 30, 1902 (Paarl, 1902).

Cook, E.T., *Edmund Garrett: a Memoir* (London, 1909).

Correspondence related to Bechuanaland, 1884.

Dachs, A.J., *Papers of John Mackenzie* (Johannesburg, 1975).

De Waal, J.H.H., *Versamelde Werke*, Deel i, *My Herinnering van ons Taalstryd* (Cape Town and Bloemfontein, 1939).

Dictionary of South African Biography, Vol. I (Durban, 1968).

Dictionary of South African Biography, Vol. II (Johannesburg, 1972).

Dictionary of South Africa Biography, Vol. IV, (Durban, 1981).

Dormer, F. L., *Vengeance as a Policy in Afrikanerland: A Plea for a New Departure* (London, 1901).

Duckitt, H.J., *Hilda's Diary of a Cape Housekeeper* (Macmillan, South Africa, 1978).

Du Toit, S.J., *Rhodesia – Past and Present* (London, 1897).

Du Toit, S.J., *Sambesia: Salomo's Goudmijn bezocht in 1894* (Paarl, 1895).

Faure, D.P., *My Life and Times* (Cape Town, 1907).

Fuller, T., *The Right Honourable Cecil John Rhodes: a Monograph and a Reminiscence* (London, 1910).

Garrett, E., *Afrikanerland and the Land of Ophir* (Johannesburg, 1891).

Garrett, E. and E.T. Edwards, *The Story of an African Crisis* (London, 1897).

General Directory and Guide Book to the Cape of Good Hope and its dependencies (The Cape Almanac) (Cape Town, 1875).

Green, G.A.L., *An Editor Looks Back: South Africa and Other Memoirs* (Cape Town and Johannesburg, 1947).

Hancock, W.K and J. van der Poel, *Selection from Jan Smuts Papers*, Vol. I, June 1886–May 1902 (Cambridge, 1962).

Hansard, Cape Colony House of Assembly debates.

Headlam, C., (ed.), *The Milner Papers* (London, Toronto, Melbourne and Sydney, 1931).

Hofmeyr, A.J.L., *The Story of my Captivity during the Transvaal War, 1899–1900* (London, 1900).

Hofmeyr, J.H., Private Papers, The South African Library, Cape Town.

Houghton, D.H., and J. Dogut, (eds.), *Source Material on the South African Economy*, Vol. I, 1860–1899 (Cape Town 1972).

Index of the Reports from the Select Committee on British South Africa, with Digest of Evidence, ordered by the House of Commons, to be printed 13 July 1897, HMSO (London 1897).

Imperialist [Verschoyle, J.S.], *Cecil Rhodes: a Biography and Appreciation, with Personal Reminiscences by Dr Jameson* (London, 1897).

Joelson, A., *The Memoirs of Kohler of the K.W.V.* (London, 1946).

Leipoldt Papers, University of Cape Town.

Le Sueur, G., *Cecil Rhodes: the Man and his Work* (London, 1913).

Lewsen, P., (ed.) *Selections from the Correspondence of John X. Merriman, 1870–1890*, Vol. 1 (Cape Town, 1960).

Lewsen, P., (ed.) *Selections from the Correspondence of John X. Merriman, 1890–1898* (Cape Town, 1963).

Lewsen, P., (ed.) *Selections from the Correspondence of John X. Merriman, 1899–* (Cape Town, 1966).

Malan, F.S., Private Papers, The South African Library (Cape Town).

Men of our times, old colonists of the Cape Colony and Orange River Colony (Johannesburg, Cape Town and London, 1906).

Michell, L., Collection, Rhodes House (Oxford).

Michell, L., Private Papers, Government Archive (Cape Town).

Molteno, J.T., *The Dominion of Afrikanerdom* (London, 1923).

Murray, R.W., Senator., *South African Reminiscences* (Cape Town, Port Elizabeth and Johannesburg, 1894).

Murray, R.W. (Limner), *Pen and Ink Sketches in Parliament* (Grahamstown, 1964).

Orpen Collection, Government Archive (Cape Town).

Orpen, J.M., *Reminiscences of Life in South Africa from 1846 to the Present Day* (Cape Town, 1964).

Radziwill C., *My Recollections* (London, 1904).

Report of the Select Committee on the Scab Bill, 1894.

Rhodes Papers (Oxford).

Rive, R., *Olive Schreiner: Letters, 1871–99* (Cape Town and Johannesburg, 1987).

Sampson, V., *My Reminiscences* (London, 1926).

Sauer, H., *Ex Africa* (London, 1937).

Shaw, G., (ed.) *The Garrett Papers* (Cape Town, 1984).
Schreiner, T.L., *The Afrikaner Bond and Other Causes of the War* (London, 1901).
Sibbelt, C.J., Papers, University of Cape Town, BC50.
Solomon, V., *Selections from the Correspondence of Percy Alport Molteno, 1892–1914* (Cape Town, 1981).
South African Almanac and Directory for the year 1832 (Cape Town).
Sprigg Papers, Rhodes University (Grahamstown).
Standard Encyclopedia of Southern Africa (Cape Town, 1974).
Stead, W.T., *The Last Will and Testament of Cecil John Rhodes* (London, 1902.)
Solomon, V., *Selections from the Correspondence of Percy Alport Molteno, 1892–1914* (Cape Town, 1981).
Te Water Papers, Government Archive (Cape Town).
Tindall, B.A.,(ed.), *James Rhodes Innes: an Autobiography* (Cape Town, London and New York, 1949).
Trekkers Gids (Mashonaland, Ngami, Bosman) (Paarl, 1894).
'Vindex' (pseud. John Verschoyle), *Cecil Rhodes: his Political Life and Speeches, 1881–1900*, (London, 1900).
Williams, R., *How I Became a Governor* (London, 1913).
Wright, H.M. (ed.), *Sir James Rose Innes: Selected Correspondence (1884–1905)* (Cape Town, 1972).

NEWSPAPERS

Afrikaanse Patriot, Di[e] (Paarl).
Albert Gazette met verband met de Bondsman (Burgersdorp).
Barkly and Diggers News (Barkly West).
Beaufort West Courier (Beaufort West).
Burgersdorp Gazette (Burgersdorp).
Cape Argus (Cape Town).
Cape Times (Cape Town).
Dagblad, Het (Paarl and Cape Town).
Diamond Fields Advertiser (Kimberley).
Express, De (Bloemfontein).
Graaff Reinetter, De (Graaff Reinet).
Nieuwe Middelburger, De (Middelburg).
Ons Land (Cape Town).
Onze Courant (Graaff Reinet).
Oosten, Het (Somerset East).
Paarl, De (Paarl).
Review of Reviews (London), February 1892.
South African Telegraph (Cape Town).
Volksbode (Cape Town).
Volksstem (Pretoria).
Zuid Afrikaan, De (Cape Town).

BOOKS

Agar-Hamilton, J.A.I., *The Road to the North: South Africa 1852–1886* (London, New York and Toronto, 1937).

Amphlett, G.T., *History of the Standard Bank of South Africa Ltd., 1862–1913* (Glasgow, 1914).

Anderson, B., *Imagined Communities: Reflections on the Origin and Spread of Nationalism* (London, 1983).

Armstrong, H.C., *Grey Steel: Jan Smuts, a Study of Arrogance* (London, 1937).

Arndt, E.H.D., *Banking and Currency Development in South Africa (1652–1927)* (Cape Town and Johannesburg, 1928).

Baker, H., *Cecil Rhodes by his Architect* (London, 1934).

Barlow, T.B., *The Life and Times of President Brand* (Cape Town and Johannesburg, 1972).

Booysens, B., *'Ek heb geseg', die Verhaal van ons Jongeliede en Debatsvereenigings* (Cape Town, 1983).

Burrows, E.H., *Overberg Outspan* (Cape Town, 1952).

Christopher, A.J., *Southern Africa* (Folkestone, 1976).

Cloete, B., *Die Lewe van Senator F.S. Malan* (Johannesburg, 1946).

Coetzee, J.A., *Politieke Groepering in die Wording van die Afrikanernatie* (Johannesburg, 1941).

Colvin, I.D., *The Life of Jameson* (London, 1922).

Cranford, F.S., *J. Smuts: a Biography* (London, 1945).

Davenport, T.R.H., *The Afrikaner Bond: the History of a South African Party, 1880–1911* (Cape Town, London and New York, 1966).

Davenport, T.R.H., *South Africa: a Modern History* (Bergvlei, 1987).

De Dosdari, C., *Cape Dutch Houses and Farms* (Cape Town and Amsterdam, 1953).

De Kiwiet, C.W., *A History of South Africa: Social and Economic* (London, 1941).

De Kock, M.H., *Selected Subjects in the Economic History of South Africa* (Cape Town and Johannesburg, 1924).

De Waal, J.H.H., *Die Lewe van David Christiaan de Waal* (Cape Town, 1928).

Du Toit, A., and H. Giliomee, *Afrikaner Political Thought: Analysis and Documents*, volume i, *1780–1850* (Cape Town and Johannesburg, 1983).

Du Toit, J.D., *Ds. S.J. du Toit in Weg en Werk* (Paarl, 1919).

Du Toit, P.S., *Geskiedenis van die Onderwys in die Kaaplolonie* (Pretoria, 1982).

Engelbrecht, S.P., *Thomas Francois Burger: a Biography* (Pretoria and Cape Town, 1946).

Fleischer, D., and A. Caccia, *Merchants and Pioneers: the House of Mosenthal* (Johannesburg, 1983).

Flint, J., *Cecil Rhodes* (Boston and Toronto, 1974).

Fraser, J.G., *Episodes in my Life* (Cape Town, Port Elizabeth, Johannesburg and Uitenhage, 1922).

Galbraith, J.S., *Crown and Charter: the Early Years of the British South Africa Company* (Berkeley, Los Angeles and London, 1974).

Garvin, J.L., *The Life of Joseph Chamberlain* (London, 1932).

Gellner, E., *Nations and Nationalism* (Oxford, 1983).

Green, J.E.S., *Rhodes Goes North* (London, 1936).

Gross, F., *Rhodes of Africa* (London, 1956).

Hancock, W.K., *Smuts: the Sanguine Years, 1870–1919* (Cambridge, 1962).

Hanekom, T.N., *Die Liberale Rigting in Suid Afrika: 'n Kerkhistoriese Studie* (Stellenbosch, 1951).

Henning, C.G., *Graaff Reinet: a Cultural History 1786–1886* (Cape Town, 1975).

Hensman, H., *Cecil Rhodes: a Study of a Career* (London, 1901).

Herrman, L., *A History of the Jews in South Africa* (Johannesburg and Cape Town, 1935).

Hobsbawm, E.J., *Nations and Nationalism since 1780: Programme, Myth, Reality* (Cambridge, 1990).

Hofmeyr, J.H., *Jan Hendrik Hofmeyr (Onze Jan)* (Cape Town, 1913).

Hofmeyr, N.J., *De Afrikaner Boer en de Jamesom Inval* (Cape Town and Amsterdam, 1896).

Hole, H.M., *The Making of Rhodesia* (London, 1926).

Hroch, M., *Social Preconditions of National Revival in Europe* (Cambridge, 1985).

Immelman, R.F.M., *Men of Good Hope: the Romantic Story of the Cape Town Chamber of Commerce, 1804–1954* (Cape Town, 1955).

Jourdan, P., *Cecil Rhodes: His Private Life by his Private Secretary* (London, 1910).

Kannemeyer, J.C., *Geskiedenis van die Afrikaanse Literatuur* (Pretoria, 1978).

Kaplan, M., assisted by M. Robertson, *Jewish Roots in the South African Economy* (Cape Town, 1986).

Keppel-Jones, A.M., *Rhodes and Rhodesia: the White Conquest of Zimbabwe* (Pietermaritzburg, 1983).

Kilpin, R., *The Romance of a Colonial Parliament* (London, New York and Toronto, 1930).

Knowles, L.C.A., and C.M. Knowles, *The Economic Development of the British Overseas Empire*, Vol. iii (London, 1936).

Kotze, D.J., *Positiewe Nationalisme* (Cape Town, 1968).

Kotze, J.G., *Biographical Memoirs and Reminiscences* (Cape Town and Cape Town, 1933).

LeCordeur, B.A., *The Politics of Eastern Cape Separatism, 1820–1854* (Cape Town, 1981).

Leipoldt, C.L., *300 Years of Cape Wine* (Cape Town, 1952).

Lewsen, P., *John X. Merriman: Paradoxical South African Statesman* (Johannesburg, 1982).

Lockhart, J.G., and C.M. Woodhouse, *Rhodes* (London, 1963).

Lovell, R.I., *The Struggle for South Africa, 1875–1899: a Study in Economic Imperialism* (London, 1934).

MacDonald, J.G., *Rhodes, a Life* (London, 1928).

Malherbe, E.H., *Educational Administration in the Cape, Natal, Transvaal and the Orange Free State* (Cape Town, 1925).

Marais, J.S., *The Fall of Kruger's Republic* (Oxford, 1961).

Marlowe, J., *Cecil Rhodes: the Anatomy of Empire* (London, 1972).

Maylam, P., *Rhodes, the Tswana and the British: Colonialism, Collaboration and Conflict in the Bechuanaland Protectorate, 1885–1899* (London, 1980).

McCracken, J.L., *The Cape Parliament, 1854–1910* (Oxford, 1967).

Michell, L., *The Life of the Right Honourable Cecil John Rhodes, 1853–1902* (London, 1910).

Millard, A.K., *Plantagenet in South Africa: Lord Charles Somerset* (Cape Town, London and New York, 1965).

Millin, S., *Rhodes* (London, 1933).

Newman, W.A., *Biographical Memoir of John Montagu* (London, 1855).

Olivier, S.P., *Many Treks Made Rhodesia* (Bulawayo, 1975).

Pama, C., *Bowler's Cape Town: Life in Cape Town in Early Victorian Times, 1834–1868* (Cape Town, 1977).

Pollock, N.C., and Agnew, S., *An Historical Geography of South Africa* (London, 1963).

Porter, A.N., *The Origins of the South African War: Joseph Chamberlain and the Diplomacy of Imperialism, 1895–1899* (Manchester, 1980).

Rademeyer, J.I., *Die Land Noord van die Limpopo in die Expansie Beleid van die Suid Afrikaanse Republiek* (Cape Town and Amsterdam, 1949.

Redgrave, J.J., *Port Elizabeth in Bygone Days* (Wynberg, 1947).

Ritchie, W., *The History of the South African College, 1829–1918* (Cape Town. 1918).

Roberts, B., *Cecil Rhodes and the Princess* (London, 1969).

Roberts, B., *Cecil Rhodes: Flawed Colossus* (London, 1987).

Robinson, R., and J. Gallagher, with A. Denny, *Africa and the Victorian: the Official Mind of Imperialism* (London, 1961).

Rotberg, R.I., *The Founder: Cecil Rhodes and the Pursuit of Power* (Johannesburg, 1988).

Schoeman, K., *Olive Schreiner: 'n Lewe in Suid-Afrika, 1855–1881* (Cape Town and Pretoria, 1989).

Scholtz, G.D., *Die Ontwikkeling van die Politieke Denke van die Afrikaner*, deel iv, *1881–1899* (Johannesburg, 1977).

Scholtz, J. du Plessis, *Die Afrikaner en sy Taal, 1806–1875* (Cape Town, 1939).

Schreuder, D.M., *The Scramble for Southern Africa, 1877–1895: the Politics of Partition Reappraised* (Cambridge, 1980).

Schumann, C.G.W., *Structural Changes and Business Cycles in South Africa, 1806–1936* (London, 1938).

Schutte, C.J., *De Hollanders in Krugers Republiek, 1884–1899* (UNISA, Pretoria, 1968).

Shaw, G., *Some Beginnings: the Cape Times, 1876–1910* (Oxford, 1975).

Siepmann, H.A. (ed.), *The First Hundred Years of the Standard Bank* (London, 1963).

Smith, A.D., *The Ethnic Origins of Nations* (Oxford, 1986).
Smuts, J.C., *Jan Christiaan Smuts: a Biography* (New York, 1952).
Solomon, W.E.G., *Saul Solomon, The Member for Cape Town* (Cape Town, 1948).
Templin, J.A., *Ideology on a Frontier* (London, 1984).
Turrell, R.V., *Capital and Labour on the Kimberley Diamond Fields* (Cambridge, 1987).
Van der Poel, J., *The Jameson Raid* (Cape Town, 1951).
Van der Poel, J., *Railway and Customs Policy in South Africa, 1885–1910* (London, 1933).
Van der Walt, A.J.H., J.A. Wiid and A.L. Geyser, *Geschiedenis van Suid Afrika* (Cape Town, 1951). Vol. 1.
Van Jaarsveld, F.A., *The Awakening of Afrikaner Nationalism* (Cape Town, 1961).
Van Jaarsveld, F.A., *Omsingelde Afrikanerdom: Opstelle oor die Toestand van Ons Tyd* (Pretoria and Cape Town, 1978).
Van Niekerk, L., *De Eerste Afrikaanse Taalbeweging en sijn Letterkundige Voortbrengsten* (Amsterdam, 1916).
Van Zyl, D.J., *Kaapse Wyn en Branwyn, 1795–1860* (Cape Town, 1974).
Walker, E.A., *Lord de Villiers and his Times* (London, 1925).
Walker, E.A., *W.P. Schreiner: a South African* (London 1937).
Wepener, B.J., *Een Model Afrikaner, of het Leven van Thomas Philipus Theron* (Potchefstroom, 1900).
Williams, B., *Cecil Rhodes* (London, 1921).
Wilmot, A., *The History of Our Own Times in South Africa* (London, 1899).
Wilson, G.H., *Gone Down the Years* (London, 1947).

ARTICLES

Abraham, I, 'Western Province Jewry, 1870–1902', in G. Saron and L. Hotz (eds.), *The Jews in South Africa: a History* (Cape Town, London and New York, 1955).
Aschman, G., ' Oudtshoorn in the early days', in G. Saron and L. Hotx (eds.), *The Jews in South Africa: a History* (Cape Town, London and New York, 1955).
Auerbach, J.W., 'Commerce, J.W. Jagger', in R.M. de Villers (ed.), *Better than they knew* (Cape Town, Johannesburg and London, 1972).
Bickford-Smith, V., 'Cape Town at the advent of the mineral revolution (c.1875): social and economic structure', in C. Saunders, H. Phillips, E. van Hyningen and V. Bickford-Smith, *Studies in the History of Cape Town*, Vol. 6 (Cape Town, 1988).
Bickford-Smith, V., '"Keeping your own council": the struggle between houseowners and merchants for control of the Cape Town Municipal Council in the last two decades of the nineteenth century', in C. Saunders, H. Phillips, E. van Hyningen and V. Bickford-Smith, *Studies in the History of Cape Town*, Vol. 5 (Cape Town, 1984).

Bradlow, E., 'The culture of a colonial elite: The Cape of Good Hope in the 1850s', *Victorian Studies*, Vol. 29, No. 3 (Spring 1986).

Bundy, C., 'Vagabond Hollanders and runaway Englishmen: White poverty before Poor Whiteism', in W. Beinart, P. Delius and S. Trapido, *Putting the Plough to the Ground: Accumulation and Dispossession in Rural South Africa* (Johannesburg, 1986).

Davenport, T.R.H., 'The "Settler" Ministry, 1878–1881', Dugmore Memorial Lecture (Grahamstown, 1984).

Davenport, T.R.H., 'The consolidation of a new society: the Cape Colony', in M. Wilson and L. Thompson, *The Oxford History of South Africa*, Vol. i (Oxford, 1969), p. 277.

Dreyer, A., 'Hollandse Joernalistiek in Suid Afrika Gedurende die 19 de eeu', OL, 8 Apr. 1930, p. 14.

Dubow, S., 'Land, labour and merchant capital: the experience of Graaff Reinet District in the pre-industrial rural economy of the Cape, 1852–1873' (University of Cape Town, Centre for African Studies, 1982).

Du Toit, A., 'Puritans in Africa? Afrikaner "Calvinism" and Kuyperian Neo-Calvinism in late nineteenth century South-Africa', *Comparative Studies in Society and History*, Vol. 27, No. 2 (1985).

Du Toit, A., 'The Cape Afrikaners failed liberal movement, 1850–1870', in J. Butler, R. Elphick and D. Welsh, Democratic Liberalism in South Africa, its History and Prospect (Cape Town, 1987).

Elphick, R., and H. Giliomee, 'The origins and entrenchment of European dominance at the Cape, 1652–c.1840', in R. Elphick and H. Giliomee, *The Shaping of South African Society, 1652–1840* (Cape Town, 1989).

Giliomee, H., 'Aspects of the rise of Afrikaner capital and Afrikaner nationalism in the Western Cape, 1870–1915', in W.A. James and M. Simons, *The Angry Divide: Social and Economic History of the Western Cape* (Cape Town, 1989).

Giliomee, H., 'The beginnings of Afrikaner Nationalism, 1870–1915', *South African Historical Journal*, Vol. 19 (1987).

Giliomee, H., 'The beginnings of Afrikaner ethnic consciousness, 1850–1915', in L. Vail (ed.), *The Creation of Tribalism in Southern Africa* (London, 1989).

Herman, L., 'Cape Jewry before 1870' in G. Saron and L. Hotz (eds.), *The Jews in South Africa: a History* (Cape Town, London and New York, 1955).

Houghton, H., 'Economic development, 1865–1965', in M. Wilson and L. Thompson, *The Oxford History of South Africa*, Vol. ii (Oxford, 1975).

Katzen, M.F., 'White settlers and the origins of a new society, 1652–1778', in M. Wilson and L. Thompson, *The Oxford History of South Africa*, Vol. i (Oxford, 1969).

Kirk, T., 'The Cape economy and the expropriation of the Kat River settlement, 1846–1953', in S. Marks and A. Atmore, *Economy and Society in Pre-Industrial South Africa* (New York, 1980).

Mabin, A., 'Concentration and dispersion in the banking system of the Cape Colony, 1837–1900', *South African Geographical Journal*, Vol. 67, No. 2 (1985).

Mabin, A., 'The course of economic development in the Cape Colony, 1854–1899: a case of truncated transition', paper presented to Economic History Conference, Economic History Society of South Africa, Durban (17–20 July 1984).

Mabin, A., 'The underdevelopment of the Western Cape, 1860–1900', paper presented at the conference on Western Cape – roots and realities, University of Cape Town (16–18 July 1986).

Peires, J.B., 'The British and the Cape 1814–1834', in R. Elphick and H. Giliomee, *The Shaping of South African Society, 1652–1840* (Cape Town, 1989).

Phillips, H., 'Cape Town in 1829', in C. Saunders and H. Phillips, *Studies in the History of Cape Town*, Vol. 3 (Cape Town, 1984).

Rosenthal, E., 'On the diamond fields', in G. Saron and L. Hotz (eds.), *The Jews in South Africa: a History* (Cape Town, London and New York, 1955).

Ross, R., 'The rise of the Cape Gentry', *Journal of Southern African Studies*, Vol. 9, No. 2 (1983).

Ross, R., 'The Cape of Good Hope and the world economy, 1652–1835', in R. Elphick and H. Giliomee, *The Shaping of South African Society, 1652–1840* (Cape Town, 1989).

Ross, R., 'The origins of capitalist agriculture in the Cape Colony: a survey', in W. Beinart, P. Delius and S. Trapido, *Putting the Plough to the Ground: Accumulation and Dispossession in Rural South Africa* (Johannesburg, 1986).

Schutte, G., 'Company and colonists at the Cape, 1652–1795', in R. Elphick and H. Giliomee, *The Shaping of South African Society, 1652–1840* (Cape Town, 1989).

Smith, K.W., 'From frontier to Midlands: a history of the Graaff Reinet District, 1786–1910', Occasional Paper No. 20, Institute of Social and Economic Research, Rhodes University, Grahamstown (1976).

Van Jaarsveld, F.A., 'Dr J.W.G. van Oordt (1826–1904) – Erflater van 'n wereldgeskiedenis aan Suid Afrika', *Tydskrif vir Gewetenskappe*, Vol. 23, No. 1 (March 1983).

Wilmot, A., 'The Africander Party, its origin, its growth, its Aims', in L. Crenswicke, *South Africa and its Future* (Cape Town, 1903).

THESES

Bitensky, M.F., 'The South African League: British Imperialist organization in South-Africa, 1896–1899' (MA thesis, Witwatersrand University, 1950).

Dalcanton, C.D., 'The Afrikaners of South Africa: a case study of identity formation and change' (PhD thesis, University of Pittsburgh, 1973).

Davenport, T.R.H., 'The Afrikaner Bond, 1880–1900' (PhD thesis, University of Cape Town, 1960).

De Swardt, A.H., 'Rhodes and die Afrikaner Bond' (MA thesis, University of Stellenbosch, 1941).

De Villiers, A.J., 'Die Hollandse Taalbeweging in Suid-Afrika' (PhD thesis, University of Stellenbosch, 1934).

Drus, E., 'The development of education at the Cape from 1859–1892' (MA thesis, University of Cape Town, 1940).

Du Plessis, J., 'Colonial progress and countryside conservation: An essay on the legacy of Van der Lingen of Paarl, 1831–1875 (MA thesis, University of Stellenbosch, 1988).

Garson, N.G., 'The Swaziland question and the road to the sea, 1887–1895' (MA thesis, University of Witwatersrand, in *Archive Year Book for South African History*, Vol. ii, 1957).

George, M., 'John Bardwell Ebden, his business and political career at the Cape, 1806–1849' (MA. thesis, University of Cape Town, 1980).

Grundlingh, M.S., 'The Parliament of the Cape of Good Hope with Particular Reference to Party Politics, 1872–1910' (DPhil thesis, University of Stellen-bosch, 1945, *Archives Year Book for South African History*, Vol. ii, 1973).

Henning, C.G., 'A cultural history of Graaff Reinet, 1786–1886' (PhD thesis, University of Pretoria, 1971).

Jenkins, S.J., 'The Administration of Cecil John Rhodes as Prime Minister of the Cape Colony' (MA thesis, University of Cape Town, 1951).

Lamond, M.S., ' "Ichabod": a consideration of the Cape Town elite at the end of the last century' (BA Honours thesis, University of Cape Town, 1985).

Mabin, A., 'The making of colonial capitalism: intensification and expansion in the economic geography of the Cape Colony, South Africa' (PhD thesis, Simon Fraser University, Vancouver, Canada, 1984).

Malan, C.C, 'The origin and establishment of the Afrikaner Bond (until 1883)' (B.Ed. University of Cape Town, 1927).

Marincowitz, J.N.C., 'Rural production and labour in Western Cape, 1838 to 1888, with special reference to the wheat growing districts' (PhD thesis, SOAS, University of London, 1985).

Marshall, M., 'The growth and development of Cape Town' (MA thesis, University of Cape Town, 1940).

Mendelsohn, R., 'The Cape and the Drifts crisis of 1895' (BA Honours thesis, University of Cape Town, 1971).

Orman, S.L., 'Sir David Graaff, businessman and politician, 1881–1910' (BA Honours thesis, University of Cape Town, 1983).

Purkis, A.J., 'The politics, capital and labour of railway building in the Cape Colony, 1870–1885' (PhD thesis, University of Oxford, 1978).

Rush, D.W., 'Aspects of the growth of trade and the development of ports in the Cape Colony, 1795–1882' (MA thesis, University of Cape Town, 1972).

Sank, Y.P., 'The origins and development of the Cape Progressive Party, 1884–1898' (MA thesis, University of Cape Town, 1955).

Scholtz, D.A., 'Ds. S.J. Du Toit as kerkman en kultuurleier', (PhD thesis, University of Stellenbosch, 1975).

Scully, P., 'The Bouquet of freedom: social and economic relations in Stellenbosch District, 1879–1900' (MA thesis, University of Cape Town, 1987).

Smith, A.J.C., 'General elections in the Cape Colony, 1898–1908' (MA thesis, University of Cape Town, 1980).

Streak, M., 'The Afrikaners as viewed by the English, 1795–1854' (PhD thesis, Rand Afrikaans University, 1972).

Sylvester, D.A., 'Capital, class, race and Rhodes: the forces at work behind the Franchise and Ballot Act of 1892' (BA Honours thesis, University of Cape Town, 1985).

Trapido, S., 'White conflict and non-White participation in the politics of the Cape of Good Hope, 1853–1910' (PhD thesis, University of London, 1970).

Van den Berg, O.C., 'Cape Dutch opinion on events in the Transvaal, 1876–1877' (BA Honours thesis, University of Cape Town, 1967).

Van Huysteen, J., 'The Non-European Franchise, 1872–1892' (MA thesis, University of Cape Town, 1952).

Van Jaarsveld, F.A, 'Die Veldkornet en sy aandeel in die opbou van die Suid Afrikaanse Republiek tot 1870' (MA thesis, University of Pretoria, *Archives Year Book of South African History*, Vol. ii, 1950).

Van Reyneveld, T.A., 'Merchants and Missions: development in the Caledon District, 1838–1850' (BA Honours thesis, University of Cape Town, 1983).

Van Schalkwyk, P., 'The response of the Afrikaners to the policy of anglicisation in the Cape Colony, 1806–1870' (BA Honours thesis, University of Cape Town, 1990).

Vanstone, J.P.V., 'Sir John Gordon Sprigg: a political biography' (PhD thesis, Queen's University, Kingston, Ontario, Canada, 1974).

Vienings, T., 'Stratification and proletarianization: the rural political economy of the Worcester District, 1875–1910' (BA Honours thesis, University of Cape Town, 1986).

Viney, C.E., 'A new look at the Logan crisis – with special reference to the role played by C.J. Rhodes and J.X. Merriman' (BA Honours thesis, University of Cape Town, 1975).

Worger, W.H., 'The making of a monopoly: Kimberley and the South African diamond industry, 1870–1895' (PhD thesis, Yale University, 1982).

Index

331

INDEX

Rotberg, R.I., 7, 9
Rudd concession, 114

Salisbury, Robert Arthur Talbot Gascoyne-
Cecil, 3rd Marquess of, 63, 127
Sauer, J.W., 46, 125, 182, 193, 212, 286
Sauer family, 99
Scab Act, 96, 199, 200–10, 216, 224, 243, 253,
263, 267, 275, 288
Scanlen, T.C., 64, 66, 89, 96, 99, 201
Schermbrucker, Colonel F., 67
Schoeman, J.H., 276
Scholtz, D.A., 35, 36, 48
Schreiner, Olive, 214, 285–6
Schreiner, W.P.: 1893 election, 186, 187, 188;
Jameson raid, 238, 249; anti-Rhodes
campaign, 244; Afrikaner party leadership,
249–52, 259, 290; relationship with
Rhodes, 268–9; no-confidence motion,
283, 288; 1898 government, 290, 300,
302
sheep, 18, 21, 24, 26, 36, 200–10
Shippard, Sydney, 8, 118
shipping, 22
Simonstown, 19
Sivewright, J.; relationship with Rhodes, 113,
140, 217, 248; railway scheme, 118; Sprigg
government, 124; Logan affair, 182–3,
185; 1893 election, 186, 187; 1896 cabinet,
243; Peace Motion, 268; no-confidence
vote, 271; 1898 election, 286, 289
Slagtersnek Monument, 257
slavery, 23, 33
Smartt, Dr T.W.: 1893 election, 186; Scab
Commission, 202, 207; Jameson raid, 248;
Peace Motion, 268; no-confidence
motions, 271, 284; 1898 election, 286–7
Smith, A.D., 41
Smith, J.H., 175, 223, 250
Smuts, Jan: education, 29, 68, 211, 295;
Bond membership, 68; on Rhodes's
relationship with Afrikaners, 123, 214,
215, 218; defence of Rhodes, 211, 219;
Jameson raid aftermath, 262; quoted, 279;
Stellenbosch meeting, 294; on Rhodes,
294–5; nationalism, 295
Solomon, R., 186
Solomon, Saul, 85
Somerset, Lord Charles, 23–4
Somerset, East, 256, 302
Somerset West, 256
Sotho People, 88
South African College, 29
South African League, 71, 258, 280, 300
South African Whaling Company, 28
South West Africa, 136, 194, 208
South West Circle, 274, 280

Spirit Distillery Company, 28
Sprigg, Sir John Gordon: government, 45, 49,
66–7, 88, 124–5; Cape parliament debate
(1884), 56; Bond support, 59, 93, 97, 218,
268; relationship with Rhodes, 113, 114;
Rhodes's Government, 139, 141, 156, 183,
185; Scab Act, 202; on Afrikaners, 215;
1896 cabinet, 243–4; government, 268, 275,
284; no-confidence vote against, 271;
Redistribution Bill, 282; 1898 election, 284,
286, 290
Standard Bank of British South Africa, 20
Stead, W.T., 299
Stellaland, 89, 91–5
Stellenbosch: urban development, 16;
Retief's origins, 28; Seminary, 31; election
speeches, 58, 113; Bond congress, 162;
anti-Rhodes meetings, 262, 293, 294;
Upper House elections, 280; 1898
elections, 289, 293–4
Stiglingh, H.D.: De Beers assault, 160,
161–2, 164, 166, 167; relationship with
Rhodes, 174, 186, 187, 188; 1898 election,
292
Strop Bill, 140
Supervision Committee, 186, 187, 192, 266,
277–8, 289
swart gevaar, 62, 66
Swaziland, 114, 119, 126, 140, 178
Swaziland convention (1890), 125, 178, 183
Swellendam, 16, 19, 24, 56, 188

Tanganyika, 8–9
te Water, F.K., 28
te Water, Dr T.N.G.: Adendorff trek
controversy, 154; relationship with
Rhodes, 155; 1893–4 election campaign,
186, 187; anti-Scab movement, 207;
Jameson raid aftermath, 243–4;
no-confidence vote, 271, 276; anti-Rhodes
campaign, 274, 276; election 1897;
resignation, 283, 285; on Jubilee
celebrations, 302
telegraph service, 19–20, 101, 177
Theron, T.P.: Bond secretary, 64, 184, 186;
Bond congress (1887), 70; Railway
Extension Bill, 111–12, 113; chartered
company, 120, 121, 123, 126–7, 139;
relationship with Rhodes, 162, 176, 184,
211, 251, 282; trek committee, 195;
Scab Act, 203, 207; Jameson raid
aftermath, 251, 256; 1897 Bond congress,
265; anti-Rhodes campaign, 274;
Redistribution Bill, 284; nationalism, 296,
303; loyalty to crown, 301
Theunissen, 205, 264
Thom, Dr, 31

337